ANNY

A Life of Anne Isabella Thackeray Ritchie

Henrietta Garnett

Chatto & Windus
LONDON

Published by Chatto & Windus 2004

2 4 6 8 10 9 7 5 3 1

Copyright © Henrietta Garnett 2004

Henrietta Garnett has asserted her right under the Copyright, Designs
and Patents Act 1988 to be identified as the author of this work

First published in Great Britain in 2004 by
Chatto & Windus
Random House, 20 Vauxhall Bridge Road,
London SW1V 2SA

Random House Australia (Pty) Limited
20 Alfred Street, Milsons Point, Sydney,
New South Wales 2061, Australia

Random House New Zealand Limited
18 Poland Road, Glenfield,
Auckland 10, New Zealand

Random House (Pty) Limited
Endulini, 5A Jubilee Road, Parktown 2193, South Africa

The Random House Group Limited Reg. No. 954009
www.randomhouse.co.uk

A CIP catalogue record for this book
is available from the British Library

ISBN 0-7011-7129-4

Papers used by Random House are natural,
recyclable products made from wood grown in sustainable forests;
the manufacturing processes conform to the environmental
regulations of the country of origin

Typeset by Palimpsest Book Production Limited,
Polmont, Stirlingshire
Printed and bound in Great Britain by
Biddles Ltd, King's Lynn

For Linda Fowler

Contents

List of Illustrations

Line drawings in the text

Title page: Anny's monogram, from her seal on the back of an envelope.

The drawings taken from the letters of William Makepeace Thackeray (WMT), Anny Thackeray Ritchie (AIT), Minny Thackeray Stephen (MS) and Leslie Stephen (LS) are reproduced by kind permission of Eton College Library.

End-papers: MS, The Ritchies arriving in Paris, and accompanying letter with key to figures.

I am grateful for permission to reproduce the following photographs and illustrations: Eton College Library: title page monogram, 2, 9, 10, 11, 17, 20, 21, 24, 25, 27, 29; J. Paul Getty Museum, Los Angeles 3, 5, 7, 18; Julia Margaret Cameron Trust, 4, 12, 13, 14; Lincolnshire Country Council, Tennyson Research Centre 22, 23, 28; National Museum of Photography, Film & Television, Bradford 6; Belinda Norman-Butler 16, 18, 29, 30; Science and Society Picture Library, Science Museum, London 19.

Part I
The Desolate Sisters

The faces and the forms of yore
Again recall, again recast;
Let your fine fingers raise once more
The curtains of the quiet past;

And then, beside the English fires
That sing and sparkled long ago,
The sires of our departed sires
The mothers of our mothers show.

ROBERT LOUIS STEVENSON
TO ANNY THACKERAY

'If I could help you, Katharine, by the memory of what I felt –'

'Yes, tell me what you felt.'

Mrs Hilbery, her eyes growing blank, peered down the enormously long corridor of days at the far end of which the little figures of herself and her husband appeared fantastically attired, clasping hands upon a moonlit beach, with roses swinging in the dusk.

'We were going in a little boat out to a ship at night,' she began. 'The sun had set and the moon was rising over our heads . . . It was life, it was death. The great sea was around us. It was the voyage for ever and ever.'

The ancient fairy tale fell roundly and harmoniously upon Katharine's ears.

VIRGINIA WOOLF, *Night and Day*, 1919

I

Thackeray . . . was in this house on the Monday before the Thursday on which he died and was in famous spirits and full of fun. On the Tuesday he dined at the Garrick and those who saw him then saw almost the last of him. He came home that night. On the next day – Wednesday – he was so poorly as to keep to his bed all day. His eldest daughter went into his room about the middle of the day and saw him. His servant looked after him the last thing at night. At midnight his mother, who slept in the next room, heard him retching violently, and when we were at breakfast the next morning a servant came to us from the house to say that 'Mr Thackeray was dead.' I shall never forget the day which we passed at the house – we went there of course – or the horror of seeing him lying there so dreadfully changed.

CHARLES COLLINS TO HIS BROTHER WILKIE, 17 FEBRUARY 1864

The sudden death of the writer William Makepeace Thackeray at his magnificent house at 2 Palace Green on Christmas Eve, 1863 came as a terrible blow to his friends and colleagues. For his daughters, Anny and Minny, it was a tragedy. Half in love with him during his lifetime, Anny remained in love with his memory for as long as she lived. Thackeray's death marked the end of a way of life which neither of the sisters would ever lead again.

It was a way of life made possible only by Thackeray's charisma and the conceit that he lived in an imaginary eighteenth century, modified to please his particular taste. While remaining utterly true to himself, he managed to portray an image of the man he wished he had been rather than the contemporary literary gentleman that he actually was. It was a convincing performance to a certain extent, but his conception of the eighteenth century was inevitably that of someone living in the nineteenth century.* His appetites and affections were prodigious, his fondness for good living insatiable. His notion of good living was determined by his highly developed sense of aesthetics and his idiosyncratic sense of humour. This was all very fine until carried to excess: and excess was one of Thackeray's most common failings, which he confessed to with disarming candour.

His London home at 2 Palace Green was 'the reddest house in all the town . . . I want if I can afford health & time to write the life of Queen Anne in that room with the arched window wh. has a jolly look out on noble Kensington Garden elms . . . it's a famous situation & will be a little competency to the girls who inherit it'.[1] Thackeray had the original building knocked down when the structure proved unsound and it was completely rebuilt in the style of Queen Anne. Set back from the avenue of elms, the house overlooked Kensington Palace and the immense sweep of the park beyond. His friends had teased him and called it 'Vanity Fair' in imitation of his bestselling novel. In a way, they were right, for it was an ostentatious monument to blatant and opulent luxury. But it was magnificent. It was beautiful. Here he held his splendid dinners, with Anny acting as his hostess, entertaining his friends from the London literati who included the Tennysons, the Carlyles, Robert Browning, Frederic Leighton, Monckton Milnes, Mrs Gaskell, Dicky Doyle and Edward FitzGerald. He delighted in their appreciation – for they did appreciate, no matter how much they teased – the style in which he had appointed his house with elegant eighteenth-century articles, handsome furniture, paintings, china and pieces of plate. Palace Green was a testimony to his success, the evidence of his determination to leave a legacy to his daughters.

The fact that Thackeray had been chronically ill for years did not mitigate the shock of his death. His friends, his family and his manservant had all grown so accustomed to his bouts of bad health, which he had done his best to play down, that they had become inured to his condition. As Anny wrote soon after, 'We thought it was only a little

---

* I am indebted to the late Quentin Bell for pointing out to me that when Thackeray illustrated *Vanity Fair*, he could not bring himself to draw his characters dressed in the costume of the period he had set them in, but portrayed Becky Sharp in a crinoline rather than in Regency dress.

attack . . . It makes me sick to think how blind we were – we *would* have it that he was better - & indeed he had no attacks this autumn but he was constantly ill in one way & another & yet so brave & bright at times & so very tender but it has been a sad & anxious time & though we would have it that he was better we were thoroughly wretched and did not care to look forward.'[2] Thackeray had suffered from an urethral stricture which was abominably painful and eventually led to a venereal infection. But it was not the infection which killed him: he had 'overdined, oversupped, overvisited' for too long. The attack he had suffered during the night had caused the rupture of a cerebral vessel. He died, in the end, from an apoplexy. He was fifty-two.

Day had scarcely broken and it was not yet light. Thackeray was discovered by his manservant, Charles Pearman, who went in through the dressing-room and found him lying in his vast bed, his arms flung up above his head. When Charles went for help, the servants sent up a wail of lament. Later, Anny recorded that she heard a strange crying in the house while she was dressing. She left her room and met Charles on the landing.

'He is dead, Miss,' he said. 'He is dead.'[3]

Her grandmother, Mrs Carmichael-Smyth, who had come to live with them, appeared, and the commotion began. Anny's younger sister Minny, disturbed by the racket, joined them. Mrs Carmichael-Smyth said she had heard Thackeray retching violently in the night from her room which was next to his.[4] No one could say for how long that first wild outpouring of grief went on. They abandoned themselves to expressions of extreme despair without the least shade of embarrassment. They lived in a more demonstrative, less inhibited age than ours even if, paradoxically, it was also hidebound by convention.

Anny was twenty-six, Minny twenty-three. Both sisters appeared younger than they really were. Anny was no conventional beauty, but there was something about her, a vitality so engaging, that in spite of her bland round face like a penny-bun and her stout figure, she was undeniably attractive. It was by her voice and gesture, her sudden laughter, that she captivated her companions. She had a lazy eye and winked inconsequentially, but she gleamed with intelligence and appreciative humour. She was very much her father's daughter or, as Edward FitzGerald put it, 'a chip off the old block'. Minny's attractions were more obvious. Pretty and slight, she had a wayward grace, a tilted nose, a determined chin. 'One day she would look like the young girl she really was and, on the next, twenty years older, so varying were her moods and expression. To those towards whom she felt no sympathy, she appeared cold and reserved, for she was sincere almost to bluntness; but beneath this exterior was a most tender and loving heart. She was one of those people who do not like: they love and are beloved in return.'[5]

Both girls had inherited their Irish mother's auburn hair and colouring, with 'brilliantly white teeth and delicate complexion one minute with the soft tint of the china rose and then again as white as a lily which gave the impression of the most exquisite freshness'.[6] Minny was much more reserved on first acquaintance, but her manner was as engaging as her sister's, transposed into a minor key. There was an indefinable complicity between the sisters which made them appear more similar than, in fact, they were.

Someone sent a servant running down the Avenue into the busy streets of Kensington to the small house where the sisters' close friends, Charles and Katie Collins lived, interrupting their breakfast with the news. Katie had known the sisters since they were children and they used to go to one another's parties. As they grew up, she and Anny had formed a particular allegiance which would last all of their lives. Katie hurried off to Palace Green while her husband went to break the news to her father Charles Dickens, before he should learn of it by chance. Charles Collins then joined Katie at Palace Green and, weeks later, wrote an account of that dreadful day to his brother, the novelist Wilkie Collins.

Charles Pearman observed that the noise of the weeping women grew quieter after Katie arrived. He nursed his own grief silently. He and

Thackeray had been not only manservant and master but friends. Their relationship had that symbiotic element peculiar to their positions and Charles was jealous of it. He had travelled with Thackeray on his second lecture tour of America, had looked after him with uncommon devotion when he was ill, had written letters to his dictation. There was nothing, it seemed, that he did not know about his master's habits, his tastes, his ways with a joke. He knew that the girls would probably blame themselves for their father's death, that they would both need care, and he foresaw that Anny particularly would make herself wretched. She had, after all, been the apple of her father's eye. She had not merely inherited from him her talent to write, but had cultivated it. Since adolescence, Thackeray's elder daughter had acted as his amanuensis, a literary apprenticeship that nurtured the bond between them. Anny had already published an essay called 'The Little Scholars' in *The Cornhill Magazine* * and was the author of a novel, *The Story of Elizabeth*, published in 1863, which was so popular that Thackeray said it tore his guts out.[7] The irony that his duties were doubled now that his master was dead was not lost on Charles Pearman.

Charles Collins arrived at Palace Green. Henry Cole of the South Kensington Museum followed and so did Mr Merivale, the Under-Secretary of State for India. Both these men were close friends of Thackeray and their children, too, had grown up to be friends of Anny and Minny. Other visitors came and went. In the end, numb and scarcely knowing what they did, the sisters allowed matters to be settled for them. Katie and Charles Collins begged them to come and stay. It would be too much for the girls, let alone their grandmother, now grown hysterical, to remain at Palace Green. Henry Cole, that most amiable of men, persuaded them to accept the Collins' offer. He insisted. Meanwhile, there was the funeral to arrange.

Charles and Katie Collins had their work cut out. The only spare bedroom in their small house was given over to the old lady, Mrs Carmichael-Smyth. Anny would have it so, if Katie did not mind. Katie would not have minded so much if Mrs Carmichael-Smyth did not sit

---

* Edited by Thackeray. ' . . . & in the meantime comes a contribution called "Little Scholars", which I send you and which moistened my parental spectacles. It is the article I talked of sending to Blackwoods, but why should Cornhill lose such a sweet paper because it was my dear girl who wrote it? Papas, however, are bad judges – you shall decide whether we shall have it or not!' WMT to George Smith, Ray IV, p. 156.

mumbling her prayers out loud over and over again; if she did not drop her homoeopathic remedies on the carpet; above all, if she would keep quiet. It was hard to imagine, looking at her bulbous cheeks and her widow's cap and weepers, that she had once been a beauty but she still held herself as straight as a poker. There was something magnificent about her, after all.

Anny remembered everything in vignettes, in pictures. Long ago, she and Katie had made particular friends. Children's parties at the Dickens' house were terrific affairs, not altogether real, but shining in her memory as brilliant and wonderful.[8] Later, they had gone on holidays together, paddling in the waves on the beach at Boulogne, gathering shrimps, collecting shells and feeling the sea breeze ruffle their hair. Anny would never forget that only two nights before, her father had come in from a carriage ride, asked for brandy and hot water, for he was cold and tired. The maid, Fanny, prepared it for him and then her grandmother made a dismal allusion to a carriage coming up to the house like a funereal coach. She had said it was bad luck. Anny was seized by an inexplicable fear mingled with rage, but then Katie arrived at Palace Green and they set off together to pay a visit to the Coles.[9]

Anny felt quite at home in the Coles' house, which she had been familiar with since childhood. When she and Minny had come to live with their father in London after being looked after by their grandmother in Paris, they had at first found everything very strange. They had liked the Coles immediately. Henry Cole had been a protégé of Thomas Love Peacock and, as a young man, had drawn for him and helped to write critiques of music. Later, Henry Cole became involved in the Anti-Corn Law League, eventually becoming its secretary. He was also intrigued by mediaeval art, was the author of a series of children's stories under the name of Felix Summerly, and designed a prize-winning teacup, milk jug and saucer which was manufactured by Minton and proved immensely popular. He had played a prominent role on the executive committee of The Great Exhibition of 1851 and went on to become General Advisor to the Exhibition in 1862. There was scarcely a scheme in the quantity of new schools of art, music and science going up in South Kensington in which Henry Cole did not have a hand.

The Thackeray sisters had made friends with the Cole girls at once. Tishy, Henny and Mary Cole had an upstairs parlour given over to their private use which, Anny could remember, had been their schoolroom. Long ago, Anny and Tishy had spent hours writing plays there, plays which they had acted out later in finery borrowed from Mrs Cole's wardrobe and the dressing-up box in the attic. Often, the Merivale children joined in. Then Minny shone briefly as a star, proving herself an unexpectedly talented actress, with young Herman Merivale as her partner. Once, Tishy and Anny, with childish priggishness, formed a 'Society for the Stoppation of Starvation'.[10] Mrs Carmichael-Smyth, who was not remarkable for her sense of humour, had objected to the 'Society' on the grounds that it was improper for her granddaughter to send out begging letters to people she hoped to persuade to become benefactors. But Anny paid no attention to her grandmother and told Tishy to write to the Prince of Wales and ask him to be Patron of the Society and to give them fifty pounds. Like most children's schemes, this came to nothing. Years later, on that evening just before Thackeray's death, Anny and Katie and the Cole girls had laughed and gossiped in a happy fizz, anticipating Christmas.[11] If Anny and Katie both felt they scarcely knew a happier family than the Coles, they did not say so. Aware of each other's feelings, neither girl wished to pain the other. Katie's father, Charles Dickens, had quarrelled with his wife and forced her to leave his house and their children. For years, Anny's mother had been the victim of a mental illness which obliged her to live in retirement, secluded from the Thackeray family.

Charles and Katie Collins did not celebrate Christmas with the showy extravagance Dickens had long insisted on. For one thing, they could not afford such lavish fripperies, and for another, such festivities were anathema to Charles. He was a nervous, melancholy man who shrank from excessive demonstration. In the attic where he worked when he was at home, the light fell diffused and ghostly through oblongs of silverleaf applied to the skylight. Wooden blocks for engraving were stacked at one end of the long table. The small garret studio smelt of ink and turpentine and paint.

But even if the Collinses were in the habit of spending Christmas quietly, they could not ignore it altogether. The funeral would not take place until 30 December. For the whole of that week, time seemed suspended in the incongruous observances of the Nativity and Death. If the mid-Victorian Christmas celebration had become an occasion for Bacchanalian junketing, the mid-Victorian funeral had reached its zenith as an extravagant display of mourning. Thackeray had made it plain to his family and friends that he detested the modern fashion for such ostentation. He had found the funeral of Hallam repugnant and had been appalled by its vulgarity. He disdained the pomp of the black hearse – the coffin decorated with an embroidered velvet pall – drawn by black horses rigged out in black ostrich feathers and followed by a procession of black carriages in the same livery, the hollow fuss of the Mutes decked out with bands and weepers and mourning bandanas. Anny and Minny, with the help of their father's friends, made every arrangement to ensure that he would be given the simplest funeral possible. He was to be buried, as he had said he wished, beside their sister Jane, who had died in infancy and lay beneath a pale marble slab at Kensal Green.

During that funeral week, mourning dress had to be made and gowns of black paramatta edged in crepe had to be cut out, fitted and stitched. For no matter how simple the funeral, the convention of mourning dress was *de rigueur*. There was a great deal of to-ing and fro-ing between the Collins' house and the Coles' establishment and the great house at Palace Green. Gardiner and Fanny, who waited on the sisters, and the servants who were part of the Cole household, went back and forth with large, flat parcels of black cloth from that vast Emporium of mourning in Regent Street, the London General Mourning Warehouse.[12] Streams of friends and acquaintances came to call and offer their condolences. As the news of Thackeray's death spread, hordes of public mourners, many of his fans, and crowds of the morbidly curious, gathered to press themselves against the gates of the house at Palace Green, jamming the Avenue.

They brought flowers, wreaths and oddly touching tributes of homage to the man whose works they loved. The rise and fall of the crowd was insistent. Perhaps no one in that crowd knew what it was they wanted other than to manifest public grief for a man they had never met, but whom they felt they knew from having read his novels and seeing his likeness in the paper, but they certainly demanded something grand and the arrival of Tennyson supplied it.

Tennyson cut a tremendous figure. He gave the crowd the satisfaction of sensation and lived up to the popular expectation of a poet's image. Memorable for his slightly mad appearance, he looked dark and brooding and sported a wild cloak and straggly beard. He won the people's hearts by not arriving in a closed black carriage. He walked up the muddy avenue and the crowd parted to make way for him. Word had it that he had learned the news of the death of his friend on Christmas Day and had come from his home on the Isle of Wight.[13] His friendly, familiar presence comforted the sisters beyond words.[14]

It was not the custom for women to attend funerals. There was a general fear that women, less practised in controlling their emotions in public, might break down. The sight of the cortège, the arduous procession, the length of the service were all considered beyond the endurance of what was then termed the weaker sex. Any display of violent grief, of loud sobbing, noisy demonstration, or, even worse, a woman fainting by the graveside was to be avoided.[15] Decency and decorum must be preserved at all costs.

Anny, though, was above convention. She insisted she would go and Minny concurred. Strangely enough, Minny, who was always regarded as the frailer of the sisters, appeared to be calmer and more self-possessed than Anny, but they both looked pale in their black gowns and had dark rings beneath their eyes. They had already undergone more than most girls in their position were ever exposed to, and Mrs Cole worried that the strain of the funeral might prove to be the last straw. But when she consulted her husband she was surprised. Despite his natural dislike of public attention being drawn to women, he threw her reservations to the winds.[16] Anny and Minny were not typical of other girls of their milieu. Their upbringing had been highly unconventional and these were extraordinary circumstances.

Accordingly, the two sisters made the long drive from Kensington to Kensal Green with Mr Cole in his carriage, the blinds drawn down. It took over an hour to get to the cemetery, and none of them were prepared for the vast crowd of over two thousand people who had assembled there. Friends and well-wishers had turned out in large numbers: Tennyson, Dickens and Charles Collins, Browning, Carlyle, Trollope, Millais and Cruickshank, together with the entire staff of *Punch*. They massed against the tombstones, dressed in black from head to foot, clasping black silk top hats against their buttoned frock-coats, and formed one great canopy of black shrouding the burial ground. But what stunned the sisters was the presence of a large gaggle of prostitutes whom their father had frequented, unknown to them. Dressed in garish colours, their faces painted and preening their blue and scarlet feathers, these women strutted around the freshly carved slab of York stone so that it was impossible for the indignant, more virtuous mourners to get close to the grave. The dignified, simple ceremony which had been planned was a shambles.[17] Neither of the sisters ever referred to it later; nor did the Press at the time: 'One of the most touching sights that could be witnessed were his two young daughters, veiled in crepe, advancing from the crowd that pressed against the grave, taking a last look at the coffin and then suddenly turning away.'[18] The tribute of the Jezebels, quite likely as sincere in their sentiments as the rest of Thackeray's acquaintance, went unsung.

The drive back to Kensington seemed interminable. In the carriage, the smell of dye from the yards of new paramatta which made up the girls' gowns was disagreeable and overpowering. The ordeal of the last week since their father's death was over, but the bereavement of the desolate sisters had only just begun.

2

Thackeray had left his affairs in a mess. For a man who was known to be anxious to leave his daughters well provided for, it was a remarkable oversight to have died intestate. Henry Cole and Mr Merivale discussed the matter with the barrister, James Fitzjames Stephen, and Charles Norman, the banker and a friend of the family. Fitzjames came from another milieu which impinged on the circles Thackeray frequented. His father, Sir James Stephen, had previously held the same office now occupied by Mr Merivale. Fitzjames was a scion of the Clapham Sect, his principles a reflection of his illustrious and Evangelical forebears, the Wilberforces and Venns.[19] He was a mountain of a man, immensely tall with piercing blue eyes and a craggy nose, unafraid to speak his mind.

There was no gainsaying him, but he had an unexpectedly charming smile.

The four men agreed that the magnificent house at Palace Green, the pride and joy of Thackeray and his daughters, would have to be sold along with most of its beautiful, valuable contents. A Trust must be formed to provide for the girls: this to be shared with their mother. For Thackeray's widow was still alive, living in Camberwell, in care and insane.

It is indicative of Thackeray's character that he never made his wife's condition a secret. In those days, madness, the causes of it − or of any aberrant behaviour − were so little understood that it was a subject terrifying enough to be virtually taboo. But Thackeray had never turned the girls' mother into a bogey half hidden in the shadowlands to terrify her daughters. Her tragedy had taken place so many years before, that by the time of Thackeray's death it seemed like a story from the distant past.[20] And it was such a sad and painful story that, although it was never actually hushed up, friends of Thackeray and his daughters did not care to refer to it, if only out of concern for their feelings.*

Born into a prominent Anglo-Indian family in 1811, Thackeray was heir to half of the vast family fortune gained by supplying the East India Company with elephants for generations. He managed, by his own bad luck at cards, compounded by the collapse of the Bank of India, to become penniless by the time he was twenty-three. In Paris, he fell in love with Isabella Shawe, originally from Doneraile, a magically beautiful house in County Cork, Ireland. Her father had been Military Secretary to the Marquis of Wellesley in India. By the time Isabella was ten, the now widowed Mrs Shawe had taken her family to live in Paris for reasons of economy. Isabella was enchanting. She was tiny and exquisite and exceptionally musical. She was as much in love with Thackeray as he was with her, but there was a snag: money, or to be precise, the lack of it.

Mrs Shawe was not having it. And who, really, could blame her?

---

* Charlotte Brontë had unwittingly caused some dismay when she dedicated her bestselling novel, *Jane Eyre* to Thackeray in 1847. Since Jane Eyre falls in love with her employer, Mr Rochester, whose mad wife is kept secretly in an attic, the parallel situation, whilst being far from identical, was too close to the bone for the dedication to be appropriate. Poor Charlotte Brontë, who had no idea of Thackeray's domestic circumstances, was devastated when she discovered her blunder. But her attitude to madness, however dramatised for the sake of her story, is far more typical of her time than Thackeray's, which was infinitely more humane. Another example is Wilkie Collins' subsequent and in some ways more spine-chilling treatment of the subject in *The Woman in White*.

Thackeray had accomplished nothing more spectacular in life than to lose a fortune: Mrs Shawe wanted a son-in-law who could acquire one. She fought tooth and nail to prevent the match and there were dreadful scenes. The lovers defied her and were married at the British embassy in Paris on 20 August 1836.

Thackeray took Isabella to live in London with his mother, Mrs Carmichael-Smyth, and her second husband, a retired major, rather a fuddy-duddy, but affable enough. For Isabella, it was a case of being taken out of the frying-pan only to be cast into the fire. Although not a virago like Mrs Shawe, Mrs Carmichael-Smyth was an obstinate, self-opinionated woman and was just as vexing in her way. She was an ardent, proselytising Calvinist, and her faith in the powers of homoeopathy was just as strong as any of her religious beliefs. When Anny was born a year after the Thackerays' marriage, Mrs Carmichael-Smyth insisted on being present. Thackeray grew alarmed and got hold of an orthodox doctor. Anny survived, but both mother and daughter's lives had been put at risk. Fortunately for Isabella, the Carmichael-Smyths were obliged to go and live in Paris where it was easier to eke out the Major's small pension.

Barely a year later, Isabella gave birth again. Jane was born in July 1838, but died the following March. They buried her at Kensal Green.

Thackeray and Isabella survived that tragedy. They lived in higgledy-piggledy domestic harmony, delighting in their funny, precocious daughter Anny and their charming, somewhat bohemian existence in their little house in Coram Street. Thackeray found it difficult to make both ends meet and Isabella was hopeless at housekeeping. One day there might be oysters and a fine steak and kidney pudding she got from the cookshop for dinner, the next there would be nothing but scrag and bone. Thackeray sometimes grumbled, but more often he indulged his pretty wife and, somehow or other, they rubbed along more than tolerably happy. He must have known that his enormous vitality and gigantic reserves of energy were exhausting for most people and certainly for Isabella. He still visited an old flame, an ex-governess in Paris named Mlle Pauline, but was not sure if Isabella knew about it. In any event, that contented yet perilously fragile household could never have survived without the presence of Brodie, a warm-hearted Scotswoman, who was nominally Anny's nurse but who looked after all of them and kept things going.

A year after the death of Jane, Isabella had another baby who they named Harriet Marian and called Minny. And then suddenly everything went wrong. Thackeray had been working extremely hard, writing and illustrating. He needed a break. The ex-governess had gone to Belgium. He wanted to join her and go on a spree. Isabella begged him not to, even though she may not have known the reason he wanted to go,[21] but her husband did not listen. He went.

When he got back, Isabella had sunk into a decline and nothing he could do would alleviate her apathy. He asked advice and took her and the children and Brodie to the seaside. Although he had spent too much money in Belgium, there was just enough left to take them all to Margate. But it was too late. Isabella was walking along the seashore with Anny when she turned on her, violently, and tried to drag her daughter into the sea and drown her in the waves. Something, perhaps the terror in Anny's eyes, stopped her just in time. They staggered out of the waves which beat against the strand. Thackeray, who had seen it all from a little way off, rushed to their side,[22] terrified by the madness in his wife's wild eyes.

He was practically at his wits' end himself. In a last desperate bid to restore Isabella to her senses, he hurriedly made arrangements to get money to take her to Ireland. Mrs Shawe must try to help her daughter. He would write a book about Ireland. His publishers would give him an advance. But while he was waiting for that, his wife was raving mad in

17

one room in Coram Street and Brodie was protecting the children from her in another.[23]

On the voyage out, Isabella flung herself into the Irish Sea and was twenty minutes floating in the water before she was even seen. She was found on her back, paddling with her hands. Thackeray knew then that his wife was irretrievably mad. He spent the rest of the voyage keeping vigil over Isabella, preventing her from making further attempts on her life.

When they got to County Cork, Mrs Shawe behaved monstrously. She refused her daughter admittance to Doneraile Court and sent the family packing. She heaped coals of retribution on Thackeray's head, declaring he had only himself to blame, and slammed the gates behind him.

Thackeray took his wife and children on to Paris to the mercy of his own mother, Mrs Carmichael-Smyth. Nothing could be more different from Mrs Shawe's repudiation than the welcome given them by Thackeray's mother. A self-opinionated old bigot she might have been, but, *au fond*, she was good. She put her shabby old house in the Avenue Sainte-Marie at their disposal, a house where she and the Major spun out their lives as though in *Cranford*, *en voyage* to the measure of laxatives and catechisms to be repeated daily.[24] She would take care of the little girls while her son found a place to care for his distracted wife.

Thackeray sought help for Isabella at Ivry, Marienburg and Chaillot before he found a solution back in England. She was given the best medical care, and eventually placed with an excellent woman, Mrs Bakewell, in Camberwell.[25] Thackeray resigned himself to settling down to a bachelor's existence in London, determined to earn enough money from his writing to afford the care of Isabella and one day to have both the little girls back to live with him.

For the meantime, the Thackeray sisters stayed with their grandmother at Paris. Mrs Carmichael-Smyth meant to be kind but she was strict, and Anny and her baby sister had never known regular ways, let alone any form of discipline. Their grandmother tried – not very successfully, for Anny was a wilful child with rebellious ways – to turn them into little Calvinists. But she also taught them that their mother was a poor, sweet woman, much to be pitied. Their grandmother was not wrong, but a certain confusion spun itself into Anny's young head. She could remember when her pretty mother used to sing and play at cats' cradle with her and she could also remember when that same person had tried to plunge her beneath the waves.[26] Minny was too young to remember Isabella but Anny never lost her early bewilderment entirely. She continued to visit her mother, who lingered in her sorry catatonic state for another fifty-three years. Somehow, Minny never did. But then, Minny never did anything she didn't want to do, although nobody ever noticed that, so beguiling were her ways.

3

A land of old upheaven from the abyss
By fire to sink into the abyss again;
By fragments of forgotten people dwelt,
And the long mountains ended in a coast
Of ever-shifting sand, and far away
The phantom circle of a moaning sea.

TENNYSON

After Thackeray's funeral, the sisters went first to stay with an old friend of their father's, the photographer Julia Margaret Cameron, who had moved to Freshwater on the Isle of Wight. They left their grandmother in London and took the train to Portsmouth. Gardiner travelled with them, for it would have been unthinkable for them to have gone unaccompanied. There were no corridors in the train and no refreshments for sale and they had taken nothing with them. At one of the stations, the train stopped and they all got out and sat in a small, cheerless waiting-room. It was a filthy night and a storm was in full spate. Nevertheless, Gardiner dashed out into the storm and came back with brandy and something for her young ladies to eat. They got back into the train and journeyed on, but it was a bad crossing and they were all exhausted when they reached the island.

The island was their haven and the people on it their redeemers. The fact that it *was* an island added to its charm and lent the illusion of safety, as though the sisters had been saved from a shipwreck and welcomed on the strands of Prospero's shore. Years before, Mr and Mrs Tennyson had 'discovered' the Isle of Wight and settled in a fine old house, Farringford, at the head of Freshwater Bay. 'We crossed in a rowing boat,' Mrs Tennyson wrote in her journal. 'It was a still November evening. One dark heron flew over the Solent backed by a daffodil sky.'[27] But that was ten years ago. Now the island had become a fashionable resort, invaded not only by Queen Victoria at Osborne, but by hordes of sightseeing Cockneys bent on enjoying a good day trip and hoping to catch a glimpse of the illustrious Poet Laureate. They were not the only ones. Julia Margaret Cameron and her husband, Charles Hay Cameron, of whom Tennyson remarked that his beard had been dipped in moonlight, had been neighbours of the Tennysons at Putney. An ardent admirer of the poet, Mrs Cameron determined to follow in his footsteps and, somewhat to the Tennysons' dismay, bought on sudden impulse two cottages which she had most imaginatively altered and joined together by a remarkable tessellated tower. She called the house Dimbola after her husband's coffee plantations in Ceylon. She had landed herself literally on the Tennysons' doorstep.

Julia Margaret Cameron confounded comparison. Anny wrote later: 'It is impossible to describe Mrs Cameron; she played the game of life with such vivid courage and disregard for ordinary rules; she entered into other people's interest with such warm-hearted sympathy and determined devotion, that though her subjects may have occasionally rebelled, they generally ended by gratefully succumbing to her rule, laughing and protesting all the time.'[28] Lavish by nature, her extravaganzas had been encouraged when her husband was appointed the first legal member of the Supreme Council of India. Since the Governor had no wife, Julia acted as First Lady hostess and was thus given full rein for her exuberance.

Mrs Cameron was one of the seven famous Pattle sisters. They were famous for their beauty, verve and eccentricity and they were famous for their infamous family history. It was said that their grandfather, Ambrose Pierre Antoine, Chevalier de l'Etang, had been an Adonis at the Court of Versailles shortly before the French Revolution. Some people said that he had been discovered in flagrante with Marie-Antoinette on the staircase – others said it was merely a Marquise, one of her ladies-in-waiting. Whatever the facts, the Chevalier was exiled to Pondicherry which, although it may have seemed a blow at the time, proved to be a blessing in disguise, for otherwise he would have undoubtedly died in the Revolution's Terror. In Pondicherry, he married a beautiful French woman, Thérèse Blin de Grincourt.[29] Thérèse had Bengali blood, which may have partly accounted for the striking looks of her descendants. The Chevalier made a successful living running a stud farm for the fabulously wealthy Nabob of Oudh. One of his three daughters, Adeline, a ravishing beauty, married an exceedingly wicked Englishman, James Pattle, who had been born in Bengal. Pattle was said to be the greatest liar in India and a reckless gambler. After Adeline had given birth to seven daughters, her husband finally drank himself to death. Thérèse outlived the Chevalier and spent her widowhood at Versailles where her granddaughters, the seven Pattle sisters, were shipped off to visit her at intervals.

For some obscure reason, Adeline took it into her head that her husband should be buried in England. She gave orders that his corpse should be preserved in a barrel of rum and that full mourning dress be made for herself and her daughters. The barrel of rum containing the late James was stood at the head of the intricately carved crinoline staircase in their house. The night before they set sail for England, Adeline went upstairs to kiss her daughters goodnight when the barrel exploded – the bung had been banged in too tight. The corpse shot out and drenched Adeline in the rum. She told her factotum to repickle the corpse and not to make a hash of it this time. When they boarded the ship, it took four strong men to carry James Pattle into the hold. Some said that the barrel exploded again at sea and that the second sight of the corpse sent Adeline off her head and she died raving mad. Others said when the ship docked at Southampton, Adeline remarked that whereas it had taken four strong men to heave the barrel into the hold, it only needed one young powder-monkey to take it down the gangplank. On being questioned, the embarrassed Captain confessed that the rations of rum being insufficient, the sailors had drunk the barrel dry.[30]

Such stories may be apocryphal, but what is irrefutable is that all seven of the Pattle sisters caused a sensation in Society a few months after their arrival in London. Thackeray had met them in Paris in his youth, where they used to stay with their grandmother Thérèse. A little in love with each of them, particularly Virginia, his 'pretty Theodosia', he was enthralled by the sisterhood collectively. None of them conformed to the fashions of the time. They boasted they had never worn a crinoline in their lives. Instead, they trailed around in amazing velvet draperies as though they had floated off the walls of a *quattrocento* chapel in Florence, chattering to each other in Hindustani. The sight of one Pattle sister would have been remarkable. To encounter seven of them in the same ballroom was overwhelming. 'They did not in the least trouble themselves about public opinion (their own family was large enough to contain all the elements of interest and criticism). They had unconventional rules for life which excellently suited themselves, and which also stimulated other people. They were unconscious artists, divining beauty and living with it.'[31]

The most beautiful of them all was Virginia, who married the Earl of Somers and lived a fine aristocratic life at Eastnor Castle. Another sister, Maria, married an Anglo-Indian doctor, a tolerant and invisible sort of fellow called Jackson: he never grumbled at her possessive passion for Coventry Patmore, then a highly fashionable poet and author of *The Angel in the House*, and she bore him three daughters, their only son dying young. The youngest of Maria's daughters, who would one day play a major part in Anny Thackeray's life, was called Julia after her aunt, Julia Margaret Cameron.

A third sister, Sarah Pattle, married Thoby Prinsep, an eminent administrator for the East India Company. The Prinseps set up an establishment at Little Holland House, now Melbury Road, South Kensington, a charming old farmhouse on the estate of the dreadful Lady Holland. Often called the Enchanted Palace, '. . . it was a place after Mrs Prinsep's heart. Its rambling rooms and corridors just suited the untidiness of her mixed French and Irish [*sic*] descent. It could not be denied that it was too far out, too far to be fashionable, but Mrs Prinsep decided to snap her fingers at fashion in this matter as she had done in dress. She would make it fashionable to live outside London.'[32] Gathering the rich and famous and artistic around her, Sarah ran something as close to a French Salon as anything that then existed in England. It was at Little Holland House that Thackeray, Tennyson, FitzGerald, Millais, Holman Hunt, Burne-Jones, Woolner and Ruskin, to name but a few, spent their evenings spouting poetry, holding forth on art, and enjoying their hostess' lavish hospitality, her offerings of curry, claret, and cups heaped with strawberries and cream, together with her insistence on all things beautiful. G.F. Watts, 'Il Signor', as they called him, was such an habitué that he stayed with them for years on end. Years later, George du Maurier based the character of Taffy, one of the bohemian painters living in Paris in his novel *Trilby,* on Mrs Prinsep's son Val, the painter.* Julia Jackson, Maria's daughter and Sarah's niece, spent many of her formative years with the Prinseps at Little Holland House.

Three of the sisters in particular stood out. If Virginia was beautiful and Sarah dashing, their sister Julia Margaret was gifted. They were known in London Society as Beauty, Dash, and Talent. While Virginia collected members of the peerage and Sarah the cognoscenti, Julia Margaret collected famous men and fair women as some children collect stamps. She herself was the ugly duckling of the family. Her six sisters, all swans, were remarkable for their beauty; Julia Margaret resembled a toad. But she was a toad with a jewel in her head. On her fiftieth birthday, in December 1863, she was miserable because her beloved husband (O! She *did* love him!) was looking after his coffee plantation in Ceylon. Her daughter, also called Julia, then gave her a camera remembering her mother's earlier fascination with the theory of photography which she had become involved in as early as 1836 through her friendship with the astronomer Sir Thomas Herschel. 'It may amuse you, Mother, to try to photograph during your solitude at Freshwater.'[33] Julia the younger was married to the banker Charles Norman, who was currently helping to sort out Thackeray's legal estate. Her gift of the camera was an unqualified success and it changed Mrs Cameron's life completely. She took up photography with the first flush of ardour common to a new craze. But Julia Margaret was a fanatic. She never stopped. From that day, she was as one possessed, luring her friends and neighbours, or 'victims' as Tennyson called them only half mockingly, to be her models.

The camera itself was an unsophisticated affair consisting of two boxes large enough to contain large and heavy glass plate negatives. This box then had to be stood on a tripod and the tripod skewered into the ground. The light must be right, the sitter beguiled. And it wasn't just any old sitter. The sitter must be beautiful and then decked out with Angel's wings

---

* It saddens me to reflect that it is too late to point out to the late Quentin Bell that, like Thackeray, du Maurier could not bring himself to dress his characters in the costume of the period he had set them in, but portrayed Trilby in the clinging clothes of the 1880s, rather than the crinoline she would have worn in the 1850s — a minor observation which I believe would have amused him.

and rosebuds, lilies, roses, carnations . . . dolled up with pasteboard crowns, saucepan scourers to serve as haloes, fair women with flowing locks pinned up with the remnants of silver paper dress-making patterns to put high-lights here and there.* And then the wretched model must keep stock-still and never bat an eyelash (which would result in a smudge), until Mrs Cameron hallooed and dashed off with the huge plate into the chicken house which she had converted into a darkroom. Mrs Cameron used the wet colloidon process. This involved a lot of obnoxious fluids being poured over the glass, which she then washed off before drying the plate and smearing it all over with varnish. It was an exceedingly smelly business. Then she had to hope for the best and pray that the sun would shine, for the frame must be exposed to the sun for hours on end until the picture appeared, as though invisible ink were revealed. Then she printed it onto paper coated with egg white. Quite often, the plate smashed.

In January 1864, while the Thackeray sisters were staying, and only a month after being given her camera, Mrs Cameron triumphed by photo-graphing Annie Philpot, the daughter of a local farmer. She called the portrait 'Annie – my first success'. Anyone more loveable, more infuriat-ing than Mrs Cameron would be hard to imagine. She was a woman of extremes. Generous to a fault, she bombarded her neighbours, the Tennysons, with gifts of rolls of bright cerulean blue wallpaper, not at all to their taste, with unsolicited legs of mutton, and with the unrequested loan of her Erridge piano for Edward Lear to play. When Carlyle received an enormous Bible out of the blue, he knew it was only the Devil or Mrs Cameron who had sent it. Easy to mock, hard not to caricature, Mrs Cameron was, for all her gush, one of those rare creatures who positively enhance life. She was not all mere exuberance. No one could have been kinder to the desolate sisters or given them a more generous welcome, warm yet sensitive.

It was bitter weather that January.[34] Minny kept indoors but Anny went out for long walks on the Downs breathing in the salt sea mist and getting her hair tumbled in the wind. Her bonnet would not stay on and she scattered hairpins on the short, sheep-nibbled turf. In her unhappiness, all colours appeared faded, their sparkle lost. She seemed to see dark shapes and the ghosts of funerals passing along the Downs. Sometimes she would

* Dress-making patterns were then made of silver paper in order to preserve them. Many people shared dress patterns as they did newspapers and gazettes. That the patterns were made of silver paper ensured that they would last longer than our tissue paper equivalents.

walk down the sandy lane to Freshwater Bay. There was a small hotel there, but no visitors at this time of year, so she had the shore all to herself. Even the boats were drawn up and turned over, their black hulls like silhouettes of shark fins cut out clearly against the waves. There was at Freshwater Bay a peculiar rock formation called Stag and the Arch, joined by a third stack sticking out of the sea. She found the rock and the waves banging against it strangely consoling. And in the evening, as they brushed each other's hair, the sisters exchanged confidences, 'as women talk most openly in the dimly lighted bedroom at curling time'.[35]

Mrs Cameron's son, Hardinge, tried to coax Minny out of her wretchedness and to interest her in painting, for Minny was a talented amateur artist and a witty one too. But now she moped and was not inclined to draw. Everyone noticed how thin and pale she had grown but, although they were all very kind, only Anny could make any impression on her sister.

For Anny, one great source of comfort was the proximity of the Tennysons. Her father, who had known the poet since they were students together at Cambridge, had always claimed that Tennyson was the wisest man he knew. He was certainly one of the kindest. In spite of his bizarre appearance, he was refreshingly ordinary, involved in the minutiae of the dailyness of life. This did not preclude his interest in the stars, in botany, in geology, to say nothing of his poetry. Nor can it be denied that he had inherited his own share of the Tennyson 'Black Blood' and the consequent propensity to be moody and despondent. But he made a point of walking over from his great house, Farringford, across the fields from Friar's Pit, in his vast black cloak and squashy felt hat in order to try and cheer the sisters. He walked through the park and came into Dimbola through a special gate. Mrs Cameron had built this gate for him so that he did not have to run the risk of being spotted by the hordes of his hated Cockney fans (not that there were any at this time of year, and even during the summer months he greatly exaggerated their number). He sat in the extraordinarily beautiful drawing-room that Mrs Cameron had created. She had decorated it with blue and white wallpaper, inlaid mother-of-pearl furniture and rush matting on the floor. The entire house had a curiously Eastern air to it, emphasised by the quantities of intricate carving painted white, which lent it the look of a Maharaja's palace. It was lit by candles and oil lamps and by the flutter from the flames in the fireplace.

One afternoon, Tennyson brought his wife. Emily Tennyson was a remarkable woman. She was everything that Mrs Cameron was not. Where Mrs Cameron gushed, Mrs Tennyson sat in silent sympathy. Mrs Cameron

Anny

wore flamboyant red and violet robes; Mrs Tennyson was as demure as any Quaker and habitually wore gowns of soft, pale grey wool. And yet there was an unlikely intimacy between them.

Mrs Tennyson, even if she did sometimes find Mrs Cameron exhausting, was very fond of her. 'I should have been dreary,' she wrote, 'as I have to write all day and cannot see to read by candlelight, had not dear Mrs Cameron come to me by night for an hour.'[36] Now in her fifties, Emily had grown so lame that she seldom left her sofa, but, anxious to visit the sisters in their bereavement, she went to Dimbola in the little carriage with her eldest son, Hallam, driving. Both the Tennyson boys were exceptionally good-looking. When they were younger, Emily had dressed them in romantic smocks with scalloped lace collars, and they wore their hair in long wavy locks. Lewis Carroll thought Lionel, the younger son, the most beautiful boy he ever saw. He feared the effect the hothouse atmosphere at Farringford might have on the boys. '. . . Mrs Tennyson and the boys I saw, and the rooms full of works of Art intense. She is a strange woman: I love her from the little I have seen, almost monastic in her shy retirement, plain drapery, and worn heavenly face. But those boys . . . My heart bled and my soul yearned to them. They filled me with a love sadly deep even at first sight . . . You say they have "*la Maladie du Siècle*" already. But Good God! do you know what form this will take with one or both of them?'[37]

However the rarefied atmosphere might affect the Tennyson boys, it was one which the sisters, especially Anny, flourished in. Freshwater was to become their refuge and Mrs Cameron their somewhat improbable Fairy Godmother. But they could not bask in the blissful environment of Freshwater for ever. They were obliged to rouse themselves to depart and face the dreadful business of going through their father's papers, and then to start house-hunting.

They stayed with Katie and Charles Collins in London and found Kensington empty and gloomy. All the houses they looked at seemed horrid.[38] It was a relief to go and stay with their cousins, the Ritchies, at Henbury near Ottery St Mary in Devon.

4

My Cousin German came from France
To learn me the Polka dance.
First the heels and then the toes,
That's the way the Polka goes.

ANON

The Ritchies were a large and exuberant family, witty and talented and great favourites with the Thackeray sisters. They were related through Thackeray's aunt Charlotte who had married John Ritchie in the previous generation. Their son, William Ritchie, was Thackeray's first cousin and had held an important post in the East India Company. After his untimely death at Easter in 1863, his wife Augusta had brought her children to live in the West Country. There were eight young Ritchies: William, Blanche, Eleanor, Augusta (always known as Gussie), Emily (always known as Pinkie), Gerald, Edward (known as Odoo) and the brightest of them all, Richmond, who had dark curly hair and velvet brown eyes and was often called Whizz. It was a fitting soubriquet for, although he was only eight, he had already gained a scholarship to Eton.

There is often something very special in the relationship between cousins. Not siblings, the element of rivalry is eliminated. There is that glorious knowledge of belonging to some clan, of sharing the same jokes, of being perfectly at home and yet at the same time privileged guests. So it was between the young Ritchies and their much older first cousins once removed, the Thackeray sisters. Still in a state of shock, Anny and Minny could relax at Henbury without having to keep up appearances. Besides, it was a relief to be in the country. Anny found a morbid comfort in the melancholy of the bare hills, so very much in harmony with her own sorrow.[39]

Anny and Minny went to Henbury shortly after leaving Freshwater. A fire was ready lighted in their bedroom. It was already twilight and the curtains not yet drawn. The sisters sat and stared at the flames. From the drawing-room below, they could hear the strains of Blanche playing Mozart on the piano. She played remarkably well, though not so well as Pinkie, who could easily have performed professionally. From across the fields, the village church bell began to ring. There was a tap on the door and

Mrs Ritchie came in. She sat between the girls, the immense skirts of her black silk gown sinking into a great black pool around her. She stayed with them and talked to them so kindly that they drew comfort from her such as they had not found before.

The next morning, however, Anny and Minny went out into the winter weather and cried their hearts out under a tree among the crows. Walking back along the lane, it seemed to both the sisters that all the leafless trees, their branches delineated against the pale sky, looked like people whom they knew. Birds circled the bare, shiny ploughed fields. They wandered slowly along until they reached the house again.

The cousins were being very jolly in the drawing-room. It was a large, comfortable room with books and paintings and the grand piano. Deep bow windows, with wooden seats large enough to curl up in, overlooked a flat expanse of green lawn, now desolate with winter bareness. The cousins were all in fits of laughter. Blanche had recently taken up Latin. Now she stuck herself out of the window so that all that could be seen of her was the back of the great bunched-up bundle of her crinoline and petticoats and the soles of her black silk shoes. She was chanting nonsense Latin at the top of her voice.

'Chichuler Pintrees adorer chicerbro chichentreen.'

Anny and Minny, who had scarcely recovered from their outburst of sobbing beneath the trees and their melancholy walk back, suddenly got caught up in the gale of their cousins' frivolity.

'What a beast you is, Odoo.'

'I don't care if I *are*. Minny, do dror a Rod for Polly Pickles.'

'O!' she said, 'that would be too painful.'

After a pause, Odoo added, ''as Mr Young tried mild persuasion?'

Blanche came out of the window. 'Is that a Whackeray?'[40]

Through the window, Anny could see faggots piled up against the trees, a wagon and horses dragging along the lane and, beyond, a distant rider. They could hear the throb of a train from across the fields. A gun went off. It was the shooting season.

And then, the refreshing, convivial atmosphere of Henbury was disturbed by the arrival of their grandmother. Their brief respite was over. Mrs Carmichael-Smyth argued fiercely about religion with Anny and Minny, the last thing likely to console either of the sisters in their distress. 'Terrible religious discussions. Grannie's religious views were always very intense and she took our different habits of thought passionately to heart. It used to make us downright miserable to see her so unhappy. Minny would be downright ill and I used to get half-distracted.'[41]

The old woman believed that it was her duty to make her grand-daughters see things her way. Her way was a narrow path and strictly Calvinist. Thackeray had been much more liberal in his outlook. Years before, when the sisters were staying with their grandmother at Paris, he wrote to Anny: 'I should read all the books that Granny wishes, if I were you, and you must come to your own deductions about them as every honest man and woman does . . . And so God Bless my darlings and teach us the Truth. Every one of us in fact, book, circumstance of life sees a different meaning & moral and so it must be about your religion.'[42]

At that time Anny wrote in her journal, 'Perhaps things appear differently to me, to what they do to every other mind? Perhaps Minny sees the trees blue not green and Amy [Amy Crowe] thinks them red.'[43] But in reply to her father, she wrote, 'I am afraid Grannie is still miserable about me, but it bothers me when the clergymen say that everybody ought to think alike and follow the one true way, forgetting that it is they who want people to think alike, that is, as they do. Monsieur Monod tells us things about the Garden of Eden, which he proves by St Paul's epistles. I don't understand how God can repent and destroy His work, or how He can make clothes as He did for Adam, or shut a door, as they say He shut Noah in, and it is things like these that they think one must go to Hell for not respecting and believing. I am sure when Christ says "My Words" He means His own, not the Bible as Grannie says, but I don't know what it means when He says that He did not come to destroy the world but to fulfil it, and so I suppose everybody is right & nobody knows anything. Minny and I can love you and Grannie with all our heart & that is our business.'[44]

Nothing had changed since then. Anny was, after her own fashion, very devout and remained so all her life. She continually made Good Resolutions which she seldom kept, and frequently seized on some Biblical text to set her right. This year, 1864, she had written, 'No more bills. Be grateful. Be cheerful and do not be afraid. Fewer Bonnets.'[45] She continually told herself to be economical, an injunction she never obeyed. She could not bear the religious controversy between herself and her grandmother. She was genuinely attached to the old woman, but was too sincere and passionate in her views to turn the other cheek. Minny didn't seem to care about religion one way or the other, but the terrible discussions made her ill.

Whilst their father had been alive, it had been just about tolerable to have Mrs Carmichael-Smyth living with them in the spacious apartments at Palace Green. But now that was to be sold and the sisters must find a more modest house. It was the very thing that Thackeray had feared. Unfortunately, the girls no longer had any choice in the matter. One day at Henbury the sisters walked out, wrapped up against the cold, to a Roman camp with a crest of pine trees. Suddenly they saw Pinkie galloping over the hills on her pony. A little rabbit ran away. 'The world seemed so big & empty that it sickened one a little.'[46]

Anny dreamed constantly of her father. Once, in her dream, he said, '"While I was with you I was sorry for you but not now." I used to have such vivid dreams that I woke up feeling as if I had been actually with him. He used to tell me not to exaggerate my feelings.'[47]

Her dreams always seemed as real as anything else and made a deep impression on her. The morning before Thackeray died, she dreamed that 'I was with Papa climbing a very high hill. We went higher & higher so that I had never seen anything like it before. And Papa was pointing out something to me which I could not see & presently left me & I seemed to come down alone. He said "Write to Mr Longman."[48] I said, "I have written."'

She could not help feeling guilty, a frequent affliction among the bereaved. If only she had done something, been more observant of his condition, she thought perhaps he might have lived. She had even had a premonition of his death in this dream and done nothing about it. For if that very hill where she could not follow was not Death or Heaven, she did not know what it was. She may not have realised that her father was leaving her a gift, a legacy for her to spend during the rest of her span on earth. His direction was clear. It was to write to the publisher, Mr Longman.

'Dear Papa where you are can you hear, can you see us —

'If with my whole life I could tell you once more that I love you & know that you forgive me.'[49]

Reluctantly, the girls went back to London and stayed again with Charles and Katie Collins. The house at Palace Green was up for sale. They sold the horses and the carriage to Mrs Ritchie, who gave a good price for them. They had to go to Palace Green to pack up their personal things, sort papers, and they, 'Chose our dear old household Gods — came back sad enough'.[50] It was a miserable business. Their father's friends, the Coles, the Merivales and the Procters did their best to help, but nothing could mitigate their melancholy. To make matters worse, Anny was incapable of managing the simplest business transaction but refused to admit it. She continually forgot things, imagined things that hadn't really happened, and mislaid vitally important papers. Minny, with her neat, quiet methods, was far more efficient, more objective, less emotional. But then she hadn't been the apple of her father's eye.

Thackeray's friend and publisher, George Smith 'rode round to offer £10,000 for all Thackeray's copyrights, thereby earning the girls' undying gratitude and making the best bargain of his life'.[51] It was just as well that the girls had no idea they were being taken advantage of. However, although George Smith was a shrewd businessman, he was also the most enlightened and influential publisher of his day. As a writer, Anny would be better served by him in the future.

They left London to stay with Adelaide Sartoris at Warnford in Hampshire. Mrs Sartoris and her sister, the actress Fanny Kemble, were both old friends of their father's. The Thackeray sisters had known them since childhood when Mrs Sartoris had been the internationally renowned opera singer, Adelaide Kemble, and Fanny had, like her aunt Mrs Siddons, taken the stage by storm.

At Warnford 'there were great terrace walks . . . The mansion stood among broad spreading trees. There was a ceaseless cawing from the rooks overhead: a deep wide lake with fish in it lay in light and shadow, with fringes of dogwood growing, crimson-tinted and waving against the banks'.[52] If Warnford was stately, its mistress was no less so: '. . . that fine and original being, so independent and full of tolerance for the young, sympathising even with *misplaced* enthusiasm, entering so vividly into a girl's unformed longings. When I first knew her, she seemed to me to be a sort of revelation; it was someone taking life from an altogether new and different point of view from anything I had ever known before'.

Striking, rather than beautiful, Mrs Sartoris had a long nose and deeply hooded eyes. She had acquired not only all the *embonpoint* associated with a diva, but a foreign accent while touring Europe as an opera singer. She had what can only be called 'presence'. Intelligent, witty and compassionate, she once wrote what seemed to Anny to be the keynote of her convictions: 'Now, to love anything sincerely is an act of grace, but to love the best sincerely is a state of grace.'[53]

Mr Sartoris was a highly cultivated and very rich businessman, devoted to his wife. Although very different characters, there was a similarity between Mrs Sartoris and Mrs Cameron, if only in that they were like no one else. Both women were exceptionally gifted and both of them had an enormous effect on Anny. They lived in an age of extreme conformity which tolerated extreme eccentricity. They were at once unfashionable and extremely popular. Sir Henry Taylor wrote of Mrs Cameron, '[she] had driven herself home to us by a power of loving which I have never seen exceeded, and an equal determination to be loved . . . She pursued her objective through many trials, wholly regardless of the world's ways, putting pride out of the question; and what she said has come to pass and more; we all love her.'[54] Of Mrs Sartoris, Anny wrote, 'If any woman ever loved beauty and reverently turned to the very soul of Nature, it was Adelaide Sartoris. I remember once long ago wondering when she burst out suddenly in her passionate, emotional way. She stood by a hedge of roses in her garden and began saying how dear to her was each plant and flowering shrub, how growing things spoke to her more intensely as time went on, and how for her Nature came to mean more and more, and the life of cities less and less. It seemed a wonderful thing to me then, that any one so fitted for the world – full of human life and enjoyment – should grasp the moment quite as this woman did, either in acceptance or in renunciation.'[55]

It would seem, then, as if it was the fashion for middle-aged artistic and unfashionably eccentric women to be married to generous, benevolent and self-effacing husbands and to enthuse romantically, ardently, about love, life, and beauty as they trailed through their gardens in flowing draperies.

Like Mrs Cameron, Mrs Sartoris was very kind. Even so, both sisters were wan and worn out and still in a state of shock. Ever since their father's death, they had been constant visitors. It is exhausting to be a perpetual guest, however accommodating the hostess, if one is distinctly miserable.

They sat in the lofty drawing-room with the oil lights burning. Mrs Sartoris was installed at the piano singing Gordigiani's passionate complaint. Anny looked at the yellow curtains, the tall cabinets, the high chimney piece and the fire smouldering in the hearth. Everything was harmonious and bright except that her heart ached. Minny sat leaning her head against the chimney. 'Grief amidst carving and splendours, it puts me in mind of Mendelssohn's Wedding March.

'Mrs Sartoris in her own room, sitting at an open window with a stone terrace. China and tapestry on the walls within, without the old court. The rooks fly round and round, there are green hills beyond the fields; one seems stifled and closed in on every side, and I feel as if some day the hills will come rolling down and close and overwhelm the house.

'There is a fountain on the terrace, and brick steps wet with rain lead down to the lawn. The rooks are flying in the air, ever so high. I hate them. One little bird trilling freshly in the rain. He makes me feel more idle and more sad. Let's improve our minds and read something.'[56]

Anny saw the advertisements for the sale of the house at Palace Green in the paper, as they sat reading in the lamp-lit room. Walking out on the terrace by the fountain with Mrs Sartoris' daughter May, they saw the fields and the meadow bathed in evening light. Suddenly, looking up, they saw a new moon. May asked her mother for a bit of silver to turn in her pocket. 'Mrs Sartoris replied, "Certainly child, if you ask her for anything." I said, "There seems nothing left to ask for any more." Mrs Sartoris answered, "Ask for peace."'

But Palace Green was to be sold and it was a bitter pill for Anny to swallow, so closely did she associate its magnificence with the memory of her father.

On 2 March, they crossed the Solent again. Mrs Cameron lent them her guest cottage. The next morning they drew back the curtains, opened the window and 'let in Freshwater with floods of sunshine filling the bare little room of our lodging. To the grocer's bought bread & jam. Breakfast at an open window'.[57]

They determined to stay for a fortnight. They needed some respite from their grandmother. They agreed that it would be folly to write to her offering any kind of explanation since she was bound to contradict anything they said. But until they had some place of their own to live, it was out of the question to have her traipsing about with them wherever they went.

Mrs Cameron's generosity was legendary. She could also be extremely thoughtful. Before she moved to Dimbola, she and her husband had lived on Putney Heath in a small house they shared on occasion with the Tennysons, but which Mrs Cameron had kept on for convenience when she wanted to be in London. She offered this to the girls while they went house-hunting. And it was very likely Mrs Cameron who suggested that it would be less exhausting for their grandmother to spend that time at Paris with their father's cousins, Jane and Charlotte Ritchie. Mrs Carmichael-Smyth still had a coterie of old friends in Paris and the change would do her good.

On the Isle of Wight, Anny and Minny saw a good deal of the Prinseps, who lived across the way at The Briary with the painter Watts. Mrs Prinsep's sister, Mrs Jackson, was staying.

Anny also fell into the habit of going for long walks with Tennyson across the Downs. He strode along, wrapped in his great black cloak, and Anny found it hard to keep up with him. He spouted poetry in the strong, burry Lincolnshire accent which he never lost. Quite often, his broad black hat blew off in the sea breeze and they would bowl after it before it was carried away in a gust of wind. Later, she recalled how she 'walked with Tennyson along High Down, treading the turf, listening to his talk, while the gulls came sideways, flashing their white breasts against the edge of the cliffs, and the poet's cloak flapped time to the gusts of the wet wind'. She recalled that Tennyson 'with his short-sighted eyes, can see farther than most people. Almost the first time I ever walked out with him, he told me to look and tell him if the field-lark did not come down on the wing'.[58] Those walks with Tennyson, listening to his absorbing conversation and breathing in the salt sea air, did Anny a power of good.

5

Eventually they heard that Palace Green had finally been sold for £10,000. It had been bought by Henry Huth, an immensely rich banker whose family was of German origin. His passion in life was collecting fine copies of rare editions of books. Mrs Huth appeared at first to be more formidable than she really was. She was an intellectual snob, but with a kind heart, who liked collecting great men with famous names. She was an ardent follower of the mathematician, Henry Buckle, and enjoyed having him hover around her as though she was the Queen Bee. Aware what a wrench it was for the sisters to have to part with their home, Mrs Huth was determined to make it up to them. She proved a good and loyal friend and was particularly fond of Minny. The sale of Palace Green was indeed a wrench. But it was also a relief. 'Salt mist over the sea, little waves, everything gentle and sad but not desperate. Woke up without heartache, that too made me wretched. I will pray for a faithful loving heart whether it aches or not.'[59]

The plan for their grandmother to go to Paris had seemed easy at Freshwater, but once in London the notion stretched the imagination. Mrs Carmichael-Smyth was furious. Before they moved to Mrs Cameron's house in Putney, Anny and Minny had temporarily taken lodgings at 36 Brompton Square. The second night after their return they dined with their grandmother and they had the most dreadful row. After dinner, the girls went together to visit their father's grave in Kensal Green. 'But Papa is not more there than *here*.' The next evening they dined with Mrs Carmichael-Smyth again. 'Trouble again. I asked G why she had been angry with us. M cried out: DO be quiet G left the table and said she would never get over it.'[60] She did get over it, but the quarrel made them all wretched.

The fact is, even if nobody recognised it, the girls were never alone. They had two maids, Fanny and Gardiner, living with them, apart from the servants who came in daily. They were always accompanied by a maid who followed them whenever they went out to take messages, call or visit. It was an element of their lives which would have been unimaginable to be stripped of, of having someone continually hovering around like a soft, almost invisible veil. There is a smudge, a faintly blurred focus between the individual and any direct contact to be made with the shopkeeper, the cabman, the people in the street. There is always the presence of another party. And when the servant, with whom one may very well be on intimate terms, retires, an elderly lady, a surrogate aunt or some other form of chaperone will take that place, the transition achieved so harmoniously, so smoothly as to go unnoticed. The servants and chaperones were rarely mentioned. That would have negated the complicit understanding that their presence was non-existent. Later on, Anny and Minny had as many as five servants living in the house, not to mention those who came and went by day.

Meanwhile, there was the problem of the disposal of their effects. Anny instinctively clung to her father's belongings. Her tenacity was poignantly expressed in another letter to Mrs Cole. 'My dearest Mother Cole. I wonder what I should do without you? There is another box at Lubbocks with *my things* & a teapot I should like to sell as we shan't want three . . . Perhaps the little sugar bowl may be inside the box. Papa always used it & so we want to keep it . . . Perhaps if we sell the teapot we could keep the cup, but I don't care very much for it & Mrs Cole shall decide only we want a little Relic or so – To look as if we had seen better days.'[61] In the same letter, she went on, 'I'm afraid poor dear Granny is very hurt & disappointed that we have put off coming & indeed I am too not to come to her, but Minny got so *pale* & *limp* at the notion of coming back just yet that I had not the courage to force her. I don't think Granny knows how miserable it is for us: Father, home all vanished in one moment – or she would not think it heartless to shrink so from coming back before all this last horrid thing is over.'

Almost as soon as the sisters were installed at Putney, Minny fell ill. She begged Anny not to attempt to write and explain to their grand-mother, but she had to keep to her bed. When Mrs Carmichael-Smyth came to spend the day Anny found herself praying for a little courage and for peace. A more welcome visitor was Mr Merivale who came over and spent the day reading *Measure for Measure* aloud to the girls.

Putney was then a small village, pleasant and peaceful, but near enough to London to go up by a short train ride. Friends of Thackeray, Mr and Mrs Prescott, lived nearby at Clarence House. He was the leading partner in the banking firm with which his family had been connected for four generations. His brother was the Governor of the Bank of England. 'Singularly generous and unselfish in his disposition, he grudged no trouble when he could do a service to any person who had a claim on his regard, or when he could give pleasure to a friend.'[62] Clarence House was 'a comfortable old house, handsome large library & famous Burgundy & Claret in [his] cellar'.[63] They had a lovely garden and 'a kind big house filled with boys, girls, sick and sorry people and we went there constantly. Mrs Prescott . . . was extraordinarily kind.'[64]

Putney did them good, although Minny remained very weak. 'I am sitting under the trees, a big bumble bee and a lovely throstle singing, cows cropping the field. Minny said, "Anny, while we are bodies, it is no use pretending we are spirits." '[65]

They were obliged to go up to town fairly often to see Mr Cole and Mr Merivale about business, lawyers and possible houses. After one such visit, Anny recorded laconically, 'It was about this time that we adopted little Ellen, whose tipsy mother was half killing her in front of our own house at Palace Green.'[66] It is not at all strange that she refers to her old home as if it was still hers, even though it now belonged to the Huths. What is startling is that the sisters should have seen a little girl being beaten by her drunk mother and, without so much as a by your leave, taken her off to live with them. What the mother thought when she recovered from her hangover is hard to conjecture. What happened to little Ellen remains a mystery, since she is never mentioned again. It is quite possible that she proved too much for them, had lice in her hair, or they simply got bored of her. It is equally possible that they placed her in some charity school or institution, for both sisters were, like most young women of their class, involved in doing good works at what they called 'ragged schools'. It never occurred to them that their behaviour might seem high-handed, not to say arrogant. Drunk working-class mothers were not considered fit to have any say in the fate of their children, and the impulsive and possibly ill-considered whims of well-meaning upper-class young women with no knowledge of caring for children took precedence.

And then Mr Cole came up with a suggestion that seemed the solution to their practical difficulties. He advised them to buy a house in South Kensington, 8 Onslow Gardens. When the girls were children, South Kensington had been a country district with lanes and green fields and nursery gardens to supply Londoners with fresh fruit and vegetables: '. . . we used to go for straggling walks on early summer mornings with our playfellows, the Coles, who lived in the terrace close by. We used to start about six o'clock and bring home branches of hawthorne blossom to decorate our school-rooms and to remind us that it was May time.'[67] By 1864, the district was being developed into an up-and-coming residential area for the middle classes. The houses were all brand new stucco town houses built around squares or 'gardens'. The gardens were still heaped with builders' rubble and not yet planted. Many of the houses were still covered in scaffolding and the din of the constructors was deafening. In spite of these temporary inconveniences, Mr Cole was persuaded that the purchase of the house at Onslow Gardens would be a good investment and that the district was close enough to Kensington proper for the sisters to keep in touch with their old friends. They paid £1,800 for it and it belonged to them jointly.

Anny wrote to her maternal aunt, Jane Shawe, '. . . Grannie is at Paris & we are thinking of going over to see her as soon as we have got things straight, but everything has to be waited & waited for.

'We have got a house to live in close to Onslow Sq. called Onslow

Gardens. – It is very fresh and open & though there are a good many rooms they are not large ones. There's a balcony & a bath and a little study for me to write in someday – at all events to write my letters & improve my mind.

'We are both quite well though Minny is very thin – I hope you & M. like this fine weather as we do, it seems to comfort and soothe & bind up one's aching wounds somehow . . .'[68]

To her father's American friend, Mrs Baxter, to whose daughter Sally Thackeray had been very much attracted, she wrote, 'I must write you one line tonight before I go to bed. I have not written before because I can only write about Papa & sometimes I *can't*. When I am worried & troubled about things then it seems a sort of desecration . . . Our home where you were once to have come is sold – we have kept only enough furniture for a small house where we are going to live with my Grandmother we believe. Friends are kindness itself, there is money enough because Papa was always working for us, and our pain is far, far less than it has been – It seems to us that sorrow at first is not sorrow but a terrible physical suffering. We could bear anything with only Papa to talk about it, but to go stumbling & falling without him is weary work. My little Minny is asleep now too sad to keep awake tonight – But she is much better thank God & the aching leaves off for a while now & then – Only she looks so thin and wan at times that I can't bear it . . .'[69]

An annoying incident, the result of a muddle, of mismanagement of the sale of Thackeray's effects, upset Anny and she held herself responsible. There was a shabby-looking old desk which Thackeray had kept in his bedroom. Nobody thought to look inside the desk and it was knocked down for a few shillings to the nearest broker. When the broker got it home, he discovered a mass of letters written by Thackeray to his mother, copies of various important letters he had written to well-known people, and a stash of letters written to him by distinguished writers and politicians. The broker could hardly believe his luck. He went to the painter, Julian Porch, who knew the Thackerays, hoping that Porch would be able to strike a hard bargain with them. Julian Porch, however, was an honest man. He at once recognised the value of the papers and went straight to George Smith who, by judicious threats, brought the broker down from two hundred pounds to twenty. Anny blamed herself very much.[70]

In June, the sisters and their cousins, Selina Shakespear and Isabella Irvine set off to Paris. They had conceived an ambitious plan of travelling with Mrs Carmichael-Smyth and Thackeray's first cousins, Charlotte and Jane Ritchie, to the Pyrenees.

While considerably older than Anny and Minny, Charlotte and Jane had been on intimate terms with the sisters since those far off days when the girls had spent their childhood with their grandmother in Paris. Charlotte and Jane had spent most of their lives there. Both spinsters, now respectively forty-three and forty-one, trotted about the little old *rues* of Paris with baskets of home-made delicacies and the latest poetry, doing good but not in a dull or dingy way. People felt positively better for seeing Jane and Charlotte. They radiated merriment and had a typically Ritchie way of cracking wry jokes out of the sides of their mouths like walnuts. Their house in Paris became a regular port of call for English intellectuals travelling abroad, although they never had any pretensions to running a stylish salon, such as that of their friend Mme Möhl.

In 1864, the Pyrenees had not yet been colonised by tourists or made popular to the public imagination. Pau was a fashionable resort, much frequented by the English, but the mountainous region beyond Pau was ignored by tourists. It was an unlikely choice for a holiday venue but, nothing daunted, the seven women, all related, set forth with their maids and vast amounts of luggage on 28 June. They made a lively, if eccentric party. They reached Poitiers that evening and Anny responded to its charm at once. They spent the evening strolling in the streets, admiring the turrets of the château, and observing old women sitting in the doorways working at their spinning-wheels. They were abroad, on holiday, and the weather was warm. It was the first time since Christmas that the strain of bereavement seemed to slacken, and they could enjoy the way in which people who lived in a more southern clime could linger in the starlight and gossip in the streets.

They travelled on to Bordeaux and finally reached Bigorre, high up in the mountains near the Spanish border, exhausted. The inhabitants had never seen anything like them. They were all still in full mourning for Thackeray and the sight of these women in their voluminous crinolines like so many vast black umbrellas was a strange phenomenon. When they set off the next morning to explore the place, they caused a sensation. 'So many of us in our Black that people took us for a community of nuns and Grannie was the Abbess.'[71] They began to settle down and enjoy themselves, planning picnics, sightseeing trips and other excursions. The relief from the constraints imposed by English Society because their first year of mourning was not yet over was intoxicating.

Anny discovered another source of happiness: she was beginning to write again. She had conceived a novel in her head, *The Village on the Cliff*, and for some part of each day she stole off to a quiet room in the inn to write. It was by far the best therapy she could have thought of. When George Smith wrote on 9 July to say that Thackeray's bust was to be put up in Westminster Abbey, Anny could not conceal her pride and delight at such a tribute being paid to her father. But despite such moments of euphoria both sisters were still fragile and their moods continued to swing up and down.

Anny and Minny went for long scrambles over the wild, bare mountains. They were overwhelmed by the beauty of the spartan, savage scenery. The hills were covered in wild thyme and alpine flowers and everywhere was the sound of running water, with frequent waterfalls cascading into lower pools. The heat was terrific. 'Came back through a pretty valley. Rather sad for M. was out of spirits.' A few years later, Anny used her knowledge of the Pyrenees landscape in her short story, *To Esther*, which appeared in book form with four other stories in 1869.

On 18 July, Anny noted, 'My dear Papa's 53rd birthday. To the marble works – slabs silences desertion – my heroine shall go to the marble works (forgot to send her).'

In the evenings, they sat up late by lamplight on the wooden gallery which ran around the inn and identified the stars blazing in the southern sky. The nights were hot and they were plagued by mosquitoes.

One memorable excursion was made by Anny and Minny with Charlotte. They hired a pony cart and a driver and set off to have a picnic luncheon on the Col d'Aspen. They were nothing if not enterprising. The view was stunning, 'a sea of shining hills'. Coming down, they were made dizzy by the scent of the pungent umbrella pines and were entranced by seeing small, dark brown, furry wild pigs roaming about. The sunset was extravagantly beautiful. 'I remember watching Charlotte's *radiant* expression as we drove along.'

On 25 July they crossed the border and spent the day in Spain. 'Everywhere fleas – red caps – long arid roads – smart peasants – black mantillas.' They went to an old Templar church where they all had to take off their shoes at the entrance. When the Angelus struck, everybody, including the hordes of beggars, went down on their knees and prayed. They lunched by a lake and on their way back to Bigorre, they saw 'a dream of an old church and tower on an arid hill, an open door – Lilac mountains, an old crumbling yard and cloister – an old crumbling priest. A sudden conviction of Death in all this beauty.'

On 28 July the maids packed up the luggage and they left Bigorre. It was a cloudy day and they started back by way of Luz-St-Sauveur towards Argèles. They travelled by coach and the horses bolted. The coachman could not stop them. The road was stony and winding and they galloped all the way until they were stopped by people at the inn where they were to spend the night. The next day they drove on to Lourdes 'where the B.V. appears', before reaching Pau in the middle of a heatwave.

At Pau, the party split up. The holiday had been an unqualified success and an exotic interlude during that year of mourning. At five o'clock in the morning on 30 July the sisters took the train to Paris with their grand-mother. Waiting at the station, the girls observed four people on a rooftop, still up from the night before, playing whist.

The plan was for the girls to extend their holiday with their grand-mother at Arromanches on the Cherbourg peninsula while the new house at Onslow Gardens was being made ready. In stark contrast to their sojourn in the Pyrenees, their stay at Arromanches proved a disaster.

They had booked into an hotel within walking distance of the seaside resort and opposite the house of an old friend, Marcia Hamilton. As soon as they were installed, all hell broke loose. Mrs Carmichael-Smyth made a terrific scene and the girls burst into floods of tears and Anny was 'in an agony of self-reproach — deserved enough'. It is possible that their grandmother, worn out by travelling in the Pyrenees, lost her temper *because* the girls had been enjoying themselves. What is certain is that she reverted to those 'terrible religious discussions' and made the sisters' lives a nightmare. By 20 August, Anny wrote: 'Grannie looks very ill. Minny says *she* herself is half mad. We want to do our duty, seeing no one makes it so much worse . . . torn & crazed between the two dear ones so miser-able & so fearing for the future.' 19 August: 'Granny very low. Fear it is my conduct, am determined to spare her. G. in the evening suddenly burst out upon us. It was horrible torture.'

The coast at Arromanches is wild and beautiful. Small painted boats brought in the fish daily. They found the sound of the waves beating against the rock soothing and the northerly winds refreshing. But none of the picturesque characteristics of Arromanches could mitigate the sisters' misery or dilute their grandmother's obsession. Later, Anny wrote, 'I think we were mad almost — I was foolish and hasty but so miserable . . .'

Minny, who suffered quite as much as Anny, began to grow ill. But she could, on occasion, help her sister. 'Such a dreary walk along the sands carrying a great load so it seemed to me. M. jumped over a rock & I followed and the load seemed lighter.'

The girls made a habit of walking into Arromanches from the hotel to get their letters. One morning, Anny discovered she had lost her purse. She was always losing things, but the girls were now in such a state that it seemed to be the last straw. Suddenly, they looked up and saw Herman, Mr Merivale's son and friend of their childhood. He was holidaying nearby with friends. The relief of seeing someone they liked and knew and trusted, and who belonged to that vanished, happy world of the past, was enormous. The sisters burst out with all their troubles and Herman was staunchness personified. He had long had an unrequited crush on Minny and would have done anything to help. He lent them money to get their letters, listened to their woes and tried to cheer them up as best he could. He walked back with them to their hotel. Anny immediately found her purse under a table. Herman's presence made everything immeasurably better. Mrs Carmichael-Smyth grew calmer. The next evening he took the girls out for a walk over the sands in the moonlight. They listened to the splashing of the incoming tide and identified the stars and spoke their hearts out. But Herman had committed himself to travel on with his party of friends and was obliged to leave the next day. Anny had a 'good cry which always comforts me & brings my dear Papa again'. They did the only thing possible. They left their grandmother at Lisieux and crossed from Le Havre to Southampton.

On St Michael's Day, 29 September, the sisters moved into the new house at Onslow Gardens: '. . . it wasn't nearly as sad as we feared. It was like coming home again.' These were brave words. But a month after moving into Onslow Gardens, Anny wrote more mundanely, '. . . We are very peaceful, us two together, a little lonely as you may think. It is like living at an inn, and does not feel as if it were home exactly, but when we look at Papa's picture on the wall and sit at his table, and see things which were his, then it becomes a strange bit of a wreck saved out of the past. . . . It is a gusty grey Sunday, out of [the] window there is a green square and then unfinished houses & scaffolding. This house was Hobson's choice.'[72]

But Anny was pleased with her study, and Minny, who had an uncommon flair for making houses pleasing, chose a pretty grey wallpaper for the drawing-room which, when the chintz curtains had been hung and their china ornaments put in place, was very attractive. The dining-room was poky, but the bedrooms airy and there was a bath and every convenience. Of course, they had to buy a few things for the house. Anny went off into the city with Fanny in search of a dining-table. In the very shop they went to, they found her father's old table from Palace Green for sale. The sight of it gave Anny a queer feeling, but it was so large it would never have got into the new house in one piece.

In those early days they saw a good deal of the Coles, the Merivales and the Procters, all friends of their father and part of what he called his 'set'. Mrs Procter was a formidable woman, bombazine personified. Her husband had written poetry under the name of 'Barry Cornwall', but then gave it up and was made a Commissioner in Lunacy. He was gentle and amusing and had a genius for recognising true talent in other people's writing.*

Another of the sisters' constant companions was Jane Carlyle. She had had a soft spot for both the Thackeray girls since they were children, and Anny in particular was very fond of her. Now, this spirited, intransigent Scotswoman made a point of taking them out for drives in her carriage, since the girls had been obliged to sell their own. But the sisters had reservations about driving out with Mrs Carlyle. Her homely brougham, upholstered in blue cloth and dark morocco against the dirt, smelled horridly stuffy. Anny's feelings about Carlyle himself were ambivalent. Shortly after her father's death, she met 'old Thomas on his horse and he suddenly began to cry. I shall always love him in future, for I used to fancy he did not care about Papa'.[73] But years later she wrote: '. . . At this moment I am furious with him, cross-grained, ungrateful, self-absorbed old nut-cracker. He who could have such beautiful thoughts should have lamented not his fellow men but his own egotistical puerilities.'[74]

And then there were the Brookfields. William Brookfield had been up at Cambridge with Thackeray, was excellent company and a notorious mimic. He took Holy Orders and eventually became chaplain-in-ordinary to Queen Victoria. Witty, gifted and blessed with a sense of humour, he invested his sermons with a degree of uncommonly amusing anecdote. But even he could be flummoxed. When Anny and Mrs Cameron went together to hear Mr Brookfield preach, 'Mrs Cameron led the way into the gallery and took up her place in front exactly facing the pulpit. When Mr Brookfield appeared, climbing the pulpit steps to deliver his sermon, his head was so near us that we could almost have touched it. Mrs Cameron chose this moment to lean forward and kiss her hand to

* The Procters' eldest daughter, Adelaide, 12 years older than Anny, had written poetry since childhood. At the age of 18 she began to publish her verse under the name 'Miss Berwick' in Dickens' magazine, *Household Words*. One can imagine her delight when Dickens went to the Procters' house in Bedford Square and recommended that they should read the 'pretty poem by Miss Berwick in the forthcoming Christmas Number.' The following day, she revealed her identity. Adelaide was afflicted with delicate health and died in 1864. Although her poetry is largely forgotten now, in 1887 'the demand for Miss Procter's poems in England was in excess of those of any living writer except Tennyson.' DNB.

him repeatedly. Poor Mr Brookfield sank suddenly down on his knees and buried his face in the pulpit cushion.'[75]

In 1841 William Brookfield married Jane Octavia, the youngest daughter of Sir Charles Elton of Clevedon Court, Somerset. Immediately after her marriage her friends nicknamed her JOB. She was a cousin of Arthur Hallam who died tragically young and who was immortalised in Tennyson's poem *In Memoriam*. Before his appointment as chaplain to the Queen, Brookfield was nominally rector of Somerby-cum-Humby where Tennyson was born and grew up. The connections were very close. Brookfield was popular not only with his congregation, but also with some of the most eminent men of his time – Tennyson, Hallam, Carlyle, Sir Henry Taylor, James Spedding and, more significantly, Thackeray.

One of the results of Isabella Thackeray's tragic illness was that Thackeray could not divorce her, but was compelled by law to remain the husband of a woman who had been declared insane. This was an impossible situation for a man of such physical appetites. 'It's *a* woman I want rather than any particular one'.[76] He had resolved his dilemma by resorting to prostitutes and by falling into fantasy love affairs with conveniently built-in obstacles. These were nearly all with married women. He fancied that he was in love with Mrs Brookfield. She was beautiful, amusing and erudite. He flirted with her. She enjoyed this and reciprocated. The affair was almost certainly not consummated, but Thackeray went too far, thoroughly annoying his old friend, William Brookfield, who declared he was sick of Thackeray's attentions to his wife and forbade her to see him again. The Brookfields patched up their domestic differences, had a daughter and called her Magdalene. It was only when Thackeray fell victim to the cholera that the ban imposed by Brookfield was lifted and Mrs Brookfield and Mrs Procter between them nursed Thackeray back to health. That Anny knew about her father's liaison is clear from the fact that she was his literary amanuensis from the age of fourteen and read Mrs Brookfield's near daily letters aloud to him.

Now that Thackeray was dead and the girls ensconced in Onslow Gardens, Mrs Brookfield moved house to be close to them in South Kensington. 'All this terrible year she has been so good to us all three that I do not know how we could have dragged through without her.'[77]

The sisters suffered not so much from the absence of a guiding hand as from too many beckoning them in subtly different directions. Naturally sociable, they lived their lives against a backdrop of well-meaning people, some of them remarkable, whose opinions were bound to conflict. It was not through diffidence that they made no effort to make new acquaintances of their own choosing. It simply did not occur to them. Young ladies in their position in society were brought up to be friends with those of their parents' choosing. Now that their father was dead and their mother remained in care, they had no choice at all. The Thackeray sisters were chaperoned by respectable matrons who were socially secure enough to afford eccentricity. But however liberated the sisters were, they did not bend the rules to their own making or encourage any breach of decorum.

The new home at 8 Onslow Gardens was a depleted household. Sims, the coachman, had accepted a job with an old lady; Charles Pearman, Thackeray's manservant, had been offered a post by the thoughtful Mr Cole at one of his museums in South Kensington. Gardiner and Fanny both stayed on, and there was a live-in cook, but Gardiner did not stay long. Anny, who always made a point of getting on extremely well with her servants, was disappointed, but knew that Gardiner had dreamed of living in the country for a long while. It was a comedown not to keep a manservant and Anny minded it very much. Minny did not seem to notice.

The plan had always been for their grandmother to live with the sisters, but since their return from Arromanches in September, they had enjoyed a reprieve, as Mrs Carmichael-Smyth had stayed on in Paris. At the beginning of November, the girls had to come to terms with the fact that their grandmother *would* come back to London and live with them. They did not look forward to it.

But Mrs Carmichael-Smyth was curiously changed and mellowed: sorrow and contemplation had altered her. Neither of the sisters realised at once how frail she had grown, but there came a time when their grandmother's vitality began to ebb almost visibly. She spent most of her days beside the fire in the drawing-room, sometimes mumbling her prayers, but for long stretches of time just sitting, plucking at the fabric of her black skirts, pleating it again and again between thumb and finger.

One chilly afternoon in late November, Anny suggested a walk and together they went out, wrapped up against the cold. 'She said she had changed her mind about many things, especially about religious things, and that she could now sympathise far more than she had once done, with what my father used to think and say.'[78] Listening to her grandmother's admission, a feeling of peace stole over Anny. It was as though they had come to an understanding at last. They walked slowly back home in the foggy, yellow light.

Not long afterwards, on a Sunday afternoon, the old lady was sitting in her chair near the fire as usual, reading the Psalm for the day. She said she didn't feel very well, that she was tired. But instead of going to bed, she put aside her Prayer Book and began to tell the sisters familiar stories of her youth, which they had heard so often before that they seemed like legends from a half-mythical past. Anny meant to write it all down, but somehow she never did. Their grandmother's tale was a strange one, and it passed down as one of the many links of their family legend.

It was almost as if she was talking about someone else, but she always insisted that every word she said was true and had really happened to her. She was born Anne Becher, and had been brought up by her dreadful old grandmother, Mrs Becher, in a house on the river at Fareham. Old Mrs Becher was not only very strict but quite unscrupulous and had ambitious schemes for her ravishingly beautiful granddaughter. She allowed Anne to go to a ball at Bath. The Peninsular Wars were at their height and Bath was teeming with handsome young officers. For a lively young girl like Anne, who was only fifteen, a ball at Bath was the most delight-ful event imaginable. The fashions of the time, high-waisted frocks – flimsy affairs – showed her figure off to advantage. The officers were resplen-dent in uniform and the other gentlemen wore pantaloons and riding boots, just as though they had been out hunting. But when Anne fell in love her grandmother was furious. Anne was smitten by a young captain who was not only penniless, but who had no prospects. Mrs Becher whisked her granddaughter away from Bath back to the monotony of life at Fareham. Undaunted, the captain hired a boat which he moored at the bottom of the Bechers' garden. He intended to elope with Anne, but old Mrs Becher thwarted his plans by locking her up in her bedroom. There, Anne could hear the sad plashing of the river running past the house and see the fields of cabbages stretching beyond, and began to wish that she had never been born. But worse was to come. Unknown to her Mrs Becher told the captain that Anne had reconsidered things and never wished to see him again. She told Anne that the captain had suddenly died of a fever. Curiously sympathetic, she said that she didn't want Anne to eat her heart out over what could not be reversed. She declared she would go to the expense of sending the girl all the way to India to stay with kind relations. She said that time as well as diversion would heal Anne's broken heart.

Anny and Minny always sat quite silent at this point, mesmerised by the idea that their own grandmother had been so young and flighty that, despite her broken heart, she had travelled all the way to India wearing her *green velvet riding habit*. It was this as much as anything else about their grandmother's story that intrigued them. For, though neither of the girls rode, they knew perfectly well that no other costume is quite so becoming. And what they knew to be irrefutable was that there was no opportunity at all for the young Anne Becher to ride a horse on board ship.

Anne's relatives received her in style. They brought her out in Calcutta, where she spent her time in a whirl of balls and dinners and junketings in the shimmering Eastern haze. To Anny and Minny it sounded like a fairy tale. People wore gorgeous clothes and military bands played marches and dance tunes beneath the date trees. It was primitive and entrancing. The jungle was close to the palaces and tigers roamed when they went on picnics, which were nothing like English picnics at all but elaborate, extravagant affairs with native bearers and attendant servants. Sometimes the picnics went on for days. The heat was intense. This was the life people at Bath pretended they were leading, but this was more real, more splendid and a great deal more uncomfortable.

Dazed yet elated, young Anne Becher caused a sensation among the heady circles of the East India Company. And then one of her beaux began to court her in earnest. He used to ride up to her verandah on a great white horse and serenade her as though she were a princess out of the Arabian Nights. His name was Richmond Thackeray and his family had made their fortune by supplying the East India Company with elephants. This was precisely the kind of marriage old Mrs Becher had dreamed of for Anne. The wedding became legendary.

After their wedding, Richmond took Anne to live in a great house in the swamps near Calcutta. The outside walls were overlaid with a façade of crushed seashells and gleamed with mother-of-pearl. Anne's life was very splendid but, although in a different way, as monotonous as it had been at Fareham. She discovered Richmond to be a remarkable, convivial man with lordly ways, and she grew fond of him. Curiously, she accepted without difficulty the fact that he kept a beautiful native mistress and their several children on his estate. There was one little girl in particular who seemed to be Richmond's favourite. Anne's acceptance of the situation would have been unthinkable in England, but this was India and life seemed more like being at the play. Besides, it was so hot.

Presently, Anne became pregnant. Her confinement was not expected until after the rainy season had ended. Richmond was called away on business and his mistress went on a visit to an aunt and took her children with her. Anne remained behind. But the monsoon broke early and Anne suddenly felt the first pains of premature labour. Panic-stricken by the storm, the servants ran away. Left all alone in the vast compound,

Anne gave birth to a son in a tiny, cramped little room no bigger than her grandmother's kitchen scullery at Fareham. When the servants eventually came creeping back, they found Anne in a state of collapse, half-clasping the baby, who had been born with an enormous head.

Richmond was delighted by the boy and called him William Makepeace after the child's grandfather. The horrors that Anne had been through he dismissed. Her confinement had been badly timed. Monsoons were always violent. Of course the servants had run away. They always did. But when the doctor came, he told Richmond that the size of William's head had very nearly killed Anne, and that on no account must she have more children.

Richmond's career continued to prosper and he was frequently called from home. He had been appointed Collector of the Twenty-Four Pergunnahs, a much coveted post in the Company. On his rounds, he met and made friends with a young officer who seemed an excellent fellow even if he was a bit of a bore. Richmond brought him home to dinner. Anne had already been ensconced in the Great Saloon for some time, entertaining the other guests – officers and members of the Company and their wives – and when she looked up to acknowledge her husband's return, she found herself gazing straight into the eyes of his guest: none other than her penniless captain, Henry Carmichael-Smyth.

Neither of the lovers knew whether it was a sense of moral duty or an uncommonly astute move on their part which impelled them to acquaint Richmond with the facts. Richmond, who possessed not only great determination, but an undeniably pronounced sense of humour, said that he would not stand in a fellow's way. But he made it clear that all the proprieties must be observed. Couldn't the Captain be a decent sort, not draw attention to himself, and just hover about? The Captain rather thought he could. This suited the lovers very well, but it also suited Richmond. Anne had begun to bore him. He was genuinely enamoured of his mistress and extraordinarily fond of his little half-caste daughter. What no one had foreseen, however, was that only three years later, when William was four, Richmond went out hunting in the swamps and caught the fever. He was buried in Calcutta and as soon as decency allowed, Anne married her Captain and became Mrs Carmichael-Smyth. Many years later, long after his own death, William's half-sister lay in the tomb beside their father, far, far away in the shimmering Indian heat.[79]

When their grandmother finished her story Fanny knocked and said that supper was ready. Mrs Carmichael-Smyth said grace and they all sat down. She would take only a little broth, but after the girls had finished their soup, she insisted on helping them both to all the choicest bits from the dishes on the table and looked at Minny very long and tenderly. Anny and Minny each took a little champagne, but their grandmother refused it. The sisters felt they had never known her so harmonious and, in her heart, Anny thanked God that this was so.

'At 10 o'clock – we had ceased talking and I had read from the Christian Year for the day and she had been reading the Psalms to herself for the last time. She got up and looked at the clock and said it was time for bed. Then she gave me a great long tender kiss and then another and went away and as she went I thank God that I remember saying thank God in my heart.'[80]

'And then as we were sitting by our fire we heard a little noise and a minute after Fanny called us – And all was over.'[81]

Mrs Carmichael-Smyth had died.

Their grandmother's death came as a new sorrow which acted as a balm on the old one. Even so, the old lady had been the sisters' last link with the past and they were worn out. They could not face the crowds and the strange and vacant faces staring at them in yet another funeral procession driving all the way to Kensal Green. They could not face very much at all.

It was the Sunday before Christmas and their father's cousin, Jane Ritchie, who had been with them to the Pyrenees, was over from Paris on a visit to her numerous relations. She went to them directly and sat up with the sisters in one of the bedrooms and they all three listened to the men down below hammering nails into Mrs Carmichael-Smyth's coffin.[82] The old lady was buried at Kensal Green on Christmas Eve, exactly one year after Thackeray, her son, had died.

Jane whisked the girls off to Brighton. It was by far the best thing she could have done. Apart from their Ritchie cousins and their poor, mad mother, they were now quite alone. The sea air did them good. Minny said she was sick to death of wearing crepe and now they must go on wearing it for at least another twelve months. O! The horrid crepe! That ghastly year was over, but they had no heart to peer far into the future. '. . . I think for the present we shall live on at Onslow Gardens – the future must settle itself – I have no heart to make plans or schemes.'[83]

6

Anny immersed herself in her writing. She worked hard on her novel *The Village on the Cliff*, which first came out in eight monthly instalments in *The Cornhill* from July 1866 to February 1867 when it was published in book form by Smith, Elder. Early in January 1867, George Eliot wrote to Anny saying how much she had enjoyed her Clarence article in *The Cornhill*.[84] Anny was finding not only solace in writing but pleasure in recognition. It was a good beginning.

She had already written several articles for *The Cornhill*, the first of which was 'The Little Scholars'. About three charity schools in London, it had first appeared in the May issue of *The Cornhill* in 1860 and was republished with other essays by her, in the volume *Toilers and Spinsters* in 1874. 'The Little Scholars' is an observant piece of journalism, not in the least sensational, but quietly objective. Her description of the Jewish children in the slums of Spitalfields is refreshingly unprejudiced, given the general attitude then prevalent. 'Little Jew babies are uncommonly like little Christians; just as funny, as hungry, as helpless, and happy now that the bowls of food come steaming in.'[85]

Anny's first novel, *The Story of Elizabeth*, was serialised in *The Cornhill* between September 1862 and January 1863, when it was published in book form while her father was still alive. The book was an immediate success. Her contemporaries found its freshness and avoidance of the melodramatic refreshing. 'Vividly comes back to me,' wrote the novelist Rhoda Broughton many years later, 'the memory of my astonished delight when *The Story of Elizabeth* burst in its wonderful novelty and springlike quality on my consciousness, written, as I was told, by a girl hardly older than myself.'[86]

Readers recognised a new and authentic voice in Anny Thackeray. She dedicated the book to Julia Margaret Cameron. It is set in the Paris of Anny's childhood and Boatstown, a recognisable version of Freshwater. The heroine Elizabeth's mother, Mrs Gilmour, is only eighteen years older than her daughter and, unknown to Elizabeth, is her rival. Mrs Gilmour is secretly in love with Sir John Dampier, an impoverished and disingenuous baronet who is attracted by Elizabeth. Mrs Gilmour prevents Elizabeth from seeing Dampier and then, driven by her love of power and admiration, marries the strict but not unkind popular Protestant preacher,

Stephen Tourneur. Elizabeth is doomed to live a life of the dullest monotony at Tourneur's seminary, characterised by prayer and a frugal diet of cabbage soup. 'Madame Tourneur was already at her post, standing at the head of the table, ladling out the cabbage soup with the pieces of bread floating in every plate. . . . There was a small tablecloth streaked with blue, and not overclean; hunks of bread by every plate, and iron knives and forks. Each person said grace to himself as he came and took his place. Only Elizabeth flung herself down in a chair, looked at the soup, made a face, and sent it away untasted.'[87]

Anny's descriptions of the life of the *petit bourgeoisie* in the suburbs of Paris is minutely observed and convincing, but she never attempts the gentle satire Elizabeth Gaskell excelled at in *Cranford*. Her perfect sincerity is evident. Elizabeth goes for an illicit carriage drive in the Bois de Boulogne with Dampier and then steals out to the opera with him – scandalous behaviour which would ruin her if she were discovered. She is. To save his face, Dampier announces that Elizabeth is his fiancée, but then has to confess to her that he is engaged to her best friend, the heiress, Laetitia. The confession nearly kills Elizabeth who succumbs to a fever. Dampier's Aunt Jean, a benevolent spinster, goes to nurse Elizabeth and, after her recovery, invites her to convalesce at Boatstown. Jean Dampier has another nephew, Will, a parson and muscular Christian who is as honest as his cousin is unscrupulous. Will suspects Elizabeth of being a worldly minx who set out to ensnare Sir John, but then he falls for her himself. In an unexpected *dénouement*, John is jilted by Laetitia who marries Will; Mrs Gilmore, now Mme Tourneur, is tortured by agonising boredom, and Elizabeth marries Sir John Dampier. Despite his loose morals and caddish behaviour, she is very happy with him. Impetuous, wilful, and a far cry from the simpering heroine typical of many Victorian novels, Elizabeth is loveable.

Having begun with an unlikely but fascinating theme – the rivalry between mother and daughter – Anny simply lets it peter out so that by the end of the novel the reader has forgotten it promised to be a dramatic tale of revenge. The subject was thought sufficiently shocking for the critic in *The Athenaeum* to attack her because 'it turns upon a subject which is, or ought to be, quite inadmissable for a novel: the antagonism of a mother and daughter, both rivals for the love of the same man . . . it trenches on the sin of incest'.[88] Instead of pursuing her initial theme, Anny introduces Jean Dampier, the prototype of a cross between a fairy godmother and a surrogate mother who will appear again and again in Anny's novels as well as figuring in her life. In real life, Anny was guided and influenced by Julia Margaret Cameron, Jane Brookfield and Mrs Procter. In her novels, the same role is enacted by Jean Dampier in *Elizabeth*, Lady Sarah in *Old Kensington* and Miss Williamson, who figures in various of Anny's short stories as well as making a fleeting appearance in *The Village on the Cliff*. When Virginia Woolf wrote *Night and Day*, which came out just after Anny's death in 1919, she modelled Mrs Hilbery's character on Anny and makes Mrs Hilbery perform precisely this role of moral and spiritual matriarch. If the structure of *The Story of Elizabeth* is weak and depends too much on coincidence to be convincing, Anny's description of French provincial life and her gift for writing colloquial dialogue in both French and English save it. Elizabeth's evolution from a wilful, petulant girl into a thoughtful, contented woman, and Anny's refusal to reform Sir John Dampier contribute to making it a spirited first novel.

Anny's heroines are orphans or governesses at the mercy of the world, and in her second novel, *The Village on the Cliff*, Catherine is both. When her employers discover her unrequited passion for their nephew Dick, a Pre-Raphaelite painter, they dismiss her to another post with their French relations who live at the Château Tracy at Petitport. Petitport is recognisably Arromanches where Anny and Minny spent such a miserable time with their grandmother in 1864. Anny makes use of her upbringing which was largely spent in France, and once again the picture she succeeds in evoking of French country life and the tightly knit community of the de Tracy family at the château, the local dignitaries such as the Maire, Monsieur Fontaine, his avaricious in-laws the Mérards, and the Curé drinking Calvados, is a delight. Catherine is a feeble, sweet-natured girl who has no more say in her fate than a piece of toffee paper swept up by a street cleaner. By contrast, Reine, the self-assured, attractive and shrewd French country girl is one of Anny's most successful characterisations. Catherine and Reine are immediately drawn to each other. 'It was a princess keeping the cows. There she stood, straight, slender, vigorous; dressed in the Sunday dress of the women of those parts. . . . As for her eyes, they were quick dancing grey eyes, that looked black when she was angry – clouds and lightening somebody once told her they were, but the lightening became warm sunlight when she smiled upon those she liked.'[89] Although both girls occupy lowly positions, they both have aristocratic connections. Reine is descended from the d'Argouges family while Catherine has a pair of well-connected wealthy aunts who choose to ignore her. Both girls are in love with Dick.

In describing Dick's studio, Anny anticipates George du Maurier's novel *Trilby*, set in bohemian Paris, by twenty-eight years. Du Maurier based the character of the painter, Taffy, on Val Prinsep. Dick's studio 'was a great long room, with a cross-light that could be changed and altered at will: for which purpose heavy curtains and shutters had been put up. There was matting on the floor, and some comfortable queer-shaped chairs were standing round the fireplace. The walls were panelled to about four feet from the ground, and from hooks and nails and brackets hung a hundred trophies of Butler's fancies and experiences. Pictures begun and never finished, plaster casts, boxing-gloves, foils, Turkish pipes and scimitars, brown jugs of graceful slender form, out of Egyptian tombs. Bits of blue china, and then odd garments hanging from hooks, Venetian brocades of gold and silver, woven with silk, and pale and strange-coloured stuffs and gauzes, sea-green, salmon-colour, fainting blue, and saffron and angry orange-browns. English words cannot describe the queer, fanciful colours.' Dick himself was 'one of those weak-minded natures . . . gentle and kind-hearted, and chivalrous after a fashion.'

While still cherishing dreams of Dick, Catherine allows herself to be married off to the Maire, M. Fontaine. 'He was absurd, prosy, fussy; he had all sorts of tiresome peculiarities, but he was incapable of a harsh or unkind action.' A funeral is still being conducted in the church when the wedding party arrives – a sign of ill luck which alarms Catherine. But her marriage is not unhappy in spite of being harangued by Madame Mérard, with her ferret eyes, whose chief interests are the price of butter and winning at cards in a game with the Curé. Fontaine is kind to Catherine, although she is dismayed when he accompanies her piano-playing very loudly on the cornet: '. . . she took care afterwards to select the calmest and most pastoral and least impassioned music in her reper-tory. When she came to passages marked *con expressione* with *arpeggios*, or when she saw *fff*'s looming up appallingly in the distance, she would set her teeth and brace up her courage for the onslaught.'

On one of his visits to France, Dick paints a melancholy picture of 'a wash of brown transparent sea, a mist of grey sky and some black-looking figures coming across the shingle, carrying a drowned man . . . It was unlike any of the pictures [he] had ever painted before. There was no attempt at detail, everything was vague and undetermined but the waves came springing in, and it seemed as if there was a sunlight behind the mist . . .'. Like the unlucky funeral on Catherine's wedding-day, the paint-ing is prophetic. A storm blows up and Dick and Fontaine go to the rescue. Seeing an object floating on the water, Fontaine thinks it is a drowning fisherman and dashes into the sea. It turns out to be merely a barrel. Fontaine is killed by the impact of the barrel in the storm. Catherine inherits Fontaine's money as well as a legacy from her family in England. Dick toys with the idea of marrying her after she has left Petitport for a comfortable house in Richmond. But Catherine discovers her own strength in directing him back to Reine who, though ill and unhappy, has not been able to forget him.

Anny had her detractors as well as her fans. Even though *The Village on the Cliff*, which she dedicated to Minny, ran into three editions in February, March and July of 1867, the year it was published, Anthony Trollope wrote in his autobiography that, although he much admired the work of Anny Thackeray and Rhoda Broughton, 'Miss Thackeray's characters are sweet, charming, and quite true to human nature. In her writings she is always endeavouring to prove that good produces good, and evil evil. There is not a line of which she need be ashamed – not a sentiment of which she should not be proud. But she writes like a lazy writer who dislikes her work, and who allows her own want of energy to show itself in her pages.'[90]

In January 1865, when Anny was beginning work on *The Village on the Cliff*, Trollope and his wife invited the sisters to stay at their house at Waltham Cross near Potter's Bar. 'It was a sweet old prim, chill house wrapped in snow.' The Trollopes had the imagination to ask the young Merivales to make up a house party and they managed to give their guests a thoroughly jolly time. Later, Anny recalled '. . . in the bitter cold dark morning hearing Mr Trollope called at four o'clock. He told me he gave his man half a crown every time he [Mr Trollope] *didn't* get up!'[91] Their visit to the Trollopes was the sisters' first taste of cheerfulness for a long time. Their state of frozen misery was beginning to thaw at last.

At Easter, the sisters returned to Freshwater and the island cast its spell on them again. 'It is so heavenly Lilac down here. There are nothing but poets and painters everywhere, and it is all gold and delicious up over the Downs.'[92]

'It is the funniest place in the world. Last night Mrs Cameron invited us to tea to meet Mr Jowett and his four young men.' The four young men were students of Jowett who was a professor of Greek at Oxford. Mrs Cameron had given him the long-term use of a cottage near Dimbola, The Porch. 'We went and found them looking at photographs in a bedroom, rather shy apparently, with Charlie Cameron's little combs and brushes all lying about. We then went on to the Prinseps next door, the four young men each carrying a candle, and Mrs Cameron's maids in three little knitted waistcoats carrying a huge box of photographs. There we all sat round a table and looked at the pictures, while the young men each had a tumbler of brandy and water.

'Everybody is either a genius or a poet, or a painter or peculiar in some way. Poor Miss Stephen says is there *nobody* commonplace? We drove in to meet her the day before yesterday, and found three cousins with whom she had come. They are at the Hotel, but rather bored and bewildered.'[93]

'Poor Miss Stephen' was the sister of James FitzJames Stephen, the barrister who was helping to untangle the legal muddle of Thackeray's estate. Her name was Caroline Emilia. Her friends and relations called her Milly.

It was small wonder that Milly was bewildered. She came from an Evangelist family renowned as members of the Clapham Sect, which although they were relatively liberal, meant that she had never been to the opera or the theatre, let alone a ball. She had been well educated at home, but in a most unworldly way, and brought up to believe that Jesus was an invisible, omnipresent and loving member of her family. Even when she thwacked her boiled egg with a silver spoon, decapitated it and dipped her buttered soldiers into the runny yolk, He was there. She loved Him and He loved her. It was as simple as that. She had never seen the like of the uninhibited goings-on at Freshwater in her life before.

Mrs Cameron had lent the Thackeray sisters a set of self-contained rooms so that they had a charming little drawing-room and a small dining-room which both opened on to the garden. But they generally all ate together in Mrs Cameron's dining-room and Anny complained that their dinners were 'shocking bad'.[94]

Anny was working hard on two short articles for George Smith. Mrs Cameron was obsessed by her photography. Jowett and his students were studying at their Greek across the way. Watts was busy painting at the Briary and Tennyson writing poetry over the fields at Farringford. It was this mixture of work and fun which lent the place its singular charm.

'. . . Mrs Cameron sits up till two o'clock in the morning over her soaking photographs, Jowett's lamp also burns from a casement, and the four young men are intently studying one another. I have not quite finished my little holiday, for I had promised to finish two little articles for Mr Smith, but it is very different writing with a pencil on a Down top, with the sea and a lark twiddling most beautifully overhead, to a two-pair in London.' They devised all sorts of entertainment and small expeditions. 'I cannot tell you how much we enjoy it all; of a morning the sun comes blazing so cheerfully, and the sea sparkles, and there is a far-away hill all green and a cottage which takes away one's breath it looks so pretty in the morning mists.' They always had a good appetite for breakfast, which was invariably eggs and bacon.[95] 'Then we go to the Down top. Then we lunch off eggs and bacon. Then we have tea and look out of the window, then we pay little visits, then we dine off eggs and bacon.' Anny was sufficiently her father's daughter to weary of such a monotonous diet.[*]

Minny spent her afternoons reading Froude aloud to Mr Prinsep at the Briary. A staunch conservative in public life, who had fiercely opposed Macaulay's proposal of substituting English for the ancient Oriental languages as the mode of instruction in India, Thoby Prinsep was immensely charming in private. A great patron of some of the most eminent artists of his time, he was once described as 'large and philosophic in mind, grand in his stature, his learning, his memory, his everything, even to his sneeze! (once received with an encore from the gallery of a theatre), childlike in his gentleness and in the sweetness of his nature . . .'[96] Like most of the settlers at Freshwater, Thoby Prinsep cut a curious figure, wrapped in quantities of coats whatever the weather and wearing a high-coned hat with a veil.

After dining off eggs and bacon, Minny and one of the other young ladies would sit by the fire draped in picturesque Indian shawls lent by Mrs Cameron, while Anny and Milly Stephen strolled about in the moonlight, improving their acquaintance. Before going to bed it was the custom to gather together over cups of strong Ceylon tea poured out by Mrs Cameron. Some of them took something stronger.

In a letter Anny described a typical evening: 'Tonight we are going to tea at the Tennysons to meet these dreadful young men again. They give whoops & make us jump, & have just been presented with two photographs by Mrs Cameron, besides the tumblers of brandy & water. The only other young man here is our cousin, who is a misogynist, and when he sees us coming he rushes away across a field, or if we call he leaves the room . . .'[97]

Evening gatherings at the Tennysons' were an institution. 'The house at Farringford itself seemed like a charmed palace, with green walls without, and speaking walls within. There hung Dante with his solemn nose and wreath; Italy gleamed over the doorways; friends' faces lined the passages, books filled the shelves, and a glow of crimson was everywhere; the great oriel drawing-room window was full of green and golden leaves, of the sound of birds and of the distant sea.'[98]

The round table in the drawing-room was laid with a white cloth and set with dishes piled high with fruit and with crystal glasses and decanters

---

[*] It is worthy of a footnote to point out that the favourite food of Mrs Cameron's greatnieces Vanessa and Virginia Stephen, when they were children, was bacon and eggs.

full of port and wine. Tea was poured by Mrs Tennyson. They sat around in the window seats, on sofas and chairs, in the pools of light lent by the flickering oil lamps.

Tennyson was given to taking large quantities of wine at night. It made him feel more cheerful and put him at ease in company. He liked to sit next to his favourite girl of the moment and stroke her hand. Sometimes, he might suddenly let down her hair. Although this would have amazed and alarmed Milly Stephen, had he ever taken such a liberty with her, it was all very harmless and there is nothing to indicate anybody minded such attentions. On the contrary, such forms of avuncular flirtation were not only acceptable but positively enjoyable. Eventually, and almost inevitably, he would read aloud his own poetry and the company sat in rapt attention, no matter how many times they had heard him utter the same verses before. That he was a genius, none of them doubted. They bathed in the reflected light of his brilliance. Their lionisation made the poet feel every bit as good as did the wine.

But their adulation of Tennyson and Mrs Cameron did not prevent the sisters from seeing the comic side of things. Both of them had a strong sense of humour. Anny wrote to George Smith about Mrs Cameron, '. . . She paddles in cold water till two o'clock in the morning . . . [she] says, "Why does not Mrs Smith come to be *photographed*? I hear she is *Beautiful*. Bid her come and she shall be made *Immortal*."'[99]

This prelude to the recovery of the sisters' happiness was overshadowed by the sudden news of Mr Prescott's suicide. That affable man who had always made them welcome at Clarence House and of whom they had seen a good deal when staying at Mrs Cameron's cottage at Putney, had slit his throat with a razor. The poor man, 'best known in private and social life as one of the most kindly and hospitable of men' had 'been in a desponding way for the last three weeks'. At his inquest, after a short address from the coroner, the jury returned the verdict 'that the deceased had destroyed himself while labouring under mental derangement'.[100]

The sisters were devastated. They decided it would be better for Minny to go to be with Mrs Prescott and her daughter Sophie, at Clarence House. Both girls were immensely sympathetic, but Minny had a quiet way with her, a calmness and resolution of manner, which made her more suited to be of comfort to the shattered widow and her daughter.

Her visit did comfort the Prescotts, but it left her exhausted and she returned to the island thoroughly worn out. Almost immediately, she developed agonising toothache. It was a wisdom tooth and she wrapped her swollen face up in a shawl. Then Anny felt unwell and the next day, the doctor came. 'Both of us ill. Mrs Prinsep brought us soup into our bedroom in a silver saucepan.'[101]

Whether it was owing to the contents of Mrs Prinsep's silver saucepan or not, the sisters recovered swiftly. By the time they left the Island, Anny could write, 'It has been very pleasant and sunshiny here and we feel as if we should like to live on here in lodgings all the rest of our lives.'[102] It was a prophetic remark, for Freshwater continued to be a haven of peace and happiness for the rest of Anny's days. Moreover, she had made a new friend, Milly Stephen, who would affect both the sisters' lives indirectly but profoundly.

★

Who so walks in solitude
And inhabiteth the wood,
Choosing light, wave, rock and bird
Before the money-loving herd,
Into that forester shall pass
From these companions, power and grace.

RALPH WALDO EMERSON

Milly Stephen might at first seem an unlikely friend for Anny. It is said that opposites attract. Thoughtful and shrewd in her observation of others, Milly was an essentially passive person. She had been in love with a student, but there was no engagement and the young man went to India without ever declaring his love. Milly's appetite for life gradually atrophied, her health uncertain. Shortly after her return from the Isle of Wight, Milly's mother, Lady Stephen, asked the Thackeray sisters to lunch at 19 Porchester Square in Bayswater. Lady Stephen was the daughter of the Revd. John Venn, and came from a long line of Evangelical clergymen who were at the heart of the Clapham Sect. She was 'a handsome, amiable person with a strong disposition to look always on the happiest side of any matter'.[103] Since the death of her husband six years earlier, she had lived very quietly with Milly, who already showed every sign of turning into an old maid. The previous year, their small household had been joined by Milly's younger brother, Leslie, a convoluted character who, having been a don of mathematics and a parson at Cambridge, had left the university and hoped to support himself as a man of letters. It was at this lunch that the sisters first met Leslie. Certainly, they made a strong impression on him, an interest which both girls returned.

It would be hard for anyone not to be impressed by Leslie Stephen, whether favourably or not. His very appearance was striking. He stood tall and resolute, his bright orange beard remarkable as were his piercing blue eyes, keen as a falcon's. Robert Louis Stevenson had once compared him to an illustration of Robinson Crusoe's goat, and the likeness was, indeed, wonderful. His nose was thin and craggy and his lips were thin, hidden almost entirely by his beard and whiskers. Everything about him was long and thin and disconcertingly jerky. He had suffered all his life from highly strung nerves and was tortured by the most appalling, awkward shyness. He spoke of himself, not very appealingly, as a skinless man. He was certainly nervous on this first meeting with the Thackeray sisters. 'I vividly remember how they came to luncheon with my mother at Porchester Square and how I talked about novels to Anny and how I ingeniously observed that I liked my old favourites the best; and, upon being asked what novel then was my favourite, I replied *Vanity Fair*. I was speaking the truth and hope she saw it.'[104] The truth, down to the last scruple, was of paramount importance to Leslie. He fairly quivered in his passion to express himself with the utmost regard to accuracy.

While Leslie was at Cambridge, he had subdued his highly excitable emotions by exhausting himself physically. He rowed. He walked. He transformed himself from being a sickly creature into an impressive athlete.

When Leslie walked, he didn't merely go for a stroll as other men do, through the five-acre, down the lane and home through the woods. He thought nothing of walking from Cambridge to Newmarket for his lunch and back; from Cambridge to London for his dinner. Not only did he find such activities a release for himself, but he positively encouraged such habits in others. As much as his friend, Charles Kingsley,[105] Leslie was an advocate of Muscular Christianity. If exercise was good for Leslie, then it followed that it must be good for all men. And, indeed, it was a fine sight to see Leslie and a few like-minded parsons whirling around like so many dervishes, divesting themselves of dog-collars, buttons, and even their jackets, while their hats flew off onto the normally staid green of Cambridge's Parker's Piece.[106] As a don and tutor, he also whipped up enthusiasm for such pursuits in his students. These scions of the English upper classes, hobbledehoy youths in tweed jackets and wide-awake hats, who were destined for the Law, the Church and the Empire, must now row themselves into a muck sweat, pulling their oars up and down the effluent waters of the river Cam. They must tramp hour after hour through the muddy Fens, scaring the water vole, leaving the startled cow to rumi- nate in the meadow. The effect which this intensely nervous and rigor- ous man had on his students − as well as upon subsequent generations − was profound.

And then, quite unexpectedly, Leslie lost his faith in God. He claimed that he had never had any. He declared that he could no longer believe in the validity of Noah's Ark. But the truth was not as simple as he persuaded himself. Rather as a traveller, who must change his currency into legal tender for the new frontier, Leslie really did forget all the vexa- tions which that transaction had cost him. His new creed was one which he continued to cling to with all the ardour of his lost one. He believed every bit as much in not believing as he had in his earlier faith. That his conversion to agnosticism had not been easy was evident to anyone who knew him well. There were even rumours that he contemplated suicide, but his true friends knew that this was unlikely. His mother, Lady Stephen, proved remarkably tolerant. Milly didn't think Leslie had ever taken God seriously enough from the start. The day before he took Holy Orders, Milly had begged him to give up the plan, '*not from any suspicion of his having any doubts*, but from my own strong sense of the absence in him of any decided "vocation" for which we had been accustomed to think of as the most sacred of callings . . . The only reply I got was "Oh never mind − it's all right" & so on − I was never satisfied . . .'.[107]

Leslie's conversion did not fundamentally change his attitude to life.

He remained as morally serious as the most devout Christian. But what did change were his circumstances. In order to be a Fellow at Cambridge, it was obligatory to be a man of the cloth. His principles forced him to resign his Fellowship and his career at Cambridge was at an end. In 1863, the American Civil War was at its height. Like his grandfather, the first Sir James Stephen, a passionate abolitionist, the mere concept of slavery was anathema to him. His father, the second Sir James, had drafted the legislation whereby the British had legally abolished slavery. Leslie was exasperated by reports he read of the Civil War, particularly in *The Times*. The prevalent view of the ordinary Englishman was essentially in favour of the Southern cause, for reasons both economic and sentimental. Thoroughly impatient, Leslie decided to go to America and find out the situation for himself. He reached Boston just after the Battle of Gettysburg, and there he met some distinguished men: the poet, scholar and politician James Russell Lowell, the art critic and writer Charles Eliot Norton, and the famous lawyer Oliver Wendell Holmes (who had been severely wounded in battle).[108] He travelled as far west as St Louis, then east to Washington, where he was very much impressed by President Lincoln, before returning to Boston where his friendships with Lowell, Norton and Holmes flourished: he remained in close contact with them for the rest of their lives.

Back in London, Leslie went to live with his mother and sister. The Stephen household offered a completely different atmosphere to the one he had grown accustomed to at Cambridge. '. . . I find I can pick up a pretty good living by writing for the papers, and like the work so far. Meanwhile it is rather an effort to turn out of a warm easy place like Cambridge, where I had been vegetating for near fifteen years in comfort. I had a luxurious set of rooms. I walked about in a gorgeous cap and gown, and every one that I met took off their hats to me. Now, in London, I find that people don't instinctively recognise me. I can walk down the Strand without causing any visible sensation . . . The change is, I believe, good for me, because an English university is only too pleasant a place for a bachelor.'[109]

He had hoped to go in for the law, but wrongly believed that, as a parson, he was not eligible. His brother, FitzJames, always known in the family as Fitzy, did not enlighten him. Later, Leslie did try for the law, but half-heartedly, disliked it and soon gave it up. But it was Fitzy, a former contributor to Thackeray's *Cornhill Magazine*, who put Leslie in the way of journalism. He introduced Leslie to the editor of *The Saturday Review* and then, fortuitously, a new daily afternoon paper, *The Pall Mall Gazette* came out and Leslie became one of its most regular contributors. The paper was a success, with G.H. Lewes, Trollope, Charles Kingsley and Matthew Arnold among its contributors. Leslie had landed on his feet as a man of letters.

The Thackeray sisters had already heard of him through their literary friends, but they were equally struck by his position as newly-elected president of the Alpine Club. The glamour then attached to that position was dazzling. By the mid-nineteenth century, mountaineering in Switzerland had become a highly fashionable and prestigious pastime for gentlemen, and the Alpine Club had an international reputation. Leslie first started climbing in 1855 in the Tyrol and the Bavarian Highlands, but became a serious alpine enthusiast when he took Milly to Switzerland with their friends the Russell Gurneys in 1857.[110] From then on he spent part of every summer climbing in the Alps, and in 1861 he was the first man to conquer the Shreckhorn. On his first visit to the Alps, he had been smitten by the power of the scenery:

> . . . the rushing snow
> The sun-awakened avalanche – whose mass
> Thrice sifted by the storm had gathered here,
> Flake after flake, in heaven-defying minds
> As thought by thought is piled, till some great truth
> Is loosened, and the nations echo round,
> Shaken to the roots, as do the mountains now.[111]

But Leslie was impelled not to write verse, but to conquer those peaks. It was very simple. He loved the mountains, but he loved them better when he was at the top. What fascinated Leslie was the mountain in relation to man and vice-versa. He wasn't merely interested by that mountain, but liked to identify that orange smudge as Seiler's Inn where he had spent the night, stretching out in a narrow bed not nearly long enough for his height, and where, unbelievably, he would return dizzy from exhaustion, and spend yet another night. That black dot must be the cook scuttling about in the yard. The sheer absurdity of the altered proportions lent an entirely new sense of perspective. Leslie was capable of letting out whoops of laughter from a sudden wave of exhilaration merely because he, too, on top of the mountain, was a member of the human race as much as the cook beetling about with potato peel in the yard far down in the valley below.

But when he went on an expedition, he did the thing thoroughly. He was responsible and serious and took only the best guides. No one sang the praises of the guides louder than Leslie. He was no fool and submitted to their counsel, for they were men who had hunted the chamois as boys and who could read the signs written in the skies, indecipherable to the amateur climber. Of all the guides, his favourite was Melchior Anderegg. Theirs was that strong and inexpressible bond that is formed after having shared some overwhelming physical experience. Words play no part in such relations – pity poor Fitzy who talked his head off when on a climb with Leslie. Leslie never invited him to climb again. Leslie was popular with the guides and his fellow climbers: a man to be depended on and looked up to. It is true that his extreme shyness frequently manifested itself in a coolness tantamount to rudeness. But that was back at the Inn. Those years spent tutoring his students, urging them to prefer mud and muscle to beer and brothels, had taught him how to hit the right note with his peers. He knew when to skylark and he knew how to lead.

No one who made an ascent with Leslie ever forgot his presence of mind when climbing those stairs of ice, his long legs striding ahead like a pair of compasses, until at last they reached the top and hoisted a flag, marked the spot with stones, yelled out a cheer for victory. No one ever forgot how he stood tall and triumphant, lighting his pipe for a whiff of shag tobacco. His influence was greater than he knew, for through that rock of morality ran a deep vein of compassion and kindness. He encouraged younger men, but never minimised the dangers of mountaineering. Those dangers were very real. But to lie on the summit of a new and first-rate pass was a wonderful and glorious pleasure which, in the very nature of things, could be but rarely enjoyed.

On that level, Leslie's love of the mountains was very simple. On another, it was complicated by the emotions with which he imbued the slopes. The mountains were very tangible, but they also stood for various milestones in his life. For Leslie, the logical rationalist, was also a passionate sentimentalist. He said one thing and felt another, and both these things were true. He was all he said and yet so much more, and so many sides to his nature flatly contradicted themselves that hardly anyone, not even those who loved and knew him best, could recognise him in all his humours. Magnificent on a mountain, he was an altogether different man in a drawing-room.

Yet he was very much a ladies' man, and both the Thackeray sisters were susceptible to his charm. They had various friends in common, including George Smith, the Merivales, the Seniors and Mrs Gaskell.[112] That they had not met before may simply have been because Leslie had only given up his Fellowship at Cambridge the previous year. Yet there was a subtle social difference. The Thackerays moved in more elevated, more cosmopolitan circles. They were also significantly richer than the Stephens and could afford entertainments which were not only beyond the Stephens' income, but discouraged by their religion.

Leslie was fascinated and attracted by both Anny and Minny. Yet, when he met them by chance a few days later in the Geological Museum at South Kensington, he fled from them. The girls did not know what to think.[113] Two days later, they received an invitation from Lady Stephen to go to tea. It was a fitful beginning, pregnant with uncertainty.

7

Although the sisters were beginning to recover from the grief of two bereavements in one year, they were not ready to take up the positions allotted them in their new life. Anny, in particular, could not let go of the memories of her father and, indeed, clung to them jealously for the rest of her life.

In May they made an expedition to Cambridge with one of their father's cousins, Mrs Bayne, to visit his old rooms at Trinity. They saw his name written in the old college books and got into conversation with a kind clergyman who remembered Thackeray drawing pictures at a water-party and in Edward FitzGerald's rooms.[114] These old traces of Thackeray's youth brought her father back to Anny more vividly than ever. When they returned to Onslow Gardens, it seemed to her as though they had almost travelled from one century into another. Moved by the visit, she took down her grandmother's Bible and began to read the Book of Job. She read 'a few words that Job spoke in his utter desolation – Today I have felt like Job, so much is gone & yet all is dearer & nearer only that it is gone. It seems to me at last as if more happiness & more peaceful times were in store. Amen if it is so, if not pray God to make us know him as we should know him, love him & wait in peace & trust until the end. What it is, this great end is very awful to realise, sometimes I feel as if it was our home, & then again as if it was only a strange country – But this is the strange country please God.'[115]

Anny was unhappy, but she was not morbid: her religion comforted her and prevented her from giving way to despair. What she wrote then was in a private diary, meant for no other eyes than hers. In public, she comported herself as best as she could and with no little success. It would have seemed to her a tremendous burden upon others to have behaved any differently, and she could not bear that her particular sorrow should be an imposition on anyone else. If Minny caught her looking a trifle blue she sympathised, and acted as a tonic after the fashion of the most understanding of sisters. Prone to depression, Anny was living a precarious kind of existence. The small craft of her life was as emotionally perilous as a matchbox bobbing about in the Bay of Biscay. And yet Anny, as much as Minny, could resurface from sinking into memory and enjoy the present to the hilt.

When the painter John Everett Millais and his wife took both girls to the National Gallery, they could not help but burst out laughing when Millais shook his fist angrily at Raphael's Madonna.[116] And when Mrs Prinsep took them to see the Summer Exhibition at the Royal Academy, they both enjoyed themselves enormously.

On 1 June, Leslie Stephen arranged a boating expedition down the Thames as far as Henley. He invited the Thackeray sisters and Fitzy and his wife Mary went with them. It was a completely new experience for

Anny and Minny and they thought it glorious to be rowed by the Stephen brothers. It was a heavenly day, and Anny admired the green riverbanks waving with lacy white cow-parsley. They dined in a restaurant overlooking the river at Maidenhead. Then Leslie and Fitzy rowed them all the way back, everyone tired and perfectly happy.

On 8 June, the publisher George Smith and his wife invited the sisters to dine with them at Hampstead. Mrs Gaskell and Leslie were among the other guests. It was at this dinner that Leslie began to fall in love with Minny. Mrs Gaskell, who was a most observant person, couldn't help noticing, and afterwards predicted that Minny would marry him.

However transparent their feelings for one another may have been, Leslie behaved with caution. He dithered. 'I was shy, diffident, and fully impressed with the conviction acquired at Cambridge that I was an old don – a superannuated bachelor standing apart from all thought of domestic happiness.'[117] He was thirty-three years old.

While Leslie's self-denigration was sincere, his belief that he was an old fuddy-duddy ineligible for marriage was not the whole story. He could not afford to marry Minny. Having left the comforts of Cambridge for Grub Street, he was making a living by journalism. Although he was proving successful, he lived free of charge in his mother's house at Bayswater. He had not got enough money to set up a separate establishment with Minny. Leslie was obsessed by money. He knew that Minny was richer than he was and he knew that she had been brought up to have expensive tastes, although anyone less self-indulgent than she would be hard to imagine. Since the Married Women's Property Act had not yet been passed, Leslie would automatically acquire Minny's money by marrying her.[118] To a man of his scruples, the notion was repugnant. He would have preferred it if she did not have a penny. So he dithered. Nothing was spoken of immediately, which was not a comfortable state of affairs.

At the end of June Anny and Minny went down to Kent to stay with Mrs Jackson at Saxonbury, near Frant. Maria Jackson was one of Mrs Cameron's sisters and the girls had known her ever since their father used to take them to Mrs Prinsep's soirées at Little Holland House. Mrs Jackson was a semi-invalid who suffered acutely from arthritis. Charming and gentle, she was extremely fond of poetry and immensely concerned with her own health and other people's. To care for her beauty did not appear to her to be vanity so much as a duty, for she believed her considerable good looks to be a gift from God. '. . . I still seem to smell the exquisite cleanliness of that toilette. The delicious soap – what was it?

something that no one else used I am sure – and her hands dabbling in the water, already so clean and transparent that surely they couldn't need washing. The powder – I think she must have had quite a lot of French coquetterie, should one call it? – at any rate she had no Victorian feeling against such aids. Her hair had to be brushed with a soft baby's brush till it shone again and then her deep-set brown eyes seemed to become bright too . . .'[119]

The Thackeray sisters were familiar with Maria Jackson and her obliging husband, the doctor. Although they had met their youngest daughter, Julia, at the Little Holland House gatherings, they had never really got to know her well until now. Julia was nine years younger than Anny and six years younger than Minny. It makes a considerable difference when you are eighteen to be with a little girl of nine, but when that child has grown to be a young woman, it becomes possible to be on equal terms. At Saxonbury, Anny and Julia hit it off immediately. Coventry Patmore came to dine and Anny wrote in her journal, 'and I fell in love with Julia, a vision of beauty, quick, sweet, practical and like a dream'.

Julia's beauty was legendary. Holman Hunt and Woolner had both fallen in love with her and proposed in vain. Julia Margaret Cameron, her aunt, photographed her frequently and she was the model for the Virgin in Burne-Jones' painting *The Annunciation*. She was quick-witted, thoughtful and naturally optimistic. It was small wonder that Anny liked her. Their friendship would have important consequences for them both.

In August, the sisters went to stay again with their Ritchie cousins at Henbury in Devon. The weather was lovely, the countryside beautiful, and romance was definitely in the air. 'The idyll of Frank and Blanche had begun – met Mr Cornish in a turnip field.'[120] Frank Warre Cornish was an attractive, owl-like and intelligent scholar who was then employed as an assistant master at Eton, later becoming vice-provost and librarian. Small and frail, with gentle voice and manners, he was the perfect foil for Blanche Ritchie. At eighteen, Blanche was a remarkable girl whose sparkling sense of the ridiculous and totally original perception of what would otherwise have remained humdrum, made her irresistibly attractive.

Robert Browning, now in his early fifties, had been very much in love with Blanche. He had been on the point of proposing to her when Frank, on learning this, 'went to him and begged him not to go to Henbury till after he had been, & that after a short consideration he had consented to this'.[121] But Frank need not have been worried that Browning would queer his pitch. Whilst she enjoyed his adulation, Blanche, who had high opinions of herself, would never have consented to play second fiddle to the legend of Elizabeth Barrett Browning. She loved Frank, and even if married life at Eton meant living in a smaller pond than Browning's, at least she would be the larger fish.

All summer long, the Ritchie boys played cricket on the lawn with Frank and everybody went on picnics to the seaside. Anny wrote: 'The great moon. *The cows up on the Hills.* Violet seas and Pearl Island. B's blue veil ahead with Mr Cornish. *On the sands* red caps hauling nets W[illy], G[erald] and R[ichmond] up to their waists in water. On the steamer discordant music – smooth waters – fun and frivolity.'[122]

It was into this Elysian summer that what Anny called the 'bombshell' broke. To be more precise, it was not just one bomb, but a series of explosions which sent them reeling back into the terrifying void of chaos from which they had so recently struggled free.

When Anny and Minny had still been in the schoolroom during their early teens, Thackeray had hit on the bright idea of asking Amy Crowe, the daughter of his friend, the painter Eyre Crowe, to live with them as their companion. The arrangement was a success and solved the vexed question of governesses which Thackeray had considered the bane of his life. Amy was only a few years older than the sisters, but sufficiently 'out' to be considered in the light of a chaperone. They all became inordinately fond of one another. Thackeray treated Amy as though she were a favourite niece and nicknamed her 'Little Dorrit'. And then Amy fell in love. She fell in love with Thackeray's cousin, Edward Thackeray, a gallant and ferocious soldier who had been awarded the Victoria Cross for capturing the Kasmir Gate at Delhi during the Indian Mutiny of 1858. Everyone was pleased for Amy, but wretched at the thought of her parting from them. After having given away the bride, Thackeray was so grieved that he went to see Millais for consolation and spent most of that afternoon in tears.[123] The sisters kept up a correspondence with Amy as frequently as the posts allowed, and were delighted when her first child, Margie, Anny's goddaughter, was born. That summer of 1865 they were looking forward to hearing of the birth of her second child.

But then came 'the dreadful news from India. Amy sank from fever after Annie's birth. It seemed as if I had known of it long ago.'[124] The sisters were broken-hearted. Anny and Minny at once decided to care for the children. Nobody – not Mrs Ritchie, Mrs Brookfield, Mrs Cole nor Mrs Procter – found anything very extraordinary in the notion that they should become involved. Their only previous experience of looking after children, apart from their ladylike and somewhat haphazard attendance at the 'Ragged Schools', was the episode of little Ellen, the waif who had been beaten by her tipsy mother. But Ellen had vanished without trace from the sisters' lives. Of course, they would have help – maids, nannies, nurses. Edward would contribute towards his daughters' upkeep. But Margie was barely a year older than her baby sister Annie, who was only just over a month old by the time they arrived in Europe.

Anny and Minny left the Ritchies at Henbury without making any practical arrangements to receive the motherless babies. They went on a spontaneous spree, first to stay with Adelaide Sartoris at Warnford, then north to stay with Monckton Milnes at his magnificent house, Fryston, in Yorkshire, and eventually came back by way of Somersby where Mr Brookfield had his country parish in Lincolnshire.

On 2 October, they set off for Paris to meet Edward Thackeray and the children. Anny and Minny stayed with their father's cousins, Charlotte and Jane Ritchie and their companion Félicie, whom they loved as a member of the family. The occasion, fraught already, was made even more distressing by the discovery that Jane Ritchie was seriously ill.

On their return with Edward Thackeray and the two children, not surprisingly Anny recorded, 'Confusion – nurses . . . We settled down by degrees, Edward making allowances for the children.'[125]

The sisters had been about to recover a modicum of happiness. Minny knew, or thought she knew, that Leslie was in love with her. But the death of Amy and the arrival of the children overshadowed that half-glimpsed ray of light. The household was put into turmoil. The servants were upset in their ways. Nothing went right. Edward veered between misery and wrath. Anny wrote, 'Poor fellow, his gentleness and tenderness is quite affecting. I can remember so well Papa bringing us to Paris & how we cried all night – These little things only wail, they have never ceased for six weeks and are quite worn out, but I hope please God quiet and care will set them up again . . . Minny says "Now, Anny don't you find our experience with puppies valuable?" She is delightful with them & knows exactly what to do.'[126]

Almost as soon as the children began to settle, the sisters learned 'the sad news of Jane's hopeless illness'. They had known of her condition, but nobody had expected the end to be so soon. Anny's reaction was typically impulsive. She would go at once to be with Jane at the end and try to comfort Charlotte. She had her bags packed and was already at the Halion, a hotel convenient for catching the boat train, when Mrs Ritchie intercepted her and, much against Anny's will, persuaded her to return home.

When Jane Ritchie died, Anny broke down altogether and took to her bed. 'It seemed to us all those days as if Death haunted our life.'[127] They had suffered tragedy after tragedy and they could not bear much more. Emotional, impulsive, quick to sympathise, Anny had a propensity to extreme depression. She was an unpredictable mixture of scattyness and wild flights of fancy, combined with a peculiarly original and idiosyncratic sense of fun. Some people have the makings of a saint and can bear the burden of grief with serenity. Anny was not one of them. She may have cared too much to be able to bear very much reality, but she was fated, despite her extreme enjoyment of life, to be haunted by tragedy.

Both the sisters were consoled by an invitation to the unveiling of their father's bust, sculpted by Marochetti, in the Poets' Corner of Westminster Abbey. It was a proud moment for Anny, although she took exception to the length of his side whiskers, hewn in marble, which she declared were too long.*

One day in 1865, quite unexpectedly, Katie Collins came to call at Onslow Gardens. It was some time since the sisters had seen her, but she burst

---

* Years later, Anny's niece by marriage, Molly MacCarthy (née Warre Cornish) conjured up the picture in her book, *A Nineteenth-Century Childhood* how 'for years . . . Aunt Anny has deplored the length of the whiskers on each side of her father's bust . . . They spoil the likeness for her and she has longed to have them clipped, as so at last she has begged Mr Ford (the sculptor) and has implored the Dean to let her have her wish, and have them shortened. So now chip, chip, chip fly the bits under the white bloused assistant's chisel. Mr Ford stands by, very cross, for he does not like undoing another sculptor's work, and if the daughter of Thackeray had not happened to be such a charming old lady it is probable she would not have had her way. She laughs; admits that there is something absurd about the commission but is firm that it shall be carried out; so she talks to him without paying any attention to his crossness, and makes him at last smile as he superintends the work. Finally the bust is flicked over with a cloth, as after a shave, and it is carried up into the nave and back into its own niche, and the silence and dignity of the Abbey receives it back again. We all survey the bust in silence, and then disperse. Aunt Anny is a little emotional as she gets into the victoria, smiling at her tears, then weeping a little at her smiles; she is triumphant, for it has been a great relief to her mind.' I am grateful to the Reverend St John H. Mullett, who, since neither he nor I were tall enough, got hold of a very tall and helpful verger, who reached up to feel WMT's whiskers in the Abbey and confirmed that, indeed, he could feel the roughness on the bust where the whiskers had been hacked off by Mr Onslow Ford's assistant.

out breathlessly, 'I know you will shrink from it, but I want to take you to the reading of *Copperfield* at St James's Hall. It is the last London reading, I have your places: I asked them to be kept for you.'[128] Dickens' reading of his novel was a thrilling and unforgettable occasion. He read magnificently and seemed to turn into the very characters whom he had created. '. . . On this special evening, it was for all the rest I heard his voice . . . He seemed holding the great audience in some mysterious way from the empty stage. Quite immediately the story began; Copperfield and Steerforth, Yarmouth and fishermen and Peggoty, and then the rising storm, all were there before us. It was not acting, it was not music, nor harmony of sound and colour, and yet I still have an impression of all these things as I think of that occasion. The lights shone from the fisherman's home; then, after laughter, terror fell; the storm rose. Finally, we were all breathlessly watching from the shore, and (this I remember most vividly of all) a great wave seemed to fall splashing onto the platform from overhead, carrying away everything before it, and the boat and the figure of Steerforth in his red sailor's cap fighting for his life by the mast. Someone called out; was it Mr Dickens himself who threw up his arms? It was all over, we were half laughing, half crying with excitement; being at the special time still very much wrought up, remembering the past, naturally our emotions took shape.'[129]

After the performance, Katie took them backstage where Charles Dickens held their hands with the kindest clasp of greeting and comfort. They were overwhelmed by his effusiveness.

At home, the presence of the children helped to cheer the sisters and give them a sense of purpose. A nurse and a nursery-maid took the main charge of the little girls, but Anny and Minny rapidly became very fond of them. Minny in particular had an extraordinary yet perfectly natural way with children. She didn't condescend but seemed, quite effortlessly, to enter into all their amusements as well as their sudden, boiling furies, and showed herself to them just as she was – tender, gentle, funny and affectionate. By January 1866, they had managed to establish a regular pattern to their days, and Anny began to get on with her novel, *The Village on the Cliff*.

Blessed with a talent for domestic organisation, Minny was a good housekeeper. Anny's notions were grand, but vague. Without Minny's ingenuity, the household would have been at sixes and sevens. Minny enjoyed paying very precise attention to those details which make up the whole. She also had the wit to laugh at Anny's more impulsive blunders. Her spirited attitude to life made her remarkably attractive, but she could prove unexpectedly thorny, or suffer from a sudden melancholy which it never occurred to her to disguise. Cautiously, by fits and starts, they began seeing people again. They gave small, intimate dinner-parties for their close friends. Minny generally devised the menus and gave the cook her orders, although sometimes these might be countermanded by Anny. At one such dinner, the guests included Katie and Charles Collins, young Walter Pollock and the diarist Arthur Munby.[130] Munby took Katie into dinner and was impressed by all the arrangements and the quality of the dinner, although he was a trifle startled when the fish was brought in. It was a splendid grayling, sent as a present to the sisters by Millais, who was a keen fisherman. The grayling lay in state upon its dish. Anny, who as head of the house, naturally took it upon herself to do the carving, hesitated. When the company wondered why, she confessed that she dared not carve it for fear it should bark. She was among friends who appreciated her tangential and original turn of mind.

Not all of Anny's vagaries were so inconsequential. Like her father, she was wildly extravagant and was the first to admit it. But, unlike Thackeray, she seemed to have no understanding of money. In spite of the muddle about Thackeray's will, he had left his daughters very well provided for. Anny's spending was not only reckless, but she could never account for it. Certainly, there was very little to show for it. She could not check herself from frittering money away on things they could very well have done without. She spent on clothes, on expensive dinners, on 'ruinacious bonnetts' [sic],[131] on travel, on books, and on almost anything that caught her fancy on the spur of the moment. She gave a fair amount away; she simply did not *think*. And then, when the bills came in, she would be filled with remorse and vow to reform, and of course she did nothing of the kind until the next lot of bills came in, and the whole performance was repeated.

That January, 1866, Anny really had outdone herself. Fortunately, they were able to solve their problems by letting the house at Onslow Gardens to Mrs Ritchie and her large family for six weeks. The sisters went with the children and the servants to stay at a small farm in Surrey where they were able to rent lodgings cheaply.

In the summer, for the first time since her father's death, Anny felt like celebrating her birthday in the grand old style to which he had accustomed her. She gave an elaborate picnic lunch, set out on tables beneath the great shady trees at the inn at Leith Hill near Abinger Hatch, and invited a number of people, mainly old friends of the family, to share it with her. The luncheon was provided by the keepers of the inn. The sun shone. The guests arrived in carriages from the station. After they had eaten, Mrs Sartoris sang Gordigiani magnificently, and they all strolled about, talking, offering each other fruit, refilling their glasses and enjoying themselves. Among the guests were Lord Leighton, Val Prinsep, the Merivales, the Coles and Jeannie Senior. Also present were Julia Jackson and Leslie Stephen.

It was the first time that Leslie met Julia. He was standing on the little green before the inn, talking to his old friend, Jane Senior, known more intimately as Jeannie.[132] Julia was standing near them among a small group of girls. The other young women all wore very pretty crinolines with flounces. Julia never wore a crinoline in her life.[133] She was dressed in white with blue flowers in her hair and her gown was draped after the manner of the Pre-Raphaelites. Leslie could not help wondering where all her admirers were. There was a stillness, a remoteness about her which seemed to distance her from reality. Jeanie Senior asked Leslie what he thought of Julia. She was the most beautiful girl he had ever seen in his life. He thought she looked like the Sistine Madonna. He thought her features absolutely faultless, and to him they seemed to imply an equal beauty of soul and character. To Leslie, standing on that small patch of green turf, Julia Jackson appeared to embody the complete reconciliation and fulfilment of his ideas of feminine beauty. And yet, despite this other-worldly vision, it was Minny who caught his fancy. Undeniably enchanting, she was not so awe-inspiring as the divine Julia.

Anny's birthday picnic was a turning point in their lives and an occasion which none of them forgot. Leslie began to perceive that Minny was drawing closer to him. 'She showed a gentle pleasure when the accidents of the day brought us together.'[134] Anny noticed it too. In her journal, she wrote, 'Made up my mind that Leslie was serious and that he really cared for Minny.'[135]

That heavenly day, as all days must, came to an end, and in the evening the entire party drove in carts pulled by great farm horses to the station where they took the train back to London.

'The Picnic,' decided Anny, 'was a very great success.'

8

Have you seen but a bright lily grow
   Before rude hands have touched it?
Have you marked but the fall of the snow
   Before the soil hath smutch'd it?
Have you felt the wool of beaver,
   Or swan's down ever?
Or have smelt o' the bud o' the briar,
   Or the nard in the fire?
Or have tasted the bag of the bee?
   O so white, O so soft, O so sweet is she!

BEN JONSON

For years Leslie had made a habit of spending part of every summer mountaineering in Switzerland. By chance, Mrs Huth, the wife of the wealthy banker and bibliophile who had bought 2 Palace Green, had arranged to go to Chamonix that summer of 1866 with her young daughter, Dulcie, and a cousin of Leslie's, Jeanie Dicey. Mrs Huth, stately in her sweeping gowns, gave the impression of a ship in full rig, but beneath her pretensions, she was a thoroughly 'good kind woman'.[136]

She suspected how matters lay between Minny and Leslie. She had made rather a favourite of Minny and often invited her over to Palace Green and asked her to read aloud works by her protégé, the historian and philosopher, Henry Buckle. Afterwards, she would put what Minny called corkscrew questions to her about Buckle's writing. But she had too much sense to put corkscrew questions to Minny about her love affair. Instead, she invited both the sisters to Chamonix and made it clear that it was an understood thing that Leslie should meet them at Zermatt. The little girls, Margie and Annie, would stay with their Ritchie cousins at Henbury.[137]

Leslie reached Zermatt before them. He walked at what he considered to be a leisurely pace along the route he knew so well. The previous day, he had heard from two travellers that the party was on its way. There had been gossip that the younger Miss Thackeray had asked everyone she met whether they knew of the whereabouts of the president of the Alpine Club.[138] He may have been amused and not a little conceited. He may have been a little shocked. He may have felt these things all at once. But whatever he made of it, he was in no hurry. He knew that he would have plenty of time to meet them at the pass where their routes crossed.

He saw them from the ridge, silhouetted against the sky. He hadn't imagined what a great party they would make. Naturally, they had brought their maids with them and quantities of luggage, and then there were the guides. Together with the mules, they made up a regular caravan. He walked down to meet them.

They were all in terrific high spirits. The Thackeray girls were ecstatic about the beauty of the mountain scenery. It was their first sight of the overpowering hills and snowy peaks. They had never encountered the quality of the light, which was so clear they could make out every detail like a pinprick from very far off. The acoustics of the soaring peaks made every sound articulate. And then, it was such a lovely day that it seemed absurd there should be so much snow, so thick, so like a picture book, that really it should belong to winter. If their exclamations struck a discord on Leslie's ears, for he generally insisted on silence in the mountains, he betrayed no sign. That meeting where the road winds round a little bluff near Täsh was the beginning of three of the happiest days in his life.[139] He walked back with them, the ladies riding mules, to Zermatt where they had booked rooms at Seiler's Inn.

Seiler's Inn smelt of soap and tarred pitch, of pinewood, boot polish and gravy, of laundry and ink and mothballs, of shaving soap, sealing-wax and coffee, and of a multitude of other things besides. Their rooms opened out on to a green painted verandah running round that side of the inn. The view was magnificent. The Matterhorn rose above them, mighty, majestic, more splendid, more terrible than the sisters had ever dreamed. They could make out where they had been that afternoon. They could see the little chalets which, in that extraordinarily clear light, looked as though they were made of paper.

Leslie took a fierce pride in showing the party his beloved mountains. He pointed out the peaks with the same reverence that other men reserve for the stars. He took them up the Görner Glacier. They went by mule and on foot. The alpenstocks provided by the inn were indispensable. The women wore crinolines which swung about them like Chinese lanterns. The crinoline was not such a ridiculous dress for the mountain as it might appear. The hoop itself kept their quantities of petticoats deliciously off their legs, so that it was like being in an airy bell.[140] Even so, they were undeniably cumbersome. All of the party were grateful for Leslie's attentions, and then again for being shown the mountains by an expert − not that the mountains would have changed without him, but they would have seen them quite differently.

That evening, they all stayed up very late in the little garden at the inn, sitting in the lamplight and looking at the stars, Leslie smoking his pipe. Anny wrote in her journal, 'O such a day – at night moonlight and mountains, a snowy, eerie world.'

Leslie suggested an expedition to the Riffle Horn and it was decided that he and the sisters and Dulcie Huth should go. They took a picnic made up for them at the inn. Anny thought Minny had never looked more engaging. They sat under a tree, and on a little grassy platform they picnicked in the shade. Wild flowers grew everywhere. Tufts of dianthus, delicate ferns, harebells and gentians contrasted with pale, fragile wood anemones, although it was too late for the small, sweet-scented mountain cyclamen which Leslie later associated with Minny. Sitting there, eating his lunch with the girls, Leslie began to feel his fate was fixed.[141] But the moment passed, and nothing was said.

Back at the inn, Anny got out the manuscript of her novel but couldn't write. She began to be angry with Leslie and to wish that they had never come at all. She could see Minny's feelings for Leslie were serious. She could not shake off a half-remembered nightmare she had had back at Chamonix. She prayed that it was not some ghastly omen, even though she knew that to be absurd.

They sat out late again that evening, under the stars, Leslie reciting Browning's 'Lost Leader' with a passion that quivered in his voice.

> Just for a handful of silver he left us,
> Just for a riband to stick in his coat –
> Found the one gift of which fortune bereft us
> Lost all the others she lets us devote;
> They with the gold to give, doled him out silver,
> So much was theirs who so little allowed:
> . . . let him never come back to us!
> There would be doubt, hesitation and pain,
> Forced praise on our part – the glimmer of twilight,
> Never glad confident morning again!

They sat motionless in the moonlight. Everyone felt this was a moment of great significance. Then Leslie began to address Mrs Huth, telling her quite calmly of his immediate plans. He was going to meet a fellow in Vienna and from there they would both go on to Transylvania.[142] He said this in his ordinary, rather high-pitched voice, as though what he was saying was the most natural thing in the world. They were all dumb-founded. Anny began to wonder if they hadn't all gone mad. The sisters were baffled and humiliated.

Even many years later, Leslie found it hard to account for his behaviour. If anyone came close to understanding him then, it was Mrs Huth, but she began to wish she had never indulged in this particular piece of matchmaking.

'Leslie left us,' Anny wrote in her journal. 'I feel low and anxious & can't think what to think. Is he serious, is he only flirting with my Min? I awoke and heard the gruder & L's early start and how *scared* I felt for my M.' She was anxious, and with good reason, that Minny's reputation might have been compromised, as well as being concerned for her future happiness.

Mrs Huth was magnificent. She said they should behave as though nothing had happened. For that was precisely it. Nothing had. They would all travel on as far as Lucerne and the sisters would take the train direct to Paris. But before they got as far as Lucerne, they broke their journey at St Nicholas for the night. In the glass that served as a postbox for travellers at the inn, the girls found a farewell note from Leslie, saying that he would see them in London. Immediately, everything seemed different.

Anny and Minny were in low spirits and easily agitated by the most trifling thing on their return to England. Their one source of consolation was to find both the little girls, Margie and Annie, positively blooming down in Devon with the Ritchies. It was there, in the congenial atmosphere of Henbury, that the sisters decided on an impulse to go and stay on their beloved island, at Freshwater, with the children and Gussie and Pinkie Ritchie.

But for once, the island offered no panacea. Mrs Cameron was not expecting them and had a full house. There were no lodgings vacant at Freshwater. They were forced to stay at Alum Bay, not far away, but didn't like it and found it very expensive. There was constant confusion about their rooms and who should pay for them. Mrs Cameron was too busy, taken up by her guests and her passion for photography, to show them the sympathy they craved. It was the first time they had stayed on the island without staying at Freshwater and being in the thick of things in that small world. Unhappiness made them painfully sensitive and they imagined themselves to be outcasts. Of course, they took the children down to the beach to paddle in the waves and collected the different coloured sands to show them, but in their miserable frame of mind, the very sight of other happy holiday-makers only increased their sense of isolation. Minny became so gloomy as to make herself ill. Altogether, it was a trying time. For many reasons, Anny found it a great relief when the holidays came to an end and they were installed once more in London.

It was not until late autumn that Leslie returned from tramping through Transylvania and, when he did, he still dithered. Writing about that time much later, when events and the years had turned him into a victim of chronic melancholia, even he found his past behaviour perverse: '. . . not that I was not in love, but that I was still troubled by some of my old doubts and diffidence. Indeed, I heard at last some sort of rumour that Minny or Anny felt some sort of annoyance at my conduct . . .'[143]

If they were annoyed by his prevarication, Anny was exasperated when he resorted to using his sister as a go-between. Milly went to Onslow Gardens and begged the sisters to go to Lady Stephen's. Anny sent her packing with a flea in her ear. 'I refused and said that we had been through more than enough and that I felt if Leslie wanted to see Minny he must come to *us*.'[144]

In the event, Leslie went and lunched alone at the Oxford and Cambridge Club and thought about the whole affair in what he claimed was a philosophical spirit. During his solitary lunch, he rehearsed a carefully thought-out speech he intended to make to Minny, weighing up all the advantages and disadvantages which their marriage might entail. In this somewhat lofty, if absurd state of mind, he set off to Onslow Gardens, where he found Minny alone. It is indicative of the effect Minny had on him that as soon as he saw her, all his pedantic arguments sailed out of the window. She accepted his proposal with a simple 'Yes'.[145]

Anny was upstairs in her study, trying to finish her novel. After Leslie left, Minny went up to tell her of the engagement. 'Heigh! Ho! How happy I am. God bless them both and help me to bless my darling.' The date was 4 December 1866.[146]

Everybody seemed pleased by the news, although Lady Stephen confessed she was very much surprised. 'My astonishment was great, for though I had long perceived that his manner to Minny Thackeray was quite unlike what I had ever seen in him to any other young lady, and had thought that manner was not displeasing to her, still I was far from thinking that he had a decided, steady purpose, and a mind fully made up . . . With my whole heart I welcomed her, and felt that I could truly and thankfully receive her as a daughter.'[147]

Lady Stephen's understanding of Leslie's wavering state of mind before he proposed was a very accurate assessment. Only the week before, on his thirty-fourth birthday, he had written, '. . . and I am going on languidly in everything, and doubt much whether I shall come to much good . . . I have a darned long row to hoe. It is possible that next year may make some important changes in my life; if so, may they be for the best, but my doubt on this point troubles me terribly . . . I must get enthusiastic about something. I have got enthusiasm in me, but it won't come out.'[148]

Now that he had overcome his doubts and been accepted, his enthusiasm overflowed. Three days after their engagement, Leslie dined at the Political Economy Club at St James's Hall. He became so agitated about Minny that he scratched with the prong of a fork on the Bill of Fare, 'MY DEAREST MINNY – I am suffering the torments of the damned from the God-forgotten Thornton, who is boring on about supply and demand, when I would give anything to be with you. He is not a bad fellow, but just now I hate him like poison. O-o-o-o-o!'[149]

Later that evening, back at his mother's house in Porchester Square, Leslie wrote to his American friend, Oliver Wendell Holmes, that he was '. . . unreasonably and absurdly happy . . . I am not such a don but that I can fall in love, and you will appreciate the addition which this engagement makes to my happiness, or rather its lift of me from discontent and growling into the purest happiness'.[150]

Anny declared the engagement made her very happy, but her feelings were jangled and she could not disguise her emotions. She was desperate to finish her novel, but found she couldn't write a word. 'I was over-wrought and I could see the characters of my story walking in the air very much smaller than life, like a bright magic lantern. I have heard of this odd impression from others since then.'[151]

Two days after Minny's engagement, Tennyson, who happened to be in town, came to call on the sisters. Anny appealed to him and asked him to help her with the last paragraph. Tennyson, who probably understood Anny's state of mind far better than she did herself, wrote, 'And Nature, working by some great law unknown, and only vaguely apprehended by us insects . . . brings about the noblest harmonies out of chaos. And, so, too, out of the dire dismays and confusions of the secret world come results both mighty and tangible.'[152] But even after she had sent her manuscript off, secure in the knowledge that it would be published, Anny continued in an unusually anxious state. As soon as the engagement was announced, Minny insisted, 'I hope never to be separated from Anny, except perhaps during my wedding tour. I am sure she will have no reason to regret the change in our lives.'[153]

The truth was, even if neither of the sisters would admit it, that whether or not Anny would regret it, change was inevitable. It was not so much that Anny would be separated from Minny, but that Minny was going to introduce Leslie, not only into her own life, but into Anny's too, and at very close quarters. While the sisters had separate allowances, the house belonged to them jointly. Even if Leslie had been able to set up a separate establishment for Minny, the sisters had the little girls to consider.

It was not such an uncommon situation for families to absorb, and be absorbed by, immediate and intimate relations. The presence of living-in servants helped to blur any uncomfortably sharp focus, to sand away the splinters. Nothing was ever discussed in much detail. They preferred to avoid any awkwardness, hoping that by not mentioning anything disagreeable directly, it would go away. And very often it did. Neither sister wished to pain the other and such a delicate taciturnity was entirely in keeping with their code of behaviour, professing happiness and suffering anxieties and vexations in silence. They may not have considered the price they would have to pay for remaining together, but they had all agreed that Leslie was going to move into Onslow Gardens and Anny knew that nothing would ever be the same again.

Eventually, Anny broke down. On 8 December, the girls dined at Lady Stephen's. Anny said that she was very happy, only she felt so ill. She turned out to have a long bout of influenza, complicated by slight pleurisy. On 19 December, she was still too ill to travel down to Henbury to celebrate Blanche Ritchie's wedding to Frank Warre Cornish. Minny went with Leslie. Anny stayed at Lady Stephen's, ill in bed and feverish.

By Christmas, she was back at Onslow Gardens and almost recovered. On Christmas Day, she wrote: 'My Min and I spent the evening together – squabbled, called each other names – what should I do without her to squabble with?'[154] She had put her finger on one of the luxuries peculiar to sisters.

Leslie spent the holiday at Cambridge. His visit was a farewell to a way of life he had enjoyed for fifteen years. For all that time, he had lived in an almost exclusively masculine society, and it was a society he was particularly suited to. Nothing appeared to have changed, except Leslie. All the same people were still in the same places, doing and saying exactly the same things – so much so that he had to shake himself and look at the photograph of Minny he'd taken with him to make sure that his London life and his future with her wasn't merely a dream. He spent a good deal of the time with his old friend, the blind mathematician, economist and radical politician, Henry Fawcett, who ribbed him mercilessly about his engagement.

'Miss T is the youngest, isn't she, Stephen? – Yes

'Does she write as well as her sister? – No

'Doesn't she write occasionally? – No

'Doesn't she help her sister to write?

'&c. &c. &c.

'wh. I succeeded in stopping by inextinguishable laughter.'[155]

He felt impelled to walk once more through those austere flat lands that he knew so well. 'The country, which you can see for miles, looked as if it would soon be all over blue mould, if it was not taken out of the rain. It was damp and rotten and full of nasty dead leaves – just the place for a gallows . . .' And while he walked, he was worried, not so much by his old doubts as a need to be reassured by Minny. He hoped that his old existence had 'not dried me up into a hopeless mummy "walking up and down to save funeral expenses" and with a soul that ought to rattle like a dried pea in a pod . . . It has made me lead for many years a half and half existence, like a plant grown in a cellar. I am quite conscious of the defects which such a life has produced in my character, though you have kindly overlooked them, or not found them out. But I hope that I am not yet too far gone to be revived.'[156]

He wasn't. Certainly not by Minny's methods. Her sprightly humour, compounded by a curious and unconscious vein of originality, revived him so that he was able to enjoy family life to an extent which no one could have foreseen.

Leslie spent New Year's Eve with Minny at Onslow Gardens. They sat together in the downstairs parlour. Anny, who was not yet fully recovered, stayed in bed, reading over old letters. Feeling *de trop* and rather sorry for herself, she cried and said her prayers and thought longingly of her father.[157]

In February, *The Village on the Cliff* 'came home as a book', and Anny, who had been far more nervous about it than anything she had written so far, was entranced by Frederick Walker's illustrations. 'They were so completely everything that I had ever hoped or imagined, that the sight of them gave me a fresh start, and I have always thought that *he* wrote the book not I, for the figures were to me almost miraculous realisations of what I tried to imagine the people might become. As a curious instance of a sort of brainwave, I had a nightmare one night, and saw the figure of Reine, very bright, coming *down* upon me, and when the little letter piece came next month there was the identical figure I had dreamed of, with a basket descending; no longer a nervous terror, but a delightful reality . . . My sister and I walked through a fog one evening to the studio, and he showed it to us on the block.'[158]

While Anny was absorbed by her writing, Minny and Leslie, like most engaged couples, were expected to make a round of social calls, visits and dinner parties, so that both of them became introduced to the other's set of friends and relations. Leslie found the business thoroughly muddling, simply because so many of the sisters' friends were also their relations.[159] Yet he was in such a contented frame of mind that these visits which, under ordinary circumstances, would have been a source of irritation were, on the whole, unexpectedly pleasant.

It was at one such dinner party that the sisters gave for Leslie, his cousin Edward Dicey, and Val Prinsep, that they learned of Julia Jackson's engagement to Herbert Duckworth. It was Val, who was Julia's cousin, who let the news drop. It dropped like a stone into their soup plates. To all of them gathered around the dinner table, Julia had appeared as a vision, beyond the reach of ordinary mortals. Blinded by her beauty and beguiled by her quietly compelling character, they had all, after their separate fashions, fallen in some degree or another under her spell. Collectively, they had placed her up on a pedestal and now Herbert Duckworth had plucked her down. He was known to all of them, and to Leslie in particular. Herbert and Leslie had been at Cambridge together and Leslie knew him to be a decent, unassuming fellow, straightforward and manly. There was no doubt that Herbert was a gentleman. He came from a good family. He was rich and modestly cultivated. Under normal circumstances, Herbert was immensely eligible and, in the ordinary sense, he would do. But whether he would do for Julia was what none of them could bring themselves to ask. For none of them could face the fact that Julia, for all her extraordinary qualities, was far more conventional than they cared to confess. To have done so would have seemed like an act of treachery towards all that she personified. None of them put this into words for, as the soup was replaced by the fish, and then the fish by a bird, it would have seemed too fantastic. They agreed that Herbert was a very fortunate man, perhaps more fortunate than he deserved. But none of them could summon up much enthusiasm for the match. It went against the grain to acknowledge that in Herbert Duckworth, Julia Jackson had found her soul mate. They went on to speak of other things, and the subject was, for the moment, shelved.

Leslie and Minny had decided to honeymoon in the Alps, and Leslie was already longing to see his beloved mountains again, even though he wondered how he could bear to restrain himself from going on his hazardous annual climbs. As a married man, he would no longer be able to risk life and limb for his own pleasure. '. . . I must say I shall grudge the deprivation, even though it will be jolly loafing about the valleys. Think of smoking a pipe on the Wengern Alp, with masses of Alpine roses, & cow & strawberries & cream, & people blowing horns into your ears, & demanding centimes for their infernal afflictions!'[160]

In May, Anny went to see her mother, Isabella, who was still eking out her shadowy existence in the care of Mrs Bakewell at Camberwell. Anny told her of Minny's forthcoming marriage, and then came home, very quiet and worn out, like an old moth, in a way which she could not account for.[161]

The wedding was set for 19 June, but although the couple had been engaged for nearly six months, they were both so careless about the actual arrangements as to shock Lady Stephen and upset Anny. In spite of Leslie's familiarity with church services, he neglected to choose a best man, which caused some confusion. Nobody had been invited formally, but a great many friends and relations came to the ceremony at Onslow Square church at eight o'clock in the morning. Old Mrs Orford, down in the basement kitchen at Onslow Gardens, said that she had so much washing-up to do that she couldn't get to the church on time, and the postman said that he was quite disgusted.[162] There were only two carriages lined up outside the church, and all the servants felt cheated and thought Miss Thackeray might have had a grander wedding, if only for their own enjoyment. And the postman said that most of the poor people went down the road to Miss Anstruther's, thinking they might glimpse Minny in her finery.[163] Mrs Prinsep helped to deck Minny out in her wedding dress: if any of the Pattle sisters were involved, the event would not be lacking in some degree of fuss, fun and excitement. Inside the church, it was almost dark. Mr Cole had volunteered to give the bride away, yet he was in Paris. Mr Merivale was ready to take his place. There was a creaky moment within the congregation and all the gentlemen stiffened their necks and the ladies tweaked their bonnet strings when the parson uttered the words, 'Who giveth?' But it was only a moment of uneasiness, and it passed. For there was Mr Cole, perfectly dressed for the occasion. How he had crossed the Channel remained a mystery.[164]

Mr and Mrs Leslie Stephen left for their wedding tour of Switzerland by way of the boat train to Boulogne, Leslie blissfully unaware that for the first and last time in his life, he was in debt to his sister-in-law for having paid the pew opener, tipped the beadle and various other offices.[165]

Anny and her friend Katie Collins packed up the wedding presents in an old *Cornhill* box. The guests left the chairs in disarray and the house quite horrible, Anny said, after the wedding breakfast.[166] Anny now left the house, which stood empty among the scaffolding, no one knowing how the new arrangement would resolve itself when the bridal pair returned from their honeymoon.

Part II
A Nest of Gentlefolk

9

It's narrow, narrow make your bed,
And learn to lie your lane;
For I'm gae'n oer the sea, Fair Annie,
A braw bride to bring hame.
Wi' her I will get gowd and gear;
Wi' you I ne'er got nane.

OLD SCOTS BALLAD

Anny expected, as did everyone who knew and loved her, that she would fall into a state of melancholy immediately after Minny and Leslie left her for their wedding tour in Switzerland. But she surprised herself as well as everyone else by being 'quite amazed and ashamed of being so happy. I thought I should not have eaten, left off crying, cared about anything'.[1] In a daze of euphoria, she flung herself into a flurry of activity. The decision to shut up the house at Onslow Gardens for the duration of the honeymoon meant that Anny had no place to call her own but must hover about staying here and there with friends and relations, all of whom made her very welcome. It was indicative of the uncertainty of the future that, shortly before the wedding, Anny had taken the lease of a cottage on Rememham Hill at Henley. She hoped to use it as a bolthole, and optimistically entertained visions of leading a solitary life there, concentrating on her writing. Leslie and Minny intended to use it as well. The little girls would benefit from the country air. But anyone less suited to the life of a recluse than Anny is hard to imagine. It was an acquisition which she could ill afford.

After closing up the house with Katie Anny left to join the children who had been staying at Eton with her father's cousins St John and Louisa Thackeray. St John was a master there. Anny thought of Minny continually and carried her sister's thimble, which she had found while tidying up the house, as a kind of talisman in her purse. The day after the wedding she had seen two birds flying away over the housetops, which made her miserable. But on her way to Eton, 'two kind little birds came flying across the park right over my head & I thought they were you & Leslie & I can't tell you how happy they made me.' She ended her letter, 'Give Leslie my love and tell him I like him much better than anybody else I ever knew for my brother.'² She meant what she said, but the fact is she had no idea what such a relationship entailed.

Eton was 'a funny little world' and one which was very congenial to Anny. Self-contained, like the royal court which dominated it, the school itself resembled a small principality. The mellow old buildings, the views leading down to the water meadows and the river, the massive outline of Windsor Castle overlooking the town, were all beautiful. It was saved from placidity by the liveliness of the boys, dressed in top hats and tails and still in mourning for George III, who were studious, frivolous, and outrageous by turns, and generally making a good deal of noise, yelling on the river. St John was a mild-mannered old fogey; his wife, Louisa, kind, but inclined to fuss. Across the way lived Anny's cousin Blanche and her husband Frank Warre Cornish, then housemaster at one of the Eton Houses, Holland's.*

Anny's cousins afforded her the closest approximation to belonging to a family that she was ever to experience. Now that the pattern of pieces which formed the small corner of her world was shifting, she valued their affection more than ever.

Like Anny, Blanche eschewed things bohemian whilst retaining a well-defined sense of aesthetics. She had already created a distinctive if rarified atmosphere at Holland's, which she had furnished and decorated very attractively. Interesting books, Moxon and Tauchnitz editions, lay on occasional tables. Vases of freshly cut flowers, eighteenth-century china, chintz curtains, contemporary Pre-Raphaelite paintings and a bowl of sweet

---

* Although, through familiarity, Anny always refers to Frank Warre Cornish's 'house' at Eton as Holland's, it is always called Holland House by those at Eton, not to be confused with either Holland House, Kensington, owned by Lord and Lady Holland, or, more importantly, Little Holland House, which Sarah and Thoby Prinsep rented from Lady Holland and made their home, with the painter and sculptor G.F. Watts.

smelling potpourri, made the ambience very different from the other masters' more spartan quarters. Both the cousins shared very much the same taste, one which Thackeray had cultivated and which they continued to nurture. Blanche wrote romantically of her memories of girlhood visits to Palace Green: '. . . the beautiful red house shaded by tall elms on Palace Green; the pieces of plate, china, and furniture collected by Mr Thackeray, when it was easier than it is now to make genuine last-century purchases, "brand new and intensely old", as he would describe some Louis XVI clock or *geridon* [*sic*] just brought home − all these old-world things seemed to me a part of the spell.'

Blanche was becoming an original, sophisticated woman, whose trenchant witticisms were to become a byword at Eton, designed to amuse the masters however much they disconcerted the boys. Enthusiastic, abhorring the commonplace and delighting in family jokes, the Ritchies and Warre Cornishes, like other complicated families, had a private language of their own. 'Washing it off the block' meant giving up all reference to a subject which had begun to bore; 'Aunt Sister' signified the sudden inability to face a stranger. 'Point-device' was an old-fashioned term which they used to mean people who were smartly dressed, or well turned out. 'Hell's Delights' meant unavoidable, daily household tasks.[3]

It was in what appeared to be their similarities that the difference between the cousins lay. Both talked the same language, both enthused and startled their acquaintance by their vivid observations. But Anny did not say what she thought for effect, although, as often as not, she was more effective than her younger cousin. Anny was not calculating or clever in the same way as Blanche. Anny was nothing if not sympathetic. Leslie, for whom the term was a derogatory one, went so far as to say, 'Anny . . . is little short of the angels. She has real genius so far as genius can be made out of affection and sympathy. She sympathises indeed so quickly that people who don't know her sometimes doubt her perfect sincerity. The doubt is a perfect mistake.'[4] If Blanche was malicious where Anny was not, Anny could laugh at herself and 'embrace oddities, and produce a charming laughing harmony from incongruities'.[5] Both of them played at being *la grande dame*, but Anny's rule was more merciful and less designing.

Blanche's elder sister, Gussie, was staying with the Warre Cornishes, and their young brother, Richmond, Anny's godson and a schoolboy at Eton, ran in and out. Richmond was precocious and had won a King's Scholarship for Eton when he was only eight. He was now an attractive youth of thirteen. The cluster of cousins, the gaiety of the celebrations in the summer term kept Anny's spirits flying high. The distractions were numerous and varied.

George Eliot and G.H. Lewes came on a visit. Inevitably, the presence of the famous novelist caused great excitement. George Eliot had expressed her admiration of Anny's own writing, saying she couldn't resist reading Anny's stories, even if she ought to be doing something else. 'I am obliged to fast from fiction,' Eliot wrote, 'and fasting is sometimes known to weaken the stomach. I ought to except Miss Thackeray's short stories, which I cannot resist when they come near me.'[6] Anny couldn't help quivering with adulation. 'George Eliot was in the playing-fields yesterday when Blanche said two hideous forms came walking . . . very quietly and all doubled up.'[7] George Lewes asked Blanche if Minny hadn't been very much agitated during the wedding ceremony. When Blanche said not, he enquired, 'And Anny, how did she bear up?' At which Mr Cornish 'opened his eyes and gave a start of surprise.'

Anny took Gussie to inspect the cottage at Henley. When she had first seen it, it had looked enchanting. Now, the whole place seemed different. It was all barred up and deserted. The grass had grown high where the lawn had been. The agent was out. The old woman who was supposed to have the key couldn't find it and mumbled things Anny couldn't make out. Anny was not easily deterred, but even she had to confess to being disappointed.

Back at Eton, Anny decided to go to Paris for a week's frolic with the Coles, the Merivales and Pinkie Ritchie. She could leave the little girls with St John and Louisa. Meanwhile, 'the baby has left off crying, the boys have subsided and Louisa has come skating in. I must do a little conversation, mustn't I, with my hostess?'[8] She couldn't help teasing Minny about her new married status, which now took precedence over Anny's own. 'A number of cards for evening parties have come tonight. Mrs Percy Wyndham, Lady Pollock, etc.[9] I shall wait for you to chaperone me – a giddy young thing like me can't go about alone, can she, darling?'

Richmond and the little girls went with her as far as the station, where Richmond got her a second-class ticket up to London. But, absentmindedly, Anny got into a first-class carriage, 'so when I had travelled up with all the Court ladies and the R. family and footmen and red baize, it was humiliating to be seized on by the guard as a fraudulent passenger'.[10]

In London, Anny stayed with Lady Stephen and Milly at Bayswater. The Huths asked her to go to Antwerp with them, and she was rather tempted until the thought of tagging on alone with them determined her to stick to her other plan of going to Paris. She felt ill at ease staying with Lady Stephen, confused and jumbled. Not for the first time, her existence seemed like so many fragments of a mosaic shifting heaven knew where, lacking in any apparent purpose.

The honeymoon couple had stopped briefly in Paris for Charlotte Ritchie to meet Leslie (she approved), before travelling on by train to Basle. It was a solid way of travel – the carriage upholstered in plush and the woodwork beautifully joined, the mirrors shining. They prided themselves on travelling light, but still took vast amounts of luggage, packed and folded away in great leather trunks. Portable desks, writing equipment, guide books, binoculars, a pair of compasses, Leibig water, medicines, boots and shoes, gloves, collars, handkerchiefs and hats – the hats packed in hatboxes – a steel crinoline hoop for Minny, packed flat like a Chinese lampshade; tweed suits, knickerbockers, a black velvet smoking-jacket for Leslie; underclothes and enough suits and dresses for every envisaged occasion. Because of the inconvenience of the crinoline, women wore travelling costumes which afforded them marginally more room to move. These dresses, though by no means so exaggerated in their fullness, were still voluminous, and the petticoats numerous. But the shorter skirts, looped up with braid to reveal a glimpse of white lace and slightly more leg than was more usually acceptable, looked very fetching on Minny.

There were quantities of waiters and people on hand, whose sole purpose was to facilitate the traveller's journey. The trains were efficient and remarkably punctual, which appealed to Leslie. Minny enjoyed their utter modernity. She was not so beguiled by the picturesque as Anny. The trains had sleeping-cars and dining-cars and every sort of luxury. The food was plentiful, served formally with a plethora of silver domes and salvers. It was not bad, a little tired, the menu monotonous. Course followed course: the sauces, white and brown, alternating invariably. The soup was ladled by the waiter from a tureen; toast in racks, croquettes and cutlets were all piled high on peaks of starched napery. They were offered wine, champagne, mineral water and digestives. They ate what the waiter served them. It was something to do. The train steamed through Europe.

They spent one night in Basle. Minny had forgotten how pretty it all was. They dined at the hotel off mutton chops, Minny wearing her married lady's cap, and after dinner they went to a café on the river and watched the world go by before going to a concert given by the choir in the red Cathedral. Minny thoroughly enjoyed the music, and even Leslie, who claimed not to be able to tell the difference between 'God Save the Queen' and a polka, was infected by her pleasure.

Minny wrote to Anny daily. The habit of writing letters was deeply ingrained and, for young women of their class, it was *de rigueur* to spend a good part of every morning keeping up one's correspondence. Apart from the telegram, letters were the only means of communication. The post was frequent, and there were several deliveries a day. Minny couldn't help worrying about Anny and was frequently vexed by Anny's vagueness and changes of plan. She left off her letter from Basle to go and pack. 'Leslie is always ready to help me pack but his notions of folding are rather vague.'[11]

They reached Berne the following day and stayed at the Faucon, where the sisters had stayed before. But this time, Minny and Leslie took a grander room, overlooking the main street. She was furious to notice what she called a 'vulgar horrid little Paragraph' announcing the marriage, which Fitzy had put in *The Times*. Otherwise, she was able to declare, 'I like being married much, much better than I thought I should and I have thought I should like it for the last six months. A husband is a thing very, very like a sister only he doesn't interfere with one's sister at all.' It poured with rain, but neither Minny nor Leslie cared at all.

And then they were in the mountains, on Leslie's old stomping ground at Grindelwald. They found their hotel charming, with a garden full of yellow roses running down to the very edge of 'these great megatheriums of mountains.' There was a quaint little summerhouse, done up in green velvet and furnished with stuffed birds in glass cases. They would go and sit there, or else in a little bower in the garden, and listen to the avalanches, 'wh. go pumping like sacks of coals down a coal-hole every few minutes'. Minny urged Leslie to go for his walk, leaving her at the hotel. She put him on his honour not to do anything very dangerous and promise to be back punctually. He was. He came back with gentians and forget-me-nots and never let Minny guess what it cost him to forgo his mountaineering.[12] Minny, who tired easily, spent the afternoons lolling about in her crinoline, wearing her blue and grey French costume. Occasionally, she peered through the eye-glass to see if she could glimpse Leslie on his walk. She knew she wouldn't be likely to accompany him often. The maid, Fanny, had forgotten to pack her stout boots, and had sent her to the Alps with nothing but a pair of dancing shoes. Minny was furious. It never occurred to her to buy a pair of boots locally, for all her boots and shoes were specially made for her. Perhaps it was just as well that Fanny, who was currently in Paris waiting on Anny, announced that she was going to get married and gave in her notice. Pretty, literate Fanny had, on occasion, written to Thackeray's dictation. She left with Anny's blessing, her departure another break with the past. But, unlike Anny, Minny was not concerned with the past. She was living in the present and enjoying every minute. When Leslie came back on the dot with the flowers, he pretended to be offended when Minny said she hadn't missed him in the least. He sent the gentians in a letter to Anny instead, and added, '. . . all the same I am fond of her and of you'.[13]

Like Anny, Minny was thoroughly cosmopolitan, well-travelled, spoke excellent French and was fluent in German and Italian. She was perfectly at home in foreign hotels, knew how to get what she wanted, and was adept in making their visit comfortable in a thousand little ways. It was not for nothing that the sisters had spent much of their childhood in Paris and in being taken about Europe by their father. It was early days yet, but it was already obvious that marriage was indisputably the making of Minny, while Leslie now reaped the benefit of all her cunning contrivances.

By 30 June, Minny could write to Anny from Interlaken, 'Darling, I should like you to be married once, just for a week to see how very pleasant it is, and then I should like your husband to disappear.' But she went on in more serious vein, 'It seems almost incredible that people should be able to fit and understand each other quite perfectly, as we have done directly. I believe that if people really care for each other, however shy they may be to others, they will never be shy to each other. It seems as if Leslie & I had lived together all our lives, like you & I, & had never been separated & never will, as please God you & I never will. Darling, when you are on one side of me & Leslie on the other, it seems to me that I shall have no earthly anxiety & as perfect happiness as ever anyone had in this world. When you are away from me, I cannot help being just a little anxious & afraid that you are not quite happy, but I know that it will make you happy to think of me & my Lez. I cannot talk of what he is, anymore than I could of you, or Papa, but I feel as if we should all be very happy in Heaven together some day, & indeed, life is more like Heaven than life to me just now.

'Monday morning. Pouring with rain.'

Anny took the boat train to Paris with Arthur Prinsep, and spent a week of jollifications there. Paris in 1867 had changed enormously, irrevocably, and pretty much entirely, from the city of Anny's childhood. This was a natural consequence of the continual upheaval of French political life. Whereas England had enjoyed a relatively stable economy, France had suffered from a staggering number of reversals of government, with the strange result that Paris had, by now, become 'a town of exhibition, placed under glass, hostelry to the world, the object of foreigners' admiration and envy, impractical for its inhabitants, but unique in the comforts and pleasures of all kinds it offers to the sons of Albion'.[14] Gone were most of the dirty, dingy *petits rues* which Anny had known all her life. The old house on the Avenue Sainte-Marie had been pulled down, and that space scythed through by the hideous, modern designs made by Baron Haussmann. The *Maison du Bon Marché*, possibly the most sophisticated department store in the world, typified the frivolity and grandeur that had become the hallmark of Paris under the Second Empire. Anny was out to have some fun, and this was certainly the right place for it.

She stayed with the Coles, who had rented an apartment, and saw a good deal of Charlotte, who kept open house for the English visitors, 'South Kensington in the dining-room, Paris in the drawing-room'.[15] Anny cheered herself up by being generally extravagant. She was moping, in a way that she didn't care to explain to herself, as a result of Minny's marriage, and spending money acted as a panacea. She shopped at the Bazaar, went to restaurants, to the theatre, was tempted – and succumbed to – the purchase of bonnets, gloves and impractical kitchen gadgets to amuse Minny. Being summer, picnics were the rage. At one of them, it poured with rain and everyone was drenched to the skin, their petticoats sodden, their bonnets ruined, but good-natured about it. And all the time, Anny was missing Minny very much. 'I got into an absurd fash at the picnic, thinking you were wet through somewhere in the rain, not seeing you come up with any of the people. It was only for a minute & I have *never* minded being away from you so little though I shan't be sorry when the last three pens are worn out darling & I see your dear old round face again & Leslie's long one.'

And then she had a disturbing dream. It was not a nightmare, but echoed that deep memory of being dashed into the sea by her mother when she had been little more than a baby at Margate. 'I dreamt of you all night long and a seashore and Papa, and Baby somehow jumped out of my arms and rushed into the sea, it was a melancholy happy sort of dream.' It was a dream which tugged at her most profound early fears.

The sensational death of the Emperor Maximilian in Mexico, betrayed and executed after a brave defence of Querétaro, meant, as far as Anny could see, that, 'Everyone is to go into mourning . . . five days black & twenty-one mitigated grief. It is the least they could do as they took away the armies & got him shot.'

But nothing could hinder the round of festivities. Anny gave a wildly expensive dinner party for all her friends at the fashionable restaurant, La Cascade, in the Bois de Boulogne. She wrote of being whirled about in little carriages, 'me with a Spanish bonnet and a yellow rose!' There were more picnics. 'Tishy is cooking for tomorrow cakes & tarts to be eaten at Versailles. Henny does the accounts, Isabella keeps house . . .' She ordered herself a new black silk gown and another for Minny. All her life, Anny was preoccupied by clothes. She wore low-heeled slippers made of soft, black leather and elegant suede gloves, and always carried lace-edged handkerchiefs. She never wore the latest fashions, for she would have considered that vulgar, but she was very particular in her dress, even if she tended to favour over-fussy trimmings. Her slippers and gloves, she always bought in Paris.[16] Minny's taste was simpler, more discriminating. Anny, who always found it difficult to pace herself, overdid things and felt seedy in consequence. Mrs Cole sent for the doctor. It was nothing serious, and Anny made light of it. 'The Coles are rather doctor mad. But their kindness is quite untellable & I do love them & laugh at them a little wee bit but much most love them.'[17]

In Switzerland, Leslie took Minny over three high mountain passes in the company of a guide. They passed chalets and cows with bells 'and there was always a view',[18] and they frequently stopped to drink milk and eat bread and honey. The bread and honey and the climate suited Minny. '. . . she looks so blooming that she is ashamed of it. "What do I mind?" she says. I mean her cheeks are red and blowsy like a milkmaid's refreshed with wine. "Anny will think this vulgar." Poo! Besides it is true.'[19]

Despite the glory of crossing the passes, it was a relief to reach a good, clean hotel. The doorkeeper was 'an elegant sort of card-sharper in yellow boots & blue trousers'. They found there was company staying. 'One awful woman six feet high & as Broad as she was long & very hideous in a short frock then there were the clergymen – My love, we have come into a swarm of clergymen like mosquitoes & all with chimney-pot hats. Lez looks at them as if they were toads & they smile at him unctuously & try & enter into vapid conversation, & we are going to stay here all Sunday too . . .'[20] Leslie and Minny changed for dinner to impress the clergymen – he in patent leather shoes and his black velvet smoking jacket, she in her crinoline and the blue and grey French costume she liked so much. Leslie never bothered about his clothes at all, but Minny couldn't help taking an immensely wifely satisfaction in his distinguished good looks. They drank champagne and the clergymen drank tea. Leslie seemed to have completely forgotten that although he had resigned his Fellowship at Cambridge, he was, technically speaking, still a parson himself. Having

given up his belief, it came naturally to him to sneer at the faithful, possibly to confirm his own agnosticism.

They stayed at the same hotel at St Nicholas where Minny had found the note from Leslie, saying he hoped to see her in London after coming back from Transylvania. It was difficult to believe that had been only the previous summer. On this visit, it seemed much quieter, but the landlord and his daughters remembered Minny and persisted in calling her Mademoiselle, which ruffled her feelings. At Zermatt, she found six letters from Anny waiting for her. None of them was dated. Always methodical, Leslie tried to arrange them in order by the postmarks so that Minny could read them in the right sequence, but even he found it impossible.

By now, Anny was back in London, again staying with Lady Stephen and Milly. Minny found herself thinking a good deal about the cottage at Henley and how it should be furnished. It did not bother either of the sisters that, although Anny had taken the lease, Minny should have the last word in its decoration. Since the death of their father Minny had 'played the part of wife' in the sisters' small household, and played it very well, making it a pleasure for the servants to carry out her instructions. 'She was more reserved and less impulsive by nature and without Anny's peculiar gift of sympathy,' Leslie remembered. 'Her sense of humour was more predominant, if not precisely stronger, and enabled her to see some things more clearly. She had not the peculiar, or, as I thought, excessive optimism which I have ascribed to Anny. She judged by her instincts, for she was not more of a reasoner than Anny; but her own instincts were calmer and more sober. The quality which first of all attracted me was one which she also shared with Anny, but which was more obvious in her from her less impulsive temperament: I mean an absolute and unqualified simplicity and sincerity in which I never saw her surpassed. She was utterly incapable not only (like Anny) of ever affecting, but (unlike Anny) of ever appearing to affect, a sentiment which she did not feel.'[21]

Unlike Anny, Minny was thoroughly practical. But although it was not in the nature of either of the sisters to mind who took charge of things − for they had shared everything so far during their lives − it didn't bode well for Anny's future independence − if, indeed, she was to have any. Minny couldn't help worrying that Anny, who was both extravagant and impulsive, might not make a good many rash purchases in her absence. 'You mustn't (*this is a strictly private letter*) buy any four-post beds for me & Leslie for it would be very uncomfortable for us as he sleeps with nothing on at all except a sheet & I like heaps of clothes.'[22]

At Zermatt the weather broke and they kept to the hotel. There were a good many other guests staying at Seiler's Inn, among them 'two fast young ladies. I like them but Lez thinks them loathsome. They are going on at a great rate with a couple of knickerbockers whom they have picked up & have an old father who always seems to retire to bed & leave them. They are jolly girls.'

They travelled on over the Hannen Moös and stayed at a dirty little inn and enjoyed it and ate goat's cheese and wandered into a church decorated with Virgins and empty except for six black crows. In the churchyard, they found the sexton digging what they took to be a grave and were relieved to find it was only potatoes. 'Dear Min, thank God, seems to be very well,' Leslie told Anny, 'and if she is half as happy as I am is enjoying herself more than I ever did in my life before.'[23]

Writing to Anny about clothes − she intended to leave her blue piqué at Paris to have it shortened – Minny wrote, 'About maids, Lez & I both think we had better make ourselves comfortable as we don't think we shall have any children & when we do we can make different arrangements, & I hope the maids will dress alike in Swiss costume.'[24]

Returning to St Nicholas, Leslie was touched to see a letter from Anny stuck in the famous glass. But he was appalled by the tourists, even though Minny protested this was not a radical sentiment. 'I don't care – I should have liked to fence out all foreigners & snobs & their wives from this one valley.' Minny was more bothered by fleas. 'I prefer any number of snobs to one flea. Signed, Mrs Leslie Stephen.' But she didn't have the last word. 'Alas!' wrote Leslie. 'If Cockneys come even now what will it be in a few years?'[25]

After staying for a few days at St Moritz, where they unexpectedly ran into their friends the Huths and Jeannie Senior, Leslie and Minny caught the train to Paris and returned to England on 1 August. They went straight to Lady Stephen's before taking the train down to Henley, where Anny met them at the station.

The reunion was a happy one. Of course, they had heaps to talk about and gossip to catch up on as well as relating their adventures. And in

August, the cottage at Henley was charming. The grass had been cut and the garden tidied up. The cottage was picturesquely covered in ivy and consequently a trifle damp, but with a view over the meadows and the river and across to Henley itself, with a church spire just visible through the trees. The plan was for Leslie and Minny to spend six weeks or so there, Leslie occasionally going up to London by train.

It was an unusual start to married life, but then theirs was an unusual situation. The household consisted of Anny, Leslie and Minny, the two little girls, Margie and Annie, to say nothing of the maids, Leslie's collie dog, Troy, and a rabbit. Leslie and Anny spent part of every day writing while Minny kept house. Unless it was raining, they generally took a boat on the river, Leslie rowing. Leslie was unaccustomed to finding happiness in the small details of daily life, and found himself in a domestic paradise. 'I am almost happier & more comfortable than a man ought to be in this world. For, to say the truth, I believe myself to have been very much in want of a wife & to have been not a little spoilt by my donnish existence at Cambridge. It always tends to shrivel up a cove's faculties to live as a bachelor in a bachelor society with very little external communication. He gets rusty & stupid & morose; & even a comparatively family & social existence in London had not undonned me. I was wanting to take root, & am only thankful that I have done so to my heart's content. In short, I am very happy indeed & don't mind saying so.'[26] He might have been speaking for all of them. Even if the presence of a sister-in-law does not seem a likely ingredient in a happy marriage, Leslie and Anny were growing genuinely very fond of one another. That they were as different from each other by temperament and habit as it is possible for two people to be, may very well have contributed to their attraction for each other. It also, inevitably, accounted for an inability to understand each other's values fully. But the tension this would bring was not evident at the start.

At the beginning of October, Leslie and Minny left Henley to start their married life at Onslow Square. Anny's spirits drooped. It was too cold to go boating on the river, and, in any case, she couldn't handle a boat by herself. She hadn't noticed how many earwigs there were and it was impossible to ignore the damp. She moped. It was madness to think she could stay there alone for the winter. If anybody depended on the stimulation of the society of other people, it was Anny. By November, she was back in Onslow Gardens.

London in November was very dreary and sooty and dirty. The fogs were dreadful, with 'regular pea-soupers' – the yellow light thick and impenetrable. Sometimes great brands of torches were carried to light the street. One could hear the warning bells of cab horses indistinctly and only just make out their ghostly shapes. The acrid smell made one choke and clung to clothes long afterwards. There was something both obnoxious and melancholy in the smell: particularly after having changed into something fresh, it was very unpleasant to smell the grime which had to be brushed off the false hem attached to the long skirts, which acted in the manner of a fender against the dirt.

Minny soon discovered that she was pregnant. She had always been delicate and now had to spend most of her time lying on a sofa, forbidden to exert herself. Leslie expressed his feelings well: '. . . I cannot help saying that Providence might have arranged things better. It seems infernally hard lines that a woman should have such a burden to bear, but repining is obviously useless as there is no possibility of getting an amendment carried to the present order of things.'[27] He was beginning to find that the demands of family life obliged him to keep his nose to the grindstone 'penny-a-lining' for *The Cornhill*, *Frazer's* and *Macmillan's*. He was persuaded to read for the Bar, but his heart wasn't really in it and he found the practice of eating dinners at his chambers, a requirement of the barrister's training, an insufferable bore. 'That infernal question of money may possibly drive me into any opening that occurs but I prefer sticking to my work if I can.'

Anny, too, spent part of her time writing, but went out frequently to dinners and parties, to galleries, concerts and the theatre, and kept up like a spinning-top with her circle of friends. She had dinner with Julia and Herbert Duckworth, now living in his father's town house at Bryanston Square. She found that she was more than ever under the spell of Julia's charm and extraordinary beauty, and grew fond of Herbert, impressed by how radiantly happy they seemed to be.

Thackeray's old friend, Colonel Hamley, was a frequent caller at Onslow Gardens.[28] He was a genial old face from the past, with an unexpectedly ironic sense of humour that appealed to Anny. He took her to the theatre and, coming away after the play, they saw the opera house in flames, a dramatic sight which Anny never forgot. It was with Colonel Hamley at Onslow Gardens that Anny had the following conversation:

Col H: I never quite understand anybody.
A: Oneself least of all. I believe other people know one a great deal better than one knows oneself. I try to keep a diary but it always seems sham.

Col H: It is just chance whether one is self-conscious or not. There are the two roads and it is all a toss-up which you take.

A: I should like to change souls with my friends now and then for a few minutes.

Col H: You wouldn't be any the worse for that unless you could remember afterwards.

Minny (calling from upstairs): While you have been amusing yourselves I have been listening to them nailing up the poor old lady's coffin next door.[29]

At the beginning of the New Year, 1868, Anny found, as usual, that she had spent too much money. And as usual, she made good resolutions. She meant to keep them when she made them, but somehow she never did. She was worried about Margie who was going through a difficult phase and resolved to spend more time with the little girls. One thing she was determined on – to let the cottage at Henley. It was lonely and expensive.

Staying with Mrs Prescott at Clarence House made her melancholy and brought back the ghosts of the old days. She had vivid memories of her father standing by the fireplace. She sat and listened to Mrs Prescott playing Marcello on the piano in the twilight.[30] The curtains were not drawn. A friend, a paralytic man, beat time. Anny was in a pensive mood.

As soon as she got back to Onslow Gardens, she had a bitter quarrel about nothing with Minny, which ended with them both in tears. It was over as soon as it started and they both agreed to forget all about it, but Anny was in a nervous state and everything seemed jangling and discordant. She felt unaccountably morbid and lonely, and went for long walks with Mrs Brookfield through the squares of South Kensington in the moonlight, in spite of the icy weather.

Towards the end of February, she was invited to stay with the Rothschilds at their vastly opulent house, Mentmore, in Bedfordshire. Almost as soon as she got there, a telegram came, urging her home. Minny had given birth prematurely to a boy: the child had died and Minny was very ill. Beside herself with worry, Anny dashed back to London. Leslie hung about feeling helpless, silent and miserable, his devotion evident. It was an anxious time for them all.

The little girls were sent to stay with the cousins at Eton. Lady Stephen, who had grown very fond of Minny, was in and out of the house with her cheerful commonsense, and she and her daughter Milly did succeed to some extent in lightening the gloom and Minny began to recover. But the recovery was slow and it was not until April that she was considered strong enough to convalesce at Freshwater.

Their anxiety drew Leslie and Anny closer together, but it was an intimacy bound inextricably with jealousy. Both felt that they knew Minny best. And, in a way, they were not wrong. Anny knew Minny as only a sister could. Leslie knew her as his wife and as the woman with whom he was very much in love. But they failed to see that Minny offered very different aspects of her self to the two people she loved most. Neither Anny nor Leslie were of much practical use at nursing Minny, although both were touching in the extreme in their love and concern. What they could not express was their own true affection for each other. Anny's demonstrativeness made Leslie recoil, while his reserve and silence were beyond her comprehension. Both were hypersensitive and inordinately emotional, but whereas Anny recognised that this was true of her, Leslie was never able to acknowledge it in himself.

Anny saw things as a series of impressions, rather as though she viewed life through the window of a railway carriage, the line running in and out of short tunnels, affording quick and unexpected glimpses of a cow in an orchard, a child on a beach, a sudden aspect of rooks wheeling round a church spire, or a woman pegging out the washing. Her impressions were extremely vivid, her point of view entirely her own. But she failed to connect. Her perceptions lay scattered, like the beads of a necklace left unstrung.

Minny was convinced that Anny was brilliantly talented. She was highly indignant when Fitzy wrote a less than enthusiastic review of Anny's novel, *The Village on the Cliff*, for *Frazer's Magazine*. 'Fitzy,' she declared, 'does not see that Anny is a genius!'[31] Leslie's view was a pretty fair assessment. 'Anny, for example, is about the most uneducated person I ever knew. She has not two facts in her head & one of them is a mistake. But certainly I think her one of the best & most attractive people I ever met & worth a dozen senior wranglers & the whole staff of professors at Girton & Newnham. What I said of her want of education is what I should say (I suppose) of a first-rate musical performer who had a bad violin. His talent might be first-rate but I imagine that his music would be spoilt for most people. Anny always reminds me of an admirable painter whose brushes or colours or something or other are so confused that all her outlines are muddled & indistinct. She would not lose her genius if she were as clever in her workmanship as Miss Austen; but she would be incomparably more successful.'[32]

Even if the merits of Anny's impressionism did not register with Leslie, and however perceptive he was about her failings, he erred on the side of folly when, egged on by Fitzy, he rashly tried to reform her. It may have been a latent vestige of his Evangelical education and upbringing, which he never succeeded in casting off entirely, that prompted him to try and change her ways. He couldn't get it into his splendidly logical head that if he changed her, she would no longer be the same woman who had won his affections while exasperating him with her haphazard, chaotic, but loveable ways. It wasn't so much that she wasn't willing, but that she was totally incapable of either learning to govern her impulses, or allowing herself to be governed by anyone else.

Their visit to Freshwater was a qualified success. Minny began to recover her health almost as soon as she got to the island. Mrs Cameron welcomed them to Dimbola and the Prinseps could not have been kinder at The Briary, while the Tennysons gave them the run of Farringford. For the sisters, the island worked its usual magic. But the rarified atmosphere in this small colony of poets, painters and photographers was anathema to Leslie. It was a great relief to him when Fitzy came to spend a few days and they could tramp across the Downs, smoke their heads off and chop logic until they were blue in the face.

As a sickly, highly-strung youth, Leslie had learned reams of Tennyson's verse off by heart. He had been so deeply moved by the poetry that he became worryingly excitable and worked himself up to such a pitch of frenzy that the family doctor forbade further poetry reading. But, although he continued to admire the poetry, Leslie showed not one jot of idolatry towards Tennyson. 'He is the queerest old bloke, to speak irreverently, that I ever saw. He is heavy in his looks, sleepy & absurdly shy. He lives . . . in dread of the outside world & never seems to think or talk about anyone except himself. He would grumble by the hour together about the villains who cheated him by asking exorbitant prices for land at Freshwater & by building houses overlooking the grounds & about the damned cocknies who follow him about & stare at him & creep into his garden & steal the pencils he may have left about. Many of the said cocknies seem to me to live only in his imagination, as he is very blind & whenever he sees a rustic in the distance, swears he is a cockney in pursuit.'[33]

Minny's near brush with death had shocked all three of them. Her slow recovery made Leslie realise just how dependent he had grown on her. The possibility of losing her was dreadful, and even though the danger was now over he remained possessively anxious and protective. That is not to say that any of them lacked optimism. They were an unusually spirited trio and full of plans for the future.

IO

Where lies the land to which the ship would go?
Far, far ahead, is all her seamen know,
And where lies the land she travels from? Away,
Far, far behind, is all that they can say.

ARTHUR H. CLOUGH

It had long been one of Leslie's dreams to return to New England and introduce Minny to the friends he had made on his first visit in 1863. They were the Brahmins of Boston, the social and intellectual elite, that 'harmless, inoffensive, untitled aristocracy'[34] to which Oliver Wendell Holmes, Charles Eliot Norton and James Russell Lowell all belonged. Leslie had kept in touch by regular correspondence and numbered them amongst his closest and most influential friends. As Minny grew stronger, Leslie began to make practical plans for the journey, persuaded that the change would do her good. He had some money saved from before his marriage, and it would be enough to pay for the trip. If physically frail, Minny had a decidedly adventurous nature and was all for going to see the New World. But although they pressed Anny to accompany them, she refused to go.

This was partly tact. Anny realised that after the loss of their baby, Leslie and Minny needed to be alone. But she herself needed, if not to be on her own entirely, to have some time apart from Minny and Leslie. She had not imagined that Leslie's intensely masculine presence in the relatively small house at Onslow Square would prove so disturbing. She had not imagined anything very much at all. No one could have foreseen either how well Anny and Leslie would get on, or to what degree they would rub each other up the wrong way. There were times when Anny could hardly bear the sounds of Leslie's boots clomping on the stairs, when she hated the smell of his pipe tobacco, when he irritated her beyond words.[35] His presence put a stop to those cherished moments of intimacy she had enjoyed with Minny when, by candlelight, they had exchanged confidences while brushing and plaiting their hair before bed. She was exasperated by her brother-in-law's insistence on the accuracy of the smallest fact, by his curbing of her enthusiasm, his reining in of her more fantastic statements – like the time when she claimed, one morning at the breakfast table, that there were forty million unmarried women in London alone.[36] A few noughts here or there might be of the essence to Leslie, but they meant nothing whatsoever to Anny. The sisters called Leslie 'the cold bath' from his habit of drenching her schemes and fancies with his chilling criticism.[37]

Although they were both candid to a fault, neither Anny nor Leslie could bring themselves to acknowledge that the seeds of their contention lay in the rivalry of their affection for Minny. They were reduced to prevarication, masking the real reason. So the root of the matter was left ignored, to grow into a tangled hedge, ineradicable and impossible to penetrate. Even in those early days, there was sufficient tension beneath the surface for Anny to need to get away, and for Leslie and Minny to acquiesce with some measure of relief.

The Stephens' visit to America marked the beginning of a passage to some level of independence in Anny's life. She had tried and failed to set up an alternative *pied-à-terre* at Henley. She was reluctant to repeat the mistake. Instead, she learned how to be a singular individual, swimming in and out of a shoal of friends and relations. She took her writing seriously, and that gave her a sense of purpose, although she never managed to master the discipline of regularity. And her writing provided a perfect explanation for her spending time away from home since she was generally quite legitimately engaged on 'research' for material or local colour for her current novel.

Just after Leslie and Minny had decided to go to America, Anny received an invitation from the fabulously wealthy American, Russell Sturgis, an emancipated Brahmin if ever there was one, to spend a long visit at the luxurious Oatlands Park Hotel in Surrey. The timing could not have been more felicitous. It was exactly the kind of invitation designed to appeal to Anny; deliciously comfortable, filled with stimulating company, and she would be able to take the little girls.

Oatlands Park, near Weybridge, was built in 1794 for the Duke of York, and converted into a grand hotel in 1856. It was here at Oatlands, with its terraces and double windows giving out on to wide vistas of lawns and parklands planted with broad-leaved trees, that Russell Sturgis received his guests. Sturgis came from a well-known family of Boston merchants. After increasing his fortune in the China trade, he returned to New England, a widower, intent on retirement. But he remarried and, with his new family, emigrated to London and joined the banking firm of Baring

Brothers. As the 'entertaining partner',[38] he led a lavish lifestyle, with a London house at Carlton House Terrace and an enormous place, Mount Felix, in Surrey. Sturgis was a cultured, fastidious man with a penchant for literature and a fondness for entertaining writers. In the past, Anny had often stayed at Mount Felix with her father, feeling thoroughly at home in the midst of its lavish splendours and magnificence, and making friends with the young Sturgis boys, Howard and Julian.

She was equally at home with the inner circle of Sturgis' guests, who included William Wetmore Story, his wife and daughter Edith, and Tom Appleton and the Dexters. Anny had first met the Storys years earlier when, as an awkward girl in her early teens, she and Minny had been taken by their father to winter in Rome. They had stayed in a vast apartment above a pastry-cook's in the Via Condotti and saw a good deal of the Anglo-American ex-patriates then staying in Rome.

William Wetmore Story was a sculptor and poet. His wife, Emelyn, was a sympathetic and graceful woman.[39] As a young man, William had studied law, had then gone to Italy to sculpt, and stayed. He had mellowed since Anny had first met him. He was beautifully, expensively clean, not a whisker of his moustache or his pointed beard out of place. He was undeniably attractive, his eyebrows dark and thick, his nose straight, his expression very much alive, intelligent and alert and marked with an unmistakable air of benevolence and good humour. At any moment his face might suddenly crease with amusement. He wore a silk cravat pinned with a jewel, a cameo chosen for sentiment.

The Storys had had two children. The boy, Joe, had died in 1853, and their quiet grief moved and saddened the ex-patriate community in Rome. The girl, Edith, survived. Anny never forgot how, towards the end of that winter in 1854, she and Minny had come down with scarlet fever just after Joe's death. Anny remembered her father drawing the characters for his book *The Rose and the Ring*, which he had written for Anny and Minny and the Story children, weaving the enchanting fairy story around them, and reading it aloud to the convalescent sisters by Edith's bedside between daylight and dusk. Those days seemed a lifetime ago. But they all remembered them as they walked between the trees at Oatlands Park and reminisced before the first bell sounded, a sign for them to change for dinner.

Anny had always equated Tom Appleton with the barrels of shiny, red American apples he used to send the Thackerays for Christmas, and for having introduced her father to the delights of the rocking-chair. An almost exact contemporary of Thackeray, Tom Appleton was an influential member of Boston society and a gifted amateur painter, collector, writer and wit. He was the first man of that circle in Boston who dared to grow a moustache. His sister Fanny was married to the poet Longfellow. His father Nathan, one of the founders of the American textile trade, had died one of the wealthiest men in Massachusetts. All these Bostonians were extremely rich. They were millionaires tinged with a streak of their Puritan inheritance. They took it for granted that it was the philanthropic use they made of their money that mattered, rather than the possession of great wealth for its own sake.[40] Discriminating and generous, Tom Appleton was a decided asset to the party.

As for the Dexters, old Mrs Dexter settled into the background quietly enough, content to admire the scenery and accept the filial tributes paid by her son in true Bostonian fashion. Tom Dexter was an attractive, experienced man of the world.[41] He was amused by Anny and she readily responded to his charm. He swiftly succeeded in making the little girls, Margie and Annie, devoted to him and, by playing with the children, made his advances to Anny doubly dear. Oatlands was the ideal place in which to conduct a flirtation. The women dallied in the dappled light, the immense circumference of their skirts glowing white like mushrooms gliding over the grass, holding aloft their white parasols lined with green silk. Wandering through the grounds with the children to play gooseberry, Anny was in a fair way to fall for Dexter irretrievably. While at Oatlands, she received almost daily letters from Minny, who was experiencing the real thing in considerably less comfortable circumstances.

★

> And this is good old Boston,
> The Home of the bean and the cod,
> Where the Lowells talk to the Cabots,
> And the Cabots talk only to God.
>
> JOHN BOSSIDY
On the Aristocracy of Harvard

Minny and Leslie sailed from Liverpool on board the SS *China* on 8 August 1868. Herman Merivale travelled with them. His sister Ella, one of Minny's closest friends, had married Pierre Freeman, an attaché to the British ambassador, and was living in Washington. The ten days' crossing was a choppy one and Minny, never a good sailor, suffered in consequence. They were held up in Customs and had to pay duty on a bonnet trimmed with gorgeous feathers which Minny had brought at the request of Annie Fields, the wife of the Boston publisher and friend of her father's.

Her first impressions of New York were distorted by the fact that she was feeling seedy and exhausted. She thought the people looked pinched and careworn and found the children 'poor little pale things with great starting-out eyes'. On the whole, it seemed to her a very sad place. To Leslie, who had first been there in 1863, just after the Battle of Gettysburg at the height of the Civil War, New York appeared very much as it always had, with the one difference that it was peaceful instead of being involved in a war. They stayed at the Clarendon Hotel, which was extremely comfortable, with a bedroom in the French style and a parlour in which to receive visitors and a private bathroom, which astonished Minny. She never did get used to the wonders of American plumbing. 'Everything here is done to save trouble, all the water through spouts goes everywhere.'[42]

The first people to call on them were the Baxters, who had befriended Thackeray on his lecture tour of America in 1855 when he had fallen for their elder daughter Sally. The Baxters had suffered considerable losses during the Civil War and now Sally was dead. Minny was much taken by their younger daughter Lucy, whom she compared to Julia Jackson but more dark and pensive. Leslie and Minny went to spend a day with the Baxters in their little white frame house in the country, virtually a shrine to a way of life extinguished by the Civil War, filled with mementos of the past. 'These people affect me more than I can tell you,' she told Anny. 'They sit there in their tiny sitting-room with Sally's picture, her dead husband & the little child who died – & Papa's – & they read the old letters & talk of old times when they were prosperous & kept a big open house. You can fancy how sad it seems.'

Most of the other people Leslie had hoped to see in New York were either away or dead or in mourning. It was not an auspicious start. Leslie's plan was to visit the Adirondacks, fit in some climbing, and write a paper for the Alpine Club. But first they went up the Hudson to Saratoga by steamboat on their way to see Minny's friend Ella Merivale, who was spending the summer on Lake George. Minny revelled in the luxury of the steamboat, which had marvellously comfortable drawing-rooms full of armchairs and great looking-glasses, and there were little booths where gentlemen could get their hair cut and their shoes shined. The journey up the river was beautiful, but by Saratoga Minny was already groggy with a bad cold she couldn't shake off. They booked into an enormous hotel crammed full of people, with children running about in their little top boots. Minny was appalled by how early the Americans got up; she breakfasted in bed, nursing her cold. When she did go down she found the other guests gathered in great gas-lit saloons like enormous waiting-rooms, some of them dancing. Somehow she had harboured a notion that American ladies spent a good deal of time sipping cocktails through straws. She was bitterly disappointed not to spot one.

The Freemans were staying in a rackety boarding house run by a parson turned innkeeper. People said his preaching was pretty good, but his inn-keeping shady. The first thing that greeted them was the overpowering stench of skunk, which pervaded the entire place. Minny was delighted to be reunited with Ella and to meet the children, but her cold soon developed into influenza, which put paid to any enjoyment. The place was draughty, their bedroom door wouldn't shut, the windows were broken and the bed was a 'horrible bundle of old straws'. There wasn't a drop of wine in the house and the wretched landlord could provide nothing to tempt Minny's appetite. Leslie took to fishing. In the evening, he and Pierre sat down meekly to a six o'clock tea and sipped cold water with their dinner. The waiters were worse than hopeless, and the vagaries of the weather did not help. It was hot as blazes one moment, and the next they were drenched to the skin from a cloudburst. The worst thing for Minny was that the rain got into all her carefully packed luggage and soaked all her clothes. 'You mustn't believe a word I say about America,' she wrote plaintively to Anny, 'because I have seen everything through a pocket-handkerchief & in this beastly climate it seems almost impossible to get rid of colds . . . The real truth is that I am excessively disappointed that I am afraid I must give up going to the Adirondacks.'

It was tantalising to have come so near and yet be so far. Leslie bore the setback to his pet scheme nobly and did not grumble, but Minny was miserable at being the cause of his bungled plans. For his part, Leslie was beginning to feel the folly of having brought Minny to such a rough place so soon after her convalescence. He was worried, contrite, and as attentive to her needs as he knew how. While she lay on the flimsy bag of straw for a bed, Leslie drafted an article about New York for *The Saturday Review*.

They left Bolton, and after a night in a luxurious inn where Minny curled up in bed with a glass of sherry punch, they decided to go on to Boston. Stopping at Albany on the way, they found the place was over-run by a huge democratic convention. By the skin of their teeth, they managed to get a room at the Delevan Hotel. Their travels seemed dogged by an unlucky star. After breakfast, Leslie went out to get his hair cut, '& came back all over with little oily ringlets . . . I do think after this our luck will change & that we shall have a good time – but our first fort-night has certainly been dampening'. Even though the Delevan was crowded, it was comfortable, and Leslie tried to make up for things by ordering champagne for dinner. To Minny's delight, they could also indulge in the risqué cocktails: 'A cocktail costs ninepence, Leslie & I have them continually through two straws. It is so nice drinking through straws that I don't think I shall ever drink any other way.' But in spite of this brief respite, they had not seen the last of their troubles.

They boarded the train for Boston at nine o'clock in the evening. Minny was plagued by a hacking cough and was restless until Leslie made her comfortable in the sleeping-car and tucked her up with shawls and pillows against the draught. At two o'clock in the morning, the conduc-tor roughly shook all the passengers awake and announced that the railway bridge was on fire and the train must be abandoned. 'Then down came Leslie's long legs & down came boots & crinolines, in the half-darkness we bundled up our innumerable wraps, poor Lez staggering along with the great bag & bundles of cloaks & I plodding on behind him trying to keep my scattered garments together.' Luckily, there was a bright moon, but they had to walk over a mile before they reached the burning bridge which was ablaze with petroleum containers that had exploded. At last, they got into another train which took them to Boston.

They went straight to the Tremont House Hotel, where Minny soaked in a hot bath before breakfasting in their room. Leslie went out and came back immediately with Oliver Wendell Holmes, then a flourishing young lawyer. He had been badly wounded during the Civil War, but was a lively, affectionate fellow and very fond of Leslie. He was delighted to meet Minny, made a favourable impression on her, and said that everyone was expecting them.

In the afternoon, Leslie walked over the bridge spanning the Charles river, and went on to Elmwood, the Cambridge home of his lifelong friend James Russell Lowell: poet, scholar, editor, critic and sometime statesman. On his first visit to America, Leslie had spent a week with Lowell at Elmwood, revelling in its quiet beauty and splendid library. Now Lowell, who later called Leslie 'the most loveable of men',[43] insisted that he should bring Minny to Elmwood where she was welcome to stay for as long as it took her to recover. Touched by Lowell's kindness, Leslie lost no time in installing Minny in the comforts of Elmwood.

Set back from the street by an expanse of rough grass planted with trees, Elmwood was a spacious, white, timbered house with an imposing portico and a carved, white balustrade above it. Behind the house, Mrs Lowell grew tomatoes and melons as well as potatoes, aubergines and sweetcorn. They kept a cow and some chickens which scratched about in the long grass. The bedroom set aside for Minny was an oak-panelled, blue-tiled room, equipped with luxurious washing facilities, delicious old-fashioned armchairs and an enormous four-poster. For the first few days, she was perfectly happy to lie in bed, occasionally bestir herself to sip sherry and suck horrible lozenges for her cold and drowse away, slipping from one doze into another.

Approaching fifty, Lowell, like many other Americans, had lost a number of his family in the Civil War. Leslie never met Lowell's first wife, a New England beauty, who had died in 1853. Of their four children, only one survived. His second wife was 'a kind, house-keepery little body but always tying up tomatoes or being sent for into the kitchen'. She had formerly been governess to his children. Minny was grateful for her kindness, but didn't take to her: '. . . she isn't at all poetic or intellectual, but she is a good-natured little woman, only I do dislike people to marry for company anybody who turns up after having delightful wives, don't you? If I was an intellectual wife in heaven, I should be disgusted, but I don't think I should mind nearly so much if my successor was up to me . . .'

Like Leslie, Lowell had a passion for reading omnivorously, and they were both happy to spend hours in Lowell's library, possibly the most attractive room in the house, reading, smoking, making the odd remark or joke which might lead to impassioned discussion as they sat absorbed, turning the pages of volume after volume.

Neither Leslie nor Minny wished to alarm Anny unnecessarily about Minny's health, but the fact was her illness was a good deal more serious than they let on. Old Doctor Holmes, who had retired from practice, came to tend her and dose her with some elixir which sent her fast asleep. But Minny's cough continued and worried both the doctor and Leslie sufficiently for a second opinion to be called for.

Leslie began to dream of leading an existence similar to Lowell's somewhere in the country back in England, not too far from London. He shared his vision in a letter to Anny. It consisted of, '. . . a nice little house, say at Weybridge, a pleasant garden where I could dig potatoes – a library like this where I am writing – & a quiet life. None of your London society but a good sleepy, cheap existence. I should write something solid & you should compose the most beautiful novels . . . The objection to this place is that it is rather more of a country place than a capital. It's still provincial in spirit & there is something rather small about it compared to London. This is true even of New York or in some respects a little more true of New York. It's like Manchester I should guess & a Manchester without a London to look up to. Now, in my dreams there is always a London in the background – to say nothing of an Anny in the foreground – so that there is no danger of my taking root here or turning my dreams into reality . . .'

Minny, like so many patients, was bored. Longing for some distraction, she asked Lowell to rustle up some American novels to amuse her. 'He . . . got me the most deadly things . . . All the ladies are called Humility and the gentlemen Kejasariah & other Scripture names, & they spend their whole days in the kitchen cooking & singing hymns, & on Sundays they go to church & died without marrying anyone. They draw a fearful picture which I believe to be true.'

As she began to recover, Minny first grew famished, then frustrated, and began to show all the petulant symptoms of a convalescent. 'All over America the food is a trifle scanty . . . I am rather fearfully thinking that I shall hardly be able to keep my invalidness up to the mark of breakfasting in bed.' Anticipating getting up and about again, she sent for her trunk of clothes from New York, but dreaded their getting soaked again.

Until they arrived she stayed in bed and seethed against the perfectly innocent Lowells and all things American, until she finally gave vent to her spleen in a letter to Anny when Leslie was safely out of the way in Boston: '. . . never will this country be at one at all until they have learnt to dine. It is perfectly monstrous & ridiculous. I now see what it is that makes them so savage against each other & us, it is hunger – & they think it is righteous wrath. Darling couldn't you send me over a tin of pork-pie or something – or if you are at Freshwater some of those bad lobsters which were so delicious? They have a horrid habit here of nibbling at some beastly stuff called popcorn – most nasty, exactly like the inside of quill pens a little burnt. They say it is delicious. I expect I shall soon be nibbling at my boots & Leslie asked me for a packet of gloves this morning in a most suspicious manner.'

There were some distractions: she was well enough to receive a visit from Mrs Ticknor, the wife of the well-known publisher. Minny was enchanted by her and described her to Anny as a 'Boston swell'. Admittedly, Minny was somewhat puzzled by the stream of compliments Mrs Ticknor paid her about her cleverness and genius, until it struck her that Mrs Ticknor had mistaken her for Anny. Minny was delighted by the muddle and both women laughed and made firm friends. Mrs Ticknor amused her further by telling her how Thackeray had suffered a great deal of discomfort in America. When Minny said he had never complained of any, Mrs Ticknor said, 'I mean in the way of attentions.' She was refer-ring to the bevvies of beauties who had fallen for him.

In spite of their kindness to her, Minny never felt completely at her ease at Elmwood, because of her aversion to Mrs Lowell. Soon Leslie, diplomatically, accepted an invitation from the Miss Westons who lived at Weymouth, a small country community outside Boston.

The Westons were connected to Leslie's Dicey cousins. While on their wedding tour in Switzerland the previous year, he and Minny had come across the Miss Westons' brother and his wife. They and their two little girls were now also staying at Weymouth. There were three Miss Westons. They led an exemplary life. Miss Dora kept the house spotless and ran it in true New England style, proud of her pickles, the produce of her garden, her beeswaxed furniture and her unstinting contributions to local charities. Their mother the Miss Westons kept firmly in bed, out of sight, upstairs. Minny was entranced by their 'storybook' existence, and was fasci-nated by their household arrangements, especially the central heating, which was quite novel to her. 'The rooms are warmed by great holes out of which a fiery heat rushes. I like it. Then the windows are open, &

outside there is the loveliest day you ever saw, a sort of beautiful warm sunny frost, something like the South of France in winter, only with all the trees out & here & there one turning scarlet.' It was already past the middle of September.

The Miss Westons were currently going through a craze for reading Jane Austen. Minny thought Lucy Baxter exactly like Anne Elliot in *Persuasion*. Leslie reserved any wild enthusiasm but recommended Jane Austen to Anny. 'I see [her] merits but I feel more than ever it is flat blasphemy to set her up as an object of worship after the fashion of some of my friends. However, she is good reading for you, because her merits are such as you might study to advantage – especially the careful way in which the stories are worked out.'[44]

If Minny was happy to admire the Miss Westons' domestic arrangements, Leslie admitted to a certain tedium. Unlike Elmwood, there was nobody for him to enjoy a stimulating conversation with. The brother was a morose fellow, made sulky by the *Cranford*-like style of his spinster sisters' ways. His idea of a good time was to stay up late into the night, drinking whisky and chewing tobacco. He inveigled Leslie into keeping him company. Leslie obliged, even though he regarded chewing tobacco as a calumny. But it gave Leslie a chance to smoke his beloved pipe and nor was he averse to the whisky.

By 24 September Leslie was able to write to Anny, 'I must send you a line to say that Min is now perfectly well & bright – which is the first time I could say so conscientiously since we landed. Her cough is gone & she talks & laughs like herself & I am quite happy to see her. I don't mean that she was ever so ill as last winter; but she was a good deal knocked up by her cold & by travelling when we reached Boston. Since then she has steadily been reviving & for the last day or two has fairly been at the top of the hill.'[45]

Now that Minny was, if not over, at least on top of the hill, her thoughts turned very naturally to the state of her clothes, which she had chosen with such care back in England, which had cost a considerable amount of money, and which had got sadly spoiled by getting soaked *en voyage* before she had had any opportunity to wear them. She was quick to take advantage of the Miss Westons' central heating and had them all unpacked and hung up to dry and pressed into some semblance of their original shape.

Leslie seized the occasion to go into Boston to hear the female preacher, the Reverend Olympia Brown. Despite the fact that Minny accused him of not liking women to be 'rational', he came away impressed. 'The church this morning was something. The young lady who preached was much like a neat person behind a counter in a London shop. She reeled it off as correctly as possible & certainly preached far better than most British parsons ... she didn't believe in hell & said you ought not to be a Christian in order to be the President of the United States, nor to avoid railway accidents because you would probably be disappointed if you did & I agreed with her as far as she went.'[46]

The Miss Westons preened themselves and their central heating on having effected Minny's cure. Now that she was well enough to go into Boston society, Leslie booked rooms in a fashionable boarding-house run by a Mrs Putnam, an enterprising woman who had written a cookery book, gave excellent dinners and was very fat – 'a melancholy sort of fat'.[47] On their arrival they were shown into a spartan parlour furnished with old-fashioned horsehair chairs and sofas, which made the shades of her great-grandmother, Mrs Becher, rise up before Minny.

In late September Boston was looking strikingly beautiful. Bright with the vivid colours of early autumn, the warmth of an Indian summer still lingered. Minny was immediately reconciled to it. It was a prosperous and bustling city which, she thought, seemed 'to take a pride in itself and keep everything neat & clean'. The houses on Beacon Hill, where most of Leslie's friends lived, were notable for their 'individual façades, the large clear windows of the curved fronts facing each other "like candid inevitable eyes"'. The principal streets were thronged with horse-drawn carriages and other vehicles, and busy with pedestrians apparently intent on risking their lives beneath the noses of the cab horses while crossing the street. The clatter of iron-shod hoofs on cobbles was tremendous, and the entire place was redolent of the smell of horses mingled with cabbages, tea, fish and saddle-soap. Commerce was thriving after the lean years of the Civil War. Admittedly, there were still traces of conflict: wounded soldiers, some of them beggars, were to be seen on the crowded, plank-covered side-walks. But almost everything yet invented was available, as well as a good many which had not been, but which were advertised. There were confec-tioners, haberdashers, candy stores, ice-cream parlours, saloon bars, grand hotels, and more dubious lodgings. Even twenty years later, Henry James was struck by the 'numerosity' of the women in Boston. He wrote of a 'deluge of petticoats' and a 'sisterhood of shoppers'.[48] The same was true in 1868 when Leslie and Minny were there. It cannot have been due entirely to the fact that the Civil War had left so many widows and spin-sters. It was best explained by the powerful role women played in Boston Society. Minny was amused by some of the American Christian names.

'Preserved Fish', 'Return Jonathan Migs' and 'Westminster Abbey' were among them. 'Preserved' Fish was a little boy adopted by Mr and Mrs Fish.

Leslie's Boston friends were almost exclusively literary, all related or connected so intricately that neither Leslie nor Minny could follow the 'huge labyrinth of cousinhood [who] all go back to the days of the Mayflower'. They lived in restrained grandeur, their manners impeccable, their motives of the highest philanthropic order. Their houses were beautiful, old and comfortable, with handsome libraries and famous burgundy and claret in their cellars. They mixed culture and housekeeping in a fashion that delighted Minny, and their Puritan streak appealed to the Evangelical streak latent in Leslie. The men dressed mainly in black and, resplendent with whiskers, might read aloud from improving books while the women, as demure as the fashions allowed, seemed intent on their fine sewing. But there was about them a freedom of thought, an uninhibited questioning and frankness in their discussions, which the Stephens found refreshing.

They were frequently invited to tea, to dinner and to every kind of party. Minny, who was a convincing actress herself, developed theatre mania. Leslie did not share her enthusiasm, except for the rare occasion when he considered the actress to be a great beauty, but he never discouraged her going to the play without him.[49] She went with Mrs Bangs to see Edwin Booth play Hamlet. Although she found him handsome and rather like Mr Brookfield to look at, she was disappointed, for Booth was a much acclaimed actor who had played Hamlet for a record run and she had expected greater things. 'He is a fidgety actor & made Hamlet nothing but a ferocious madman & not an interesting young man.'[50]

In return for all the hospitality, Minny decided to give a luncheon party, and spent some trouble confabulating with Mrs Putnam on the menu. They finally agreed on a deceptively simple cold lunch – deceptive only in that everything was of the very finest quality and deliciously cooked – of cold fowls, lobster salad, oyster scallops, ice-cream and champagne. Among the guests were two of the Misses Weston, Oliver Wendell Holmes *père et fils*, and Mrs Fields. It would have been splendid if Mrs Fields had worn her gorgeous feathered bonnet, although it is unlikely. The cream of Boston society kept their latest acquisitions of European finery for at least two years between tissue paper in their clothes presses before wearing them, such was their aversion to vulgarity. The lunch party was a success.

In spite of his love for Boston, Leslie could never reconcile himself to

William Makepeace Thackeray, by E. Edwards.

Anny Thackeray, May 1870, by Julia Margaret Cameron.

Minny Thackeray, May 1865, by Julia Margaret Cameron.

Sir Henry Cole, 1865,
by Julia Margaret Cameron.

'The Dirty Monk', Alfred Tennyson,
May 1865, by Julia Margaret Cameron.

Dimbola, Anon. 1871.

Julia Margaret Cameron,
by G.F. Watts, *c*.1852.

Julia Margaret Cameron playing
her Erridge Piano, 1863,
by Oscar Gustave Rejlander.

Richmond, Willy
and Blanche Ritchie.

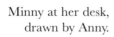

Minny at her desk,
drawn by Anny.

Félicie.

'The Stars in her hair were Seven',
Emily 'Pinkie' Ritchie, May 1870,
by Julia Margaret Cameron.

Margie Thackeray, 1866-9,
by Julia Margaret Cameron.

Leslie Stephen, 1872,
by Julia Margaret Cameron.

Minny,
by G.F. Watts.

anything approaching luxury for men. He was as deprecating about Tom Appleton's house, for example, as Minny was full of admiration for Mrs Bang's arrangements at Longwood. Leslie was not one to mince words. 'And really Tom's house is disgustingly luxurious for a bachelor. It seems as if you only have to turn a screw anywhere to have hot water, or cold water, or gas, & a clean shirt, or to be shaved, or to have your hair cut. As he can also summon spirits it must be a kind of magical establishment.'[51] Minny was equally capable of plain speech. '. . . You have no idea of the comfort & beauty of a well fitted American house. [Mrs Bangs' house has] about the same number of rooms as ours but the whole is fitted up with real wood – all the doors & shutters & panels & staircases are made of this beautiful dark wood. Then there are bathrooms & washrooms & cupboards without number, a great cedarwood closet to make anything smell nice that they put there. Then there are lifts & speaking-trumpets & every possible thing.'[52]

Leslie was eager to be in New York for the forthcoming presidential elections. Ulysses S. Grant was running for office after President Johnson had been impeached, brought to trial and acquitted. Leslie was a true political animal and rightly thought there 'would be more row' there than at Boston.[53]

The night before they left, Minny went to the theatre with Mrs Fields, Pierre Freeman and Herman Merivale. Leslie went for a final smoke with Lowell whom he liked 'far better than anyone here and better than most people in England, he is much the best informed man I have met about literature & such, & has any amount of shrewdness & humour . . . Also he is a warm-hearted cove, though he doesn't apparently care to see many people'.[54] Leslie's description of Lowell could equally have applied to himself. The two parted after Lowell had walked him to a corner of the street where they had left each other on Leslie's first visit to America, '. . . & felt quite sentimental'.[55] Leslie's curious combination of detachment and sentimentality is typical of him. All his life, he held certain places to be sacred for entirely sentimental reasons: the street corner where he left Lowell, the grassy knoll at Täsh where he had been on the brink of proposing to Minny, the Wengen Alp, and many other places. He despised sentimentality in others, but indulged in it himself to a great degree. Such conflicting emotions are partly what made him such a complicated, fascinating and vulnerable man.

On their return to New York they stayed at the Clarendon Hotel again. Leslie was caught up in the political scene and enjoyed the electioneering to the hilt, as he did any good argument or physical battle against the elements. In those days of letters of introduction foreign arrivals were announced in the newspapers, and Leslie and Minny were courted by American society on two counts. Leslie was much in demand as one of the first investigative journalists of the recent Civil War, and won the heart of free-thinking North Americans. Minny had the cachet of being her father's daughter. Each was popular on their own account.

Minny's own political views may have been somewhat muddled, but the fact is that she hated any war and, of all wars, one which divided a country in two was the most abominable. '. . . I can no more sympathise with people for hacking at each other & blowing out each other's brains for 4 years than I can sympathise with Queen Mary's religious frolics. I am quite sure that war must go out with civilisation, it's too horrid, & when you come to a country like this where people haven't yet recovered from killing their neighbours and being killed you see how brutal it is . . . It's bad enough here & in the South it must be a hundred times more horrible.'[56]

Minny, whose attitudes often altered according to her own sense of wellbeing, reversed her early impressions of New York and was fascinated

by the people who called on her and invited her out. She was much absorbed by the new fashions: '. . . I wish you could see these little ladies tripping up & down Fifth Avenue in their tremendous toilettes. They usually wear a velvet surtout of bright colours all looped and festooned up and satin petticoats.'[57]

After decades of women's contours being aggrandised to an extraordinary degree by the hoops, petticoats and general impracticalities of the crinoline, the bustle was beginning to make its appearance. Minny understandably longed for one and felt positively shabby without. She also admired one of her acquaintance's exquisite pale tea-rose coloured silk gown worn with coral and red ribbons around the neck. Minny had to snap her fingers at such salmony finery and make do with her old lace tippet, even though she remarked, 'No one has lace here, & I think they think it an eccentric antimacassar.' But if she was envious of the women's fashions, she held the local transport in contempt. She found the streets rowdy and loathed the overcrowded omnibuses, which were the only means of getting about since it was considered 'fast' for a woman to take a cab by herself.

Such niceties didn't trouble Leslie in the least. He was completely taken up by the election. He noticed it was much quieter than in London, partly because the number of polling places precluded vast queues, and partly because all the liquor shops were closed for the day. Nevertheless, 'the most remarkable experience was at Tamanay [*sic*] Hall where the Democrats collected. There was a huge crowd of the roughs of New York packed as tight as herrings in a barrel – I was one of the herrings and the others smelt decidedly strong'.[58] At the Republican meeting, the crowd was enthusiastic and cheered and sang. It got too much for Leslie, who took himself off to eat oysters at the Century before going on to the Union League Club, where he stayed till one o'clock in the morning. He was delighted by the outcome and genuinely glad that Grant was elected, he told Anny, but observed that '. . . in New York it is simply a fight between the Rowdies and the Atheists (in a political sense) on one side, and the Brains and Fanatics and genuine Yankee Spirit on the other'.[59]

Minny was more interested in gossip than politics. 'I heard a funny story about Mr Emerson and Margaret Fuller today from Mrs Baxter. They went together to see Miss Fanny Essler, the great opera dancer, & were captivated by her *al la transcendental*. She gave one kick that quite upset Mr Emerson who said – "O, Margaret, this is poetry". She then gave another still higher, upon which Margaret said – "O Ralph, *this* is religion." I'm afraid you think it horrid of me to laugh at Mr Emerson, he really is a dear old boy . . .'[60]

From New York they went to spend a week with new friends, Alfred Pells and his family at West Point on the Hudson river. They were both spellbound by the beauty of the landscape, and Leslie found some consolation for having missed the Adirondacks by striking out for immense walks with young Pells through the gloriously coloured forests to the heights beyond. 'Last night was as cold as old boots and we found some snow on the top of the hill today. The fact is that this is one of the most beautiful places I ever saw.'

Not so Washington. Minny found it more like a 'horrid dream' than anything else she could think of, and Leslie called it 'a God-forgotten sort of hole'. They saw a good deal of Ella Freeman, whose charm and vitality succeeded in captivating Leslie even though he and Minny found her husband Pierre an obnoxious bore. The Lowells were on a visit too, but the highlight of the Stephens' stay in Washington was a meeting with President Johnson, General Grant, the President Elect, and Chief Justice Chase. Leslie had a ten-minute 'chat' with Grant and thought him 'a good round pebble of humanity looking tough enough for his part, though I did not recognise as perhaps I should have done, any remarkable radiation of genius about him'.[61] For her part, Minny was quite won by President Johnson. 'My heart melted to him in an instant, he looked so tired and fagged.'[62] Having narrowly escaped impeachment, Johnson was serving out his term of office until Grant's inauguration. There was every reason for the man to look jaded, but he reciprocated Minny's admiration. 'When we were going away,' she told Anny happily, 'he went up to the chimney-piece & took a nosegay of flowers out of a china pot & said to me with the air of a melancholy prince, "Will you allow me to give some of our flowers – I have nothing better to offer you" & I concluded by thinking him a most ill-used man.' The flowers given her by the President and Leslie's chat with General Grant helped to mitigate the beastly mud and mosquitoes of Washington.

Their friends John and Eliza Field (not to be confused with the Boston publisher John Fields, and his wife who was the possessor of the bonnet) were a well-off, 'cultivated, childless couple who spent their lives in travel and leisure'.[63] They lived in a large, comfortable and well-appointed house in Philadelphia and both Minny and Leslie enjoyed the week they spent there. As usual, Minny was fascinated by the way the Americans ran their homes. She intended to bring back plans of some of the houses she had seen and at one point declared an ambition to be an architect. 'I should so like to be a house-builder & don't see why not.'[64] Even though Minny never realised this ambition, she was preoccupied by domestic architecture and household planning for all of her adult life. The surviving plans she made, even though few of them materialised, are evidence of her talent and imagination.

The only thing which marred their pleasure was a letter from Anny announcing that she planned to accept an invitation to stay with the Storys in Italy almost as soon as they returned. They both protested. Leslie made his feelings quite plain. 'I don't like to feel that I shall be the cause of separating you & Min for six months in one year. Think of it!'[65] Minny was more diplomatic, suggesting that Anny should postpone her visit until March in order to avoid the horrors of the east winds howling in England at the equinox. As usual, Minny got her way.

And then it was time for the Stephens to leave America. They sailed on the SS *Scotia* and had a miserable crossing. Minny was laid up for the entire voyage. Leslie spent most of his time on deck, smoking, but there was nobody interesting for him to talk to, and he became bored and irritable. They landed at Liverpool on 6 December. They were not altogether sorry to be back in England and at home once more in time for Christmas at Onslow Gardens.

II

'The first time I saw your horse,' Azamat went on, 'when he pranced under you, and jumped, dilating his nostrils, and flint sparks sprayed from under his hooves, something strange happened inside my soul, and since then everything became dull to me.'

MIHAIL LERMONTOV *A Hero of our Time*

On 17 August Anny paid one of her fairly regular visits to her mother, who was still living in the care of Mrs Bakewell. At that period of her life, Anny went to see her mother about three or four times a year. These visits, though necessarily somewhat sad, were not altogether depressing. Isabella's sad and gentle existence touched Anny's naturally affectionate heart. Since Thackeray's death, she had made a point of making her mother's comfort one of her immediate concerns. Minny avoided any share in the responsibility, but Leslie was a reliable and constant support and occasionally of practical help. As time went on, Anny's fidelity to what at first she perceived to be her duty, became a source of pleasure as she began to glimpse her mother's personality, not obscured entirely by the partial eclipse in which she lived.

By September, when Minny and Leslie were in America, Anny and the little girls were at Freshwater. In the beauty of those familiar surroundings, listening to the waves lap against the shore and reassured by the company of people she loved, Anny began to recover. Dexter had trifled with her feelings at Oatlands Park and she felt she had made a fool of herself about him. Dexter had not exactly jilted Anny, but it felt like it, and she had minded so much she could hardly bear for him to be anywhere near the children any longer. Edith Story had tried to comfort her, and told her it was an old story with Dexter and he shouldn't be let loose on society. But it was the first time anything like that had happened to Anny, except once, years ago, when she was a young girl in Paris and she had had a crush on a curate – but she didn't really count that. At Freshwater she began to work again, writing a short story, *Sola*, about a young girl who is unlucky in love. She liked the work and the rhythm of daily writing, which she always found so much easier on the island than she did in London. Writing and walking along the seashore and climbing the Downs with close friends soon proved healing to a bruised heart. She was able to think she had had a lucky escape and to consider herself fortunate to be her own mistress.[66]

Anny's intimacy with Mrs Tennyson began developing into a closer bond. Emily Tennyson could see that Anny was unhappy and it was not difficult for her to guess why, even though she knew the reasons were multiple. Emily was dedicated to her husband, an immensely demanding man; she was dedicated to her children, to the happiness of others, and to worthy causes. Yet despite her air of frailty, she combined her noble aspirations with a resounding common sense. She was practical and busy. Both the Thackeray sisters had always been interested in charitable causes and, chiefly under the influence of Jeannie Senior, had dabbled in good works. A modicum of philanthropic effort was expected from girls in their position, but somehow these essays always fizzled out until they were stirred to start a new worthy scheme. Minny found that her marriage precluded any possibility of her becoming an active social worker. Now, Mrs Tennyson once more appealed to Anny's better nature. In a letter to George Smith, Anny wrote, 'I am very much excited about this little dream of Mrs Tennyson's & mine, of a sort of living club for single women. I think it would cheer up some of the forlorn ones very much to have nice little apartments & a cook's shop on the ground floor.'[67] The two women had in mind, it would appear, more of a haven for the fallen than a ragged school for orphans. But even if this 'little dream' bore no more fruit than Anny's childhood plan for a Society for the Stoppation of Starvation for Children, it confirmed her friendship with Emily. 'She is very delightful and we agree in our notions of how to do good in the world,' recorded Mrs Tennyson, who appreciated Anny's 'great wit' and 'good heart'.[68] Anny benefited from her company and it was pleasant to sit and speculate about such subjects in the drawing-room at Farringford. Mrs Tennyson had a wonderfully uplifting effect as she sat, seldom idle, on her sofa overlooking the lawn and the cedar tree.

Then, in October, Anny felt unwell and the doctor was sent for. He had serious misgivings about her and diagnosed pleurisy. The notion of setting off for Italy with the Storys became increasingly attractive, only to be squashed by Minny's letter persuading her to put the visit off until March. Anny recovered surprisingly quickly, although she remained for some time in the nervy, irritable state of the convalescent. Long walks with Tennyson, and later Sir Henry Taylor, along the Downs and across to Alum Bay helped to restore her health. Another companion with whom Anny walked along the seashore was Marie Spartali, a talented Greek painter and renowned for her beauty: when Swinburne first set eyes on her, he declared he wanted to weep from rapture.* Marie Spartali was a pupil of Ford Madox Brown and had caused a scandal by having a love affair with Lord Ranelagh: both Minny and Anny were her confidantes. Two years later, she married the American widowed journalist, William Stillman. Marie's family objected to Stillman as much as they had to Ranelagh, but Minny and Anny arranged meetings between the lovers at Onslow Gardens. There was nothing quite like other people's tangled love affairs to evoke the sisters' sympathy.

In November, Anny set off to London via Mrs Sartoris at Warnford, her house in Hampshire, which she had created as a 'monument to Beauty'. But Anny was in an unusually recalcitrant mood, anxious about her writing, anxious about Minny and Leslie's imminent return from America, and her nerves still on edge after her bout of pleurisy. It did not help that the builders were in full spate, propping up the 'monument to Beauty', and

---

*When Anny first set eyes on Swinburne, she thought he looked like Apollo or a Fairy Prince 'swinging his hat in his hand, and letting the sunshine flood the bush of his burning hair'. She wept when he left Fryston Hall, where they were all staying with Richard Monckton Milnes. It has to be admitted that both Swinburne and Anny were easily moved to tears.

the two women had to walk through ladders on their way to the drawing-room where they sat on a kind of island in the middle of the floor, the workmen all round them. Anny grumbled and Mrs Sartoris scolded. To Mrs Sartoris' astonishment, Anny flew into an ungovernable rage. It was as though the dove had snarled and drawn her talons. The following day, she was penitent and they were reconciled. Mrs Sartoris gave her some sound advice. 'Read your ms *aloud* to yourself,' she said. 'Many things will then strike you, which otherwise you might pass over.'[69] 'I seem to have newly discovered that Mrs Sartoris is *extraordinarily* clever,' Anny wrote to George Smith – quite forgetting that Adelaide Sartoris had been an internationally acclaimed opera singer – 'that if she had been a man instead of a woman I don't know what she would have done.'[70] She certainly wouldn't have sung Norma.

Minny never enjoyed such close affinities with Mrs Tennyson, Mrs Brookfield, or Mrs Sartoris as Anny did. After her marriage to Leslie, Minny avoided such mentors and eventually resented what she grew to see as their interference. But Anny's need for the company and approval of these women did not lessen. Her intimacy with them had one curious effect: they prolonged her youth. Instead of threshing things out with her contemporaries and having the corners rubbed off her, Anny continued to defer to women old enough to have been her mother, and who treated her with an odd mixture of equality and the protection they had given her as a girl. Anny was already thirty-one, an age which they regarded as being pretty well on the shelf.

Anny returned to London to supervise the preparations at Onslow Gardens for Minny and Leslie's return. In between giving orders, cancelling them, and giving new ones, she saw a good deal of the Merivales, the Coles, and the Stephens. Although she was never close to his wife, Mary, Anny was becoming increasingly fond of Leslie's brother, Fitzy. It was an unlikely friendship, for no two people could have been more different. Fitzy was a great hulk of a fellow with a mighty intellect, but lacked Leslie's charm and subtlety of mind. After dining with Lady Stephen, Fitzy walked Anny home and they had a long conversation about 'the Pole Star Flash and uncertainty and making for the North'.[71]

When Minny and Leslie did return in the second week of December, Anny was dismissive about the success of their American visit. The fact is that she wouldn't have enjoyed it, and the interest of any exciting times Minny and Leslie had were obscured for her by her anxiety about her sister's health. It couldn't be denied that Minny, who had been made extremely ill by the loss of her child before setting off for America, had spent most of the time there worryingly unwell. Anny had been the recipient of a mass of letters written by Minny when she was at her lowest ebb. Leslie had been perfectly aware of her frail condition before they left, and knew the nature of the country he was taking her to. But if it was unreasonable of him to take Minny on such an expedition so soon after her convalescence, it was not because he was positively selfish so much as that he lacked that kind of imagination. This lack was to lead to subsequent suffering, but he was, in fact, one of the kindest and most loveable of men, quick to cherish his friends and family once he saw how. It was his lack of empathy rather than negligence that caused him to blunder.

They took up their places somewhat hesitantly back at Onslow Gardens. The balance in their relationships had shifted subtly in ways they did not care to define but which, after months of absence, they all recognised. Leslie now felt so much at one with Minny that he could hardly realise the life he had led before his marriage had ever really existed. Minny, who had previously appeared to be dependent on Anny, now began to realise the strength of her own character. Through her union with Leslie she discovered her own identity. The sisters remained very close, intimate and considerate of each other, but Anny began to feel desperately lonely. And if Anny and Leslie were jealous of each other, they were also immensely fond of one another. Perhaps too fond. The situation was fraught with uneasiness, not made any better because nothing was said.

Leslie could not speak about his feelings to Anny without blushing or stammering. He could not bear to 'speak sentiment' and was apprehensive of her emotional replies. But he did at least express his feelings with uncommon candour on paper and address them directly to Anny: '. . . when I think of this time two years & a bit ago, I wonder whether I am I. I was a miserable moody creature with a general impression that I was going posthaste to the devil. I am a happy cove with lots to do & liking to do it, with Min for a wife & you for a sister & on much pleasanter terms with my own family . . . I won't say what they feel about you; only without you, I shouldn't be more than a crippled creature still. I feel like a frozen animal that has been taken in & thawed by benevolent people & am sensible of being expanded & improved in every faculty I possess.'[72]

They did their utmost to respect each other's privacy. Leslie spent most of his time in his study right at the top of the house, Minny often closeted with him, while he read at enormous length and then went to his writing table where he wrote for hours, composing articles for *Frazer's Magazine*, *Macmillan's*, *The Pall Mall Gazette*, *The Saturday Review* and the

Alpine Review. He wrote about climbing, about Defoe's novels and Richardson's novels, about Ritualism, Politics and the Church. He wrote informatively, succinctly and made his subjects come vividly before his reader's eyes. He worked hard and was indisputably beginning to make a considerable name for himself in the world of letters. He was touchingly proud of his attic study. Not at all apiece with the rest of the house, it was cluttered and overcrowded with books, writing tables, a sofa, the rocking-chair he sat in, a rack of pipes within reach. The walls were hung with photographs of Alpine scenes, of a few old friends, of Cambridge. Old alpenstocks leaned against the wall beneath the stuffed head of a chamois. The room was thick with the fug of tobacco mingled with the smell of the coal-fire, and of his beloved sheepdog Troy, curled up on the mat. Leslie's taste was not aesthetic; he liked things for what they reminded him of and for what they represented. He would have been taken aback and possibly amused if he had been told that he liked objects for senti-mental reasons. It was very much a man's room and a fairly accurate expression of his personality.

Anny kept her own charming writing-room unchanged. Here she wrote voluminous letters, seldom dated, addressed to her multitude of friends. Anny had a particular knack for letter-writing. Her letters are lively, orig-inal and to the point, as much as they are inconsequential. They are vastly more readable than they are legible. It was here, too, that she wrote her 'real writing'. She wrote hastily, untidily, covering an enormous quantity of paper – old envelopes and shopping lists as well as pages of foolscap – in her round, ballooning hand. Her prose was as impressionistic and vivacious as her conversation. Sometimes she stitched her manuscripts – consisting of bits and pieces of paper of varying sizes – together with strands of silk. Sometimes, she stuck on memoranda with the white perfo-rated edge from stamp paper. Her publisher, George Smith, was frequently driven to distraction by her methods or, more accurately, by the lack of them. Nevertheless, he considered the deplorable state of her manuscripts as 'expressive of her somewhat vagrant genius . . . She was a woman of genius – with many of the characteristics – and some of the limitations, of a woman of genius'.[73] George Smith was about to bring out her collec-tion of short stories, *To Esther & Other Sketches*, and Anny had already conceived the idea for what is one of her most important novels, *Old Kensington*. She had already written to Smith saying she wanted to get on with the book, and she thought of taking it to Rome.

In this writing-room, which also served Anny as her private parlour, she could receive her visitors without disturbing the rest of the house-

hold. At least, that was the idea. The obvious drawback was that her callers, cousins, and friends like the Merivales, Mrs Brookfield, the Coles or Katie Collins, were just as close to Minny as they were to Anny. This might not have mattered so much if Anny did not have a habit of overflowing. Like the muddle of papers on her desk, she took up a tremendous amount of space and spilled from one room into another. She was quite likely to usher a visitor into the main drawing-room, perhaps to see a camellia in flower, or to show them Leslie's latest learned article. It was impossible for Minny to shelter under that most convenient of Victorian white lies, namely to pretend she was not At Home when she only too evidently was. It was an arrangement which was far from ideal.

Naturally, Anny was always present at luncheon, tea and dinner, as well as sharing those long, post-prandial evenings, whether Minny and Leslie had guests or not. On one occasion, Leslie invited Robert Louis Stevenson and the young Edmund Gosse to dinner. They arrived together, expecting a grand dinner-party with a lot of literary nabobs present. They were rather dismayed to find that they were the only guests – their dismay much increased by the unnerving silence of both Leslie and Minny throughout the dinner. Anny tried to keep up the illusion of gaiety, sailing blithely from one subject to another until she reached the topic of servants. 'I tell my maid everything,' she confided. 'Yes,' said Minny suddenly. 'And how we wish you wouldn't!'[74]

None of the difficulties was as obvious then as they became with hindsight. They were obscured by the details of quotidian life. The servants outnumbered the nominal occupants of the house; the hum of life and the stamp of feet, the shaking of wet winter galoshes, the unfurling of sodden brollies in the small 'hall', the arrival of the post several times a day, the ordering of dinners, seeing to the children, all demanded their attention.

No wonder that the Storys' invitation was attractive to Anny. This visit confirmed the precedent set by her stay at Oatlands Park. She was to make a number of extended visits away from Leslie and Minny for as long as they lived together. She genuinely enjoyed travelling and sightseeing. She nearly always took some writing with her, or used her observations of the places she stayed at to provide background material for a projected novel. The obliqueness of this attempt at finding a solution to the persistent malaise at home was as typical of the age she lived in as it was of her. She was squeamish of a more direct approach.

In 1869 Gladstone was preoccupied with the disestablishment of the Irish Church; matters in France were resolving themselves in a way which would rattle the rest of the Western world to its backbone and lead to the Franco-Prussian War; Ferdinand de Lesseps completed the construction of the Suez Canal, and Tolstoy published *War and Peace*. Anny travelled to Italy with Lady de Rothschild and her daughters. She went with them as far as Florence, and then continued overnight to Rome.

The Rome that Anny knew was magnificent. When the coachman drew up the horses outside the Palazzo Barberini, which was the Storys' home, the sleepy occupants of the coach opened their eyes and gasped. Anny described it as being 'grander than Windsor Castle with the sun rippling down all the marble steps'.[75] It was certainly a great deal more dazzling.

The Storys hadn't been able to understand Anny's characteristically muddled note about her travel arrangements and had not been expecting her early morning arrival. Nonetheless, they welcomed her enthusiastically. She was led up a vast number of stairs, through great, noble empty chambers to the old schoolroom, comforting and informal, where they plied her with a breakfast of coffee and fruit and cakes, as well as questions about her journey. After her breakfast, she wallowed in a luxurious bath of 'delicious spranking water'.[76]

The Storys were at the centre of the circle of American and English artists, musicians, poets and writers who had formed a colony of cultivated ex-patriates in Rome over the last two decades, and the names of their close friends conjure up the arts of their day: they included the Brownings, the Trollopes, Mrs Sartoris and her sister, Fanny Kemble, Longfellow, Charles Eliot Norton, James Russell Lowell, Mrs Gaskell, Madame Möhl, George Eliot, Frederic Leighton, and Henry James. But Story's genius as a host lay not in emphasising the importance of his friends' eminence, but in his mastery of understatement. Imposing though the Palazzo Barberini undeniably was, the Storys' assumed lifestyle was so deceptively simple as to allow their guests to be uninhibited by the splendour that surrounded them. Such a way of life would have been impossible to maintain without the fortune Story possessed, but for his wealth to have been conspicuous would have been to negate the wonder of the illusion he created.

His canary, hanging in a wicker cage in the window overlooking the Vatican, had possibly the finest view of the grandeur that was Rome. Vistas of fountains and statues and marble steps, and the purple shadows of the Campagna beyond, were as familiar to the bird as the husk of millet it was given to peck. Dukes and beggars, all in costume picturesque beyond belief to the English or American beholder, strutted and gabbled in the streets, together with musicians and onion-sellers, cooks, and girls laden with laundry. The imperviousness of the canary to such sights was almost as magnificent as the gorgeousness it disdained.

Sightseeing was the order of the day. Story generally escaped to his studio after sharing a late breakfast in the old nursery with Anny. While his guests explored the ruins, Story sculpted gigantic statues. He was fascinated by the problems of how to chisel marble so that it emulated the flowing qualities of falling drapery.

Anny found Rome breathtaking. 'It's a great deal bigger, grander, *Romer* than we remember it even.'[77] Like almost all of her friends, she was steeped in Ruskin, and had been familiar with the dark chocolate-coloured bindings of his *The Stones of Venice* since it had first appeared during her childhood.[78] The fact that she had met Ruskin on the occasions when he came to call on her father, made him even more real to her than the author of those volumes of resonant prose. The effect of Ruskin on Anny's generation cannot be overestimated. Even Ruskin was appalled by it, and was compelled to leave the haven of Herne Hill for the splendours of Brantwood in order to escape the mass-produced translations, which he abhorred, of the Gothic which he advocated. Visitors to Rome saw their surroundings and works of art through a lens polished by education and their contemporary reflections. Revivalism was very much in the air. George Eliot had published *Romola*, set in fifteenth-century Florence, as recently as 1863. It was illustrated by Leighton, whose perception of art itself was inextricably bound up with his contemporary view of the past. The Pre-Raphaelites were using myth and their conception of historical scenes as subjects for their paintings. Tennyson and Browning borrowed from history and legend for the background of many of their major poems. When Anny went with Edith Story to the Church of San Lorenzo, it was impossible for either of them not to see it in the context of a poem by Browning. And it wasn't merely that both girls were influenced by Ruskin, as well as being intimate friends of Browning. The average gentleman was very well read in the Classics. A thorough knowledge of Plato, Horace and Virgil in the original, together with an ability to construe them into eloquent English, was part of every public schoolboy's education. The widely read romances of Charlotte M. Yonge were frequently set in an idealised version of the past 'unknown to history'.[79] In this respect, Anny and the rest of the set surrounding the Storys were very much of their time.

During the twelve years since her first visit to Rome, Anny had matured into a cultured if undisciplined young woman of thirty-one. As a girl, she hadn't cared for the statues. Now, as she looked at them with a fuller understanding of their significance, she began to love them. 'It isn't sham make-up feeling, it's as if a new delightful sense came to me, which I didn't know I possessed . . . they drag a trail of glory with them, & I think I have been to Olympus & feasted with the Gods.'[80] In Anny's case, it certainly wasn't sham. She was too transparent to dissemble. But it was understandable, however infuriating, that on a subsequent visit to Venice when she wrote to Minny extolling the virtues of 'Tintoret', as all good disciples of Ruskin called Tintoretto, a friend of Minny's declared that Anny must have been reading the sage. Admiration of 'Tintoret', claimed the friend, was merely a phase people went through, much as they were bound to get measles in infancy.

In between the round of entertainments, Anny derived an increasing satisfaction from her writing. One of the most civilising aspects of staying with the Storys was that pleasure was enhanced by work, and vice-versa. She had taken the manuscript of her novel, for which she had not yet found the title, and was working on that as well as a series of articles about Rome. Leslie helped her to place these with the *Pall Mall Gazette*, although she would have preferred her 'scraps' to have appeared in *The*

Cornhill, the magazine her father had founded and edited.[81]

Nearly all groups of artists attract eccentrics, dilettanti and idle hangers-on. The artistic ex-patriate society at Rome was no exception. Anny was impatient of them. 'I want painted people & marble hearts just now, & don't seem to care to devote myself to all these grandly dressed strangers. I find myself wishing that the peerage of the United Kingdom could be swept away at one swoop. Lords are like meteors here in Rome, & still more Dowager ladies & their daughters.' When Lady Dunmore called, 'she called, & called, & called, for such a long time, that I thought all the bright afternoon would be over, but it wasn't & we went & fetched Mr Story from his studio, & took a drive & then went to see Odo Russell . . . he is diplomatic in large trousers & little pointed toes.'[82]

Odo Russell was a quirky, fascinating individual. The second son of the Duke of Bedford, he had been born in Florence and educated mainly by his mother. For many years now, he had been attached to the British Legation at Florence and was acting as an unofficial minister to the Vatican during one of the most critical periods of the complicated history of Italy. Extremely genial and very knowledgeable, he entertained Anny and the Storys by describing the habits of the owners of the old palace where he lived. Whenever a member of the family died, all the curtains and hangings and pictures and furniture were swept away into vast lumber rooms upstairs and left to moulder there with other decaying treasures. 'It's like a parable to hear of these people piling up & piling up. They never go & see their treasure, & only laughed at Mr Russell for wanting to explore.'[83]

The hangers-on and dilettanti were a small price to pay for such a sojourn of otherwise unmixed pleasure. As well as visiting art galleries, ruins, and churches, Anny, the Storys and their friends often took a carriage to ride out in the beautiful, unspoilt Campagna beyond the city. As the weather grew warmer there were picnics, and Anny delighted in walking over the hills and discovering wild flowers, many of which were new to her. A particular walk she remembered long afterwards was one she took with the two poets, Browning and Longfellow, after a lengthy and agreeable lunch with the Storys. Anny's rapport with Longfellow was immediate. She was attracted by his 'simpleness and sweetness'.[84] The gigantic figure he cut with his immense beard and leonine head made him instantly recognisable, so that complete strangers stopped to salute him as they strolled along.

She visited the Capitol with Edith. 'I find one of the odd effects of Rome is to set one longing, I don't know for what exactly . . .'[85] She couldn't help wondering what had become of all the great men and women of old, and whether one day people would think of the Huxleys and their contemporaries as the conquerors of their time. Coming suddenly into a marble room iridescent with sunlight and filled with rows of the busts of Aristides, Hippocrates and others, she thought they looked exactly like Mr Hunt and Mr Huxley[86] and Mr Spottiswood.[87]

If their days were devoted to work and the worship of art, the evenings were generally very sociable, with concerts and parties and 'brilliant little assemblages'. The Dexters, *mère et fils*, were very much in evidence, as were the Kings. Anny appeared to have got over her feelings for Dexter, which were complicated by a measure of wounded pride as much as anything else. He appeared to have forgotten his devotion to Mary King. Anny confided to Minny that she wouldn't be in the least surprised if Dexter and Edith didn't make a match of it. Matters were made farcical for Edith by the sudden arrival of Herman Merivale, who proceeded to fall hopelessly in love with her. She wouldn't have objected so much if Herman hadn't made such a drama of things. Poor Edith was subjected to Herman jumping out of statues and declaring passionate love for her, and then demanding tiresome, long explanations. Herman was beginning to exhibit symptoms of a nervous condition which was to dog him for the rest of his life. He was much to be pitied, though Edith's patience was sorely tried.

Intensely musical, Anny never forgot a visit to the opera, where she heard Minghetti and Grisi singing Marcello, a composer of whom she was particularly fond. She came away feeling quite intoxicated by the beauty of the music.

Tom Trollope and his wife Fanny (the sister of Nelly Ternan, the actress and secret mistress of Charles Dickens) were living at the Villa Ricorboli. They invited Anny to spend the day in Siena with them. Like his brother Anthony, the writer and the better known of the two, Tom Trollope was very hospitable, and Anny took the view that he couldn't help it if he was a bear of a man any more than he could help being regrettably vulgar. She didn't let his lapses interfere with her enjoyment.

She also spent an evening with Harriet Hosmer, the American sculptress who was notorious for her scandalous ways. Years before, Hatty had induced Elizabeth Barrett Browning, much to Browning's alarm, to dress up as a man so that they could insinuate themselves into a monastery, ostensibly to look at some frescoes. Hatty was given to singing 'savage ballads in a hoarse manny voice'[88] and got into trouble with the local police for riding about alone, without even a groom to accompany her. She rather terrified Anny, who could not feel in the least at her ease with her.

Anny enjoyed most of the evening parties, even though she worried that her gowns were not fine enough. She couldn't help wishing that her hair grew in 'thick natural plaits & scrolls alternated with elegant rows of curls, like the Italian and American ladies'.[89] She revelled in the brilliance of the scene, the stream of scandal issuing from the lips of the *marquesas*, the hideous flower arrangements they wore as corsages, and the fun of it all. She had not experienced such sophisticated society since the 'summit' of her youth, when she had acted as her father's hostess in the days of Palace Green.

It was very likely at one of their tête-à-tête breakfasts together that Story divulged the interesting news to Anny that Browning, having been attracted to Blanche Ritchie before her marriage to Frank Warre-Cornish, had now transferred his affections to Edith.[90] Distinguished though he was, and fond of him though Story and his wife were, he was not at all the kind of suitor they had in mind for their treasured daughter, their only surviving child.

Of course, being Anny, she got into terrible tangles at Rome, made dozens of social engagements she was forced to cancel and behaved in her usual 'insane fashion'.[91] She missed Minny, but her visit was unforgettable and of great consequence to her. She was beginning to form her own, independent opinions of art and of people. 'It's a new discovery I have made.'[92] The discovery was a turning point in her life.

12

If Anny's absences from Onslow Gardens lessened the tension in the household, Minny and Leslie missed her gaiety and vivaciousness. Leslie wrote to her that he was fast 'sinking into a hopeless recluse in Onslow Gardens & shall take root in my study if you don't come home soon'.[93] Minny longed sometimes for the blue skies of Rome and the chance to gad about with Anny, but she had made her choice and knew it was the right one. She and Leslie were very much in love, and it was a deeply rooted love which continued to grow throughout their marriage. And Minny was by no means dull. She constantly went to concerts with her Ritchie cousins, and made a point of going to as many performances by the violinist Joachim as she could. Many of these concerts were held in the grand London drawing-rooms of their rich friends. Joachim was a great admirer of Pinkie Ritchie's piano-playing, and it was on occasions like these that

Pinkie came as close as she ever did to playing in public. There was nothing, so far as the excellence of her playing was concerned, to have prevented her from doing so, except her own distaste for being in the public arena. Joachim certainly thought her good enough, and so did her discerning audiences in these private houses. Minny much preferred these private concerts to public recitals. The very notes themselves seemed to grace the occasion, run *triolets* through the audience who were in evening dress, the women with white camellias trembling in their hair. The cascades of notes scored by Brahms, Mendelssohn and Beethoven seemed to dance reflections on the vision of Joachim bowing cadenzas in the triple mirrors, framed in ferns and flowers, to leap and twirl on Pinkie's sparkling rings. It was delightful to sip Apollinaris water and champagne, to fan oneself from the rustle and the murmur of one's gorgeously attired neighbours. A public hall could be tiresomely uncomfortable, and there was nothing good to eat. Here, ensconced in a brocade chair, or reclining on a yellow plush sofa, the music seemed to weave in and out of the fabric of life itself.

That summer, Lord Leighton, the president of the Royal Academy, had moved the Academy premises to Burlington House. Naturally, the new galleries, which allowed for larger hanging space, caused great excitement. Burlington House was thronged with gentlemen in top hats and monocles, and with ladies in polonaises and bustles looped and draped in a positive sea of *cascades*, *chûtes* and *ondulations*, so that it was by no means easy to view the new paintings by Val Prinsep, Waterhouse, Leighton and Marcus Stone. But Minny had the advantage over the throng, for she could always go to the studios of her friends and see Val Prinsep's most recent canvas, or Watts' latest triumph. In the public galleries, the buzz of conversation was sometimes so noisy, that it seemed to make one's eyes go deaf.

Leslie never objected to her going to the theatre, or seeing her numerous friends at places to which he did not want to go himself. A lot of husbands in his position would have been selfish dogs in the manger. But then Minny herself had just the knack of not letting visits from these same friends disturb Leslie's peace of mind when they called at Onslow Gardens.

Minny's relationship with Leslie's mother, whom both the sisters called 'MyLady', was becoming increasingly important to her, to MyLady and to Leslie. Even in old age, Lady Stephen was still a handsome woman. Her fundamentally optimistic outlook was surprisingly tolerant for a Clapham Sect Evangelical. She may have been anxious and disappointed when Leslie discovered that he did not believe in God, but she never tried to proselytise; she had too much commonsense to alienate her favourite child. Her daughter Milly was another matter; Lady Stephen was profoundly distressed when Milly lost her faith in the Evangelical persuasion. She dabbled in various branches of the Church before finally becoming a Quaker. By contrast, Lady Stephen found Minny's spirited attitude to life refreshing. Minny's own brand of scepticism did not bother Lady Stephen in the least.

As a matter of course, Minny put on her bonnet and gloves before she stepped out to pay MyLady a call. Once, on her way to Petersham Terrace, she went into a church and found a christening service in full progress. 'There was a baby & a horrid old Gamp holding it as if it were a bottle & a young mother in a yellow bonnet & a blue gown & a father many feet shorter than his wife – & 2 sponsors evidently in love with each other & the lady with black grey curls all round. I listened attentively to the service & thought parts of it monotonously heathen.'[94] She wondered, if she ever had another child, whether she would be obliged to have it christened. Leslie believed, erroneously, that they would have to. Minny was clear that she would rather not. A child, of course, was what she yearned for to complete their happiness.

They were all pleased when Anny and Minny's cousin, Gussie Ritchie, told them she was engaged to Douglas Freshfield, a solicitor and well-known alpinist. He was well known to Leslie, and they all liked him. He had been instrumental in encouraging young Richmond Ritchie in his unexpected Alpine feats. Richmond was only fifteen, but amazed everybody, including Leslie, by being the youngest recorded person ever to climb to the summit of Mont Blanc. He made the ascent with his elder brother Gerald, and their achievement was entered in the records of the Alpine Club on 3 September 1869.[95] Anny, who was his godmother, was particularly fond of her young cousin, and delighted in his conquest. Then, having shown that he was capable of greatness in the playground of Europe, Richmond appeared to lose all interest. It was as though this exceptionally talented and attractive young boy had been endowed with too many gifts at birth.

For some time, Anny and Minny had both been made anxious by vague allusions from Edward Thackeray in India, to his possible return to England. Edward's daughters, Margie and Annie, had now been living at Onslow Gardens for four years, and the love and affection which Anny and Minny felt for them was very strong. Suddenly, Edward arrived home and

announced that he was going to remarry, set up house in Hampstead, and wanted the children to make their home with him and his new wife, Lizzie. Anny and Minny were dismayed. It was understandable that Edward should wish for his daughters, but his clumsiness and lack of tact verged on cruelty. There were horrible scenes, followed by still more distressing explanations which took place on the doorstep.[96] For the time being, the children went to live with their father and stepmother in Hampstead. They were pathetically missed by the household at Onslow Gardens.

Life at Onslow Gardens could never be without turbulence, partly because of the discrepancy in the attitudes of Leslie and Anny to money. It didn't trouble Minny at all that Leslie naturally assumed control over all her property and all her money. It was the normal contemporary practice and, besides, like a great many other women both before and since, she was prepared to dupe herself to a certain extent, and Leslie to a larger one, by appearing to be perfectly acquiescent. She prided herself on her economies but these were, in reality, devices which allowed her to spend money in the way she preferred. She kept the figures in her account book ruled in neat columns, but if tippets were in fashion, and asparagus in season, she would wear a tippet and offer her guests mounds of green asparagus with a sauceboat filled with melted butter. She knew how to manage the household. More importantly, she knew how to manage Leslie. And indeed, he rather liked being managed.

'The attitude of men to money is often so bizarre and diametrically opposed to their other characteristics that to generalise from it is mad.'[97] Nothing could be truer of Leslie. His attitude to money was so convoluted that his friends might be forgiven for thinking him off his head unless they began to understand how terrified he was by it. Leslie muddled money with morality, with emotion and, more significantly, with power. Much later in his life, when time and circumstance had changed him into an embittered old man, he became obsessed by it and used his authority to bully the females in his family, declaring that they were 'shooting Niagara to ruin'.[98] He never bullied Minny, although they had their occasional spats, and was able to discuss finances with her fairly equitably. But he was always determined to cut down on expenses, thought cheeseparing a virtue and extravagance wicked. It would be a mistake to say that he was a miser. On the contrary, he was remarkably generous. He often lent money to friends in need, especially to younger, aspiring writers. His attitude was partly the legacy of his Evangelical upbringing, his terror of ruin more common than people supposed.

Before the advent of Leslie, Anny had taken charge of the household accounts, often with disastrous results. At the beginning of the Stephens' marriage, Anny was accountable to Leslie for Minny's share of the household budget. This, she frequently spent. Finding the arrangement unviable, Leslie then undertook Minny's accounts, and so Anny became in debt to him. It was beyond Leslie's imagination to begin to understand Anny's approach to money. He never cottoned on to the fact that she was incapable of connecting the object of her purchase to any sum she might or might not have in the bank. To Anny, money was as unpredictable as a cloud, and might gather or puff away at any moment. But a charming Staffordshire china figure of a shepherdess in a shop window in Bond Street was very real. The fact that it would look particularly well on the mantelpiece in the parlour was far more interesting to her than the price. Her appetite for bonnets was prodigious. Her gowns were expensive, and even when the silk had been cut from the bolt and paid for, they still had to be made up and trimmed. But she ordered them and enjoyed the effect and, surprisingly, the world did not come to an end. Anny and Leslie were like the weather-man and his old woman in their little painted wooden cottage. Anny positively liked spending money, while he felt her expenditures as a personal affront. Unlike Minny's, Anny's affairs

Anny

were not in Leslie's arbitration, but he assumed control for altruistic and fraternal reasons. The rages he flew into when she overspent her allowance were partly the result of what he felt to be his responsibility. But in spite of the repeated rows, it never occurred to Leslie that his fury did no one any good.

On one occasion, when Leslie had badgered her over the bills, Anny lost patience, seized a florin from her purse, and flung it across the table at him. This was tantamount to challenging him to a duel, for it was not the actual florin, but the principle of the thing which mattered to Leslie. Anny knew this, but she was too much her father's daughter to be bothered with the finer points of what a farthing might have fetched. It was a pity, everyone agreed when it was too late, since their mutual misunderstanding distorted their views of one another and led to a coil of muddle and fury which they both made very nearly impossible to disentangle.

And then, in the spring of 1870, when the ominous intimations of the Franco-Prussian War were beginning to sound from across the Channel, Minny discovered that she was pregnant again. Her news temporarily eclipsed any wrangles they might have had about florins, and even any more far-reaching anxieties about friends and relatives in France. Minny was never very strong, and her pregnancies were complicated and danger-ous. She was constantly ailing, but none of the doctors who attended her could find out what exactly was the matter. Eventually, she became so ill as to frighten Leslie and Anny very much indeed.

They decided to rent a little house at Kingston, not far from Maidenhead, with a garden that ran down to the river. It was the house which Millais' mother had lived in, and there were still some of his early paintings hanging on the walls which Anny found troubling and even grotesque. In the evening dusk, she could not help being put in mind of his other, later paintings of Sir Isumbras and The Vale of Rest.[99] But the view of the river with the shady trees that bordered the bank was lovely, and slowly Minny grew stronger. Soon, she was able to come downstairs, even if she spent a considerable amount of time on the sofa. Later, on good days, and if the weather was fine, she was able to get out of doors and enjoy the pretty garden. As spring turned into summer, Leslie was able to take her out in a boat on the river. Nothing gave them more pleasure than for him to row and for Minny to lie opposite him on cush-ions and allow him to ferry her down the river.

From Kingston, Anny went to Bristol at the suggestion of Jeannie

138

Senior, Anny's close friend and an educational reformer, to look up material for an article for *The Cornhill* about the plight of working children.[100] While she was there, she made a point of going to see her maternal grandmother, Mrs Shawe, who lived at Clifton with Anny's Aunt Jane and her Uncle Arthur. There was no reference to any past ill-feeling. Anny was pleasantly surprised to find Mrs Shawe to be an agreeable old lady with an acerbic wit. Her aunt and uncle she knew to be eccentric, but she came away with a favourable impression of the relations of whom she knew so little.

That was a particularly lovely summer at Kingston, but in July their calm was disturbed when they heard the dismaying news that the Emperor Louis Napoleon had declared war on the Prussians. To all three of them war was a dreadful thing, and this one in particular seemed stupidly unnecessary. Anny, especially, could not help worrying about Charlotte Ritchie in Paris. In late July Minny's health had improved to such an extent that Leslie thought she would enjoy the company of a few friends from London for an excursion on the Thames. In those days, the river was immensely popular with all classes and provided all manner of forms of recreation which were affordable to almost everyone. It was thronged with pleasure boats and barges, punts, skiffs and rowing-boats. The unpolluted waters ran through the rich, moist valley, soon to be disfigured by a rash of buildings which would scar the landscape forever. Meadowsweet and Queen Anne's lace fringed the banks where the fishermen sat, casting March browns and blue uprights across the water from the shelter of their green umbrellas. Smart hotels and riverside pubs catered for day-trippers. Maidenhead was in its heyday as a boating resort, and the Regatta at Henley an event which drew the crowds. Skindles at Maidenhead was a fashionable hotel for a fancy luncheon and a game of skittles afterwards. Leslie immensely enjoyed such boating parties as the one he had arranged and felt in his element, encouraging his friends to make the most of the fun. He was keen to make things comfortable for Minny, and she knew how to better his arrangements for everyone. Leslie had all the delicacy of a true sportsman, handling the oars and shipping them with a nicety which complemented the craft. His boat, with Minny in it, shot ahead in a clean, unfettered line.

He saw her from the boat distinctly, standing at a point where the road from the railway station joined the one which followed the riverbank. It could be no one else, of that he was certain. He had never seen another woman so remarkable for her beauty, her perfect silhouette etched against the sky. There was something agitated, almost desperate, in the gesture she made to her companion that startled Leslie.[101] He nosed the boat towards the bank.

Minny identified the two women as Julia Duckworth and her sister-in-law Minna. Leslie and Minny made themselves known. Julia and Minna Duckworth were looking out for Herbert, who had missed the train on which they had expected him. Yet Julia's anxiety seemed out of all proportion. Herbert was a barrister joined to the Northern Circuit and was frequently away from home. Leslie and Minny had heard that Julia usually went with her husband. They had heard, too, that the Duckworths' marriage was said to be no ordinary union, but an alliance of uncommon devotion. Leslie was disturbed by Julia's distress. He had a sudden glimpse into a source of anguish which was too private for him to have witnessed, but which Julia had been unable to disguise. It made a deep impression on him which he never forgot.

And so the summer drew on. Minny grew perceptibly stronger. Leslie and Anny were encouraged by her progress and scribbled away at their separate writing. In September, when Anny went over to Guildford to have tea with the Merivales,[102] she heard the news on the way from the station and saw posters on the lamp-posts: the Emperor had surrendered and the French army had been defeated at Sedan. Someone went running for the paper. The servants had fetched the chairs and tables out of the house and placed them in the shade on the lawn. Mrs Merivale poured the tea. Their daughter Agnes handed round the paper-thin slices of bread and butter. But when Mr Merivale read aloud from *The Times* they could hardly digest the news at all. 'Fire and Blood and Tears' was the headline. They were stunned, and somehow the very sleepiness of Guildford seemed strangely to bring the din of war more clearly to their ears and make vivid those doomed and hopeless armies sweeping by.

Later that month, Anny went north to the Lake District to stay with the Marshalls, a large, intricately intermarried family who had made a fortune from their linen mills near Leeds before moving to a large estate at Coniston. James and Mary Marshall were well known to Thackeray and his friends. Long ago, the Tennysons had spent part of their honeymoon at Tent Lodge on the Marshalls' estate, and Mary and Emily had formed a lasting friendship. A close and dear neighbour was James Spedding at Myer House. The following year, Ruskin had bought Brantwood, also on Lake Coniston, then a small house with a few acres of stony ground before he eventually rebuilt it on a grand scale in 1872.

James and Mary Marshall lived at Monk Coniston, a lovely neo-Gothic house overlooking Coniston Water, with a castellated boathouse in the bay. With them lived their adult, unmarried offspring James, Victor and Julia. Highly intelligent, the young Marshalls had all inherited the marked family sense of humour; fastidious, teasing and philosophical. James was a keen mountaineer, Victor a gifted amateur painter, and Julia a witty, attractive young woman. There was a great deal of entertaining at Monk Coniston and most of the literati of the day were frequent guests. The countryside was breathtakingly beautiful. Wild hillsides reached up to rocks and fells dominated by 'the Old Man of Coniston'. Below lay the great sheet of reflecting water, still as glass on a windless day. There were frequent boating expeditions, walks and picnics.

On a 'gold and glory day', Anny decided on the title of the novel she was working on: *Old Kensington*.[103] They had set out to visit their friend James Spedding, best known for his colossal work on Bacon. Spedding had been up at Trinity with Thackeray, Tennyson, Monckton Milnes and Arthur Hallam. He spent a short spell in the Colonial Office, an appointment made for him by Leslie's father, Sir James Stephen. Immensely learned, he was a modest and delightful man who now lived at Myer House near Keswick. Approaching by way of Derwent Water, they had a long and enjoyable lunch.

All the holiday, Anny was in an ebullient mood. Not generally given to much outdoor exercise, she was buoyant when, on another occasion during this visit, young Harry Marshall took her for a 'delicious walk over a pass'.[104] She loved the fleeting changes of light, the rocks and falls and constant sound of running water. And then, to her intense delight, Brodie, her old Scots nurse who had looked after her all those years before when Thackeray lived with his small family at Great Coram Street, turned up. By now, Brodie was 'sweet & 80 & tender'.[105] When Brodie left the Thackerays after Anny's mother broke down, Thackeray arranged for Brodie to go into service in the Darwin household where she became Annie Darwin's nurse. Since the Darwins remained close friends of Anny's, she and Brodie had been able to keep in touch.[106] Now, Brodie had retired somewhere in the neighbourhood and heard of Anny's whereabouts. Despite her age, she insisted on acting as Anny's maid: they could be ensconced together with enough privacy to reminisce about old times. From now on, the Lakes held a very special appeal for Anny.

After a time, however, she left to go on to the Kingsleys at Edinburgh, and then to stay with her cousins, the Lows at Clatto. Crossing the Firth in an open boat to Clatto, Anny caught cold and arrived at the Lows feeling distinctly groggy. Her cold worsened and developed once again into pleurisy. The Lows, who Anny had last seen in Rome, were very much absorbed by their daughter Augusta's impending departure for India. The arrangements and purchases necessary engrossed them all. And it was at Clatto that Anny, reading the newspaper, learned of Herbert Duckworth's sudden death. Few people were so evidently in love as Herbert and Julia Duckworth, and the tragedy of Herbert's sudden death was made all the more shocking by the fact that Julia was expecting their third child. Herbert had been feeling under the weather earlier that month, and Julia had taken him to stay with her aunt, Adeline Vaughan at Upton Castle, Pembrokeshire. One Sunday, apparently quite well, he reached to pick Julia a fig from a high bough and suddenly had a stroke, was in pain, and by Monday he was dead. From being the happiest of women, Julia became the unhappiest. She longed for death. She was only twenty-four.

Anny's pleurisy became so serious as to make the Lows recommend her to return to London despite the rigours of the journey. On her way, she stopped in Edinburgh and saw Dr John Brown, the famous Scottish doctor, writer, and old friend of her father's. He saw her to the station and brought a basket of fruit and a silver fruit knife as a gift. As the train started, two of the other passengers in the carriage said they had seen everything they wanted to in Edinburgh except for Dr Brown. Anny said, 'Why, that was Dr John Brown – won't you have some of his fruit?' To her dismay, 'they took the beautiful peach in the centre of the basket, leaving me only the humbler plums. So much for affability'.[107]

By the time Anny arrived at Onslow Gardens, she had a high fever and collapsed. The doctor came and prescribed complete rest. Minny, who had grown stronger as her pregnancy advanced, took complete charge, nursing her sister with soup and sibling affection.

13

On 16 October 1870, Charlotte Ritchie made her way from Paris, which the Prussians had been holding under siege since 19 September.[108] This tiny, heroic spinster, now fifty, who had spent most of her life in Paris working among the needy as well as providing a cultural haven for her friends and relations, had managed to escape the city. Yet it was far from her intention to desert her adopted city now that most communications were cut and the Parisians starving. Anny was not yet fully recovered from her attack of pleurisy, but the cousins managed to spend time together at Onslow Gardens.

However sketchily and intermittently, Anny had occupied herself with the needs of the poor since she had put her hair up and let her skirts down. Her very first publication, 'The Little Scholars', which appeared in the May, 1860 issue of *The Cornhill*, was concerned with the plight of charity school children, and includes a vivid description of altruistic ladies dishing out dinner for destitute children. It is more than likely that Charlotte, in her well-bred, undramatic fashion, tried to enlist Anny's help in collecting relief money for the victims of the siege. Such an appeal would have won Anny's sympathies at once. Moreover, unlikely as it may seem, Anny was exceptionally well placed to act as a fundraiser, and nobody knew that better than Charlotte.

One of the most important legacies Thackeray left his daughters was the good will of his host of literary, political, artistic and influential friends. It was only the year before that Anny had travelled to Italy with Lady de Rothschild and her daughters. Since the middle of the previous century, the Rothschilds had built up their fabulous wealth and consequent influence and power by underwriting loans to needy monarchs. They were moneylenders who became the largest merchant bankers for the governments of Europe. When Paxton built the ludicrous *aggrandisement*, Mentmore Towers, for young Mayer Rothschild, Lady Eastlake declared, 'the Medicii were never lodged so in the height of their glory'. At Mentmore Towers, Mayer Rothschild included among his guests the editor of *The Times*, Delane, Gladstone, the Eastlakes,* Matthew Arnold, and Thackeray and his daughters. It was there that Thackeray uttered his pronouncement on fashion after one of Lady Eastlake's tirades: 'Female Dress,' he said, 'is often like a winter's day. It begins too late and ends too soon.' Thackeray and his daughters were also among the regular guests at Aston Clinton, Sir Anthony de Rothschild's imposing country house near Aylesbury. It was in these grandiose surroundings, more tasteful than the

---

* Sir Charles Lock Eastlake (1793-1865) & Lady Eastlake. Sir Charles was President of the Royal Academy (1850) before Lord Leighton, immensely influential in advising Prince Albert and held the newly created post of Director of the National Gallery from 1855. As a painter, he is perhaps best remembered for his 'banditti' paintings, 'The Peasant Woman Fainting from the Bite of a Serpent' and 'Christ Blessing Little Children'. Lady Eastlake (1809-93) née Elizabeth Rigby, author of works on Goethe and *A Residence on the Shores of the Baltic,* she translated Waagen's *Treasures of Art in Great Britain.* Emphatically clever and undeniably magnificent, she could be quite terrifyingly self-opinionated. When asked to reminisce about Lady Shelley, she said – 'But one didn't *know* her, even after her return.' She got on her high horse about the infamy of *Jane Eyre.*

overwhelming opulence of Mentmore, that the Thackeray sisters first met Sir Anthony's daughters, Constance and Annie. Constance was so philan-thropically-minded that for her sixteenth birthday present she asked for an Infants' School, got it, and was allowed to lay the first stone of the building. Now, at the time of the Siege of Paris, Alfred, Leo and Nathaniel de Rothschild headed the French relief efforts in England. On the French side of the family, Alphonse, the eldest Rothschild brother, squared Bismarck and, between them, the brothers underwrote the five billion-franc indemnity to Prussia. No one else but the Rothschilds could have paid such a monstrous sum so much more creditably than Bismarck had expected, and two years ahead of schedule. Anny was never involved in matters of crucial international importance, but it was through her connec-tion with the Rothschilds that she was able to carry out Charlotte's scheme of raising funds for famine relief, and thus play her small part in the relief of Paris.

Charlotte hurried back to Paris, and on 25 October Anny went to visit old friends who had been forced to flee from their French châteaux and seek refuge in England. She found Madame Marochetti, Madame de la Haûte and Madame de Saade and her daughters, all squashed up in humble lodgings in Alfred Place, but so composed she couldn't help being deeply impressed. 'It was really moving to see them all so poor, so ruined & undaunted. I had last seen Madame Marochetti in her Château Neulan-les-Muriers. Real ladies, well-bred, high-thinking & just the same as ever. A lesson to all middle-class ladies.'[109]

Three days later, Anny went to the large house at Bryanston Square which was old Mr Duckworth's town house, where Herbert and Julia had made their home. Julia's confinement was imminent and she received Anny in her bedroom. Since their last meeting, Julia had suffered the full impact of the shock of Herbert's death. Her despair was so deep that she could not speak of it. She yearned for death and had spent hours in sorrow and solitude, sleeping on Herbert's grave. The child she bore insisted on life. Julia gave up her faith in God. This denial was the least conventional act of her life, accompanied by a refusal to listen to any appeal, even from her mother. Her extraordinary beauty, even at the time of her deepest grief, made her appear more intangible than ever. Anny was one of the very few people whose presence Julia could tolerate. Merely by being there, Anny could be of comfort without intruding on the intense privacy Julia insisted on.

'What Anny has been to me I should find it very difficult to describe. When I was very much alone, the children quite small, and every day seemed a fresh burthen, she used to come; and though I could never pour out, and she never talked about myself or my feeling, she somehow took me into her life; and, by making me take a sort of indirect interest in things she did and people she saw, helped me into some sort of shelter and made things real to me again.'[110]

On that first visit, Julia rang for the tea-things and insisted on making Anny tea up in the bedroom, herself. The next day, 29 October, Anny received word that Julia had given birth to her third child, a healthy boy, Gerald. Julia gave him the additional name, de l'Etang, from a romantic attachment to her own maternal great-grandfather, Ambrose, Le Chevalier de l'Etang. Gerald was born six weeks after his father's death. '. . . I was only 24 when it all seemed a shipwreck, and I knew that I had to live on and on, and the only thing to be done was to be as cheerful as I could and do as much as I could and think as little as I could. And so I got deadened.'[111] Julia found it impossible to show her grief, so it festered on within. 'I had all along felt that if it had been possible for me to be myself, it would have been better for me individually; and that I could have got more real life out of the wreck if I had broken down more. But there was Baby to be thought of and everyone around me urging me to keep up, and I could never be alone which sometimes was such torture. So that by degrees I felt that, though I was more cheerful and content than most people, I was more changed.'[112] The trauma of death was inextricably mingled with the trauma of birth. Julia sacrificed her own wellbeing for the sake of her children, and never really recovered from the nightmare of that time. But there sprang into existence then a strong and enduring alliance between Julia and Anny that would withstand even the most unexpected tests of time.

Leslie always thought Herbert's death had turned Julia into a dissenting Sister of Mercy. Whenever anyone of her large family was ill, Julia was sent for automatically. She became an admirable nurse. Hovering over other people's sickbeds could not but help leave its trace of melancholy, and Julia gradually retreated into an existence where the 'world was clothed in drab . . . it was all shrouded in a crepe-veil'.[113] For a long time, she remained 'deadened' and numb.

After her visits to Julia at Bryanston Square, Anny took the opportunity of going to Hampstead to visit Margie and Annie Thackeray. Anny was anxious about the children and missing them very much. The little girls had not settled down in their new environment satisfactorily. The visits were deeply upsetting, and Anny suffered violent headaches in consequence. Eventually the Thackeray children would spend significant time in the Stephen household, increasingly as their father went back to India. She was also plagued by worry over her work and her concern over Charlotte's plans, which involved the collection of money from charities for the Paris relief funds. She loathed Bazaine, the Marshal of France who, trapped by the Prussians at Metz, had surrendered after a siege of fifty-four days.

'I think Bazaine is the man I most dislike and detest in it all,' she wrote to Fitzy, who was now in India. 'How awful and vivid and branding it is on one's mind, or is it turning us all to sharks? I hear of people shot and maimed, & I hardly care, & yet it's all through everything. Yesterday, when I bought a penny paper, and read of certain peace, of a congress, and of every hopeful blessing, a load lifted from my mind – but in *The Times* of today there is nothing more of this, only worse and worse news.'[114]

Then, in December, Anny was distracted by an event which concerned her more closely. She was staying at Eton when the telegram came. Minny had given birth to a daughter. Laura Makepeace Stephen was born on 6 December 1870, at two o'clock in the morning, three months prematurely. She weighed less than three pounds. This tiny little creature, hovering on the brink between life and death, had to be wrapped in cotton-wool, like Thumbelina, for the first two months of her long, ill-starred life. Anny returned home at once and spent the next three days with Minny, caring for her beloved sister and her tiny niece as best she could. The doctor reassured them, but the birth had not been easy, and Minny remained weak for a long time to come.

Laura was nicknamed Memee, and she became the centre of attention in the small household. Leslie was touchingly delighted to be a father. He had been more anxious about Minny and the effect the possible loss of a second child might have on her than he had cared to show. 'We are now absurdly happy & talking baby from morning till night. Did you ever remark what a beautiful object a small baby is? I never did before, but I see it now. As for a mother & child in the attitude of a Madonna, I can only say that the sight goes some way to reconcile me to papists.'[115]

Leslie had accepted George Smith's timely offer of the editorship of *The Cornhill Magazine* at a salary of £500 a year. It was an extremely satisfactory move. The pay was good and gave Leslie 'more leisure from the treadmill of writing'.[116] The sisters were enthusiastic, since their father had founded the magazine, and they were pleased to keep it in the family. The position held considerable cachet in the literary world: these were the days of great publishers, and George Smith was the greatest publisher of them all. The editorship of *The Cornhill* brought Leslie under the umbrella of Smith's patronage. Smith had made his own personal fortune by investing in Apollinaris water. He made money for his writers and was notably generous to them. Leslie benefited immeasurably from his interest now, and would do so incalculably later when Smith invited him to edit what was to be Leslie's triumph, *The Dictionary of National Biography*.

One of the immediate results of Leslie's new employment was that the house became a meeting place for aspiring young writers whom Leslie asked to contribute. R.L. Stevenson, Thomas Hardy and Henry James became regular visitors as well as the old familiar faces. Leslie worked hard in an age when writers were notorious for putting in prodigious hours. He sat for great stretches of time in his rocking-chair, rocking backwards and forwards and then, when an idea seized him, he would advance on his writing table and cover sheet after sheet of foolscap in his precise and accurate hand. When they were complete, he would roll them up, go downstairs, put on his greatcoat and could be seen, a remarkable figure, striding forth through the streets of London to the offices of *The Cornhill* in the City. On his return from work, there was nothing Leslie enjoyed more than the spectacle of his tiny daughter and of Minny's loving care.

Anny did not let the pleasant practice of baby-worship interfere with her visits to the French refugees, who continued to stream into London. It was an exceptionally cold winter, and one day she set off through the snow to see a poor woman whose husband was fighting in Paris. The French capital had become so remote, it seemed farther off than India. It made Anny's heart sink to read of the muddled retreats and the defeat of the National Guard on the Prussian lines. The descriptions of terrible suffering, hardship, and hunger tore her heart. The news in the papers was unreliable and often contradictory.

'It's so cold I can hardly hold my pen,' she wrote to Fitzy, '– a blue three o'clock frost with a muffin – why do muffin bells always tinkle in the frost? . . . I was so touched by the poor preacher who prayed that he might pray only for a little success before the end – just enough to raise the French from their hopeless sorrow in which they are overwhelmed. When I heard Mr – & Mr – shouting out for war the other night, I felt I could have knocked their stupid heads together. War is so different from fighting, shouting from either.'[117]

As matters grew worse and the news grimmer, Anny became increasingly more partisan. 'Who says "Women who tacitly encourage fighting are the real *mitrailleuses*", and that if *all* women set their faces against war, it would do more than all the peace conventions. It comes over one with a sort of shock to think of the horrible tortures we civilised nations inflict.

We who shudder at thumbscrews and religious persecutions, and yet think nothing of two countries going to war for the name of a province and the uniform of its militia. It is awful, awful, and please God a day of peace will come at last, of real peace, not breathing time.'[118]

Minny and Leslie shared Anny's horror of war. On his way to the Alps after the outbreak of the Franco-Prussian war Leslie had passed through Paris and, while waiting for his dinner to be brought to him in the railway buffet at the Gare du Lyons, he wrote to Minny: 'The only sight I have had of warlike affairs was a regiment marching through Paris which delayed my victoria for a time. Poor fellows, some of them looked such boys & they carried such heavy knapsacks with their little tents & saucepans & loaves of bread on their backs & it all looked so like business that I could become a Quaker on the spot. It is horrible to see the people who are going to be killed.'[119] When Fitzy wrote from India, wishing that Leslie had managed to see some of the fighting, Minny lost her temper. 'Do you suppose I should have let him go anywhere near the fighting? I don't think he is the sort of man who would enjoy the sight of a battlefield, & I don't think you are either. My own feeling of disgust at the wicked misery this war causes is so great that I would not give a sixpence towards any fund that helps to keep it up, however I am not going to talk about it for I fear that I shall only lose my temper & prevent Leslie from enjoying his pipe. Now goodbye, dearest Fitzy. I shall love you even more than I do now if you can help to teach people not to go to war.'[120]

Anny was ever more determined to take an active part in alleviating the distress at Paris. For the moment, she wrote 'a foolish little appeal for the French wounded'.[121] At the same time, she was in a state of 'utter bewilderment' about her book, *Old Kensington*.[122] It was nearly finished, and she had promised it to George Smith, but she had got in a muddle about the end. In January, Charlotte Ritchie made another brief appearance in London: in her journal, Anny noted down, 'mem re Rothschild? Bazaar Times Appeal; then Félicie (Sola?) Paris Fund Appeal; American Appeal.'

Whatever her own personal involvements and ambitions, Anny never forgot her old friends. For some time now, for example, Carlyle had become increasingly lonely. When some burglars broke into his house in Chelsea and absconded with his dining-room clock, Anny was touched and felt acutely sorry for the old man whom she had known since childhood. She dreamed up the notion that it would be appropriate for fifteen of his rich female admirers, including Lady Ashburton, Mrs Tennyson, Lady Stanley and Mrs Oliphant, to club together with her and buy him another clock. They could give it to him for his birthday present in February as a token of their respect, affection and good will. Lady Stanley was asked to be the spokeswoman and to present him with the clock. It was a dismal winter's day and the streets were filled with fog and 'greenish vapours'. All the ladies assembled in Lady Stanley's great drawing-room in Dover Street 'where the fog had also penetrated, and presently from the further end of the room, advancing through the shifting darkness, came Carlyle'. There was a ghastly moment. No one moved and no one spoke and no one knew what to do. Lady Stanley uttered her little speech, and that fell like a cold pebble into her bleak and foggy drawing-room. Anny began to wish that she had never conceived this well-intentioned idea. The silence was so painful as to be torture for her and, she could see, for the other ladies whom she had involved in this foolish enterprise. Could the subject of their idolatry not speak? In the end, the old man grunted a recognition, gruff enough to have warranted Anny's apprehension. 'What have I to do,' said the old man, 'with Time any more?' Anny was much vexed with herself and very upset to have been the cause of such a blunder. But when Minny met Carlyle a few days later, she came home and told Anny how he boasted of the clock and kept the paper of signatures of all his female admirers to show his friends. In spite of minding it very much at the time, Anny could see the absurdity of the occasion and recalled it later with wry good humour. She was very fond of Carlyle, but her opinion of him reflected his own, complicated character.

On 10 March 1871, Anny finally sent off her corrected proof of her long and autobiographically based novel, *Old Kensington*, to George Smith. The next day she went to Mentmore to stay with Mayer Rothschild. Sir John and Lady Leslie were there, Lord Dudley, and the Duchess of St Albans. When she got home, she went, in complete contrast, to see her mother at Camberwell. She had at last got her passport to Paris, and nowadays, generally, she always tried to see her mother before she did anything significant.

On 14 March, Anny crossed to Le Havre with a distant cousin, Alice Probyn, on one of the last boats to leave for France, and continued by train (in a Thomas Cook carriage) to Paris. Alice spent the entire journey reading her Morning Psalms in a corner seat. Looking out of the window, Anny saw the Prussian helmets 'gleaming in the villages – blossoms on the fruit trees and the snow lying on the ground everywhere'.[123]

Charlotte and Félicie came to meet Anny at the station. Félicie was ostensibly Charlotte's maid, and had been with Charlotte and Jane, who had died six years earlier, since Anny's childhood. But Félicie's role was, in reality, much more important. She was an attractive, intelligent woman, and a great friend to all the family, who loved her dearly. But in spite of their welcome, Anny found 'all dim & grey – everyone in black – empty streets'.[124]

It had been one of the coldest winters within living memory. On 21 December, the night-time temperature was −14C.[125] People were dying in the streets from cold and from hunger. There was food, but it was scant and unevenly distributed; there was no notion of rationing, so that those who went hungry were driven to madness. Although the city was under siege and much of it destroyed beyond recognition, a semblance of ordinary life, of people behaving as they always had, struggled on.

If people ate in restaurants, and a surprising number did, they might be offered the meat of elephants, yak or zebra, which had been killed in the zoo at the Jardin d'Acclimatation. Others had to make do with stews of rat or cat or vermin – undercooked because fuel was dear. For a moment, the illusion of ordinary life was almost convincing. But not for long. The stench, even in the frozen streets, swiftly put paid to that. And then the crazy behaviour, the idiot gestures, the drunken women, the terror of it all, dispelled any semblance of ordinary life. It was very, very frightening indeed.

Paris had been cut off from nearly all communication for months. There was no reliable mail, no telegrams guaranteed to arrive. Carrier pigeons were used, but could not be depended on. For political messages, tiny strips of film, whose images had been wonderfully reduced to microscopic size, were attached to the legs of the pigeons. If any of the birds arrived at their destination, the minute strips of film were projected on to magic lanterns, and then it was anyone's guess who could interpret them. It is possible that the appalling conditions in which the French found themselves only served to enhance their extraordinary native gift for invention. For they not only sent pigeons off into the air, but politicians too. The besieging Prussians were astounded to see huge balloons sailing away from the imprisoned city. One of them carried Gambetta, the Minister of the Interior. These amazing flying objects were made from whatever the half-maddened inhabitants of the city could rustle up; old bits of waxed calico, pumped up by gas and fuelled by coal. The baskets containing the passengers were attached by rope to the main structure. Surprisingly, the Prussians only managed to wing five of the sixty-five manned balloons which left Paris under the siege. But the balloons were unreliable, unwieldy, and if few people knew how to navigate them, still fewer were prepared to risk their lives in such a dicey enterprise. It was on such frail and flimsy hopes as these that the fate of Paris depended.

None of this was immediately evident to Anny. What was evident to her was the grim and ghastly contrast between what had been so safe and so lovely and what had now become the stuff of nightmares. On 16 March she and Charlotte drove to Versailles. Threatening notices in German were stuck on all the walls. On the way back, she saw St Cloud, one of the familiar entries into Paris, now burned out and destroyed. Yet at the same time the sun was shining, and people were singing in the streets. A Frenchman leaned over to her and said, '*Ecoutez-les! Ils chantent avec leur pays en ruins!*'[126] The next morning, she was woken up by the noise of the cannon going off at Belleville, a suburb on the edge of Paris. All the noises were very loud, not in the least bit like anything Anny had ever associated with Paris. She was aghast, but she managed to scribble down, in short, staccato dashes in her journal: 'News of a Revolution – murder of the generals, *People acting* in the streets as they all described it to one another. Woman comes up, *Vous etes Anglaise. Fuyez, fuyez!*

'March 22, To Madame Mohl's in the sunshine, met hurrying crowds of figures who looked as if they had come straight out of the French Revolution. Massacre in Place Vendome. Charlotte and I were out together, we rushed across fire to the guns to escape. We took refuge in the Church of St Roche; Rue St Roche crowded with people turning out to fight, others running away, while others stood joking on their balconies.'

Anny had had enough. She was determined to leave Paris. As a matter of course, she asked Charlotte and Félicie if they wouldn't like to go back to England with her. Undefeated, they refused to leave Paris, and Anny wasn't all that surprised. The train seemed to rumble on forever, yet it kept stopping. At Roûen, Anny was petrified by Prussian officers who became bullying and obstreperous. 'Was ist geschehen in Paris?' It was lucky that she was a lady, and so they did not pester her more. After all, she had her precious documents upon her person. She took the boat to Newhaven, and then, quite strangely, everything was perfectly ordinary again. There were no more guns. Nobody dashed about or were half starved or had terror on their faces. When she got back to Onslow Gardens she went immediately to bed, exhausted and distressed.

As soon as she was rested, she went straight to Aston Clinton to stay with Sir Anthony de Rothschild. The violinist, Joachim, travelled with her on the train. The splendour of the place and the solid luxury of it all could not have been a stronger contrast to the scenes she had just witnessed. She was able to give an account to Sir Anthony. Everyone was fascinated and came up to her, asking about what she had seen in Paris.[127] Back in London, too, she was in great demand to describe what she had seen. At a party at Lord Leighton's house, she promised Mrs Dilke she would write it all down.[128]

Anny kept her promise. She used her experience in her novel, *Mrs Dymond*. It was the last novel she wrote and it was not published until 1885, but her vivid impressions of the great horror she had lived through are recalled with poignancy and clarity:

'In those moments one saw more of life than in as many years of an ordinary existence. The people running, the groups rallying, the terrified women dragging their children into shelter. We saw a group of hateful dandies leaning over a balcony with opera glasses in their gloved hands, and laughing at the diverting sight of fellow citizens flying for their lives. . . . suddenly we found ourselves surrounded by soldiers. In a rare moment we saw that these were not Insurgents, but National Guards belonging to the party of order, with broad blue sashes round their waists. One of them, a big fair young man, stopped short, and stamped his foot in furious helpless rage and indignation as he looked up at the lounging young men on the balcony overhead. "The country in ruins, and not one of you cowards to answer her call!" he cried, shaking his fist at them with impotent fury. An older officer said something, pointed somewhere, and the little band hurried on, glittering, clanking, helpless against the great catastrophe.'[129]

14

The winter passed, and in April 1871 they all went to Freshwater, taking Margie and Annie who were with them for the holidays, as well as Laura, and staying at The Lodge. After the horrors of Paris, the island seemed more idyllic than ever. Anny took the proofs of *Old Kensington* with her. Julia Duckworth and her children were staying nearby with her aunt, Sarah Prinsep, at The Briary. Julia and Anny spent a good deal of time together, strolling on the sands, and Julia, whose mind was infinitely more methodical than Anny's, helped her to correct the proofs. She was invaluable in making things clear from Anny's disorder, and each profited from the other's company. Minny was much taken up by Memee, and both the little Thackeray girls ran about on the beach with the young Duckworth children, George and Stella. Like Memee, Gerald was still a babe in arms.

They made the usual daytime excursions, going over to Alum Bay and climbing down the rocks and boulders, wet with spray and difficult for the women to negotiate in their immense skirts and slippery, laced boots. Leslie was in his element, courteous, and graciously helping them from rock to rock. The children went bowling after the men's hats, which blew off once they regained the windy heights of High Down.

Mrs Cameron was as exuberant as ever. She cajoled her niece, Julia, into sitting for her. She rushed about with her hands stained from chemicals, and demanded attention, participation and enthusiasm. Julia sat motionless, her beauty matchless, betraying evidence of sorrow during the long exposure. These were some of the finest photographs Mrs Cameron ever took of her favourite niece. While they were being developed, Julia could retire to the more sequestered atmosphere of The Briary. But for the others there was no such refuge. Mrs Cameron had taken to writing theatricals and insisted on roping in the Tennysons. Tennyson spent hours learning her lines instead of writing his own. His son Hallam was now nineteen and about to go to Cambridge (he eventually went to Trinity in spring 1872), while Lionel was still at Eton and showed a marked talent for the stage. Julia Margaret Cameron's own sons were not so satisfactory.

On one occasion, impatient with his clumsiness during a love scene, she cried out, 'O heavens, Henry! Do you call *that* making love? Here, let *me* show you how to do it.'[130] She galvanised the young people into making up moonlight parties, dances and evening recitals.

At dinner one night at Farringford, Anny found Gerald Ritchie and his younger brother, Richmond, among the guests. Richmond was now seventeen and possessed of great charm. Since early childhood he had shown signs of great promise and now it looked as though he was set to fulfil it. His friends and family, as well as his teachers, all had high hopes of him. At Eton, he and Lionel Tennyson enjoyed an easygoing friendship. Anny's interest in her lively young cousin quickened. She found his attentions very pleasant.

She was amused and not altogether surprised to get a letter from him on his return to Eton. Ostensibly, he wrote to tell her about his brother Willy winning a scholarship. He wrote in measured tones. 'It's a capital thing for him which would enable him to carry out his favourite scheme of becoming a college tutor.'[131] But he ended on a more lyrical note. 'Coming back to Eton was perfectly charming, & I walked through the forest in the twilight while the moon's light slowly made deeper & deeper shadows & the stars came out, one by one, Jupiter first & then a lot of lesser beauties. I remain your affectionate cousin Richmond Thackeray Ritchie. You must come here in June for water parties.'

In the early summer, Anny went back to the Lake District. It was there that she heard the news of the burning of Paris. She managed to telegraph Charlotte through the Rothschilds and was reassured that she and Félicie were safe. But Anny was possessed by the thought of Paris in flames. 'Burning Sunset', she noted in her journal. She wore herself out climbing up the foothills of Llyn Ghyll. 'A gloomy prospect. Quite knocked up.' She was out of sorts, depressed and crotchety. Her novel *Old Kensington* would appear in *The Cornhill Magazine* from April 1872 to April 1873. In 1873, George Smith would bring it out in book form. But for the moment, Anny suffered from a sense of lacking purpose. Towards the end of the month, she was 'inwardly troubled & disquieted. After all it is my nature to be & can't be helped. Be sober. Be useful. Be simple. Love the unknown & raise a poor little altar to it & be thankful for small mercies'.[132] It might not sound ambitious, but for someone of Anny's quicksilver temperament, it was no easy task.

In August, she went with the Stephens and baby Laura to stay at St Gervais, near Chamonix. After the grind at *The Cornhill*, Leslie looked forward to the holiday and to climbing 'innumerable little hills but no big ones — my wife won't let me.' Minny was confident that the baby would benefit from the mountain air. Anny took her work with her.

Earlier, she had conceived the idea of retelling a selection of old fairy stories by turning them into accounts which are neither probable nor possible, but which she made plausible. These had appeared in *Five Old Friends*. Now she embarked on a second volume. There was, at the time, a great vogue for fairy tales and stories from myth and legend, often reworked. This interest was reflected, too, in contemporary paintings, such as Dicky Doyle's *Fairies in Fairyland*.[133] In Switzerland that summer, Anny wrote her version of *Ricquet à la Houppe* in her hotel bedroom, where the window opened on to a magnificent view. The story would appear later with a collection of others entitled *Bluebeard's Keys*.

That summer set the precedent for others. Minny and Leslie made a habit of going to Switzerland when they could. They were intensely happy and supremely occupied by Memee. Anny loved them both and was a doting aunt, but her situation was not altogether satisfactory. She wanted something else: but she had no idea what it was.

The sense that part of her life was over, and another part not yet begun, was emphasised by the death of her grandmother, old Mrs Shawe, in Bristol that December. Anny went to the funeral and encountered her 'cracky' Aunt Jane again. Uncle Arthur got irrefutably tipsy. Anny came away feeling thoroughly disjointed.

While she was making notes for an article on Jane Austen for *The Cornhill* Anny compared herself unfavourably to the writer and mimicked her style: '"As I must leave off being young, I find many doucers [*sic*] — for I can drink as much wine as I like. You will kindly make allowances for any indistinctness of writing by attributing it to this venial error." She never grizzled over her state, nor allowed her conscious superiority of intel [*sic*] to claim distinction in her home. Tho an artist, she had no artistic temperament. An oblique reproach on me.'[134]

The New Year of 1872 began on a melancholy note: one of the Merivale girls, Agnes Trench, was dangerously ill. 'A nice, bright, sensible girl after the best English variety & good as gold . . . she came to her mother's for her first confinement and died a few days ago of puerperal fever. They are all in the deepest distress for they had an awful time of it.'[135] Leslie escorted both the sisters to the funeral. The rain streamed down. 'A dreary Methodist preacher. All very sad.'[136] Anny went to sit with Fanny Merivale in the afternoon, and later Mrs Brookfield went to see them. Anny and Minny's sorrow was painful and inevitably raked up the past. For a New Year present, Julia gave Anny a little inlaid cabinet of drawers.

Anny tried not to mope. She was too caught up by the details of daily life to allow the blues to bedevil her for long. She couldn't help being infected by Leslie and Minny's happiness. '. . . Minny says, "O Anny, how one does like one's own child", & when Leslie comes home tired, dusty, overworked, I hear the clump, clump of footsteps running up to the nursery.'[137] Leslie was equally ecstatic. 'It is true that my baby is the best of all possible babies. That child's head contains an amount of brains wh. would astonish any humble phrenologist. She can't talk much but her expression indicates an amount of humour, & of feeling wh. few persons possess. She is not appreciated by the general public, because she does not weigh as much as some babies & the public goes by weight in regards to babies but she is a baby to be proud of to anyone who has an eye for the best qualities of human babies.'[138] Anny joined in the general adulation.

Onslow Gardens had never been intended to accommodate more than the two sisters and, at a stretch, their grandmother, old Mrs Carmichael-Smyth, together with the servants. Now that Leslie's affairs were prospering they began to contemplate moving into a larger house, which was still being built as part of the new developments in South Kensington. 'We are thinking of a new house; I am to have the ground floor which I shall like very much, and then Laura will have a whole suite of apartments if she chooses, and Leslie will be up at the top of all with a skylight and a special ventilator for his pipe.'[139]

The new property appealed to Leslie, but it was really Minny who revelled in the move. She had never had a chance to set up a home of her own since her marriage. She was fascinated by houses, their architecture and design. Wherever she went, she noticed other people's domestic schemes and contrivances, their plumbing and heating arrangements. Like Anny, she had cultivated her father's exquisite taste, but she was more practical and she was prepared to investigate the technical aspects of a problem in order to achieve the aesthetic results she desired. She hoped to incorporate some of the new ideas she had seen in America into her plans. The new house, which stood with its neighbours in a wasteland of unprepossessing rubble, had been hastily designed and would need all her ingenuity to transform it into a home of character and charm.

In April, *Old Kensington* began appearing in monthly instalments in *The Cornhill*. It met with great success. Set in an idyllic version of the Kensington she had grown up in, with every street and country lane remembered in fond detail, Anny conveys a very strong sense of place. But that place has been lost in the course of progress, and there is no return. Until now, Anny had been unusually tied to her past. She had a deep, nebulous fear that her inability to let it go would jeopardise her chances of any genuine future fulfilment. With the publication of *Old Kensington* she began to realise that there was a way of keeping true to her old associations while acquiring the emotional and intellectual freedom she was beginning to feel the need of so urgently. As she put it later, she was feeling her way to observing life from a 'double point of view and from the two ends of fifteen years'.[140]

An immediate success – it ran into five editions – *Old Kensington* is the novel by which Anny is best remembered. Her most ambitious work to date, it is a triumph of evocation of mood, memory and place. 'In those days . . . the hawthorn spread across the fields and market-gardens that lay between Kensington and the river. Lanes ran to Chelsea, to Fulham, to North End, where Richardson once lived and wrote in his garden-house . . . There were strawberry-beds, green, white and crimson in turn. The children used to get many a handful of strawberries from . . . the market gardener at the end of the lane, and bunches of radish when straw-berries were scarce . . . Sometimes in May mornings the children would gather hawthorn branches out of the lanes, and make what they liked to call garlands for themselves . . . There was a Kensington world (I am writing of twenty years ago) somewhat apart from the big uneasy world surging beyond the turnpike – a world of neighbours bound together by the old winding streets and narrow corners in a community of venera-ble elm-trees and traditions that are almost levelled away . . . Tippets, poke-bonnets, even a sedan-chair, still existed among us long after they had been discarded by more active minds . . . in Kensington Square itself, high-heels and hoops were not unknown; but these belonged to ladies of some pretension . . . advancing in powder, and hoops, and high-heeled shoes – real hoops, real heels, not modern imitations, but relics unchanged since the youth of the ghost-like sisters.'[141] Anny's evocation of this vanished world is so powerful that it could stand by itself without any story, and for the first few chapters she almost manages without one. But gradually the characters, who are never as plausible as their setting, do emerge and develop as the novel progresses.

Wrapped in layers of sub-plots and stories within themselves, the central plot of *Old Kensington* is the story of Dolly Vanborough's salvation through love and loyalty. As children, Dolly and her brother George are sent home from India to live with their aunt, Lady Sarah, in the sprawling family home, Church House, in Kensington. Nearby, the Rev. John Morgan runs an establishment where Etonians cram for Cambridge and students from Cambridge cram for their degrees. It is monitored by his thrifty step-mother, a vulgar gossip, and is the home of Morgan's orphan niece, Rhoda, who is Dolly's companion and childhood friend. Raban, an intriguing character, 'once called Dolly a beautiful sour apple. Beautiful apples want time and sunshine to ripen and become sweet'. The Vanborough children's mother, Mrs Palmer, who is remarried to an admiral on the high seas, returns. Convincingly realised and humorously observed, Mrs Palmer is supremely selfish. 'So long as she had her emotions, her maid, her cups of tea, her comfortable sofa, and someone to listen to her, she was perfectly happy.' We see the children grow up in telling vignettes of Kensington society which include tea-parties and walks in Kensington Gardens as it used to be with the high brick wall around it. Later, Anny is excellent at conjuring descriptions of Dolly and Rhoda, chaperoned by the absurd Mrs Palmer, visiting George and his fellow students at Cambridge and spending the day on the river at Henley. George, stupid but true-hearted, is captivated by the artful Rhoda who eventually carries off Dolly's fiancé and, for a time, her fortune. But Dolly's fiancé, Robert Henley, is 'an abominable prig' who insists that Dolly belongs to him and that 'a woman's work is to follow her husband. Every woman, when she marries, must expect to give up her old ties and associations, or there could be no possible union otherwise . . .' When Lady Sarah falls ill, she inadvertently saves Dolly from what bodes to be an unhappy marriage. Dolly refuses to go to India with Henley and the engagement is broken off. Through Lady Sarah's influence and her own integrity, Dolly does ripen into a sweet, mature woman and is happily married to Raban who has long been in love with her.

In real life, an episode at Eton occurred which was hushed up as much as possible, but which involved them all in varying degrees. As a pretty, ringleted child, Lionel Tennyson had been spoilt by his adoring parents. Now, he was under a cloud. Lionel had been implicated in a sexual scandal involving a very much younger boy. The boy was John Probyn, a distant cousin of the Ritchies and Thackerays, in his first year at Eton and only thirteen years old. Lionel's housemaster wrote a devastating letter to the Tennysons, which arrived at the same time as a telegram from Lionel declaring 'ALL IS PROVED A LIE'.[142] This may have reassured his parents, but did not dissuade the senior authorities from suspending him. Probyn's parents withdrew their son rather than have him expelled. Lionel was popular with his peers, but resorted to bravado in a letter to his parents attempting to exonerate himself. His troubles were not at an end, but luckily for him, notice of him was diverted temporarily when he did return to Freshwater where Louisa Prinsep's wedding had become the focus of attention.

The wedding was a tremendous occasion. The bride and her twelve bridesmaids wore primroses in their hair and their white serge dresses were looped up with flowers. Mrs Cameron provided the music and the Prinseps gave a magnificent wedding breakfast. The following night, the Tennysons gave the first ball in their new ballroom. The guests were roped in to polish the floor which they would dance on later that night. The ball was a great success. After the last waltz had been played, Minny and Anny went for a long walk across the Downs with Mr Bryce and Richmond. The moon was full and the night air very lovely. It was all very conducive to romance. When Richmond got back to Eton, he complained that he had been 'very dull ever since', and that his only occupation was croquet, varied by yawning.[143] Anny stayed on in the Isle of Wight, writing and seeing the Tennysons.

When she went back to London, Hallam came to stay at Onslow Square, and on 23 May Mrs Tennyson wrote to him there asking him if he could have a word with Lionel's housemaster about his return.[144] Something that Frank Warre-Cornish had said to Mrs Tennyson made her apprehensive. The next day, Anny went down to Eton, ostensibly to see Margie and Annie who had been staying with St John and Louisa Thackeray while recovering from the whooping cough. Anny mentioned Mrs Tennyson's anxieties about Lionel to Frank. By now, St John Thackeray was Richmond's tutor at Eton. When Anny saw Richmond there and told him what she had done, he was cross with her for having interfered, but otherwise delightful.

Anny spent the early part of that summer staying with Mrs Brookfield, going to tea-parties where she met Richmond and lunch parties where she met Julia Duckworth, and then to Aldworth in Sussex, where she stayed with the Tennysons. 'I only came here for a breath of fresh air,' she wrote to Richmond. 'This is such a lovely view, almost too lovely for my special taste. I like a cock & a hen & a kitchen garden, & some lilies & lavender quite as well as these dream worlds and cloud-capped lands. To me, they are like the sonnet, "Farewell, thou art too dear for my possessing", & I can never *appropriate* a horizon, as one does a haycock, or a bunch of river weeds, or the branches of a tree.'[145]

That summer, the only member of the household to go to Switzerland was Leslie. He went on a short trip to Grindelwald and Zermatt, leaving

Minny with Laura at The Crag, a house at Rosemerrin which they took for the summer near Falmouth in Cornwall. Laura's nurse, Louise Meineke, was in attendance; Molly Alderson, later Lady Humphrey, was Minny's companion. The house at Rosemerrin was enchanting, in a wood, like Sleeping Beauty's castle. The sea was so close that the waves could be heard within the house. Later, Anny wrote, 'How well I remember coming there after travelling all night & Minny coming along the green starry avenue to meet me; the blue sea like the silent depths of cool verdure; the pretty iron gates; the old stone house & the stone hall which M had made into a drawing-room.'[146] Anny did not stay long. She had pledged herself to look after Margie and Annie during the holidays. The little girls had had whooping cough and were still in quarantine so could not be with Laura. She took them to Lion-sur-Mer in Normandy, where her cousin Blanche Warre-Cornish had also taken a house, and close to where Browning and his sister were spending the summer.

Alone for much of that summer, Minny was absorbed by drawing detailed plans for various domestic arrangements for the new house at Southwell Gardens. She also drew, sketched and painted, for she was a talented artist and had not only inherited Thackeray's gift, but had profited from his knowledge of drawing, as well as observing his contemporary artist friends at work. She painted a still life of a salmon with mullet. She also occupied herself painting a series of decorative tiles which she planned to surprise Leslie with and to incorporate in his new study. But her most absorbing charge was Laura. Still very small for her age – she would be two in December – Laura was having trouble teething, could not sleep at night, and lay awake screaming. It took all Minny's skill and patience to soothe her. She tried giving her arrowroot and, because Laura disliked meat, fed her on peaches. She got hold of a donkey so that Laura could have the milk, and then wondered whether it wasn't the donkey who had such a strange effect on the child. 'She sat up & sang in bed until half past ten.'[147] Minny was relieved when Laura cut another double tooth, but couldn't help worrying about her progress and didn't think she was as advanced as the Thackeray children had been at the same age. Laura had developed a trait of getting into fizzy spins of excitement when she would chatter baby-talk nineteen to the dozen and whirl around singing and dancing. Sometimes Minny found this entertaining, but it could be very exhausting. Laura was beginning to be able to speak, but not much of her speech was intelligible. Leslie arrived back from Switzerland early in the morning, after having stopped off on his way back to see Anny at Lion-sur-Mer. Minny was still in bed, but Laura 'hung her head on his shoulder & shouted Papa & is SO happy with him & so am I.'[148] Louise, the nurse, took to doing Laura's hair up in a kind of pompom on the top of her head, so that Minny thought she looked like a little Red Indian, and both she and Leslie took pleasure in watching her run about with other children on the beach. It was a very happy time for both parents.

Meanwhile, Anny and the little girls, Blanche and her children, and Charlotte Ritchie and her companion Félicie were enjoying holiday life at Lion-sur-Mer. 'We were all living in "sea-coast-nookful" Normandy one year, scattered into various châteaux and shops and tenements. Some of our party were installed in a clematis-wreathed mansion, near the church tower; others were at the milk-woman's on the road to the sea. Most of the lively population of the little watering place was stowed away in châlets, of which the fronts seemed wide open to the road from morning to night; numbers of people contentedly spending whole days in tents on the seashore. It was a fine, hot summer, with sweetness and completeness everywhere . . . Mr Milsand had a little country lodge at St Aubin, near Luc-sur-Mer, and I wrote to him from the shady courtyard of our château and begged him to come over and see us.'[149]

Anny was already acquainted with the Milsands, who had a renowned

Salon at Paris. Almost everyone of interest or social standing passed through, with letters of introduction for him to open the doors of the great and famous whom they might wish to have access to. When M. Milsand came to see Anny, he brought the news that the Brownings had arrived.

Anny and Blanche spent much of that summer with the children on the beach. They went with Charlotte and Félicie and the maids, and with baskets of sand-shoes and toys, sketchbooks, refreshments and writing paper. They sat on wooden chairs set out for them by the local urchins hoping to make the odd *sous*, held parasols, wrote letters, and watched the white dab that was Margie's frock being chased by Mary-Anne's stout figure. Margie wasn't recovering from the whooping cough quite as fast as Anny would have liked, and in one of her frequent letters, Minny suggested dosing her with quinine. Anny had more faith in the fresh air, the scudding clouds, the blue skies and the grey-green waves. If they wanted to go bathing, they changed from their full, white summer dresses in the tents. Their bathing dresses were still ample enough to puff up behind them like so many moorhens when they struck out to sea. And, changing back in the tents later on, and tying the strings of their chemises and petticoats, of course the sand got into everything.

Sometimes, Anny stayed behind and wrote in the shady courtyard of the small château she had rented with the help of Edward Thackeray's contribution to his daughters' convalescent holiday. Minny wrote warning her to go through the proofs of *Old Kensington*, soon to appear in book form, with a toothcomb. 'Leslie says there is a dreadful mistake in your proofs which must be altered & which is about *fishing* in the Cam – that nobody was ever known to fish in the Cam so I suppose it must be cut out.'[150] From an oversight, the fish remained.

Blanche could be immensely entertaining. But she could be equally exasperating. Her wit was much sharper than Anny's, and it was often tinged with malice. Her demands stemmed from an exaggerated sense of *amour-propre*. When she wanted to take over Anny's more spacious quarters, Anny was glad of Minny's indignant support. 'Can't she find one rather dearer & better somewhere else for she isn't writing a book & hasn't got whooping cough & it must make such a difference to the children having a garden.'[151] Anny welcomed Browning's presence in the neighbourhood. He had never resigned his fondness of Blanche, and she was much less likely to be difficult with him there. He was busy writing his poem 'Red Cotton Night Cap Country', the title suggested by Anny, and which he dedicated to her. On a memorable day the Milsands invited them all to St Aubin:

'We started almost the next day in a rattle-trap chaise, with an escort of donkeys ridden by nephews and nieces, along the glaringly sandy road to Luc. The plains were burning hot and the sea seemed on fire, but the children and the donkeys kept up valiantly.'[152] When they reached the Milsands' they were given a warm welcome, and found Browning already waiting in the small parlour where Anny caught a glimpse of big books and comfortable seats and tables. But they made up a large party and were invited to eat a feast spread out of doors on the terrace. There was a view of the sea between lilac bushes, and the low table set in the shade was spread with dainties, glasses and decanters and '. . . a certain capon and a huge fish, lying in a country platter, curled on a bed of fennel, surrounded by a wealth of marigolds, and in its mouth a bunch of flowers.' They heard military music coming from the lane, and the daughter of the house explained that a certain regiment was passing by. Their hostess disappeared. They waited. The music continued to play, but still they waited. Madame Milsand returned, full of laughing apologies. She confessed that her larded capon had been sent to the pastrycook to be roasted, but the pastrycook's boy had absconded with it and 'it is feared, is running after the soldiers.'[153] Of course there was plenty for them to eat and drink, even without the bird, and when they had finished the last cup of coffee, the maid popped her head round the door and asked if she should serve the capon, for Pierre had just returned from the review. It was typical of that innocent, domestic sense of humour which Anny and her friends thrived on.

That autumn, and for most of the winter of 1873, Anny was unaccountably depressed. When Jeannie Senior was made a government inspector of girls' District Schools, she was overcome by an absurd jealousy. Jeannie Senior pioneered some important administrative work in setting up new systems in schools. Nobody could have been less suited to such a task than Anny. She was enjoying a particularly low sense of self-esteem. She reproached herself for being 'morbid', and then looked in the Bible for a New Year's text. 'It's the draught of fishes. If only I could obtain a single sprat!'[154]

In February 1874, Mrs Procter took her to visit George Eliot at Northbank. Although she wrote in her journal, 'such a disjointed visit. Each talking their best and neither listening to each other,' she described the visit more respectfully to Richmond. '*Scene* – a cup of tea, George Eliot in a beautiful black satin dressing-gown by the fire, snow outside & German paper-books on the table, a green lamp & paper-cutter.

'The shrine was so serene & kind that this authoress felt a wretch for having refused to worship there before. She looked very noble & gentle, with two steady little eyes. You must go and see her. I am sure she will be a friend just as I felt her yesterday, not a personal friend exactly, but a sort of good impulse, trying to see truly, not to be afraid, and to do good to other people.'[155]

The following month, Anny and the Stephens finally moved into 8 Southwell Gardens. In her journal, Anny mourned their departure from Onslow Gardens. 'Goodbye, dear old house. You have sheltered, warmed & comforted us. We were having a tea-party I remember when the vans came to move us & our cups were carried away out of the drawing-room.'[156]

The new house was only a stone's throw away in the maze of new buildings that were still going up in South Kensington. When Thomas Hardy saw it the following year, he couldn't understand how Leslie could bear to live in such a wasteland of building ground. Leslie's defence that he had grown up there was only partly true, for he had spent his early boyhood in nearby Kensington, in the quiet cul-de-sac of Hyde Park Gate South. Number 8 Southwell Gardens was a corner house, but not detached from the rest of its neighbours that made up the urban 'Gardens'. In spite of Minny's efforts, it was still full of builders. 'If this is to be my home & my future life,' Anny wrote to Hallam, 'I consider life secretly not worth living. Two gas-men in one room, a carpenter in another, tap, screw, grind, vile bell, creaks. It's like having a horrid dream and I don't know why we have so jumbled everything. Having now grumbled, I confess this is much nicer (inside) than the other little old house; my room has a sort of imposing jail-like appearance, but a young man with chintz is coming to enliven it for me this morning.'[157]

The move, however, did nothing to lift Anny's spirits. She was 'dull', 'done-up', 'unsure' of herself and 'scattered'.[158] 'Trust more and above all put your hand to the plough,'[159] she admonished herself. Even when she realised she had glimpsed the skein of a new story, she did not pick up the thread or begin to unwind it immediately. She went to dinner with Sir John and Lady Leslie at Stratford Place. Sir John began telling the story of the extraordinary life of Angelica Kauffman. He pointed out the details of the dining-room ceiling which she had painted and decorated. It was an intriguing subject and one which caught Anny's fancy. 'Thought of writing story,' she noted in her journal. But she was too dispirited to touch it then.

It was unlucky that she was in such low spirits when a variety of things conspired to make Leslie blow up. She said things she couldn't possibly mean and which meant nothing when taken and examined singly. She muddled dates and mixed up times. There wasn't one salient point she didn't alter. She had spent too much money and was going to have to spend more. Somehow or other, she was in debt to him for £100 and had nothing to tide her over at the bank. Leslie exploded. She had succeeded in thoroughly exasperating him. They had another row and it didn't do any good. To have over six foot of tweed-suited, red-bearded outraged fury expounding in the dining-room at breakfast was intimidating, but Anny refused to be bullied. She found her good-humoured Ritchie cousins full of support and understanding. It wasn't that she was blameless, but Leslie was so unquestioningly self-righteous. 'Darling, how sweet you have been to yr poor old Polonia,' she wrote to Pinkie. 'I see now that what you said is quite true, one must just accept states of things and minds and bear with them if they are not always quite comfortable and not think it is one's fault exactly and it's just the same with Leslie who I know loves me as I know I love him, and I suppose bother for each other sometimes, what then – it's no fault of anybody and if one once accepts the fact it ceases to prick and to mean more than it does mean.'[160] It wasn't a foolproof recipe for peace, but her objectivity was worth preserving.

Anny's depression continued. Even after a pleasant spell at Freshwater, she wrote in May, 'Feel very done and long for a little *internal* rest wh. will come, I suppose.'[161] In June, she and Minny and Leslie went with Laura, the nurse and the two little Thackeray girls to holiday in the Alps. The very beauty of the mountains, the lakes, the little Swiss pastures and the great, overhanging rocks crowned with snow, only served to underline her wretched state of mind. Leslie went on an expedition, climbing Mont Blanc again and traversing a new pass from Chamonix to Courmyer. He rejoined the party brown and strong and his wellbeing contrasted greatly with Anny's dejection. Seeing Minny and Leslie so happy together made Anny only more conscious of her irrational depression. She made an effort to go on with her 'Fairy Tales'. She went for a ramble with Leslie and discussed the merits of the novella as a form of writing, in between meeting cows and members of the Alpine Club. And then she experienced a form of visionary enlightenment.

Her experience was of seeing everything with a very heightened perception of detail and colour, rather as she had perceived the characters in *The Village on the Cliff* as she wrote the last page. She was certainly exhausted and overwrought and in a highly emotional state of mind. She made an effort to write down what she had seen and felt in a rambling account in her journal, coloured by pathetic fallacy and influenced by contemporary poetry and philosophy. She describes the spring flood of tiny alpine flowers as 'all indescribably frail and tender'.[162] They are purified by the mountain air and she, too, is purified and refreshed by it. She had 'a sense of God all enclosing, of his works here brought close to us' and was moved to 'feel that this *is*, and we dwellers in the town of life and of heart sometimes remember the mountain tops – and sometimes realise for one instant God's Solemn Beauty is all that *is* . . .' Even if she couldn't describe her perception more clearly, she held it for future reference. 'I have felt it tonight and write it down tho' tomorrow I may have forgotten all save that I have recognised it . . . Are not these sacraments left to descending life?' Anny believed them 'as good as love, as youth, as anything I ever wanted, and hold all those I love enfolded even as Love encloses it all.'

But the next day, she was disarmingly *terre-à-terre*. 'Remember that without any uphill thing you can't get up. Don't be weak. Every life is worth its worth, let it be itself and trust; and prayer means pulling at the rope of the guide.'[163] She did determine on two things. She resolved never to go abroad again without a companion 'to distract me from morbidness for Leslie naturally wants Minny'. She made up her mind to rent a cottage again so as to have more independence, although she would continue to make her home with Minny and Leslie at Southwell Gardens. She had forgotten how badly the experiment of renting the cottage at Rememham Hill had resolved itself. 'I wrote a letter & cried a g. deal. Very angry with myself.' Nevertheless, her depression had lifted.

On their return to England, they went to Willy Ritchie's wedding to Mrs Brookfield's daughter, Magdalene. Magdalene was married from Mrs Brookfield's house at Onslow Square, and they made up a huge party of Thackerays, Ritchies, Brookfields, Tennysons, and family and friends. In the evening, Anny and the Stephens gave a large dinner-party for old Mrs Ritchie. It was their first party at the new house, and it was a very great success.

That autumn, Leslie's mother began to show signs of failing health which, although gradual, gave him, and consequently Minny, a good deal of cause for concern. A more immediate worry was Laura's health. Having been born as a tiny little thing weighing less than three pounds, she remained vulnerable and was prone to any passing infection. With the coming of winter, she caught cold severely. Minny became anxious and took her down to Brighton, hoping that she would benefit from the sea air. Meanwhile, she ordered new stoves to be fitted into the house at Southwell Gardens. It was a good idea, but it did not come off quite as Minny had planned.

They missed the first train, got there late, and had bad luck finding suitable lodgings. Exhausted and at the end of her tether, Minny finally accepted a couple of poky rooms in a nasty house at the wrong end of town. The next-door lodger was a wretched woman who 'always comes fumbling in with a bottle of whiskey under her arm & does nothing but drink & play the piano . . . she always plays as if she was sitting on the keys.'[164] It was too cold to take Laura to the beach. Between Laura and the lodger, Minny found it difficult to sleep, got thoroughly dismal and succeeded in catching Laura's cold. She was too unwell to be able to go out or to see any of her Brighton friends. Laura's cold grew no better, and Minny thought if there wasn't any improvement in the next couple of days, they might as well go home: '. . . there is no denying that this visit to Brighton has been the most utter hash.'[165] The worse Minny felt, the less tolerable she found the rooms. When Leslie went down to see them, he seemed impervious to the discomfort. 'It is very curious but I don't think Leslie ever notices anything of that sort. Of course when one has a feverish cold one is more apt to mind such things.' Everything conspired to be most provoking. Only Laura took some pleasure in the drunk woman's deafening renditions of Mozart. Laura danced for long periods of time without stopping to the dreadful noise, whirling her dolls round in the back drawing-room, which had a slight folding door between the front parlour. When they got back to London, Minny discovered that the fireplaces had not been properly installed.

Eventually, Laura recovered and, although she never grew really robust, she had access to a great deal of nervous energy. She frequently gave vent to long bouts of chanting and singing improvised nonsense. Even if what she said didn't make much sense, she was talkative for a child of three and could chatter away in a 'wonderful jargon of German-English-baby language wh. requires a dictionary of its own.'[166] The German Laura picked up naturally from her nurse, Louise Meineke. She often became unusually noisy and voluble. She enjoyed the company of the Thackeray children, and made a willing slave out of little Annie. She had a passion for her father and adored his dog Troy. Both her parents lavished a good deal of time and attention on her. She was looked after by Louise and tended carefully by Minny. She had a definite sense of humour, and was a clever mimic. 'I was so surprised at Memee suddenly beginning to strum on the piano and shouting a long ballad all de children are mumbled down stairs

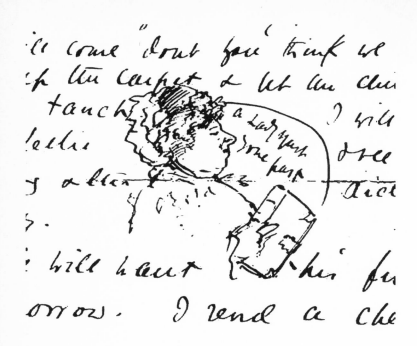

Polly put de kettle on Cooky take it off again wheres me little children gone.'[167]

The links with the past were vanishing one by one. At the beginning of February, old Mr Merivale died. Anny sat by his bedside with his wife, and later went to his funeral with Leslie. 'The wind dry and blinding. Be a dear kind prosperous sentimental old maid if you can, if you can't a cross & failing & true hearted one.'[168]

Pulling herself together, Anny decided to write her book about Angelica Kauffman in the form of fictionalised biography. As portrayed by Anny, Angelica is a gifted painter but a creature of impulse, prey to her own whims and uncontrolled emotions, and the victim of her own bad judgement. She longs for love, but cannot find it and is beguiled instead by an imposter into a bigamous marriage. Angelica's salvation is found eventually in the solace brought by true dedication to her art. The connections with her own life were clear. As much as Angelica, Anny hungered for love, and more especially for guidance. 'It may be our blessing as well as our punishment that the *Now* is not all with us as we hold it, nor the moment all over that is past. It is never quite too late to remember, never quite too late to love; although the heart no longer throbs that we might have warmed, the arms are laid low that would have opened to us. But who shall say that time and place are to be a limit to the intangible spirit of love and reconciliation, and that newfound trust and long delayed gratitude may not mean more than we imagine in our lonely and silenced regret?'[169]

Anny stuck to a fairly regular pattern, unusually so for her, writing her novel in between leading a busy social life. She was a popular guest and was frequently asked out to dinner. She met Cardinal Manning with 'his ring and aesthetic nose', lunched with the George Smiths, breakfasted with Gladstone. She went to balls and parties and concerts. She dined with the Huths and went to a tea-party at the Lehmann's. Millais, Browning and Joachim were all there. 'Ah! I saw her listening to you, Joachim,' said Millais. 'Mr Joachim teaches us to listen just as you teach us how to look & Mr Browning how to think,' was Anny's reply. 'Oh, it's all the same thing,' said Millais. 'Don't believe him, don't believe him,' said Mr Lehmann. Anny thought of them all dead and in heaven, learning each other's arts with each other's fiddles, quills and palettes.[170]

Although Anny was writing and no longer under the strain of the previous year's melancholy, she again had an underlying sense of being not altogether fulfilled, and of missing something she could not quite identify. In spite of her work and all that society had to offer, she was essentially lonely. That Easter, she went on a spree to Paris.

After the horrors of the Siege and the Commune, Paris, that reliably fickle of cities, appeared to have accomplished a complete *volte-face*, and presented the gayest and most splendid front to the world. 'The ladies, week after week, are treading the devious ways of the great shops – the *Bon Marché*, the Louvre, the Compagnie Lyonnaise; the gentlemen are treading other ways, sometimes also, doubtless, a trifle devious. Paris seems more than ever superficially, a vast fancy bazaar, a huge city of shop fronts.'[171]

Anny enjoyed herself immensely, thought Sarah Bernhardt tremendous and drove in the Bois. When Leslie came over for a few days, she had lunch with him and Robert Louis Stevenson at Bélard's Hotel. She and Stevenson had a natural affinity for one another. She was attracted by his charm and enchanting talk, and the way he kept tossing back his long, dark hair. He admired her writing and fell under the spell of her humour. Anny's Ritchie cousins were also staying in Paris, and she delighted in their company. 'It was a week of mad but delightful extravagance.'[172] Leslie left disgruntled, suffering from food poisoning and disapproval. Minny sent reams of notes filled with shopping commissions. She specified gadgets for making ice-cream, silk and lace to be made up into jackets, polon-aises and gowns, and all manner of frivolous knick-knacks which were not obtainable in London. Anny and her cousins flew about the bright, gay streets, discharging Minny's demands.

The notion of a subsequent, more ambitious holiday in Italy was talked about between the cousins, and they began to make plans. Richmond showed enthusiasm, and his presence had a marked effect on Anny. He was now in his last year at Eton, preparing to go up to Trinity in the expectation of carrying off the Newcastle Prize. He was bright, good-looking and humorous. His headmaster, Edward Lushington, thought him a 'brilliant Etonian', old for his age and of true promise as a scholar. His charm was very real and his wit quite vivid enough to cut through the self-consciousness of youth. Anny was captivated by him, and she never thought to make a secret of it. For his part, he couldn't help being bowled over by Anny who, even if she was no great beauty, was undeniably glam-orous, had the allure of fame and the attraction of vivacity. But for the moment, Anny was off to look at the châteaux in the Loire with her old friend Ella Freeman. The visit to Italy was planned for the autumn after the great heat of the summer, which made travel disagreeable.

Anny wrote to Richmond from Blois, and dated her letter *Yesterday*. 'All the old women have got their white caps on, the east wind has made every weathercock shine. I can't think how to tell you what a lovely old place this is, sunny streaked up and down, stones flung into *now* from St Louis's days, others rising into carved staircases and gabions and gargoyles. This isn't a description − I wish it were − it isn't white or crisp enough, or high enough.'[173] Her letter may not have been a 'description' in that it was no precise outline, but it was an effective demonstration of the new style already being talked of in the studios of Paris. The style became known as Impressionism, and the name stuck. It is doubtful whether Anny had ever heard of it then, but it was a style instinctively her own.

Anny was still seriously contemplating renting a cottage of her own. She considered the possibility of buying a place and discussed this with Minny and Leslie. The discussions often became heated. Anny's wilder plans tried Leslie's patience. Then she hit on the notion of renting The Porch, the cottage next door to Dimbola where Jowett and his young men had stayed at Freshwater. The choice was expedient. She knew and loved the place and was cherished by the members of that singu-lar community. It was agreed that Anny should buy some property on the Isle of Wight, with the intention of building. She was wildly excited.

She raced round the island looking for an accommodating piece of land.

London was hot. Leslie was overworked, and Minny beginning to long for the peace of the country. Lady Stephen dragged on in a state of declining health. Milly Stephen devoted herself to her mother, and a nurse was brought in to live at Petersham Terrace. Leslie suffered 'unconscionable blues'. He and Minny stayed on at Southwell Gardens. Leslie went to *The Cornhill* every day and worked late into the night. Julia Duckworth dropped in one evening when they were having 'delicious purée soup and apricot puffs' for dinner, but would not eat.[174] Laura seemed to expand in the heat, and Minny had to order her new clothes for all her summer things had grown too tight. In July, they gave a dinner party for the young Thomas Hardy who had come up to London to go over the proofs of *Far From the Madding Crowd*, which Leslie published in *The Cornhill*. The evening was 'a wild wild chaos – I tried to drown my cares in drink but it only affected my *feet* & not my head. Mr Hardy is a very damp young man and dampness I abominate . . . the Ice too was warm – the only cool things were the soup and the hot viands.'[175] Minny felt sorely tried. Anny stayed on at Freshwater.

Eventually, Leslie and Minny took a cottage at Englefield Green near Windsor. Leslie looked forward to some well earned rest, and hoped to go off for long tramps with his philosopher friend, Morley.[176] At first, Minny felt cooped up, but realised the 'vegetable existence' was good for Laura.[177] The walls were paper-thin. If Laura screamed, Minny got no sleep. The weather did not break.

When Anny wrote ecstatically from Freshwater to say that she had found a field and enclosed a plan of the house she hoped to build, Minny was scathing. She couldn't understand which field it was – the one by the butcher, or the piece by The Porch – thought it too expensive, and pointed out that Anny hadn't left any room for the stairs in the plan she had drawn. If Minny sounded less than sympathetic, it was partly because she now found herself in an unenviable position. It was becoming increasingly clear to her and to Leslie that it was no longer a good idea for Anny to continue to live with them. She drove Leslie distracted. She upset all their plans. She was altogether too unpredictable for there to be much chance of any regular domestic peace. Leslie was working too hard and was too nervous to tolerate Anny's vagaries. Nor was this the whole truth. Leslie and Minny were cherishing a new plan. They were toying with the notion of going to live at Brighton. It was within commuting distance to *The Cornhill*, and Leslie had spent part of his boyhood there and liked it, and they felt that the sea air would be beneficial for Laura. The more they thought about it, the better they liked the idea. But Minny could not see a solution. Generally, when there was an obstacle in her path, she tried to avoid it, or hoped that by ignoring it it might go away, and even she was surprised by how often the obstacles, which had seemed insurmountable, vanished of their own accord. But she could hardly expect Anny to vanish, and besides, she didn't want Anny to vanish. She loved Anny with all her heart and expected everyone else to as well. And she knew that Leslie was fond of her, it was just that they didn't rub along together. So Minny now took a completely opposite line of enquiry. The very incongruity of her activity amused her.

She started, from the heat of the day at Englefield Green, to take the stifling train up to London and go house-hunting. She found a great many houses, none of them suitable, on the market. It wasn't merely that they weren't suitable, but she had no use for any of them. She had a perfectly good house at South Kensington, and if she and Leslie were going to move it would be to Brighton. Yet her house mania filled her days. 'You can't think how enchanting they all sound . . . I was most anxious to take an old-fashioned residence at Highgate of 9 bedrooms 5 sitting-rooms, Garden, Coach House for £45 a year at once – I daresay it's the small-pox hospital or something of that sort. But we could all be vaccinated at once.'[178] It was all part of an elaborate tease, designed to distract the two people whom she most loved, as well as herself, from a more disagreeable issue. She devised a scheme whereby they could all live in some suburb with a garden, go to Switzerland for several months a year and then to Paris for a month or two in the winter: '. . . only don't say anything more about it before Leslie, or he will disagree again. He can't bear people doing anything they like.'[179]

Anny was too happy at the prospect of owning her own field to bother about Minny's problems. The island had seldom seemed lovelier. She went on a long walk from the Needles over the Downs and was dazzled by the beauty of it all. The birds wheeled in the air, only just above her head. The light on the sea danced on a thousand waves. The cocks crew the whole time. They had been ordered for dinner, but they came alive and so they were kept until everybody was so deafened that they were swiftly turned into *coq au vin*. Anny was happy at Freshwater. The only cloud on the horizon was a misunderstanding between Hallam Tennyson and Pinkie Ritchie. They had had a brief flirtation, which Pinkie had taken too seriously. Hallam had gone too far and thoughtlessly led her on. Anny blew him up. He should have been more careful and not trifled with Pinkie.

He *had* written her intimate and misleading letters, and she had been led to believe he cared for her in the way she wanted him to. Pinkie remained hopelessly in love with Hallam for the rest of her life.

15

Anny's high spirits continued into the autumn, when she went to Paris and travelled with Charlotte and Félicie and their maids to meet the rest of the Ritchies — Gussie and her husband Douglas Freshfield, Pinkie, Blanche and Frank Warre-Cornish, Willy and Magdalene, Richmond, and their mother Mrs Ritchie — at Venice. 'O darling,' she wrote to Minny, 'I'm almost too happy & *thrilling* to write. At sea the sun rose & 1000 waves began to laugh . . . you would be sitting in a clean sweet fresh room like a salad bowl with 2 domes & a campanile & a lot of roofs. We came in a dark gondola last night. Richmond met us.'[180]

The next night the company rowed out to the Lido. 'The hills lay like an amethyst crown on the horizon.' They were intoxicated by the beauty of Venice, and none of them more so than Anny, who tried to scribble down descriptions of everything she saw as material for *Miss Angel*, her book about Angelica Kauffman. Her notes were disordered and, of course, later, she wished she had taken more. But she used what she did observe to good effect in the opening chapters of *Miss Angel*. She went shopping with Gussie and Blanche and Pinkie, and was entranced 'by crystals, old laces, buckles, and gimcracks of every description . . . But perhaps the fish-stalls were the prettiest of all. Silver fish tied up in stars with olive green leaves, golden fish as in miracles. She would have liked to carry home the whole market.'[181]

They were prodigious sightseers. When they had worn themselves out looking at palaces and paintings and Madonnas in churches, they returned to their hotel and collapsed in heaps, and wrote long letters and ate delicious, long spun-out dinners. Mrs Ritchie was beginning to grow exhausted and was grateful for the homoeopathic medicines Anny had remembered she needed and had brought from England. Charlotte was made nervous by their apparent extravagance and got into a fidget trying to make small economies which failed. Douglas Freshfield, who had all the reassuring qualities of a cultivated man of the world, succeeded in calming her. They travelled on to Florence.

They made up a party of over a dozen, easily identified from a distance

the arno   out of window

The terrace

by their quantities of luggage, and the maids running in between with wraps and attentions. They did not dress in the latest fashions, but their clothes were good, expensive and graceful. The men wore impeccably cut suits, and their luggage was old, well-travelled and of the very best quality. It was not always easy for an outsider to tell where they were going, or, indeed, to be certain how sure they were themselves. They made a commotion swaying to and fro, and stopping and starting again, and then one of them would rush off and fetch something – a newspaper, a basket of fruit, a parasol, so that it was difficult to determine any sense of direction. They could be sensed long before they arrived, in twos or threes or all together. Their voices were distinctive, piercing the hum and leaving great waves of comment in their wake. They bubbled with enthusiasm, determined to find an obscure church, a fresco they had heard spoken of. They were erudite and knowledgeable, and quick to enjoy an absurdity or a joke. People deferred to them with apparent pleasure. Station masters, hoteliers, bell-boys and chambermaids all put themselves out to give some extra service, reheat the soup, leave the keys out, provide extra cushions, and all these things were done with smiles.

Anny had never disguised her fondness for Richmond. All along, he seemed to return her feelings with interest. He was attentive, amusing, did small things for her so that she felt radiant, laughed at her jokes, and noticed when she was tired. It was hard to believe that he was still a schoolboy, even though in his last year at Eton. But if they did not hide their feelings, there was no possibility of declaring them. The conventions of the age were so hidebound as to prohibit any physical demonstration, however slight. And then, neither of them really knew how seriously they should take what they felt. Anny was ridiculously inexperienced and Richmond ridiculously young.

Surprisingly, it was Charlotte who put the cat among the pigeons. The day they got to Florence, Anny felt seedy and lay down on a sofa in the splendid salon of the rooms Gussie and Douglas had taken at the hotel. Charlotte began to upbraid Anny. She begged her not to '*accapare* Richmond about wh everybody looks at from different points of view & altogether it was most irritating as I was far from well. I felt most furious'.[182] The truth was Anny did not want to be looked at and criticised from any point of view.

At Perugia the party split up, Pinkie and Anny returning together, the Freshfields and Richmond going on to Rome, and the others returning more slowly in stages. 'We are all very sorry to part. We have all been in a most absurd state of rapture, and next time, unless you come, I shall come alone, and gush less, and write descriptions for a book.'[183]

Anny reached Southwell Gardens on 30 October. She was delighted to be back at home. The business about houses and moving to Brighton seemed to be forgotten. 'My [drawing of a heart] is full of gratitude for their unchanging tenderness & love.' Her present to Laura was a little toy gondola. The very evening of her return she went to the first performance of *Hamlet* with Henry Irving playing the Prince of Denmark. It was a wild success. 'Behind the scenes audience shouting. Hamlet with his overcoat on tall and vibrating.'[184]

That autumn Anny and Richmond saw each other as often as they could. They met at Eton and Richmond came up to see Anny at Southwell Gardens. He was busy preparing for a scholarship to Trinity, Cambridge, which he would sit early the following year. Anny was occupied with *Miss Angel*, which she was still rewriting when the proofs arrived. Once again, Julia Duckworth helped Anny over her proofs. Even so, Anny continually muddled them, and when she sent them for publication in Australia they were in such a miscellaneous state that the end chapters came out before the first. When Richmond and Anny couldn't see each other, they wrote to one another constantly, and were already declaring more passion on paper than they had ever managed to express directly. Their involvement with each other was growing and developing rapidly. And yet, such an involvement was inadmissible. Anny was living in a heightened state of emotion, and the strain was sometimes very great. 'The time has seemed endless these 2 months have been so heavy - & yet I would not have been without them. Sometimes I feared that circumstance was to be stronger than will, & simply annihilate everything. Surely, all this long worry and disappointment must give one some power of enduring faith.'[185] There was no one she could talk to, since no one was prepared to admit what her feelings for Richmond might be.

But coming away from Eton one day in the pouring rain, Anny shared a railway carriage with Lord Leighton. He must have heard the gossip, for gossip there was, and guessed at her state of mind. Very gently, he said that love had nothing to do with age. Then, with great sympathy, he began to tell Anny far more than she had ever known of his own life-long love for Adelaide Sartoris. It was perceptive of him and Anny never forgot his kindness.

Very soon after, Charlotte sent her a conciliatory letter, making amends for their quarrel at Florence. 'She says don't give way to despondency and she is right. One may be just as good as a happy cheerful woman as by being a gloomy despairing one.'[186]

Richmond was inclined to shrug off the difference between their ages. He insisted they had a host of things in common, as well as a family language in which to talk about them. They shared a love of music, painting and literature, and were gradually able to talk to each other more and more freely. When she wrote to him about a concert where Joachim had played 'like a soul in bliss, like the end of that poem of Shelley's', she could rely on him to recognise that poem to be 'Prometheus Unbound'. She also knew how to amuse him. 'Joachim . . . went on in a sort of ecstatic stream in the midst of wh. he suddenly stopped & all the gallery & stalls he had carried away fell back into their bodies again. He began 3 times. The 3rd time he put his spectacles on & got through. Once more we started off after him but it was rather agonizing when he came to the note . . .'[187] By now, Richmond was staying up at Cambridge in Hallam's rooms to take his scholarship. He found her letter waiting for him in the evening. 'It makes all the difference to me & − confound all the phosphorous − I must thank you. I feel scholarships don't matter in the least. Good night dearest, yr. grateful Richmond Ritchie.'[188]

In February 1875, Lady Stephen grew very much worse. Milly had been living at home, looking after her mother with the help of a nurse. She had taken on most of the burden, but now had grown so depressed as to become almost ill. Efficient and tender, Minny made an ideal nurse, but she was never strong and, inevitably, the strain had begun to tell on her. By the time Lady Stephen died, Minny was exhausted. Leslie took his mother's death very hard and afterwards went off to the Lakes on a walking tour.

Anny had been missing Richmond very much. Towards the end of March, after Leslie's return, the Stephens gave a party at Southwell Gardens. It was a small, quiet affair since they were in mourning for Lady Stephen, but very much to Anny's surprise, Richmond walked in. Without anything being said, they reached some sort of private understanding. Very subtly, but significantly, amidst the hum of Minny's guests sitting on the sofas and discussing the latest novel, their relationship had changed gear. But in spite of being surrounded by friends, there was nobody Anny could speak to about it.

And then, quite unexpectedly, Anny discovered that she had two other suitors on her hands. Minny and Leslie had evidently been up to some ingenious matchmaking schemes in an attempt to distract her from what could only appear to them as a foolish crush on Richmond. Both of Anny's new admirers were old friends of Leslie's.

Hastings Hughes was Jeannie Senior's brother, a widower with four children.[*] It was an advantageous proposal, and Anny would have made the children a remarkable stepmother. She was flattered but declared it was absurd. Hastings was an admirable man and possessed of unusually fine qualities that made him very loveable. But Anny was not in love with him, and she was too romantic a character to entertain the idea of a *mariage de convenance*. Then Hastings repeated his proposal in a letter and, while she was reading it, she began to wonder whether she wouldn't be justified in accepting him. In a panic she rushed off to Paris and stayed with Charlotte. It was an overwhelming relief to have escaped from a situation which she feared was getting out of hand. But Hastings was not a man to give up easily. He wrote again, and sent Minny a draft of his letter. Minny showed it to Leslie. 'Leslie recommended me not to answer this letter,' Minny wrote to Anny in Paris, '& if it pleases him to think

---

[*] Hastings Hughes (1833–1909) had married Emily Clark, by whom he had four children. Emily was the niece of Nassau Senior, the political economist, and the cousin of Jeannie Senior's husband. After Anny's rejection of his proposal Hastings moved to America where, in 1887, he married Sarah Hathaway Forbes (1853–1917). For a fuller account of Hastings Hughes, see Bicknell.

your heart is being broken by this atrocious male flirt – let him think it. Only Leslie says that I had better let him know that he is not to propose again in six months – he is evidently in a marriageable humour & is much more likely to get married in 6 months than you are.'[189] Minny was quite capable of scratching with her claws and purring at the same time.

When Douglas Freshfield turned up at Charlotte's apartment out of the blue, Anny suddenly felt as though she was on an unexpected holiday. He took her and Charlotte off to the salon to see the new Millets, and then to dine at the Madeleine. Anny was still staying at Charlotte's when Leslie's friend, the Swiss painter Loppé, came to call on her. She knew Loppé and liked him. He was a close friend of Leslie's and had been on many mountaineering expeditions with him, notably to climb Mont Blanc in order to see the sunset. Loppé had carried his easel on his back and painted away furiously at the view before the sudden darkness fell and endangered their descent. To Anny's utter amazement, Loppé proposed to her. She couldn't quite believe that this was happening in Charlotte's tasteful grey and silver salon. He took her refusal philosophically enough. 'Enter M. Loppé – who proposes. L'homme propose. Dieu dispose. He drinks some soda water & goes away.'[190] She found his proposal too ludicrous to take very seriously, although she couldn't help wondering if Leslie hadn't put him up to it.

When Anny got back to Southwell Gardens on a wintry afternoon early in 1875, in time for tea, Minny told her that she was pregnant again. As the months passed, and spring turned into summer, Minny became very ill and they were all horribly anxious. The doctor recommended a visit to Switzerland. Leslie and Minny left with Laura on 1 July, and Anny joined them shortly after. In the clear mountain air, Minny seemed to revive as if by magic.

Walking up the valley with Laura to Rosenlauie, Anny felt unaccountably lighthearted. Everything seemed possible. She sat on a log by a torrent while Laura looked for a lost toad. She thought of Richmond continually. 'How I wish one could send all that one sees to you and to all other poor hard-worked people who really want it! I should like to send you a pine tree & a bunch of wild strawberries, a valley of sloping nodding flowers with thousands of glittering spiders' webs, the high up snows & far below lakes, & yesterday's yellow evening, dying rather sadly behind the pine ridge & the misty Stockhorn.'[191] When the doctor came to see Minny, Anny overheard him having a discussion about health in general with Leslie. 'He says medicines are a mere accident but that people

> I think it w
> bury it. Br
> beautiful Kr
>   Leslie
>   hat that
>   very nice
> rotten - he is
> his poncho &
> that it is a

are certainly medicinal, some are sedatives, some are tonics, some are irritants.'[192] And so it was that Anny coined one of her favourite endearments for Richmond, calling him her 'Dearest Tonic'.

At Interlaken, they were at the Hotel des Alpes. Their stay was a long one and their visit punctuated by a stream of friends and acquaintances passing through the mountains. 'All Cambridge seems to be about.' Leslie had arranged to go back to England for ten days or so, for unavoidable work. The sisters stayed on with Laura and Louise and the maids, and waited for his return. Anny enjoyed taking Laura for walks. They went out together one afternoon to climb a small hill. Laura walked stoutly on, singing one of her improvised songs. 'Up in de mountains, Up she goes.'[193] Enormous dark clouds gathered. The weather broke. It poured with rain. Anny and Laura scrambled back to the hotel through the deluge, arriving with their clothes streaming with rain. The hotel seemed abandoned and Anny found Minny sitting all alone. Anny handed Laura over to Louise and huddled up by the porcelain stove with Minny. She ordered champagne, partly because it was pleasant, and partly because it was considered an excellent tonic. The sisters began to gossip about the Ritchies and Blanche's latest baby and, inevitably, it led to talk about Richmond.

Minny took Anny to task. She said suddenly, 'You are not behaving rightly. You ought to make a little joke of things instead of taking them so seriously, even if it is disagreeable to you. There is no reason why you and Richmond shouldn't go on as usual, only without all this emotion.' Anny agreed with her, but it didn't make her any happier.[194]

On their way back to England, Anny stopped off at Paris for 'a delightful solitary flight' and stayed, as usual, with Charlotte. Once again, Douglas Freshfield was in Paris and came to dinner at Charlotte's, then took Anny to visit Madame Möhl in her famous salon.[195] Anny had known Madame Möhl for years, but could never get used to this extraordinary woman, now nearly eighty, who looked like a cross between a Skye terrier and a cut-glass scent bottle, and had such a genius for cultivating people that over the last sixty years and more, most of the leading lights of Europe had gathered in her salon. That evening, Anny found Madame Möhl and the feminist campaigner and landscape painter, Barbara Bodichon, and a circle of guests sitting round the historian Renan, 'a little round flapping sort of man who talked most beautifully'.[196] She listened to him expounding, thought he seemed like a 'very fat ill-bound grammar and dictionary all put up together' and couldn't help noticing that his shirt buttons did his wife no credit. But she was fascinated when he claimed that art, emotion and belief required participation, but that science could stand alone. 'He said that nobody was ever persecuted to prove a thing that was provable such as a problem of Euclid, but only to prove a thing that was unprovable such as religion or dogma.' After they had all begun to praise Herbert Spencer, the evolutionary philosopher and author of *The Principles of Psychology*, Anny came away in a coupé in the starlight along the river and thought of the day when Margie and Annie would be old enough to go to parties with her. Douglas also took her to the theatre 'with a moon and shooting stars and Mr Aslee in attendance with an opera hat, two little golden sugar tongs and a box of the most delicious iced fruit' which they ate during all the intervals: 'All the grand ladies of Paris were in the theatre, sitting about in boxes, with shoulders & diamonds & frizzed heads.'[197] In the daytime, Douglas took her to see the new exhibitions. It was all very splendid and very stimulating and Anny loved every moment of it.

When she got back to Southwell Gardens towards the end of October 1875, she found that Minny had gone to stay with Mrs Huth in the country, apparently not well. As soon as Minny returned, it was clear to Anny that she was very ill. But neither of her sister's previous pregnancies had been easy. Anny did not know what to think, but she could not help being horribly anxious when Minny confided in her. 'She complained of pain all the way down her back & then she would get better & seem almost as usual. On the 26 November I met her out walking and a little later she came home. She said, "It's very odd, I got almost well before Laura was born and I don't get well now." I had a strange sort of fright — a *certitude* that wherever I went sorrow would follow. It was horrible. I went to Mr Chope's church haunted by this feeling. Then I went to an empty house. They would not let me in. Then I went to see the old Valentine Smiths, they could not see me and I came home and looked at myself in the glass and the terror left me.'[198]

Anny went to Windsor to spend the night with her friend, the writer Margaret Oliphant. Leslie and Minny sat at home as usual, in a state of blissful, loving, unbroken harmony.[199] Over the last few months, they had grown closer to one another than ever. They seemed to 'recognise and to share each other's wishes and feelings at a glance'.[200] Julia Duckworth dropped in on them, but left almost immediately. Later, she said she thought her presence an intrusion on a couple so evidently bound up in one another, and had walked back home alone. But that evening Minny felt unwell and thought it best to sleep apart in a room where Anny's maid, Mary Anne, could look after her. During the night, Mary Anne called Leslie. He found Minny unconscious and in convulsions. He rushed out into the night to fetch the doctor.

A telegram was sent to Anny, urging her to come home, but not specifying why. She took the first train from Windsor in an agony of alarm. Fitzy met her at the station and told her that the baby had been still-born. 'Yes, yes, that I can bear,' cried Anny. 'It's my Minny, tell me quick, my Minny?'[201]

Then Fitzy had to tell her: Minny was dead.

When she got to Southwell Gardens, Anny took Laura in her arms and carried her upstairs to kiss Minny. 'Then it seemed to me as if my Father was in all the house & poor Leslie came up & sat by the fire in my room all night long.'

Minny had died from eclampsia, a state of acute toxaemia, with convulsive fits. She died at about midday on 28 November 1875. It was Leslie's forty-third birthday. He never celebrated it again. The present was a hideous nightmare; the future now walled up.

Part III
Intimate Relations

16

Minny's unforeseen and violent death had disastrous consequences for the three people whom she had loved the most: Anny, Leslie and Laura. The course of all their lives was altered irrevocably. But while Laura, who was not yet five years old, was mainly confined to the nursery for the time being, Anny and Leslie drove each other, inadvertently, to distraction. That two such ill-assorted people should be bound together by a grief so deep, and yet be unable to help one another, made a mockery of everything they both held so dear. Confounded by misery, all their earlier differences were now exaggerated so as to become unbearable. Each knew how wretched the other was, but there was nothing either of them could do about it. Later, Leslie admitted that Anny 'was like a person condemned to live in a den with a fretful beast & always persist in stroking it the wrong way'.[1] Morose in his misery, Leslie didn't want to be stroked by anyone at all; Anny had never felt so lonely in her life. It was an appalling situation.

Anny was so overwhelmed by Minny's death that for a time it seemed as if she would never regain even a flicker of her old zest for life. Her despair recalled her father's death and revived that old grief. 'One night I dreamt that it was Papa's funeral over again. There was a strange clanging music. I stood by the grave & people came & shook me by the hand & somehow they took his hand too.'[2] Sometimes, it seemed as if she was confused by events and that, in her agony, she could not bear the reality. 'I think I am writing to tell you that Papa is dead,' she wrote to her father's old friend, Mrs Baxter, whom Minny had met in America but who was only known to Anny through correspondence. 'It always seems to be that coming back, not anything new.' She did not disguise her longing for Minny. 'I am still so unaccustomed to it that I don't feel I think very much – only that I have the tenderest faithfullest most unspeakably loving sister that all one ever ever had . . . One day I went away for a night –

'You see it is my Fate – & she was dead when I came back next day . . .'[3]

Upstairs, in his book-lined study, Leslie was going through much the same gamut of emotions. 'My life was so happy a few months ago that it seemed to me that unhappiness was impossible. Now it is so unhappy that it seems like a dream.'[4] However inaccessible and curmudgeonly grief had made Leslie, he was painfully aware of his shortcomings. '. . . Unhappiness tries my temper. I am more fretful & irritable by disposition than you know & sometimes I bully my best friends shamefully. The problem of making sorrow ennobling instead of deteriorating is a terribly hard one.'[5] Leslie had put his finger on one of the most difficult lessons of bereavement, but neither his startling honesty nor his analytical clarity enabled him to solve the problem. Since childhood, he had been the victim of his own extreme emotions and, although he worried at them like a dog with fleas, he was no more able to shake them off now than he had ever been.

It is not uncommon for people to feel jealous and possessive of their dead, and Anny and Leslie were no exception. What made things even more poignant was that Leslie realised all the while that Anny was one of the people he found most sympathetic. 'Anny has been as brave & tender as only good women can be . . . the shock to her was great as to me & came upon a more sensitive system.'[6] But they were living in the shadow of a hideous nightmare, and Leslie could convey very little of the affection he felt, or give the reassurance which Anny so desperately needed.

8 Southwell Gardens had never been a cheerful house, and now, in the dismal winter after Minny's death, the sheer melancholy weighed on Leslie and Anny. They did their best to carry on, even though accomplishing the most ordinary of their daily tasks seemed hopeless. Little Laura mooned around, not forgotten or neglected, but bewildered by the loss of her mother. She was the child of unhappy circumstance. Leslie found his salvation in work. He trudged off every morning and took the other children, Margie and Annie Thackeray, to school on his way to the Cornhill offices. In the evening, he buried himself deep in the book he was writing, *A History of Thought in the Eighteenth Century.*

Anny struggled to pick up the threads of her own life, but they were so intrinsically tangled that the task of winding them on to well-ordered spools of neatness was beyond her. She sought comfort in her faith and her unquestioning belief in the Resurrection, sure that she would meet her sister and her father and the rest of her loved ones later on in heaven, even though in the form of spirits. Her dreams were full of reassurances from her father. But Anny could not share such consolation with Leslie, to whom anything verging on religion was anathema. That Anny should find solace from God for the loss of Minny was positively repugnant to him.

Grief was swiftly turning Leslie into a cantankerous recluse. He resigned from his clubs and avoided all but a very few friends. Without Minny to enhance his life he plunged into a state of gloom verging on madness. Anny became ill with anxiety. Leslie was genuinely anxious for her, but so wrung and strained and clumsy in his approach that he was worse than useless. It was an immense relief to everyone when Julia Duckworth, who had seen Minny the night before she died, stepped in and quietly took command.

Anny and Leslie each had a battery of well-meaning and mildly conflicting friends. Victor Marshall, Mrs Huth and the agnostic, John Morley, were among Leslie's closest supporters, while Mrs Brookfield, the Coles and her Ritchie relations hovered around Anny, offering every comfort they could devise. But with the single exception of Richmond, on whom Anny was fast developing a total, if hidden, emotional dependency, none had anything like Julia's therapeutic powers.

When Julia had been in the depths of despair after the sudden death of her husband Herbert, Anny had gone to her rescue. Now Julia came to Anny and helped her as no one else could. For there was about Julia a calmness, an almost stoic implacability that people found themselves turning to almost automatically in times of distress. She sat very still, or, when she moved around the room, always held herself very straight, making very little sound, her movements quick, practical, full of reassurance. Anny began staying with Julia, using her house at Hyde Park Gate South as a second home. The two women were never very far apart and, very gradually and slowly and painfully, Julia helped Anny to come to terms with Minny's death, even if she never wholly recovered from it.

Not long after Minny's death, when the wound was still raw, Julia suggested they should all go down to Brighton for a change of scene. Anny and Leslie and Laura, together with Louise, stayed at one set of lodgings, and Julia and her children at another, close by. Laura played with the Duckworth children, and Anny was reminded of the time she and Minny stayed at Brighton with their cousin, Jane Ritchie, after her grandmother had died. She looked at her own unrelieved black dress and at Laura's little black frock and remembered how Minny had loathed what she called the horrid crepe. The landlady cooked them appetising meals, Louise was in a good temper, and Laura's cheeks grew rosy in the sea air. Leslie went off on long walks with John Morley, and Anny wrote letters and read Heine and thought a good deal of Richmond, not caring that the lodgings were 'unutterably fusty.'[7] What was remarkable was the extraordinary ability Julia had to soothe Leslie. She did not fuss or upset him, and he was susceptible to her beauty and intelligent sympathy. She made no claims to have tamed the 'fretful beast', but he certainly growled a good deal less when she was with him. By the time they were ready to return to London, it had become understood that Julia had become a central figure in their orbit. She was never to leave it again.

Apart from Julia's influence, the only consolation during that 'miserable and terrible winter'[8] came from Richmond's visits. 'He used to come up and see me from Cambridge like new life in the darkness and gloom.' The intimacy between them was already far more developed than Leslie had ever dreamed. There had been gossip, some of it exaggerated, some of it justified, about the flirtation between them. Minny had tried, not very successfully, to scotch such rumours. She wouldn't have minded if Anny had settled to have a fling with Richmond, and not allow things to become too serious, but the objections to their indulging in anything more than a light-hearted affair were manifest. Anny was seventeen years older than Richmond. Richmond was just embarking on what his masters prophesied would be a brilliant career. They were closely related, first cousins once removed, and Anny was Richmond's godmother. Nothing could have seemed less propitious.

Richmond was born a favourite of the gods. As a child, he was quick, lively, precocious, funny and affectionate. At eight, he won a scholarship to Eton; he achieved the double glory of being in Sixth Form and Pop,* won the Prince Consort's French prize at sixteen, and was Newcastle medallist in his last year.[9] He was also president of the Eton Literary Society. He had taught himself to think for himself and to act upon his decisions at an age long before most people realise they have any choice at all. Richmond had all the nonchalance of an upper-class hero. He did not appear to work very hard for his medals and prizes but was in fact a very thorough scholar; it would have been contrary to his notion of good form to have appeared to swot, so he took care his industry went unobserved. He was well-travelled and sociable, enjoyed the theatre, exhibitions, and music. He was tolerably cynical, aware that he lived in a society where he would very seldom be asked to exercise very much choice: his reading matter, his diet, his very clothes were prescribed for him by the conventions of the day. He was a product of an elite which was far more conformist than it strove to appear. His falling in love with Anny was the single act which marked him as an unconventional man. His love did not take the romantic form to be expected of one of his years, but was protective, practical and, to Anny's delight, possessive.

Anny lived for Richmond's visits. He managed to come up to London fairly often, and they met in the drawing-room at Southwell Gardens at tea-time. They met in public and submitted to the familiar ceremony of

---

* The colloquial term for the Eton Society, originally founded to debate, but which evolved into a self-elected group of the socially elite. To become a member of Pop was the ambition of most Etonians. It implied considerable power, prestige and influence as well as the right to wear distinctive, brightly coloured waistcoats, and other dress privileges. As Jo Grimmond remarked several generations later, 'it could never have originated in the head of a schoolmaster.'

cups and saucers, the plates handed round with thin slices of bread and butter, the cups refreshed and the conversation revived. Close acquaintances dropped in: Mrs Brookfield, Mrs Huth, Marie Stillman, Leslie's Dicey cousins. Leslie shunned the gatherings around the tea-table. He found he was beginning to dislike Richmond, who seemed to haunt the house. If Richmond noticed this, he did not show it, and if he had time, he tried to linger until after the other guests had gone, hoping to have a few moments alone with Anny before catching his train. Anny pined for his letters. Unhappy, moping for her sister and leading an unsatisfactory life with Leslie, there was little else to stimulate her. Richmond kept her voluminous scrawls in a pretty old bureau she gave him and she was dependent on his notes, written in a minute script, folded in the smallest of envelopes.

They found they could write freely to each other of their hopes and sorrows and of the absurdities they had witnessed during the day. She could write to him about Minny. She even invoked Minny's blessing on their relationship, ignoring the reservations her sister had expressed when she was alive. 'I feel as if my Min was alive & always would be after people have forgotten even her name, but somehow her dear little soft hands — with healing power — will have been laid on us & her dear unselfish tender spirit will be at work — and now it seems as if we must all do our business in our respective places & ages and accept — that is all I can see . . . except not to forget to say thank God.'[10] Their correspondence steamed ahead, and very soon Anny's feelings for Richmond had become the central point of her life to the exclusion of everything else. He showed his love for her and called her his 'rock' and his 'anchor'. If nobody else would condone their relationship, Anny was keen to have the approval of her two dead loved ones, Minny and her father. All her father's relics were still sacred to her, and to send a treasured fragment of a letter from him as a gift to Richmond was a token of a very serious pledge. 'Do you know that the last time I ever saw his dear face he sent me away — I just remember going back & standing by his bedside not thinking him ill, but looking at him & you see after eleven years I find you my dear to talk to about him & to be yourself too . . .'[11]

Anny told him, too, of how she dreamed she heard Thackeray's voice, saying '*poor Nan* but now I think we shall all be together again some day & if it is not God's will, at least it has once been his will to make us all, & when I think of *them* & of Richmond & of you my dearest children I don't know how to thank God'. And so Anny began to alter very subtly the inflexions of the voices of the past. Very delicately, she darned the holes, and occasionally embroidered the dull patches, not from mischief, but because she believed so desperately in the good and beautiful, and disliked so intensely anything verging on the unpleasant.

But even if she carried a letter from Richmond as a talisman in her pocket, or had one unfinished to him lying in the blotter on her desk, Anny could not avoid the painful scenes at Southwell Gardens or the backbiting on the stairs. The old money troubles between Anny and Leslie now became magnified. Of course she overspent, and now that she had to deal with the household budget previously managed by Minny, she brought Leslie bills far in excess of the amount he expected. He lost his temper and Anny got into a miserable, nervous state. Sometimes, Leslie had swearing fits and they had scenes. They made it up and wished it had never happened, and then, of course, it happened again the next time they had to go through the accounts. She knew that she was to blame, but she longed for a calmer, less frenzied reaction to her extravagance.

She would have been far more at home with Frank Warre Cornish's method of dealing with her cousin Blanche, who was as impractical about money as Anny herself. Although Frank suffered in some degree from that malaise typical of the Victorian paterfamilias, financial anxiety, he tempered his agitation with good humour and never lost his sense of the absurd. The Cornishes' account book was known in the family as *Le Grand Livre*. If Frank grumbled at the quantity of Camembert Blanche had ordered, 'she would advance a whole string of unanswerable arguments in favour of Camembert.

'"Well, then, *wine?*"

'"Yes, but you know how deadly dull the Bishop of Camelot's dinner parties are," [Blanche] replied, "and it is chiefly because they only have water for the exhausted guests."

'[Blanche] then would suggest that all animals and birds should be instantly put down: dogs ate bones, cats drank milk, birds cracked hemp. "Now the parrot really *is* an expense . . . June – bird-seed, corn, sand. July – corn. August – hemp, corn."

'[Frank], who, she knew perfectly well, particularly liked the parrot, turned impatiently from her irony to leading the attack once more himself. And so they would go on, detail after detail proving indispensable.'[12]

The Cornishes swung from one extreme to another, veering so noticeably from a grim frugality to a regime of lobsters and ices that their friends used to ask, 'Was it fast or feast at the Cloisters when you were last there?' But although they argued over money, they laughed at themselves too, and this Leslie was unable to do. Leslie's tantrums failed to make the slightest difference to Anny's incompetence. On more than one occasion, she made matters worse by asking him to lend her money when she had overspent her allowance. He was thunderstruck when she once revealed she had only thirty-five pounds left at the bank, borrowed a hundred and fifty pounds from him, and swore blithely she would pay it back by the next quarter without having the foggiest notion where the money was coming from. By a quirk of what Leslie considered quite unmerited good fortune, she was able to keep her promise. The effect of Leslie's violent outbursts of temper on Anny was devastating. Mrs Brookfield tried to remonstrate with him. But it was Julia who succeeded in doing what no one else could. She took him for a stroll in Kensington Gardens and Leslie admitted his shortcomings and promised to try and turn over a new leaf.[13]

For the first time since her father's death Anny did not retreat to Freshwater, which had always proved a haven in times of distress. Julia Margaret Cameron had left. This garrulous, impulsive, wildly generous and often maddening genius had an immense effect on Anny; in many ways, they were remarkably similar in temperament. Now, when Anny needed her most, Mrs Cameron was no longer there. After years of accepting his wife's eccentric whims, Mr Cameron suddenly woke up to the fact that he was dying of homesickness. He was bored by Freshwater. He was bored of dipping his beard in moonlight. He pined for the strong sun of the East, and insisted on returning to his coffee plantation at that other Dimbola in Ceylon. Mrs Cameron, who, for all her adulation of other, more illustrious men, loved her husband with passion, went with him. Their departure from Freshwater caused as much sensation as anything Mrs Cameron had engineered during her long sojourn on the island. They travelled with mountains of luggage and all their chattels crated up. Teams of porters had to be roped in to heave their possessions on board, and were startled to receive enormous photographs taken by Mrs Cameron in lieu of a tip. She insisted on taking a cow with them, to prevent their catching tuberculosis on the voyage. For good measure, she took two coffins in case she or her husband should die at sea. Practical after her own fashion, she stuffed the coffins with yet more of their possessions on the chance that she and Mr Cameron might survive. Mr Cameron, who was now eighty-one and had been bedridden for twelve years, suddenly got to his feet and boarded the ship unaided. From that time forth, he was rejuvenated, so strong was his yearning to see his beloved Ceylon once more. The farewells were protracted and emotional, with ardent protestations of love to all and sundry. And so, in typically dramatic fashion, Mrs Cameron sailed out of Anny's life. They never saw each other again.

17

That spring, Anny and Leslie sold the house at Southwell Gardens for four thousand, one hundred pounds, but were obliged to wait until June to move into their new home next door to Julia at Hyde Park Gate South. Anny and Minny had invested in the house earlier, and its unexpected vacancy was fortuitous. It was a roomy house at the end of a quiet cul-de-sac off Kensington Gardens in Knightsbridge, the same street in which Leslie had spent his early childhood. Both Anny and Leslie found Southwell Gardens depressing. They said it was too big, although the new house was larger. All of Minny's household arrangements, the stoves and fireplaces she had designed and had installed in the hallway and the bedrooms, the window in the stairwell she had contrived out of dark green glass bottles, the lovingly painted tiles she had decorated when alone with Laura at Rosemerrin, now made them unhappy and were oppressive reminders of their loss.

Naturally, Leslie inherited Minny's share of the sale of the house at Southwell Gardens and her share of the house at Hyde Park Gate South.[14] It may have been because of the knowledge that he had profited financially from his marriage to Minny that he chose this time to buy a small cottage in Wimbledon for Anny's mother to move to with her caretaker. Whatever his shortcomings, Leslie was a remarkably scrupulous man. The cottage cost about nine hundred pounds.[15]

The acquisition of the cottage at Wimbledon made it far more convenient for Anny to visit her mother and she could stay overnight, if necessary, with her Ritchie cousins who now lived nearby. Anny's visits to Isabella became more frequent and more regular. Whatever the motive for the purchase, it was an imaginative gift of Leslie's.

In May, Anny went with Leslie to see the newly installed headstone for Minny's grave at Kensal Green. They had chosen the flat white marble slab to be carved by Anny's friend, the sculptor Marochetti, now living in exile from France in London. He had cut the headstone in raised lettering in memory of Minny, and decorated it with sprays of carved Alpine flowers. For the rest of his life, Leslie continued to associate Minny with the tiny, purple cyclamen she loved.[16] She had dug some up on their honeymoon in Switzerland, and coaxed them to grow in the small, grimy garden in South Kensington. When Anny went back to the grave two days later, she found 'my dear stone covered with blossoms & raindrops'.[17] She derived, in that vast acreage of monuments and tombstones on the outskirts of London, a melancholy form of consolation.

Just as they were getting ready to move house, Anny was sent for to visit her ageing aunt Jane Shawe, who was leading a wretched, half-forgotten existence at Clifton, near Bristol. Anny had always thought her aunt 'cracky', but now she was verging on insanity. Anny was moved to pity. 'I found my poor wasted old aunt sitting with her cats in her dreary room. It's a terrible thing to see . . . It's distracting to think of such a waste of life & generous feeling & power of affection.'[18] Aunt Jane harboured a passionate desire to return to Ireland where, long ago, she had been brought up with Isabella at Doneraile Court. Anny knew that this was a forlorn hope, but there was little she could do about it.

In a state of bewilderment, Anny retreated to the comfort of Clevedon Court, very much as her father might have done under similar circumstances. Clevedon Court was the stately girlhood home of her father's paramour, Mrs Brookfield, and was still occupied by her family, the Eltons. Thackeray had made it the setting for *The Newcomes*. Anny had wangled an invitation through Mrs Brookfield, and was delighted by the splendour of the place and the distraction the visit afforded from the plight of her Aunt Jane.

By June, they were on the wing. There was just time for the removal from Southwell Gardens to be accomplished before Anny, Leslie and Laura, together with Louise, went north to spend the summer in the Lake District. They went to Coniston and stayed in a small farmhouse on Victor Marshall's estate. It was close to the American, John W. Field and his wife Eliza, with whom Leslie and Minny had spent a delightful week in Philadelphia, and it was close to Ruskin, who had recently made Brantwood his home.

They arrived worn out. Leslie went off to the Victor Marshalls' at Monk's Coniston, and Anny slept on a sofa while their rooms were made ready. Leslie was touchingly, boyishly pleased to be among his beloved hills. Like Wordsworth, for whom Leslie had a deep admiration, he held that the lakes and mountains had a spontaneous affinity for what he believed to be the nobler feelings. As he put it, 'The elementary and deepest passions are most easily associated with the sublime and beautiful in nature.'[19] Anny shared his love of the Lake District and was equally responsive to its beauty, partly for the same reasons. But love the mountains as she did, she had no great liking for exercise and could not begin to comprehend Leslie's almost worshipful attitude to Pike O'Stickle and Haystack as being a sacred preparatory school for that great university of the Alps.

Victor Marshall was an unlikely choice of friend for Leslie, but he was one of the few new acquaintances to whom he had become increasingly attached since Minny's death. It is possible that their friendship owed something to the poignancy of their first meeting just over eighteen months before. Victor's brother James had been killed in a climbing accident on the Brouillard Glacier in September 1874, and Victor and his sister Julia had gone to Switzerland to make arrangements for the body. It was in a crisis such as this that Leslie's shyness vanished, and his very real kindness came to the fore as well as his natural ability to lead. In his position as ex-president of the Alpine Club, his authority was of immense practical help to both Victor and Julia in their shocked and bewildered state. The intimacy between them held fast. Jolly, comic, yet tinged with melancholy, Victor was 'a born Bohemian, spontaneously and naturally so . . . a man of great gifts, with a big, bulky figure & massive head . . . he painted and was devoted to music . . . He limped badly, having one leg shrunk & shorter than the other . . . His checked trousers used to be cleaned by being tied to a boat and rowed slowly round the lake'.[20] That April, Victor had married Tara Gordon, a Scottish heiress, 'clever, amusing & at that time an attractive little woman, with a narrow conventional soul that became more visible as the softness of youth wore off.'[21] But just then, Victor and Tara seemed enviably happy, while Julia, a formidable yet imaginative woman, was still living with them, running the household at Monk's Coniston. Various matchmaking matrons thought Leslie could do worse than to take Julia Marshall for his second wife.

The beauty of the landscape, however much they revelled in it, induced a painful melancholy in both Anny and Leslie. The crystal lake, the craggy hills and the profusion of wild flowers, forcibly reminded them of Minny who seemed 'more than ever *here*'.[22] Anny could not help longing unrestrainedly for her sister. 'It would have made Minny so happy to be here & every little flower & cloud & tint seems to ache for her.'[23] But Anny and Leslie did find a form of peace at Low Bank, the farmhouse wedged among the chestnut trees and meadows full of flowers, where they stayed. The terrible strain of the last seven months began to ease and, for the first time since Minny's death, they were able to show the genuine affection and concern they felt for each other. When Leslie moped or couldn't walk without being tired, Anny grew anxious. It was a pathetic sight to see the conqueror of the Shreckhorn defeated by the Old Man of Coniston, but Anny understood the reason for his lethargy and was moved to pity. She was very relieved that the Marshalls were so close. The company of Victor and visits to Monk's Coniston almost invariably succeeded in cheering Leslie and enlivening Anny's spirits.

Victor and Julia had kept up the Marshall tradition of entertaining and keeping pretty well open house to their friends, and now, with Tara, they were generous and hospitable hosts. Monk's Coniston was an oasis of culture and fun. Books were abundant and lay everywhere. Games of chess set out on small, inlaid tables proved absorbing, as did various card games including a very complicated and rather mad form of Old Maid. Anny and Julia, Victor and Tara all played the piano, and they played it very well. Victor and Leslie spent hours innocently amusing themselves and Laura by folding and cutting lengths of paper with swift, deft strokes which resulted in a sudden cascade of butterflies, or a stream of monkeys, attached only by their tails. These never failed to fascinate, particularly the young. Their neighbour, John Field, whom Leslie declared had a genius for friendship, was also a constant visitor. On fine days, they went sketching or enjoyed boating on the lake. Leslie punted and the Marshalls had what Anny called a lifeboat, while the painter and companion to Ruskin, Arthur Severn, floated about bareheaded in a sailing yacht.

If Leslie needed something to grouse about, it was more or less handed to him on a plate in Ruskin. Leslie always felt that he was treading on eggshells with Ruskin. He fancied that he had been criticised in *Fors Clavigera* for committing the calumny of smoking a pipe on a mountain peak, and said that Ruskin was 'one of those people who frighten me to death, and makes me want to sink into my shoes and forces me to be sulkily silent.' Yet he much admired Ruskin's writings and envied his secret for saying 'stinging' things, even if the price he paid for it, a morbid sensitivity, was one which Leslie refused to bid for.[24] He dreaded Anny dragging him off to Brantwood, and he knew she would.

Ruskin held no apparent fears for Anny. She had been used to the company of great men since childhood, and had met him on several occasions when she had acted as hostess for her father's elaborate dinner parties. They had forged a curious and unlikely intimacy. Sixteen years earlier, Ruskin had confided to Anny that he was one of the unhappiest men in the world.[25] It was a strange remark for a man of forty to make to a girl of twenty-two, but then Ruskin was a strange man and Anny, with her open and uncommonly sympathetic nature, invited such confidences.

Remembering their earlier friendship, Anny had no qualms in carrying Leslie off to Brantwood.

Leslie capitulated. He rowed along the lake and they took Laura with them. The lake was still, the light extraordinarily clear, the sun illuminating every blade of grass, every twig and leaf of the oak trees and honeysuckle growing on the near shore. Red squirrels dropped carelessly from the branches.[26] Leslie rowed with skill. He knew exactly when to dip the blades so that scarcely a drop of water disturbed the calm surface of the lake, leaving only the course of their passage in the wake behind. He cut a clean line in the direction of the small jetty. Brantwood stood high up on the slope, a large and sprawling two-storied house which Ruskin had converted to the dictates of his extremely exacting taste in the neo-gothic style. The many windows he had installed, some of them latticed, some of them with a multitude of small panes, the pristine white walls, the tall, steepled chimney pots, all reflected the rare quality of the Lakeland light. Leslie feathered the oars, and the boat struck with a hollow crunch against the stones of the tiny landing pier where a motley fleet of Ruskin's boats was anchored behind.

They scrambled out and walked up to the house through a path of fruit and flowers, carnations and strawberries, which zigzagged to the lawn in front of the Brantwood windows. Not just one, but three maids opened the door, and Anny noticed with a thrill the umbrella stand in the glass door. For all her insouciance, she held Ruskin in great esteem and quivered on recognising that the great man owned a brolly just like other people. And then her hopes were dashed: the maids told her most firmly that Ruskin saw no one without a previous appointment, that he refused to admit casual callers. Anny left her address at Low Bank Farm and then suddenly, Laura, who was bored, rushed away towards the lake and Anny was obliged to go bounding after her in a somewhat undignified fashion. Leslie rowed them back in silence along Coniston Water.

She need not have been so despondent. A few days later, Ruskin walked over to Low Bank Farm, dressed with some ceremony in a tall hat and frock-coat, spoke to her most affectionately and hospitably, struck the turf with his boot, and invited them to dinner at Brantwood. Leslie may have groaned, but Anny was delighted:

'The brightness of Brantwood, the squareness, and its unaffected comfortableness, were, I think, the chief characteristics. You had a general impression of solid, old-fashioned furniture, of amber-coloured damask curtains and coverings; there were Turners and other water-colour pictures in curly frames upon the drawing-room walls – a Prout, I think, among them; there was a noble Titian in the dining-room, and the full-length portrait of a child in a blue sash over the sideboard has become familiar since then to the readers of *Praeterita* . . . only the simplest and most natural arrangements for the comfort of the inmates and their guests, – Turkey carpets, steady round tables, and above all a sense of cheerful, hospitable kindness, which seems to be traditional at Brantwood.'[27]

That evening, 'the rooms were lighted by the slow sunset cross-lights from the lake without.'[28] Mrs Severn, who acted as housekeeper to Ruskin, sat behind a silver urn, while Ruskin, with his back to the window, filled their glasses with wine. The food was simple and excellent. They were given homemade wheaten bread and oat cakes, trout from the lake and strawberries from the garden. The strawberries were the most delicious Anny had ever tasted. The talk was every bit as good as the dinner, if not better. It seemed to take wings and fly away. Anny never could remember exactly what was said, for 'who can ever recall a good talk that is over?' but she could remember Ruskin explaining his theory that there should be 'a standard of fitness applied to every detail of life; and this standard, with a certain gracious malice, wit, hospitality, and remorselessness, he began to apply to one thing after another, to one person after another, to dress, to food, to books.' He turned to Leslie and described the shabby quality of mass-produced print that people put up with, and contrasted it with the splendour of the books he was printing for the use of the local shepherds. If this was galling for Leslie who, as editor of *The Cornhill Magazine* knew perfectly well that, however lamentable, it was not viable to produce a national magazine to the same high standard, he had too much sense to rise to the bait.

Anny and Ruskin resumed their old intimacy effortlessly. Once more, she became his confidante, and was able to put him back in touch with one of his old flames, Isabelle Maison.[29] When Leslie was irked by Ruskin's constant presence he would take himself off to the Marshalls, or smoke a pipe with his friend Jack Field. Anny continued to feel a revulsion for the mourning she and Laura were obliged to wear. She remembered how Minny had loathed it, and she knew that Ruskin had a marked aversion to women wearing black. '. . . If I had my way I should scarcely put on black. I didn't think so once. There was a great field full of lambs yesterday and chestnut trees in bud, which put me more in mind of Minny than all the gloom that ever was massed together.'[30] When George Smith sent her a present of a pair of gloves which were a perfect fit, she immediately dashed off to Brantwood to show them off to Ruskin, since she was sure he had noticed her old pair had holes and her fingers went through them, making her feel shabby and awkward. She may have been in thrall to Ruskin but, being Anny, she could not help being amused by some of the things at his 'lovely aesthetic encampment'.[31] In her thank-you letter to George Smith, she wrote, 'They are all in fits of delight over *scraps*, not the lake and the mountains, but a gooseberry or a feather off a chicken's head or something of that sort . . . Ruskin has beautiful old Bibles, and missals and above all such nice strawberries at his house. He says if you can draw a strawberry you can draw anything.'[32]

Anny missed Richmond, but they corresponded as often as the posts allowed, and she was growing more and more confident about their relationship. In spite of her inevitable ups and downs, she was beginning to thaw, to feel less numb, and was more content than she had been since Minny's death.

After leaving the Lake District, Anny and Leslie went with Laura and Louise to Seaford, on the Sussex coast. They took lodgings near Julia Duckworth's sister and brother-in-law, Mary and Herbert Fisher, and their tribe of eleven children. Julia and her own three children were staying with the Fishers. What with the consequent number of maids and nurses in attendance, they made up vast parties going down to the beach to swim, paddle, picnic, and play cricket on the sand. Herbert Fisher was tutor and private secretary to the Prince of Wales. Mary, noted for her beauty, was not remarkable for her liveliness of humour.* She could on occasion be stultifyingly oppressive, but however trying the atmosphere at the Fishers', it was outweighed by the fun all the children had on the beach and Anny's enjoyment in watching them. She also took great pleasure in Julia's company and found that she was able to confide her feelings about Richmond. It was an immense relief to be able to talk about him. Julia was not in the least concerned about the apparent unsuitability of their liaison. She was an inveterate matchmaker and a tremendous supporter of young lovers all her life. Leslie, for different reasons, would have liked to enjoy Julia's company too. But he was chagrined to realise that the beautiful, sad-faced widow was avoiding him.[33] He could not know that this was because she feared she bored him. It was beginning

---

* When, many years later, Mary Fisher was run over by a taxi and killed, her niece, Virginia Woolf, wrote to her own sister, Vanessa Bell, somewhat callously, that it seemed 'a positive stroke of genius – I mean the discomfort & self-sacrifice of it.' *The Letters of Virginia Woolf*, edited by Nigel Nicolson and Joanne Troutmann.

to dawn on Leslie, however mistily, that he was gradually growing increasingly dependent on her.

Anny and Leslie were back in London at 11 Hyde Park Gate South by the end of September. The house was still not completely ready, for the builders and decorators took far longer than had been envisaged and there were all the inevitable and vexing delays. The carpenter banging his hammer, first in the dining-room, then in the drawing-room, forced Anny to retreat to bed with a violent headache.[34] Leslie suffered too. They were both mouldy and out of spirits. The first dinner party they gave, to which they invited the Bryces[35] and Mrs Brookfield, was a dismal occasion. Everybody present was acutely conscious of Minny's absence and the evening tailed off in a minor key, leaving everybody with a feeling of awkwardness and sadness.

Exactly one day after the first anniversary of Minny's death, Richmond went up to London from Cambridge and stayed for three days at 11 Hyde Park Gate South. Anny went to meet him at the station, got there much too early in her eagerness, and had to hang about for half an hour before his train got in. In her excited frame of mind, with the crowds milling about, the noise of the steam engines, the glare of the gas lights, and the general confusion, the waiting seemed interminable. But when Richmond did arrive, he was 'very, very, very glad' to see her.[36] Leslie's sister Milly joined them for dinner. Afterwards, Anny and Richmond managed to have a 'long & *most interesting* conversation'. But however enthralling their talk, Richmond deserted Anny the next day to go and play football at Eton. She thought his behaviour base, but since Minny's death the least emotional excitement incapacitated her, and the previous evening had left her strained and done up. Foolishly, she agreed to go with some friends to the South Kensington Museum, but trailed after them in a state of exhaustion and had to go home. She felt ill and had to go to bed. Richmond looked in on her in the evening, but she wasn't fit for any more tête-à-têtes. The next day, she was well enough to lie on the sofa, but she felt wretched and unhappy. Wisely, Richmond spent most of the day out. When he went to the theatre in the evening, she felt rather hard done by, but she couldn't possibly have gone with him and would have proved dull company if he had stayed at home. When he left for Cambridge on the following day, they were sad to part.

In spite of Anny's collapse, Richmond's visit marked a significant point in their relationship. They were more certain of each other than ever. Anny was incapable of pretending anything other than she felt, but since there had been no specific proposal, there was nothing for her to announce to Leslie, or to anyone else, even though the nature of her intimacy with Richmond was becoming increasingly obvious.

18

Over the New Year 1877, Julia's parents, Dr and Mrs Jackson, invited Anny, Leslie and Laura to stay at their house, Saxonbury, near Frant in Kent. As a matter of course, Louise went with them, and Anny took her maid, Mary Anne. Saxonbury was an old house overlooking Erridge Park. Anny was continually conscious of the woodland sounds and scents. Indoors, the rooms were low-ceilinged, and the winter sunshine streamed in through the 'Goethe' windows.[37] She felt very much at home in the sleepy, peaceful environment, the rooms full of books and old-fashioned furniture, and objects from India which reminded her of her father's own Anglo-Indian origins. Maria Jackson, from all outward appearances, could not have been more different from Julia Margaret Cameron, whose favourite sister she actually was. Very beautiful, frail, tall and graceful, she had been a semi-invalid for years, and suffered from incurable rheumatism. But, ill as she was, she seemed to Anny to be much more lively and spirited than anyone else at Saxonbury. Her curiosity in the lives of others and her absolute belief in goodness was a source of comfort and inspiration to Anny. 'She loved her children profoundly & Poets & the Past & she was not religious but Religion somehow so intense so tender & merry & unworldly.'[38] In 1877 Mrs Jackson was still able to hobble about and took pleasure in her garden and at presiding at table.[39] Dr Jackson was an active, silver-haired, punctual old gentleman, 'a regular old Indian'.[40] A thoroughly conventional 'worshipper of respectability', impervious to his wife's pre-occupation with the poetical and lofty aspect of things, he was perfectly good-humoured and kindly. Despite the apparent lack of shared values, there was an evident and very real sense of deep love and affection between the two, which accounted in no small degree for the harmony of the atmosphere at Saxonbury.

In the evening, after a long siesta, Mrs Jackson would be carried downstairs, dressed in silk and wrapped in shawls, and they would all dine by lamplight. Afterwards, they adjourned to a small sitting-room. Mrs Jackson's conversation was mainly of the past, which fascinated Anny, especially since she could reminisce about Thackeray as a young man. But she also spoke of poets and poetry, and of Coventry Patmore in particular, for whom she had nursed a devotion for years. If Mrs Jackson had held initial reservations about Leslie, whose extreme shyness was often mistaken for cold sarcasm, these were soon dispelled by his genuine charm and his remarkable ability to memorise great tracts of poetry, a gift which Mrs Jackson shared. After a certain amount of general talk, she would invariably begin to quote verse, and when she left off, Leslie carried on.[41]

On the second day of their visit, Leslie learned that, like their father, his brother Fitzy had been made a baronet. The same day, Julia Marshall came over from Tunbridge Wells, some twelve miles away, to lunch with them. It was pouring with rain, and it rained so hard that Julia spent the night. Two days later, Anny drove over to Tunbridge Wells and had lunch with Julia in her house with its bow window and pretty view. They went to a toy shop and Anny bought presents for the children before getting back to Saxonbury in time for dinner. That evening Leslie confirmed Mrs Jackson's good opinion of him by reciting an ode by Swinburne.

The visit to Saxonbury was a pleasant interlude, but when they got back to London, Leslie was enveloped once again in a cloud of gloom. He was depressed and suffered from the most dreadful headaches, interspersed with bouts of neuralgia. He had not merely resigned from his clubs, but had given up going out to dinner, avoided Anny's visitors, and scarcely left the house at all except to stride off to Haymarket and buy more books from Baine's, his booksellers, or go to the office of the *Cornhill*. Julia Duckworth, Fitzy, and Milly were the only people he cared to see, with the rare exception of John Morley and Victor Marshall, neither of whom were in town very often. Sitting upstairs, scribbling away in his book-lined study at the top of the house, he emanated a terrible gloom which seeped through the floorboards and fairly suffocated the rest of the household. It was an unhealthy atmosphere for Laura, a backward but impressionable child, and it made Anny's life almost intolerable. If it hadn't been for her sympathy and natural good nature, she might have been tempted to leave. But that was precisely what she couldn't do. She was bound to Leslie, it would seem inextricably, by practical and financial ties, by the conventions of the day, and by the memory of Minny. But while Leslie remained plunged in gloom, Anny, like a stout, but charming version of Sleeping Beauty, was ready to be woken up.

Leslie had believed Minny when she had dismissed gossip about the relationship between Anny and Richmond as nonsense. By now, however, he could no longer fail to notice what was going on and viewed all symptoms of their love as ominous.[42] He was revolted by the discrepancy in their ages. He was terrified by yet another upheaval in the household.

Above all, he was jealous, and his jealousy made him moody and wretched. What made matters worse was that not only had Anny found an ally and support in Julia Duckworth, but so had Richmond. Julia was now receiving Richmond into her house, two doors away. Although discreet and a woman of great integrity, Julia did enjoy, possibly as a result of the loneliness of widowhood, dabbling in other people's affairs. But if she had a tendency to make other people's lives her business, she also had the diplomatic ability to pour oil on troubled waters.

Leslie now began to find fault with Anny quite unreasonably, and criticised her manner of dealing with Laura. Louise Meineke, Laura's German nurse, was partly at the bottom of the trouble. She was not a particularly intelligent woman, and was sly and deceitful.[43] There had been friction between Anny and Louise, and Louise took it into her head to disregard Anny's instructions. When appealed to, Leslie took Louise's side. He thought Anny far too lenient with Laura, even though he could not dismiss her success with the Thackeray children, Margie and Annie. He handled the situation clumsily, telling Louise that she need not take orders any longer from Anny. Julia, who was in and out of the house a good deal, remonstrated and told Leslie bluntly that he was not behaving properly by Anny.[44] Later, Leslie granted that Louise was 'a silly woman enough; but in my helplessness I trusted her a good deal, as she had been trusted by my Minny.'[45] But Minny had frequently found fault with Louise, and only a few months before Minny's death, there had been a blazing row.

Most rows, particularly domestic ones, can seem ridiculous in retrospect, and Minny's row with Louise had been no exception. The fact of the matter was that little Annie Thackeray had sat on Laura's hat. This provoked Louise, whose temper was no better than it should have been, to fly at Annie in such a passion that the child was thoroughly frightened. There was some doubt as to whether Louise had actually slapped Annie, who was not in her charge, but she had certainly raised her hand. Hearing a great hullabaloo from the nursery, Minny had run up the stairs and, amazed by the goings-on, '. . . told her that if she could not control her temper I should not think her fit to take care of Baby', with the result that 'Louise is lurking about to give me warning.'[46] Minny seldom made a fuss which wasn't warranted and, knowing Leslie's shortcomings, almost never involved him in domestic wrangles until after she had dealt with them. But on this occasion, she had written to Leslie in despair while he was away for a few days at Cambridge. Things were resolved but it looked bad for Louise. The incident was never referred to again, but Louise, at any rate, had not forgotten it. The present rift between Anny and Louise

a little pair of blue boots that her margins ... like at

created an uncomfortable situation whereby Anny had to live in a household where one of the servants had been authorised to disregard her. But the saddest aspect was that their altercation prejudiced Leslie in his opinion of Anny's ability to look after Laura, who was extremely fond of her aunt. Worst of all, the episode helped to poison the atmosphere at 11 Hyde Park Gate South.

They tried to pretend nothing had happened, for daily life had to go on. Leslie's blind friend, the political economist and advocator of women's suffrage, Henry Fawcett, came to lunch, and the same afternoon Anny paid a call on Mrs Merivale.

Given the highly strung characters and the increasingly wound-up circumstances, the semblance of ordinary life could not be kept up for very long, and very shortly afterwards the tension snapped. Even many years later, Leslie referred to it as 'the catastrophe'.[47] He went into the drawing-room and discovered Richmond kissing Anny. To Leslie's horror, it appeared that Anny liked it. Had he chosen to ignore the situation he could have closed the door and left them while he deliberated what, if anything, should be done. But this was not in Leslie's character. He burst in on them and demanded that they should either stop the affair or get married at once. By being so exigent, Leslie probably only hastened the inevitable. But he was confounded when Anny confronted him that very afternoon, and informed him that she was engaged to be married to Richmond.

Anny would be forty that June. If she wanted children, and both she and Richmond did, it was obvious that a long engagement was out of the question. But Richmond, who was only twenty-two, was still a student at Cambridge. Great things were expected of him. His tutors and his friends looked forward to 'seeing his name blazing among the immortals'.[48] Besides still having his degree to take, which everyone believed he would pass with shining honours, there was a serious snag to an immediate marriage. The Ritchies could hardly be said to be poor. Richmond's father, William Ritchie, had held an important post in India as Advocate General of Calcutta, with a salary of fifteen thousand pounds a year, but Richmond must work for his living. A principle was involved: it was the gentlemanly thing to do.

It does not seem to have occurred to Anny then, that she was asking Richmond to make an enormous sacrifice by marrying her. She was in love, extraordinarily unworldly, and blind to the fact that if he married her, he would automatically resign what promised to be a brilliant future. Quite what the nature of that future was, remained dazzlingly out of sight. But then, his talents were so varied that it was difficult to predict which one of the many paths open to him he might choose to follow. Undoubtedly he would make a mark whatever he did, but would not, his friends feared, soar to the heights if he cut short his time at Cambridge and made an improvident marriage. If Anny was blind to all this, Richmond made no attempt to enlighten her. He, too, was very much in love, in love with a highly popular authoress who happened to be his cousin, his godmother, and seventeen years older than himself. Nor did he seem to care that his union with Anny would flout all the conventions of the Establishment to which he belonged, not only by birth but by temperament. For her part, although by no means a bohemian, Anny was, *au fond*, no more of a true conformist than her father had ever been, and so secure was she in her small world, that to cock a snook at a convention which did not suit her came as second nature.

None of their immediate problems was helped by Leslie. His reaction to their engagement, which had not yet been made public, was bizarre. He had never made a secret of the fact that he did not care for Richmond. Now he began to display his innermost demons of self-pity and jealousy. He feared being left on his own with Laura, whom he had already succeeded in preventing from being under Anny's care. He was beginning to realise that his feelings for Julia Duckworth went far beyond those of ordinary friendship. Thoroughly bewildered, this intelligent, nervous and labyrinthine character was working himself into a frenzy. He turned what should have been a sublimely happy time for Anny into one of torment.

It was a great relief to everyone concerned when, on 16 January, Leslie went off on a much needed holiday to the Alps with his nephew Herbert Stephen, Fitzy's eldest son. They planned to join Leslie's old friend Loppé, the Swiss painter and alpinist, who had previously proposed to Anny, at Berne. Afterwards, they would go on to regain Leslie's beloved heights, climbing steadily on through the snow and ice. From Switzerland, Leslie wrote Anny eight letters, all of them affectionate, and none of them referring to her undeclared engagement. He sent messages and drawings to Laura, and in one he confessed, 'I am really surprised by my own strength and begin to think that I have been humbugging all the time. Ever since I wrote to you I have been up to my knees in snow with nothing to eat but scraps of bread and cheese and a bit of tongue . . .'[49] Yet, despite all his protestations, Leslie could not help recalling happier days in the Alps with Minny, and found that some of Tennyson's lines had lodged in his brain:

All along the valley where thy waters flow
I walked with one I loved two & thirty years ago
All along the valley while I walked today
The two & thirty years were a mist that rolled away
All along the valley by rock & wood & tree
The voice of the dead was a living voice to me.[50]

Although Leslie's absence delivered them from his badgering, neither Anny nor Richmond could take full advantage of it. Richmond was obliged to spend a week at Cambridge and Anny, exhausted by Leslie's disapproval and by her own emotions, became ill. Her doctor prescribed physic, rest, and a diet of baked apples. But when Richmond returned to London she revived momentarily, and the following evening they went for a long walk in the icy cold starlight.[51]

Leslie returned from his holiday looking much healthier and happier than he had since Minny's death. The following evening, 31 January, Richmond had a long talk with Leslie and Julia. It was astute of Richmond to include Julia, who had already shown herself to be his ally, and who clearly possessed uncommon influence on Leslie.

The doctor's prescription did not ameliorate matters for Anny. Her condition had become so bad that Leslie was shocked by her altered appearance. Anny herself admitted that she was quite overdone and it was decided that it would be better for everyone if she went to stay with Julia. Julia provided tea, sympathy, a cocoon of quiet, calf's-foot jelly, and loving care. After a few days of this tender regime, Anny could lie on the sofa in Julia's black and gold and vermilion drawing-room and receive visits from afternoon callers.

On 4 February, Mrs Ritchie and Mrs Brookfield went together to see her. Although the engagement was still unofficial, naturally both women knew of it. Mrs Ritchie had been aware of the romance between her son and Anny ever since 1874, when the flirtation had first become evident during that holiday in Italy, which now seemed so far away. She may have had reservations, foreseeing that the proposed marriage might harm Richmond's career, but she kept her doubts to herself, and showed Anny nothing but kindness. She and Mrs Brookfield had both known Anny since she was a child and felt a very natural concern for her. They invited her to go abroad with them. It was an imaginative invitation, for it would have precluded any further scenes with Leslie until it became possible to arrange a date for the wedding if, indeed, there was to be one. But, in the event, nothing came of the plan and neither Mrs Ritchie, Mrs Brookfield, nor Anny left England.

The next day, recumbent on Julia's sofa, Anny was quite oblivious of a new turn of events which would affect her directly but went almost unnoticed in the quiet cul-de-sac opposite Kensington Gardens. In the morning she was well enough to go for a carriage drive. In the afternoon Leslie called and brought Laura with him.[52] Anny, who had a forgiving disposition, was touched by his kindness. What she did not know then, was that at some point early in the morning Leslie had been striding down Kensington Gore on his way to the West End when, passing the gloomy old edifice of Knightsbridge Barracks, he suddenly said to himself, 'I am in love with Julia.'[53] This discovery came on him as a flash of revelation. Anny, who was an astute observer, would probably not have been as astounded as Leslie, for she had not been blind entirely to his increasing devotion to Julia. But Leslie, illuminated at the dingy Barracks, turned on his heel and walked back to Hyde Park Gate South. He did not have the patience to pursue his errands in the West End. He must put pen to paper and declare his love for Julia in a letter. Besides, the Balls were coming to dine.

Dearest Julia,

I am forced to say something to you which concerns me very much and you very little. It was revealed to me a little while ago that I loved you – as a man loves the woman he would marry. Your presence thrills me. You are always in my mind when I am away from you.

Now a sure instinct tells me that you have no such feeling for me. I have not the slightest illusion about this. I feel certain too that you will never have such a feeling for me. Nay, I am convinced that even if you loved me, I could hardly make you happy as my wife.

It is then hopeless for me to think of being your lover. But there is nothing which I more ardently wish than to be your friend – to be as close & trusted a friend as you will permit. I promise on my honour I will never speak to you of love again.

Why do I trouble you by speaking now? Perhaps I ought not, but I can't help it. When I am in your presence, your unsuspecting sweetness makes me love you more & more. I am haunted by illusions wh. I know – ah! so well! to be merely illusions. Yet I can't find it in my heart to keep away, lest you should think me indifferent when in fact I only feel too much. In short I don't see how to escape without your help. I write to put you on your guard against me for your own sake; to beg you to help me to be a friend without being a lover.

If you decide that I had better not see you just now or see you less often, I will obey you without a murmur. One word is all that will be enough. If, however, you trust me, I would rather continue to see you as at present. I feel that when I have given & you have accepted my promise, I shall be stronger & that with your help I shall be able to subside into an appropriate state of feeling. If you permit this, I shall know it from your silence.

But I will do whatever you tell me, if you have any commands to give. Whatever happens I shall love you (in one sense) as long as I live. I shall never be happier than when contributing in any way to your happiness. As I write, I feel half-mad & half-wicked, but I do not feel unfaithful to distant memories.

Anyhow & under any circumstance I am Your most devoted friend, L. Stephen

I am writing this (Monday) morning. I can't make up my mind to give you this before I have had one more evening with you on the old terms. Tomorrow we shall be different.*

Old acquaintances of Leslie's, the Balls had been his neighbours at Southwell Gardens, and had, for many years, rented a place not far from Freshwater. Although Minny had never attempted to disguise how much their company bored her, and had mocked them frequently, Leslie found John Ball amiable and accomplished. Editor of *The Alpine Guide*, John Ball and Leslie shared common interests. Luckily for Leslie, he had already asked Julia to make up a fourth at his table.

The dinner itself was not memorable, and if the Balls thought Leslie strangely silent, there was nothing unusual in that. At the end of the evening, Leslie gave Julia the letter, which he had managed to write between returning from Knightsbridge, visiting Anny and dressing for dinner. She threw him a glance of surprise, slipped the note between the folds of her black silk gown, and followed the Balls out of the house. Leslie pondered the consequences of his letter and was about to go upstairs to his study, when he was surprised by a knock on the door. There stood

* *Text* BL Add. Ms 57,222 This ms is Stephen's handwritten copy of his original letter, which has not survived. Paraphrased by Stephen in *MB*, p. 49, and by Jean Love, *Virginia Woolf*, pp. 78-9. I quote from Bicknell, Vol. I, pp. 188-9.

Anny

Julia, who had read the letter and returned on the impulse of the moment. They went up to his study together.

She told him that he had guessed her feelings about him accurately. She patted his shoulder gently and caressingly, and added that their marriage was out of the question, but that she trusted him implicitly, and they were not to move any further apart. They would remain on terms of closest friendship, but there was no hope of anything approaching more intimate relations between them. She left him to return to her house two doors away, where Anny was lying in bed still suffering from nervous exhaustion brought on by the very man to whom Julia had just pledged solemn friendship.

The following note from Julia to Leslie was, after her death, designated by him as 'Her reply to the opposite, I take it.'

> I can only thank you. Whatever I can be to you let me be. I hope it does not make life harder for you to hear that you are very dear to me, but I cannot bear to give you pain. Your love must be a blessing to me always. Do not tell me that I can trust you, don't you know that I do entirely? Whatever you say or do will be right to me. Do not put a strain on yourself with the idea that you may pain me by your words – that can never be. I must always care to hear all that you think and feel.
>
> Your ever affectionate J.D.*

It could have been worse. If, in some respects, Leslie was a disappointed man, he had not lost Julia irretrievably, and he did not give up hope entirely. Yet if his view of his own position had been enlightened it failed to illuminate his understanding of the situation existing between Anny and Richmond.

The impediment to Anny's marriage was not, as Leslie imagined, Mrs Ritchie's disapproval or, indeed, his own horror, but the question of Richmond's career. For even though the Ritchies had money, and even if Anny had sufficient private income for them both, everyone was agreed that if he was going to be Anny's husband, Richmond must follow a profession. There was some talk of the Post Office, but nothing was done about it, and the problem proved a stumbling block until Mrs Brookfield had her brainwave.[54] On 1 May, Anny went to call and found Mrs Brookfield's daughter Magdalene with her.[55] Now this was diplomatic of

* *Text* BL Add Ms 57,222 in the section called 'Extracts': Bicknell, Vol. I, p. 189.

Mrs Brookfield, since Magdalene had married Richmond's elder brother Willy and consequently knew better than most how matters really lay with her mother-in-law, Mrs Ritchie. She assured Anny that Mrs Ritchie would agree to anything Richmond wanted to do if only he discussed it with her, adding that Willy was anxious to be of use, and had offered to go down to Cambridge to see Richmond. And then Mrs Brookfield insisted that Anny should go with her there and then to see that Great Panjandrum of South Kensington, Sir Henry Cole. The two women went off together in a hansom and found him sitting in an armchair in his office, having only just returned from Manchester. But he was evidently expecting them, for Mrs Brookfield was no fool, and had clearly apprised him of the quandary they were in. Sir Henry had given the matter of Richmond's career a good deal of thought and, with the kindness and patience typical of him, explained the options open to Richmond as clearly as he could.

Looking at the two women seated before him – Mrs Brookfield, whom he had known since she was a young beauty, the Reverend William Brookfield's bride and the light of Thackeray's eyes – and at Thackeray's daughter, whom he had known and loved since she was a child and played with his own daughters, he was very likely reminded of his own youth. Cole had never forgotten how much he owed to Thomas Love Peacock, in whose house he and his father had lived during his own childhood. Peacock had befriended the young Henry and encouraged him to draw, as well as to study music. When, after a reversal of fortune, Peacock was obliged to seek remunerative work, he had heard of a vacancy in what was then the East India Company, and in 1819 he passed the very taxing examination.[56] Now, Sir Henry reflected, perhaps such a post was just the job for Richmond.

The Post Office, Sir Henry said, was a tiresome, humdrum drudgery of a life and did not have a particularly good social standing. It is possible that he was thinking of the writer, Anthony Trollope, who had slaved away for years in the Post Office: he was an amusing fellow and a successful novelist, but one could hardly call him a gentleman. And then there was the Record Office. That did have its advantages. There were interesting documents and interesting people and for a quiet, unambitious man, it would be ideal. But for a man of Richmond's qualities, Sir Henry was adamant that there was nothing to beat the Home Office or the India Office. Both were socially acceptable and, bearing in mind Richmond's longstanding family connections with India, it seemed clear that the India Office was the thing to try for. Peacock, he said, had been elected to it merely because of his knowledge of Greek. But then, that was a long time ago, and great changes had been made since the days of the East India Company.

Anny, who knew next to nothing about any Office, Public, Private, Home, Post or Indian, whirled away from that dear man's own office in a state of euphoria. Mrs Brookfield, too, had been so galvanised by Sir Henry's words of wisdom that, as Anny wrote to Richmond that night, 'She said if you were her son she should be wretched if you refused, & that it *had* made her so happy she became 25 she was so pleased . . . Send me a telegram for I want a sign.'[57]

Three days later, Anny went to Freshwater for the first time since Minny's death and Mrs Cameron's departure. She took the children, Margie and Annie, with her and as soon as she got there her spirits began to soar. That very day she got a telegram from Richmond. There was every likelihood that he would get a position at the India Office. The relief was immense and the excitement terrific.

What dismayed her was that Leslie, who complained bitterly how burdensome he found Anny's unofficial engagement, did not take advantage of her absence to let the matter rest. He was like one possessed, and positively bombarded her with letters of an increasingly strange nature. It says a great deal for Anny's understanding of human nature that her affection for Leslie survived the verbal battering rams which assailed her by virtually every post.

On learning of Richmond's hopes of a job at the India Office, Leslie replied, '. . . If he can I suppose that he will. Everyone seems to wish it. Assuming this, I wish to say one thing once for all. I have an extreme repugnance to talking about R. with you, because I hate all talk about such feelings and in this case my sympathy is so imperfect that I am afraid of being harried into some remark which would shock you.'[58] He was agitated by the very idea of Richmond being in and out of the house, and dreaded the Ritchies 'scurrying and bustling and talking nonsense and making scenes'. He urged Anny to get married at once and have it over and done with to spare his nerves. It did not occur to him that by insulting Richmond's family, he was also insulting Anny's own close relations and that her view of them was very different to his own. 'The Ritchies are good people in their way & mean the best I have no doubt; but they are capable of driving you mad out of pure kindness. They are young & talk as if years were of no importance. They delight in making scenes, wh. is a simple torture of your nerves. They go in for sentimentalising & speak, at the same time, as if you had the strength of a rhinoceros & were a strapping young cook of five & twenty . . .'[59]

It can scarcely have furthered Anny's cause that Leslie then went and brought his sledgehammer down on poor Frank Warre-Cornish, a perfectly innocent party, if ever there was one.[60] Leslie began a heated and perfectly ludicrous argument with Frank about whether Richmond should stay at Cambridge and take his degree, or go on reading for it in London after having left Cambridge, which, as Leslie knew, was a possible option.

It took the sensible Mrs Ritchie to unruffle his feathers. 'She talked about you & will do everything that is wanted. I have no doubt that she will consent to everything you and Richmond may determine. She said she would allow him his £200 a year & was otherwise pleasantly judicious in her remarks.'[61]

This came as no news to Anny, who had known all along that there was no serious opposition from Mrs Ritchie. Away from Leslie, in the security of the island, Anny began to see most of his bluster as mere guff. She wisely kept her own counsel, let matters cool down and began to feel that things were beginning to be less of an exhausting, dreary burden to her.

She was right to believe that fortune was beginning to smile on her again. The island was starting to work its old magic, and although she could not help recalling the times she had spent there with Minny, and missed her beloved Mrs Cameron, she let herself yield to its enchantment. The trees, already in leaf and many in blossom, seemed to Anny to be of a dazzling green. Wild flowers abounded, and she had taken congenial 'nice bowery lodgings' over the grocer's shop.[62] After all the months she had spent in Leslie's increasingly dour company, it was a wonderful relief to be in the society of the Tennysons, Mrs Hughes, and the Prinseps. So inextricably braided were the relations of that small corner of the intelligentsia, that it was in the presence of Julia Duckworth's uncle, Thoby Prinsep, that Anny finally received the telegram for which she had been waiting all along.

They were sitting in Watts' studio which stood at one end of the Prinseps' house, The Briary.[63] The studio was large, hung about with immense quantities of paintings by Watts, rather as though the walls were constructed from the pages torn from a giant's album of postage stamps. It smelt of turpentine and linseed oil as well as of old velvet, mothballs and the slightly rotten stench of the carnations and Madonna lilies with which Watts loved to adorn the place. It was an attractive and sympathetic atmosphere, and could not help reminding Anny, as well as Uncle Thoby, of those far-off days they had spent at his old home, Little Holland House, which had been torn down and replaced by the new studios in Melbury Road in Kensington. Uncle Thoby, his hair now so white that it resembled the white planed wood shavings in the grate,[64] was a man of uncommonly generous nature. A learned scholar of Oriental languages, he had spent a long and distinguished career in India: both the Marquis of Hastings and Lord William Bentinck declared he was the ablest man in the service. There was very little about the administration of India with which Uncle Thoby was not *au fait*. Anny was reading aloud to him when suddenly the postman turned up, carrying his great leather bag slung over his shoulder, and handed Anny the telegram directed by Richmond. Anny blurted out the contents to Uncle Thoby. She couldn't have been in better company. He knew not only about India, but he knew about love. After he had given her his blessing, Anny ran down the lane to tell old Mrs Hughes, and then on to Farringford. Richmond had got the position at the India Office and Mrs Ritchie had formally consented to the marriage.

Everybody, whatever their private reservations, was 'very very kind',[65] for they all loved Anny dearly, and her happiness was so great and brimming over. Two days later, the Tennysons gave a celebratory dinner for her at Farringford. It was a magical evening. The Prinseps, Mary Brotherton and

Mrs Hughes were present, and in the company of such intimate friends Anny was able to join in their reminiscences by the hour as well as to include them in speculations about her future.

Now that Anny's engagement to Richmond had at last been made public, she was swamped by 'piles and piles of letters'.[66] The general reaction was more favourable than she had feared. Naturally, no one wrote any letter of ill-will, but some of the less kind responses leaked out. Henry James was disgusted. Hallam Tennyson didn't believe it could be considered a real marriage. Millais, whose own marriage to Ruskin's divorced wife, Effie Grey, had previously caused such a scandal, was outraged. 'Preposterous! It shall not be! It shall not be!' he was heard to roar. George Eliot, on the other hand, who had always liked and admired Anny, was said to have been so deeply influenced by the event that she followed her example and married a very much younger man, Johnny Cross, in the near future. Answering a letter of congratulation from Andrew Hitchens, who had married May Prinsep, Anny wrote, 'If it were not for Richmond I should be afraid to take such a life's gift, but he knows his own mind so clearly that the blessing of affection seems to have lightened the darkness in which I am living . . . it has come like a miracle.'

During all the months of waiting and worrying, Anny had not been idle. She had immersed herself, as much as ill-health and her circumstances would allow, in writing a novella, *From An Island*. It is an exquisite form of *roman à clef* based on life at Freshwater. Anny never wrote an absolutely perfect book, but this is as perfect as anything she ever did write. Strongly reminiscent of Adelaide Sartoris' novel *A Week in a French Country House*, based on a week in the house of her sister-in-law the Marquise de l'Aigle, Anny's tiny masterpiece is set at Dimbola and takes place over a Friday to Monday. The story itself is slight, and concerns three different love affairs. Its strength lies not only in the characterisation and evocative descriptions of the island, but in the complexity of its point of view. It is written as though it were reflected in mirrors, and is seen partly through the eyes of the narrator, Mrs Campbell, a character largely based on Anny herself. The portraits of Tennyson, Mrs Cameron, Anny's cousins Pinkie and Blanche, as well as an endearing vignette of little Margie Thackeray, are telling and recognisable. The strangely misty, magical quality of the island is conveyed with rare perception, and the story told with a delicate insight coloured by flashes of humour.

Anny's imagery embraces the homely as well as the spiritual and the combination is a powerful one. She can make an observation such as this: 'Some people cannot put themselves into words, and they say, not the actual thing they are feeling but something quite unlike, and yet by no means all they would say. Some other people, it is true, have words enough, but no selves to put to them. Emilia never said a striking thing, rarely a pathetic one; but her commonplaces came often more near to me than the most passionate expressions of love or devotion. Something in the way she looked, in the tone when she spoke of the holly tree, touched me more than there seemed any occasion for. I cannot tell what it was; but this I do know, that silence, dullness, everything utters at times, the very stones cry out, and in one way or another love finds a language that we all can understand.'[67]

This is swiftly followed by the briefest of descriptions of 'Lady Jane, who was cutting up her mutton into long strips, calmly excited, and prepared for battle.' The tone is original and utterly true to herself. Much of its brilliance may be due to the fact that Anny's naturally highly strung temperament had been tuned to such a pitch that her writing poured out in an uninterrupted minor, but significant key.

And then she took the children back to London and got caught up, as Leslie had predicted, in the social whirl unavoidable for a popular novelist, the daughter of a famous one, about to make a controversial marriage.

Almost the first person she met was Richmond's brother, Willy. They met by chance whilst walking in the park, and as they talked and walked and took several turns about the Round Pond, Willy emphasised yet again how happy all the Ritchies were to welcome Anny as Richmond's bride, and that somehow, Leslie had been mistaken in his notions.[68] Anny was deeply moved. Leslie hated the constant stream of well-wishers pouring into the house at Hyde Park Gate South and, appalled by the invasion, he beat a retreat to the Lake District with Laura, Louise, and his sister Milly. They travelled by train and refreshed themselves on the journey by eating strawberries given to them by Julia.[69]

19

To all outward appearances, Milly Stephen seemed to be a whey-faced spinster, inclined to shrink from the responsibilities of life. She was tall, thin and stooping, but immensely dignified, if a little pompous, in her bearing. She invariably wore gowns of grey, generally of alpaca, cut so as to make her resemble a nun in a grey habit. It was not so much that Milly had withdrawn from worldly life as that she had never been part of it. She had been not so much her mother's slave, for Lady Stephen was no tyrant, as a devoted daughter, obedient to her mother's whims. After Lady Stephen's death in 1875, she suffered from a form of suppressed nervous breakdown from which she never fully recovered. It turned her into a dried flower, pressed between the leaves of an album which was never opened again. But Milly was no goose. Highly sensitive like all the Stephens, she had inherited the mixed blessing of being able to express herself, not directly with other people, but through the written word. She wrote very clearly and was the author of *The Service of the Poor* and *Strongholds of Quakerism*. She was attracted to the Quakers, 'finding something sympathetic in their quietism and semi-mystical tendencies'.[70] But Milly was as practical as she was mystical. Now that Minny was dead, and Anny was to marry, she thought it incumbent on her to help Leslie and to be responsible for Laura.

But while Leslie had found Anny exasperating, he now found Milly depressing. They were too alike to be of any use to each other. If, for the fun of it, Leslie put forth an argument, Milly took it so seriously that Leslie almost began to believe what he had said. If he began to doubt himself she had no idea what to do. If he felt gloomy, the tears would trickle down her cheeks. Where Anny had overstimulated him, Leslie now found Milly's meekness like a contagious form of mental influenza.[71]

Still suffering from grief, tortured by jealousy over Anny's impending marriage, and living on a see-saw of emotion in his new-found love for Julia, Leslie was now confronted by Laura's condition, which had become so pronounced that he could no longer ignore it.* It now appeared that she was mentally deficient, perverse; an idiot to Leslie's way of thinking. The realisation would haunt him for the rest of his life. Often accused of cruelty, he undoubtedly loved his daughter very dearly: if he blundered in his treatment of her, he blundered no more than the best accepted

---

* It is no longer possible to give an accurate diagnosis of what, specifically, was wrong with Laura but, with the advantages of hindsight and the disadvantages of any complete documentation of her medical history, it is very likely that Laura suffered from a form of autism complicated by Tourette's syndrome. It is equally possible that she was a victim of childhood schizophrenia, and it is almost certain that part of her troubles were caused by lack of oxygen in her head at her birth. At that time, very little was known about mental disorders, particularly in children. Even now, the causes of autism and childhood schizophrenia have not been fully determined, but neither disorder is believed to be caused due to any fault in the treatment on the part of the parents. The case of Laura is a particularly tragic one, which has never been fully understood.

medical opinion, which he went to a great deal of trouble and expense to obtain.

Minny had been anxious about Laura since her birth, and understandably so since she was born three months prematurely, weighed less than three pounds and had to be treated with infinite care. Minny looked after her with an uncommon degree of love and solicitude which Laura would never experience again. Laura detested meat. Minny never forced her to eat it, but fed her on a diet consisting mainly of goat's milk and fruit instead. What did worry Minny was that Laura's development seemed extraordinarily slow.[72] She was slow to walk, slow to talk, and slow, in fact, at reaching all the ordinary milestones of infancy. On the other hand, she displayed sudden fits of excitability, pouring out torrents of words all muddled up in English and German at such speed that they became tangled and unintelligible. Or she might take to dancing in a frantic fashion, or banging her fists on the piano. Minny seemed to understand instinctively that none of these demonstrations of what might have been interpreted as acts of wilfulness were Laura's fault, but the results of her condition.

After Minny's death, Laura was not exactly neglected but, inevitably, she was the victim of circumstance: it was a mistake on Leslie's part to have interfered with Anny's affectionate treatment of her. Laura was a pretty child, who would have been a beauty had it not been for her dull stare, but her imagination was a closed world to which no one ever found the key. She was bewildered and confused by the wretched atmosphere in the house after Minny's death. She must have missed her mother, and suffered from the rows between Leslie and Anny even if she did not actually witness them, which she very well may have done. Left to her own devices, mooning on the half-landing, she was a melancholy, baffled and angry child.

Now, aged five, her behaviour had regressed into habits which her elders found not only unacceptable, but intolerable. Forced to eat meat, she spat it out in gobbets at table. She developed a lockjaw way of talking, spasmodic utterings, queer speaking and semi-stammering, all of which contrasted strangely with her former torrents of gobbledy-gook.[73] She had fits of wild shrieking and howling, of passion and rage, and what Leslie called 'superficial tantrums'.

Leslie was bewildered and outraged by Laura's irrational conduct, yet his love for her never faltered. 'I had another argument with Laura today, but I am so far pleased that she tries to be good. That is a great change for I was beginning to doubt that she had any moral sense at all. I don't believe that the most refined of coquettes could tease more than that little mite. If Gerald ever falls in love with her he will have a bad time of it.

(iv)

(i)

(v)

(ii)

(iii)

Minny's note runs: (i) Laura Makepeace Stephen was born at 2 o'clock on the 6th of December. (the 7th, L.S.) She weighed under 3 lbs at her birth and was enveloped in cotton wool for a couple of months. She cut her first tooth at 6 months old & when she was 8 months old (ii) went with us to St Gervais & Chamonix, where she ascended the Montanvert. She said Papa when she was 6 months old & bow wow shortly after Mama when she was abt. 11 months old, but from the time she was 6 months old made very (iii) little progress for a year. As she was cutting her teeth in '72 we thought it better not to be abroad but took a house for 3 months in Cornwall & there she began to walk in September at 21 months old but said very few words & did not make much (iv) progress that winter having continual cramps at Easter and . . . & colds. We sent Laura to Freshwater where she improved. We took her again to Switzerland she was 2 years and a half old, she was very backward with her teeth & we discovered her 4 eye teeth only on the road from Geneva to Chamonix. We came home at the end of August (v) we took her to Freshwater where she was very well. Louise our German nurse went with us as well as Emily Blackwell who left us soon after we returned to town.

219

The way she puts her head on one side, like a mischievous magpie & makes a perfectly irrelevant remark with the most provoking good temper is little short of impish.'[74] He tried very hard to look on the bright side. Unfortunately, his uncharacteristic optimism was unfounded.

Laura's symptoms grew worse, not all at once, but in fits and starts which were painful for all concerned. Leslie always accounted for her condition by implying that she had inherited her grandmother Isabella's feeble mind and her great-aunt Jane's 'crackyness'. He did not care to think that if Laura's deficiencies were inherited, which is debatable, that they could have come from his side of the family. Leslie himself was neurotic, hypersensitive, disturbed, and occasionally childishly irritable. He never went mad, but at times he came very close to madness. The very idea of insanity terrified him. He blinkered his mind to the wild streak in the Stephen family, who had for generations shown signs of peculiarity quite different from, but every bit as aberrant as, those evinced by any of Anny and Minny's relations.

Milly's quiet but firm rule had a good effect on Laura. Under her supervision, Laura ceased to spit out the detested meat but 'pitched in to chicken & bacon & strawberries & cream like a glutton'. Milly undertook Laura's lessons, and on fine days, they spent the afternoons painting out of doors. Milly produced ladylike water-colours of the landscape, while Laura was inspired to paint a series of wild monsters. Sometimes, Leslie would take the child for a long walk so that she came home so tired and blowsy she seemed almost normal, and Leslie felt she was for 'all her faults such a tender & caressing little mite . . . that I feel my little thing's goodness more than before'.[75]

Milly might be dull, but her very unworldliness afforded Leslie some small amusement. They had both been discussing what Leslie called 'that infernal marriage', when it dawned on Leslie that Milly remained as bewildered by Anny as she had been on their first encounter all those years ago at Freshwater. 'She considers her as a sort of mysterious firework wh. may go off at any moment in any direction & would as soon think of living with her as taking in a bonassus for a lodger in Cheyne Walk. She wonders at R's audacity as a nervous old lady wonders at a man daring to carry a loaded pistol.'*[76]

---

* Leslie may have been dipping into Darwin. An aurochs, erroneously known as the European bison, the bonassus is a species of wild ox, a cumbersome beast noted for its mane of shaggy hair and its fatty hump. Extinct, except in zoos, the bonassus would have been a decided fish out of water in Cheyne Walk.

Julia, on the other hand, couldn't help wondering if Richmond would satisfy Anny's many and varied needs. She qualified this by adding how she could 'understand that he being enough for her she can begin life with him, for all the happiness she has had & all the sadness, she has never had any individual life. Her feelings have always been for others & she has never had any happiness all to herself'.[77]

Milly's reign lasted barely a month. Brother and sister's temperaments were incompatible, although they remained on very affectionate terms. Instead, his sister-in-law, Mary Stephen, Fitzy's wife, recommended a certain Fraulein Klappert, who had previously been nurse to her own children, to look after Laura.[78] Leslie may have realised, too, that Milly's presence would prove an obstacle to his securing Julia, with whom he was growing daily more in love.

It was not unreasonable of Anny to want to celebrate her marriage with all the conventional trappings of a lovely gown, a splendid wedding break-fast to be enjoyed by her quantities of friends and relations in reception rooms to be decorated with choice flowers, and for the toasts to be drunk in the best champagne. Above all, she wished to be married from her own home, and for the wedding breakfast to be given there.

This very natural desire triggered off a series of explosions from Leslie which landed in the form of epistolary missiles on Julia's elegant writing table in her morning-room. The contents could not fail to ricochet on Anny. In addition, he aimed several at her directly, and they wounded her

deeply. Matters were not helped that no actual date for the wedding had been arranged. The dithering infuriated Leslie still further. He still could not bear the thought of all the Ritchies and their friends. 'They will be wanting breakfasts or dinners or something & I, good gracious! I shall be as crusty as if I was having a tooth out. The thing is surely painful enough without these aggravations. I should not like a party to see me operated on for some ghastly disease.'[79]

Nearly all brides suffer from nerves before the wedding, and Anny had more to agitate her than most. To add to her worries, neither she nor Richmond had been able to find anywhere to live. Leslie immediately jumped to the conclusion that they would wish to live with him. He dreaded the idea and didn't bother to hide his apprehension. For Anny, this proved the last straw. She broke down and blew up and, in a way quite unlike her normally tolerant self, quarrelled with the very people whom she loved best.

It started with a 'horrid little scene' with Milly about the future of the Thackeray children, Margie and Annie.[80]* The spat between them was unpleasant and inconclusive. There was no time for any respite. The house was besieged by callers: Mrs Brookfield, Mrs Smith, Fitzy, Mr Synge and Mrs Dicey. The maids were worn to a frazzle by being constantly interrupted in their normal duties to open the front door and let the callers in. There were always extra places to be laid at table at mealtimes, for it was the custom among their friends to drop in unexpectedly at luncheon or dinner, quite apart from paying calls and wandering in uninvited to tea. And then the downstairs rooms grew stuffed to bursting point with wedding presents; saltcellars, eggcups, vases and toast-racks, not to mention the opulent candlesticks sent by Lady de Rothschild.

One hot afternoon, Milly came to lunch. Anny lost her voice, dashed off to an exhibition of Rembrandt etchings and wore herself out looking at ten possible houses for her and Richmond to live in, none of which was suitable. She took a cab home, returning dishevelled and out of temper. Richmond was waiting for her. Instead of sympathising, he was furious. This was the first time Richmond had lost his temper with Anny, or shown any sign of disillusionment. He, too, was suffering from nerves as well as the accumulated strain of the last few months. They had a long and dreadful scene on the balcony, which neither of them ever forgot.

---

* After Anny's marriage, the children went back to live with their father and stepmother, Edward and Eliza, but were always made welcome to stay with Anny and Richmond on extended visits.

Leslie observed shrewdly to Julia that half the trouble was that 'Anny remembers her age and R does not. Anny thinks that he ought to look up to her opinions & he does not in the least. She fancies that he ought not to interfere with her in various ways & he thinks he has a right to.'[81] Then, after more calls and dinners, Anny rounded on the unsuspecting Julia. Julia spent the next day in bed, while Anny and Richmond had another blazing row. Anny was in despair. To make matters worse, Uncle Arthur arrived two days early, the first of the wedding guests, much the worse for wear from some murky, seedy saloon.[82]

★

Last year only, the old church was still standing, in its iron cage, at the junction of the thoroughfares. It was the Church of England itself to Dolly and George Vanborough in those early church-going days of theirs. There was the old painting of the lion and the unicorn hanging down from the gallery; the light streaming through the brown saints over the communion table. In after-life the children may have seen other saints more glorious in crimson and purple, nobler piles and arches, but none of them seemed so near to heaven as the old Queen Anne building; and the wooden pew with its high stools, where they used to kneel on either side of their aunt, watching with awe-stricken faces the tears as they came falling from the widow's eyes.

ANNE THACKERAY, OLD KENSINGTON

Anny always called it a Bank Holiday Wedding. It was the only time Richmond could take off from his new post at the India Office. The ceremony took place early in the morning on 2 August 1877 at Kensington Church, conducted by the Reverend Mr Norwood. In spite of all the fuss, Leslie attended it. He cut a distinctly gloomy figure, a thin, tall cormorant dressed in the deepest mourning, who would have cast a blight on the proceedings if Anny and Richmond had not been so evidently absorbed in one another, their quarrels now forgotten. Julia, who stood next to Leslie, 'wore the thickest black velvet dress & heavy black veil, and gave the gloomiest, most tragic aspect to her side of the chancel'.[83] The rest of the wedding party consisted of jolly Ritchies and intimate friends, all delighted to celebrate the couple's marriage. The Tennysons did not go, for Emily was poorly and the poet reluctant to brave the crowd. But Lionel, in high spirits, was Richmond's best man, and Pinkie Ritchie was Anny's bridesmaid. Outwardly, Anny appeared to be very calm. Her wedding gown showed her at her best. It was elegant, cut in one sweep and tight-fitting, although her bonnet, a frilly affair of lace and muslin, rather spoiled the effect. Richmond looked the ideal bridegroom, handsome, strong and tender, and when they were asked to join hands in wedlock it seemed as though they would stand clasping each other by the hand for the rest of time. In fact, the service lasted only four minutes. It was hard on Mrs Brookfield to arrive just as it was over, and all the children in tears. Margie and Annie Thackeray and little Molly Warre Cornish wept copiously, little Annie sucking lozenges to stifle her sobs, while Stella Duckworth was still and silent 'with her mother's tragic mask'.[84] But they all cheered up at the lavish wedding breakfast back at 11 Hyde Park Gate South, and Richmond, to whom the children gravitated naturally, poured them out glasses of champagne, more efficacious than lozenges. Richmond was much to be congratulated, for in the space of a single year, he had been an undergraduate reading for the Classical Tripos, become a member of Government Office, and succeeded in marrying Anny. After the breakfast, they left for Guildford in a second-class railway carriage.

Once the event he had so much dreaded was over, Leslie did have the grace to admit what he had known all along, that he had treated Anny infamously. Even though 'the recollection of that marriage comes across me at intervals like a gritty thing one finds in one's food', he acknowledged he was 'remorseful of my repugnance to the marriage. It is not reasonable & I have a remorse as though I were not acting or feeling as Minny would have me feel to her sister . . . A & I are not really sympathetic to each other. I know that she is wonderfully good, that she has a real touch of genius & that, in short, she is in every way admirable. But I know it more than I feel it'.[85] Anny was far more perceptive than Leslie imagined. Before her wedding, she had been to see Julia and felt more sorry for her and Leslie than she could show. 'I ended by crying this time not for us,' she wrote to Richmond, 'but because it is so sad for her & Leslie & she doesn't know what to do – she said they envied us so this morning . . . & Leslie said we both looked so happy . . . I'm afraid Leslie is very, very unhappy. He says Julia has healed his wound but she cannot staunch the blood.'[86] After her marriage, Anny erased any ill-feeling she might have had towards Leslie. It was not in her nature to bear a grudge. She remained on close and affectionate terms with him for the rest of his life.

The newlyweds' trip to Guildford was not a honeymoon. That, they proposed to spend in the autumn. It was the first time in her life that

Anny had been involved with anyone who actually went out to work at a regular office job. It was not that she was unacquainted with work. Her father had been obliged to work immensely hard, writing and illustrating prodigiously before he could afford to have Anny and Minny to live with him in England. Later, she had observed him first-hand, acting as his amanuensis while he exhausted himself at his desk. But apart from visits to his publishers, and later *The Cornhill*, he did not go out to work. Most of his writing, he did at home. It was the same with Leslie, who spent most of his working life on the top floor of whichever London house he currently occupied, immersed in books from which he would later emerge to write at great length at his desk. Even when he, like Thackeray, became the editor of *The Cornhill*, he was more likely to receive his colleagues at home rather than venture forth to the office. Most of Anny's friends were either people like Tennyson, who worked intensely hard but rarely left his home, or they were the cultured rich, who did not have to work at all but enjoyed the privilege of being patrons of the arts. Now, Anny had to adjust not only to being a married woman, but being the wife of a man who took his job very seriously indeed. Her very honeymoon had to be postponed on account of his work, and even the fortnight near Guildford was interrupted by his frequent visits to his office in town.

Anny had been eagerly and largely instrumental in getting Richmond nominated for the India Office. But she knew next to nothing about the India Office and, quite frankly, cared even less; she simply realised that employment would enable Richmond to marry her. What she had failed to realise was that if Richmond went out to work, she would be left on her own, that she would miss him, that his attention would be given to an even more exacting object than herself. The realisation was a horrid shock.

She did not realise it at once. The Surrey countryside was lovely and, from Newland's Corner, they made excursions to the Hog's Back, walking sublimely happy through lush meadows and picking forget-me-nots by a brook. They drove out to Abinger Hatch, and watched the Bank Holiday couples courting as though they were in Arcadia. They went shopping, and Anny bought a writing-table and a drawing-room looking-glass for the house they had still not yet found. They had a lovely time at Sheen, wandered down an enchanted lane and were entranced by a farmyard full of pigs and chickens, with a meandering stream running through it, and they listened to that most English of sounds, the pealing of churchbells. But many years later, what Anny remembered most vividly was plodding along with Richmond through a turnip field. 'So much for impressions.'[87] Something went wrong.

Part of the trouble was that Richmond was exhausted. At Cambridge, he had been used to the company of a particularly witty and high-spirited set of fellow-undergraduates. He was a shining light in the Magpie & Stump, the debating society, together with Mrs Brookfield's son, the future actor Charles Brookfield, two of the Balfours, Spring-Rice, and Lord Colin Campbell. Howard Sturgis, Alfred and Edward Lyttelton, Hallam and Lionel Tennyson were among his closest friends. He had left the university without taking the first-class degree he had long been assured of, and suddenly found himself working in a position designed for a very much more experienced man. If he was not strikingly original, Richmond was undeniably clever. What made him stand out of the ordinary was that he combined brilliance with accuracy and thoroughness, qualities which seldom go in tandem. He would undoubtedly need his urbane humour to carry him through the inevitable tedium of his duties in the India Office.[88] Already, the demands at work were beginning to devour his time and attention. Coming back from the office on the train to Guildford, Richmond suffered some sort of nervous breakdown. It was not an auspicious start.

They went on to Frant, and saw Leslie and Julia at her parents' house, Saxonbury.[89] Leslie and Julia met them at the station. It was pouring with rain. Anny thought Leslie woefully thin, and he had what she called a soulful look in his face, which made her rather miserable. Picking her way through the puddles, and following Leslie and Julia flitting down the High Street together, the strangeness of their altered circumstances struck Anny forcibly. She looked round, and there was Richmond, absurdly young and handsome.[90] Julia was looking especially lovely, and welcomed them warmly into her parents' house. She had already prepared a beautiful five o'clock tea and sat behind the teapot, pouring out cups of scalding tea, and offering them slices of home-made bread and butter. Anny and Richmond had taken lodgings nearby and intended to spend the last few days of their holiday there. It was while she was eating Julia's bread and butter that Anny suddenly realised that she had left her entire trousseau in the train. Richmond very calmly arranged for it to be collected by Mrs Jackson's servant in the pony carriage. They may have got off to an uncertain start, but the course of their marriage was already determined.

20

By September, Anny and Richmond were installed in a rented house in Kensington. It was pleasant enough, with wood panelling in the drawing-room and on the staircase, which Anny liked, but it was only a temporary measure. They led a much more sociable life than Anny had been used to since Minny's death. Millais and Colonel Hamley often dined with them. Colonel Hamley was characteristically kind in arranging for Anny's nefarious Uncle Arthur to be taken in by the Thompsons, who now ran the small establishment where Anny's mother was still being cared for at Wimbledon.[91] Isabella had been in care, confined to a twilight existence apart since Anny was a child. Now, after years of such confinement, Isabella seemed to stir within her cocoon. She would never be able to lead an ordinary life, but she had regained a modicum of serenity, and enjoyed playing the small piano Thackeray had given her so long ago, watching the antics of the Thompsons' kitten, and recalling the past and the faces of her old friends.[92] Her partly regained animation was a source of immense pleasure to Anny. In October, she had another reason to rejoice. She was pregnant. The only shadows across her horizon were Charlotte Ritchie's final illness in the old house at Paris, and her increasing anxiety about Laura.

In July that summer, just a month before Anny and Richmond's wedding, Leslie had taken a curious step. He wrote to Fitzy and told him that he had made Richmond and Julia Laura's guardians in the event of his death, and that Julia would have the same authority over Laura as if Julia were the child's mother. He added that he intended to marry Julia, and even if she refused him it wouldn't be from want of mutual affection. He told Fitzy that Julia had agreed to undertake the guardianship of Laura, whether or not she consented to be Leslie's wife. He said that Anny's marriage would prevent her from being Laura's guardian, but of course she could see Laura as much as she liked.

Leslie had been indefatigable in his pursuit of Julia. Theirs was one of the strangest courtships in history, and his love letters to her must rank among the more bizarre of that genre. Although Leslie never recaptured the earlier, unalloyed happiness he had shared with Minny, the love he grew to feel for Julia was very deep and almost sacred. Julia was not only the most beautiful woman he had ever seen, but she possessed a charisma which left him mesmerised. Once anyone fell under Julia's spell, they never wished to be extricated. Her presence was vivid, and she had a manner of speech which was swift and staccato, her voice clear and round. She had a way of making people laugh at something that wasn't particularly remarkable, her own laughter dipping down into 'three diminishing ahs'.[93] Her fingers were long and square-tipped, and she wore exquisite jewellery: an opal ring, another of moonstones, bracelets of silver, and earrings which dangled, catching the light beneath her sad, severe, if beautiful regard. She had inherited a streak of originality from her mother and her eccentric aunts, and the mixture of absolute compliance with the rules of society and her oddly incongruous sense of humour made her very attractive. As a result of the demands of her relations, Julia was very seldom in one place for any prolonged period of time. Indeed, it was almost easier to distinguish her by her absence than by any categoric recollection. Badgered by Leslie's persistence and his incessant, carefully composed letters, she finally succumbed, and consented to marry him. They were married at the same church as Richmond and Anny had been a few months previously, on 26 March 1878, again early in the morning. They appeared as lugubrious a couple as they had at Anny's wedding, grave and thin and tall, remote from other people's sense of normal, nuptial rejoicing. They spent their honeymoon with the Duckworth children and little Laura at Eastnor Castle, the home of Julia's aunt Virginia, the Countess of Somers.

Anny and Richmond now needed a more permanent home than the one they rented at Bath Place. Like Minny, Anny had a near insatiable appetite for house-hunting. Mrs Brookfield and other members of her female acquaintance also became absorbed in the quest. Finally, in the middle of April, when Anny was heavily pregnant, she and Richmond moved into 27 Young Street.[94] It was opposite number 13, the house which Thackeray had bought with his hard-won earnings from his writing, and where Anny and Minny had spent some of their most impressionable years. Young Street was in a small backwater of Kensington, just below the High Street, and number 27, like its neighbours, was a modest, attractive Queen Anne house with bow windows and a very pretty fanlight over the front door. Its lack of convenience, antiquated domestic arrangements, narrow stairs, curious jumble of rooms and tiny, if elegant, wrought-iron fireplaces were more than compensated for by its charm, and the lovely garden at the back. It had 'an ancient medlar with a hole in it. There was also a lovely tall acacia tree. In those days, before Kensington Court, there were other gardens full of birds and trees beyond the walls and the tall spire of the church'.[95] They furnished the house with the surviving 'dear old household gods' from Palace Green days, and with more recent acquisitions, the ornaments and second-hand pieces Anny took so much pleasure in buying. If Leslie thought it sentimental of Anny to have returned to the street of her childhood, she could only point out that Hyde Park Gate South was where he had spent his infancy.

Anny gave birth to a healthy daughter on 1 June 1878, at four o'clock in the morning at Young Street. They named her Hester after Thackeray's heroine in *The Virginians*. 'All the birds were singing when Mrs Brookfield brought her to my bedside in her arms & said: "She has beautiful brown eyes like Richmond's."'[96]

Hester was christened at the old church in Kensington High Street where her parents, and later Leslie and Julia, had been married. Anny enjoyed the occasion. The ceremony was slightly delayed by Hester having a screaming fit after having been tricked out to the nines in a bonnet and gown, ribbons, lace, and other finery. Lady Martin (formerly the actress Helen Faucit, an old friend of Thackeray's, married to Sir Theodore Martin) and George Smith were the baby's godparents. Afterwards, everyone strolled back over the short distance from the church to the house in Young Street to a sumptuous tea-party, and were regaled with cake and strawberries and cream. Later in the evening, when the guests had gone and Anny and Richmond were basking in a glow of parental pride, the nurse went up to Anny and said, "'a lady, a rather strange-looking lady, appeared after the xting & threw a little shawl over Baby". When I saw the white shawl I knew it came from my dear Mrs Cameron.'[97]*

Anny was forty-one when Hester was born. Two years later, she had a son, William Makepeace Denis, always called Billy. At first glance, Anny seemed cut out for maternity. Certainly, she delighted in her children and recorded their infantile sayings and achievements with all the relish of a doting mother. But, as in so many other areas, Anny was uncommonly vague and almost fickle in her role as a mother, perhaps because she had

* The mysterious gift of the shawl is explained by the return visit of Julia Margaret Cameron and her husband from Ceylon in 1877. What remains a mystery is why Mrs Cameron chose not to attend Hester's christening or manage to meet Anny during her stay, over fourteen months. It is possible that though her love for Anny never faltered, she felt some repugnance for the Ritchie marriage. This is mere speculation on the part of the author.

lacked a mother's care herself. If she did not possess Minny's maternal qualities, her children thrived. One could no more blame Anny than one would a cat careless of her kittens. Apart from the nurses and maids, the children's most constant source of attention was Richmond. Hester, in particular, was her father's pet. Even after Richmond had worked long hours in the India Office, he made a point of spending time with the children on his return home. Anny adored them, read to them, took them to call on her distinguished aged acquaintance, but Richmond was a more dependable parent. One reason for Anny's apparent unreliability was the swift deterioration of her health. Shortly after Billy's birth, her rheumatism worsened dramatically, she became afflicted with excruciating sciatica, and later developed trouble with her thyroid gland.

Whatever the doubts had been about their engagement, Anny and Richmond were swiftly accepted as a well-matched couple among their circle of friends. Henry James, it is true, still found difficulty in surmounting his distaste for the alliance between Anny and her 'infantile husband', as he did at Anny being 'further advanced toward confinement . . . than I have ever seen a lady at a dinner party'.[98] But his prejudices wore away, and he grew increasingly fond of Anny in whose 'extreme good nature and erratic spontaneity I find something loveable and even touching. She has the minimum of common sense, but quite the maximum of good feeling'.[99]

For the most part, they saw a good deal of Mrs Brookfield and Richmond's sister Gussie and her husband Douglas Freshfield, as well as his brother Willy and his wife Magdalene. These people formed part of Anny's extended family, and they all lived within walking distance from each other in spacious old Kensington houses, set back from the main streets in sheltered, tree-lined squares and gardens. Gussie had just had a son, and together with Hester and Billy and Magdalene's daughter Adeline, the infant cousins became constant companions. Anny continued to see Laura and was frequently in and out of Julia's house, which Leslie and Laura had moved into. She kept in touch with them on a regular basis. By now, Leslie and Julia had started a new family, their four children, Vanessa, Thoby, Virginia and Adrian, being born in swift succession. Aunt Anny, as they called her, became a familiar figure to them all.

Anny made a point of going to all the new exhibitions, and enjoyed the theatre. Music was a great passion with Richmond and she went with him to most of the concerts. They gave tea-parties and dinner-parties galore, but not all of their entertainments were grand or formal by any means. Willy and Magdalene, who lived round the corner, formed a habit of dropping in of an evening, and Richmond played drafts with Willy in the gaslight. Those were simple family evenings which Richmond found infinitely relaxing after his hard day's grind at the India Office. He enjoyed the undemanding rules of the game and the gentle, humorous company of his favourite brother. Anny's At Home afternoons could equally well include Richmond's friends from Eton, Cambridge and the India Office, as well as the George Smiths, Browning, the Millais', and their close friends from very early days, Lionel and Eleanor Tennyson.

Lionel and Eleanor had known and been much attracted to each other since their early youth. Eleanor's father, Frederick Locker, was a minor poet. Her mother, Lady Charlotte, was intelligent, witty, and infinitely charming. When Lady Charlotte died, Emily Tennyson took the motherless Eleanor, a girl of eighteen, under her wing.[100] She invited Eleanor to Aldworth, their house in Sussex, and for holidays at Farringford. When the Tennysons were in London staying at their mansion flat near the Albert Hall, which Lady Charlotte had been instrumental in furnishing and decorating, they were frequently joined by Mr Locker and his daughter. Eleanor had inherited her mother's charm, wit, and intelligence. If she was occasionally petulant and wayward, she was so beguiling that it would have been churlish not to forgive her. Both the older Tennysons were much taken by her liveliness and her appetite for life, and they smiled on Lionel's increasing attachment. When Eleanor's father took it into his head to remarry, they were concerned for her. The new Mrs Locker did not seem likely to prove a sympathetic stepmother. An heiress of American origin (she insisted on adding her name to her husband's), Jane Locker-Lampson was an ardent Evangelical and disapproved vehemently of anything artistic. As for the theatre, it positively reeked of the Devil, and she would never set foot in such an iniquitous den. When Anny and Richmond went to stay at their house near Cromer, Anny described the visit as horribly spartan.[101]

In 1875, Mrs Locker-Lampson gave birth to a son, and Emily Tennyson, suspecting that Eleanor's nose had been put out of joint, invited her to accompany the Tennysons on a tour of France. At Pau, Lionel proposed and Eleanor accepted. Like his friend Richmond, he was still at Cambridge and had no prospects, but eventually, and with some difficulty, he too managed to get a post at the India Office as a junior clerk in the political department. The couple were married in February 1878, in an amazingly grand wedding at Westminster Abbey. Eleanor's aunt, Lady Augusta, had married no less a personage than Dean Stanley of Westminster Abbey, and it seemed, in some roundabout way not popular with everyone, that the grand wedding was a fitting tribute to Lionel's father, the Poet Laureate. The young Tennysons set up house at Sussex Place in Regent's Park.

Lionel and Eleanor were a sprightly and amusing couple, more up to date than Anny and Richmond (Anny's habit of living in her version of the past tended to immerse Richmond in it too). The young Tennysons gave them an entrée, which Richmond, in particular, appreciated, to a more flighty, more modern society. Since childhood, there had been an element of jealousy between Lionel and Richmond. Both children of promise, they had spent childhood holidays together, been at Eton and later Trinity together, and now they both worked at the India Office. Richmond had secured by far the better post and was showing himself to be increasingly proficient, while Lionel grew restless and fretful. It often appeared to outsiders that Richmond and Lionel were rivals at work, but both of them knew that this was not really true. Lionel's heart was not in his job. Even though he applied for the post as private secretary to Lord Derby, a position he failed to secure and which went to Richmond, Lionel was under no illusion that he merited it himself, and was able to be glad for Richmond. Fortunately for them both, Richmond was too tolerant and Lionel too graceful for either of them to allow what might have been an uncomfortable situation to affect their friendship.

Lionel made no secret of the fact that he was bored by what he called the 'red-tape bondage' at the India Office.[102] He had no alternative but to stick to it, since he was constantly strapped for cash. Anny stood godmother to the Tennysons' second son Charles. Their children played together and the adults entertained each other frequently at home. Lionel had always been stage-struck – at one time he had even considered acting professionally, like his friend Charles Brookfield – and he and Eleanor were both keen on giving theatrical evenings. Eleanor, dashing and captivating in the latest fashions, ignored any objections her stepmother might have sustained, and took part in the performances. Those evenings were great fun. Later, the Tennysons grew more ambitious, and held what were billed as 'Mrs Lionel Tennyson's Private Theatricals' in a small, hired theatre in which Lionel, Eleanor, Henry Cameron and Charles Brookfield performed.[103] Even if these events were not very successful, the members of the cast enjoyed them enormously.

Marriage did nothing to curb Anny's extravagance. She continued to spend far more than they could afford but, unlike Leslie, Richmond was remarkably tolerant. On one occasion when the Banker's Book was more unsatisfactory than usual, Anny recorded, '. . . he said he had been imprudent to marry & he was very glad he had been imprudent.'[104] If she consoled herself with the thought of Richmond's steady rise at the India Office, she had to acknowledge the unselfishly long, unstinting hours he put in at work. If Anny had been able to adapt to her new life better, it is possible that her marriage might have been a happier one, calling for less sacrifice on either of their parts.

They could not help being touched when Willy and Magdalene called round one evening, both looking embarrassed, unusually shy and apologetic. After some hesitation, Willy muttered that they had heard Richmond and Anny were in financial straits. Willy fumbled about in his pockets and produced a hundred pounds in bank notes and begged them to accept the money. Willy and Magdalene were both so eager and so obviously brimming with generosity, that Richmond and Anny compromised, although they knew that if Willy had seen the dreadful Banker's Book, he would have been aghast to know that all his bank notes put together were but a drop in the ocean. Richmond accepted thirty pounds as a present from his brother, and Anny dropped a hint to Magdalene. 'We should only pay our bills with a hundred pounds, you may as well pay yours.'[105] Magdalene agreed rather ruefully, but insisted they promised to spend the money.

Not long after that, Charles Darwin invited them to stay at Down, his rambling old house in Kent, full of curiosities. Typically, Anny muddled the day and they arrived a week before they were expected, but the butler was hospitable and the Darwins even more so, though they couldn't help laughing at Anny for her blunder. Anny was riveted by Darwin. He spoke of her father's old friend, Admiral Fitzroy, the Captain of the *Beagle*. He spoke about the migration of birds, and the habits of the tortoises on Ascension Island. He was wonderfully enthusiastic about everything, and then declared it was time for him to rest. At breakfast the next morning, he had a long conversation with Anny about Madame de Sévigné, and told her that when he was young, he and his brothers and sisters were so familiar with her letters that they nicknamed all their friends by the names of the people she described. The Ritchies left reluctantly, after Darwin had given them a tour of his garden and a close inspection of its worms. As it turned out, if Anny had gone on the day she was supposed to, Darwin would have been dead. '. . . Those two happy days were the last bright flash of that glorious life.'[106]

In February 1879, Magdalene's youngest child, Charlie, was born. Her elder children went to stay with Anny at Young Street, and they all rejoiced at Charlie's birth. Then came the news that Magdalene was seriously ill, and there followed terrible weeks with Magdalene in the throes of the fever. Mrs Brookfield took Anny to see her on her deathbed. Child after child was ushered into the room to kiss their dying mother. From behind the door, Anny could hear Richmond blowing his nose while she gazed into Magdalene's eyes. There was a little organ-grinder who used to wind his barrel organ regularly on the street corner for all the children to dance to. When he struck up his familiar tune, Anny ran out of the house and begged him, in despair, to go away as far as he could. Straw was laid down in the street to muffle the sounds of the horses' hoofs and the passing carriages. Richmond's sisters Blanche and Pinkie paced up and down outside the house, keeping up a hopeless vigil. When Mr Sartoris rode slowly by on his great horse, hoping for better news, the sisters could only shake their heads and Mr Sartoris threw up his hands in despair.[107] Magdalene was buried at Kensal Green. Not long afterwards, Willy and the children made their home with Mrs Brookfield on her family's estate at Clevedon Court, near Bristol. Magdalene's early death was a great sorrow to them all, and Richmond missed the company of his favourite brother Willy, and took it to heart very much.

Pinkie was not long returned from a visit to India, where she had stayed with her brother Gerald. There, she met Charles Lutyens, the elder brother of the architect, and they became engaged, but although a date had been made for the wedding, nobody was very happy about it. The Ritchies didn't take to Lutyens. He was said to be in financial difficulties yet, at the same time, he was unappealingly arrogant towards the Ritchies, considering they weren't grand enough, or well dressed enough. A few weeks before the wedding, his father, a much more sympathetic character, called on Gussie and implored her to have the engagement broken off, if it wouldn't break Pinkie's heart. Mr Lutyens, the father, was adamant that Charles wasn't good enough for Pinkie. Richmond was given the unenviable task of taking the message to her at Wimbledon. When he broke it to her, she started up out of her chair, more relieved than words could say. She had already broken her heart over Hallam Tennyson. When Richmond subsequently had to call on Charles Lutyens, he was sufficiently nervous to go and buy 'a new pair of chaste trousers' to face him in.[108] On the eve of what would have been her wedding day, Pinkie went to Anny and Richmond at Young Street and stayed with them for some time before she felt able to resume her life once more. Many years later, Richmond was instrumental in securing Edwin Lutyens, Charles' younger brother, the appointment of architect to the New Delhi planning commission, on condition that Lutyens should design the central buildings.

One of the inevitable consequences of Anny's clinging to the past through her continued friendships with the older generation, was her repeated sorrow at their deaths. A few days after hearing the news of Mrs Cameron's death far away in Ceylon, Anny received a parcel of extravagant gifts from her. It was typical of Mrs Cameron to contrive to remain overwhelmingly generous beyond the grave.* Anny couldn't help being amused, even though her amusement was overshadowed by sadness. Not long afterwards, Anny and Pinkie Ritchie both lunched with Adelaide Sartoris.[109] The two cousins, now sisters-in-law, spent a long and entrancing time with the elderly woman who had grown more vast and voluble than ever. She told them the sad, intriguing and convoluted story of her youth, and Anny was reminded of Lord Leighton's adoration of her. To Anny, Mrs Sartoris had always seemed to belong to a race apart. It was the last time Anny saw her.

* Mrs Cameron's involvement with things mystical did not cease after her death. Her ghost is said to haunt Dimbola to this day. It manifests itself in the reek of rotten fish.

The loss of both these women, Mrs Cameron and Mrs Sartoris, who
had influenced and inspired Anny, set up a chain of memories, both precious
and painful, which vividly recalled the visits the desolate sisters had spent
with Mrs Sartoris at Warnford and with Mrs Cameron on the Isle of Wight.
The increasing number of deaths of old friends from her father's circle
continued to sound a note of low, continuous threnody, which would have
been a source of anguish had it not been balanced by the pleasure she
found in her young family, as well as her creed of faith and optimism.

Her compulsion to write saved Anny from dwelling on the morbid. Her next choice of subject matter was one for which she seemed, at first, singularly ill-equipped. She decided to write the life of Madame de Sévigné. The idea had originated sometime in the autumn of 1877, when her old friend, the novelist Margaret Oliphant, suggested she should write it for Blackwood's series on Modern Classics. So far, Anny had been too preoccupied by marriage, maternity, and the social whirl to do anything beyond rereading Madame de Sévigné's letters. When Leslie first heard of the scheme, he was appalled. He wrote her a fierce letter imploring her to have nothing to do with it.

'Do, pray, leave Mme de Sévigné alone. I can't bear you to do things that you cannot do thoroughly well. Rd ought to make you understand the difference between cram & real knowledge. Why should you do what will put you on the level of every wretched scribbler who can remember dates & facts?'[110]

In the same vein, he gave her some sound advice about her need to research the period:

'To write about Mme de S. you ought first to be a thorough critic.

2ndly, familiar with French literature all through.

3rdly, specially well informed about the beginning of the eighteenth century including all the memoirs of the time, etc.;

4thly, to know all about editions wh. are authentic & full & wh. are not.

Otherwise you could not do anything worth doing if you were Sainte Beuve himself.

Get the literature up thoroughly, wh. will give you about 5 years' work, & you will be able to write much more than Mme de S. But if you haven't got it up, don't scamp it.

The one thing that vexes me about your work is that you haven't enough respect for [your] talents & your calling & are content to put in bits of sham & stucco alongside of really honest work.

You profess to believe me to be a critic, this is the very ABC of the doctrine. I feel it very strongly. It doesn't matter if people like me do a bit of penny-a-lining sometimes for bread & butter; but you artistic people ought to stick to your strong points.

Yr. L.S.'[111]

It was characteristic of Leslie to growl about a matter so dear to him without caring to muzzle himself.

Anny knew Leslie far too well to take umbrage. He was one of the finest editors in England, and she valued his advice and was grateful for it. Nevertheless, she went ahead and wrote the book. It took her over three years and it cannot be said that all of those years were spent in unremitting scholarship. As Leslie well knew, that was not Anny's forte. And yet the book is well researched and, when it came out in 1881, it was well received. Although Leslie was not far off the mark when he told Julia that Anny was one of the most uneducated persons he knew,[112] she was, nonetheless, extraordinarily well informed, even if in a patchy way, haphazard and lacking in method. But what she did know, she knew very well indeed. She had a remarkable ability not only to sympathise with her subject, but to convey a character as a living being without the slightest recourse to pedantry. As Julia remarked so perceptively, Anny had a genius for being other people.[113]

21

In the winter of 1882 Billy caught scarlet fever and had it very badly. Richmond took Hester to stay with Gussie and Douglas Freshfield from fear of infection, and Anny was left alone with Billy and the servants at Young Street. If Anny was not altogether a satisfactory mother on a daily basis, she always rose to the demands of a crisis where her children were concerned. But it was an anxious time and, immured in the house, fearful about her small son, and worn out from staying up late watching over him, Anny's spirits drooped. She depended on Richmond's visits. He dropped by every evening after leaving the office, and they exchanged news in the fading light, in the bare, wintry garden: it was too risky for Richmond to come into the house in case he caught the infection. That Christmas was a solitary one for Anny and Billy. They were shut up in the house and not allowed out. The sight of Richmond and Hester coming to wave at their pale, moon-faces through the nursery window from the street, was too pathetic to comfort them. A few days later, Lionel Tennyson came to call, and Anny was cheered by spending the afternoon pacing up and down the narrow confines of the garden with him.[114] His light-hearted, lackadaisical charm had appealed to Anny since he was a boy, and now, in her enforced solitude, he succeeded in enlivening her. She had just learned that Hester had fallen ill with another childish ailment and was relieved when Lionel suggested that Eleanor should go and see

her. By the time both children were on the mend, Anny had been cooped up for so long that she felt almost frightened of being with other people when Richmond took her out to a restaurant to celebrate the children's recovery. Anny decided to take the children to stay in lodgings on the South coast at Worthing, hoping that the sea air would put some colour back into their cheeks and that country cooking would fill out their lanky limbs. She herself needed a change, and their absence would give the servants a chance to fumigate the house against any lingering infection.[115]

Anny always insisted that it was the experience of the children's illnesses that bleak winter that determined her and Richmond to move to a larger house. Other people suggested that it might have been because Billy, who was growing into a young wag, had been picking up undesirable language from the regulars at The Greyhound, the pub a few doors down the road from the house in Young Street. Number 36a Rosary Gardens would be a red brick house off Hereford Square in South Kensington. It had yet to be designed and built for them, an enterprise they could ill afford. At the moment, their new house was still a castle in the air, but while Anny was at Worthing Richmond sent her a telegram confirming that he had been appointed private secretary to the Under-Secretary of State for India, Mr Kynaston Cross, MP. It was a considerable advancement and Anny was jubilant. She rushed down to the seashore with an overflowing heart and walked along the sands, her skirts billowing about her, and thanked God from the bottom of her heart. When Richmond joined them a few days later, her happiness seemed complete. She and the children had grown much stronger, and all four of them spent hours walking along the seashore, investigating rock-pools, seaweed and shells, undaunted by the cold, bracing winds. Anny and Richmond shared a euphoric relief now that the long, dismal winter was finally over. Anny was delighted when Richmond told her that when Billy's life had been in danger, he had gone ahead and put in a firm offer for Rosary Gardens. His offer, which was far in excess of their means, had been accepted.

Back in London, Anny threw herself into activity. Tennyson had agreed that she should write a personal memoir of him for publication. She was honoured by his confidence, and anxious to do it well and win his approval. Then George Smith suggested she should put a book together of four of her essays about women writers, which had appeared previously in *The Cornhill Magazine* under Leslie's editorship. It wasn't difficult for her to choose them. She selected essays on Jane Austen, Anna Laetitia Barbauld, Amelia Opie, and Maria Edgeworth.[116] The difficulty lay in her desire to tinker with them before she was satisfied that they were fit for republication.

At the same time, she was driving herself and a good many other people distracted by insisting on overseeing the plans for the new house. No one could be less suited for such a task. It was not that Anny wanted anything that was particularly hard to achieve, but she could never get it into her head that, unlike Minny, she did not have the gift of delegation. Her confused attempts to explain what she wanted only succeeded in confusing everyone else. Grates, banisters, window-sashes and doorknobs never led such a precarious existence as they did when drawn by Anny on myriad pieces of paper, which fluttered like confetti from her already disordered desk. She was, in short, an architect's nightmare. But despite all the chaos, she finished her memoir of Tennyson and, in the late spring, went down to Aldworth and handed him the proofs to scrutinise.

Tennyson read them at length and mumbled, 'flummery, flummery' and only corrected a word here and there. If Anny never learned to give clear directions, she could appreciate the poet's lesson and profit from it. 'I was not Dantë but he most assuredly was Virgil & it was a joy to have such a convincing lesson in style. Simply given and indisputably felt by me.'[117]

In May, she and Richmond went on a short holiday to Paris. It was the first time she had been there since their marriage. She couldn't help missing Charlotte very much, and thinking of the old days in the Avenue Sainte-Marie, where she and Minny had been brought up by their grandmother. But it was impossible not to be seduced by the gaiety and frivolity of the city in the spring. The lilacs were out, the cafés enticing, the streets thronged with women of all classes in the latest fashions. They went to the theatre and to the monstrous new Opera House. They went shopping, and they went to see old friends, including Pen Browning, the artist son of Robert and Elizabeth Browning, in his studio, and Ella Freeman. They went on a pleasure boat along the Seine, and they marvelled at how enormously Paris had changed during their lives yet how very little its identity had altered. They enjoyed themselves immensely and were sorry when the holiday was over.

Such jaunts, to Paris, to Antwerp, to Brussels, became a feature of their married life, and they both looked forward to them. They were precious interludes snatched from the demands of the India Office and domestic life. Holidays were no longer spent at Freshwater, although Anny kept on the lease of The Porch. Richmond enjoyed golf, fishing, and going for immensely long walks. His favourite companions were his brothers and sisters, whose company Anny, too, had enjoyed all her life.

In 1883, a plan was hatched for nearly all the Ritchies to spend the late summer near Blanche and Frank Warre Cornish's house in Devon. With their numerous children and attendant members of the households, the Ritchies made up an enormous clan. Blanche and Frank's house, The Chough's Nest, was near the small village of Lynton on the North Devon coast. It was a charmed spot, romantic and idyllic for holidays, perched high on cliffs above the sea. Behind, stretched a rolling landscape of farmland, curly lanes, and great, thick hedgerows. It was a perfect place to swim or picnic, read or sketch, fish for trout in the inland streams, or ride across the moorland on sturdy Exmoor ponies. Blanche found lodgings at a hotel, where Anny and the children were joined by Gussie and her brood and the elderly painter and illustrator Dicky Doyle, famed for his 'Fairy Pictures' and a friend of the entire family; he had designed the original cover of *Punch* and illustrated Thackeray's novel *The Newcomes*. [118] Mornings were spent with the children on the beach, their clothes stiff with seawater, sitting on rocks watching the light change between the sea and the land, or else lying among the heather on the cliffs, surrounded by ferns and grey boulders.[119] In the evenings they all gathered at the Chough's Nest, talking, laughing, drinking coffee in the lamplight after dinner, and then one or other of them would play the piano and the music streamed out into the night air. At Lynton, Anny suddenly had the inspiration for the title of her collection of essays. She wrote immediately to George Smith, 'Since I saw you, as I was crossing Lynton Moor in a storm, with the children tucked up on my knees, and the wind whirling, I thought of Macbeth's Three Witches, and then it suddenly occurred to me, that my new book ought to be called: A BOOK OF SIBYLS by Mrs Richmond Ritchie. It would also give a certain point to my volume, for the Sibyls were certainly authoresses.'[120]

For a long time, the idea had been germinating for a novel largely based on Anny's experience during the siege of Paris. She first referred to it in a letter to Richmond shortly before their marriage. It progressed

slowly, and she worked on it only intermittently. After Hester was born, she wrote to Pinkie, who was then in India, 'I don't believe Goethe himself could have written while Wolfgang was a baby.'[121] She promised Leslie that it would be ready for publication in *The Cornhill* in March 1884, but it wasn't. The move from Young Street to Rosary Gardens delayed the book further. *Mrs Dymond*, as the novel was titled, would have to wait.

They moved to Rosary Gardens in October. In spite of Anny's muddles and maladroitness, the house was very handsome and extremely well appointed. It had every modern convenience: gas lighting, speaking-tubes, a dumb-waiter for the dinners to be winched up from the basement kitchen to the elegant dining-room, hot water which gushed out of the taps to save the maids carrying the bathwater up the stairs in buckets.[122] Both Richmond and Anny were proud of it, but somehow, it lacked the charm of Young Street with its happy-go-lucky atmosphere. Ten days after they moved in, Anny smashed a small statuette of a little prince which had belonged to her father. Her carelessness made her feel like a murderess. Even though she persuaded the National Gallery to repair it, she never got over the feeling that the breakage was a bad omen.[123]

When Billy and Hester developed hacking coughs that winter, Blanche suggested that they might exchange houses as the children would benefit from the country air at Eton. Richmond knew his sister well enough to know she meant she would like to enjoy the delights of the hot water gushing out of the taps and talk to her maid down the speaking-tube, if her children didn't get hold of it first. The cold mist rising from the Thames and the dank water meadows at Eton did nothing to restore Billy and Hester's health, but Anny enjoyed the beauty of Blanche's great drawing-room, with its graceful blue majolica Italian pots on either side of the fireplace. An enormous fire was kept burning all day long, and she loved the great tapestry of the woodland scene which hung above it.[124] When Richmond was in London, she saw a good deal of Margaret Oliphant. She was entranced by the evening service at St George's, listening to the choristers singing 'Dulce Jubilate' high up in the organ loft, and she enjoyed gazing at a group of young lady violinists, whom she fancied resembled figures in a painting by Botticelli. Afterwards, she walked back across the cobbles in the wintry starlight.[125]

On 24 January 1885, young Margie Thackeray, now twenty, married Richmond's elder brother Gerald, who had settled in India. Margie, who had previously been regarded as Anny's unofficially adopted daughter would, on her marriage to Gerald, become her sister-in-law. It was one of those strange quirks of relationship which seemed to cluster around Anny and her family. Anny was delighted: of the two young Thackeray girls, she had always felt closer to Margie. Anxious that everything should be perfect for the wedding, she spent great sums of money, as much from enthusiasm as extravagance. If one ignored the bills, the wedding could be considered an unqualified success. Hordes of Ritchies and Thackerays waved the couple off at the station on the first lap of their passage to India. Although Margie was going to make her home so far away, she and Anny maintained a regular and intimate correspondence.

By February, it was no longer possible to ignore the accumulation of outstanding bills. The Banker's Book was obdurate. Richmond and Anny were forced to acknowledge that they had been too ambitious in taking on Rosary Gardens, and that it was far beyond their means at their present rate of spending. There seemed to be no obvious solution. Richmond worked longer hours at the India Office. Anny struggled to read the proofs of *Mrs Dymond* and make the necessary corrections. Leslie asked her to write an article on Elizabeth Barrett Browning for *The Dictionary of National Biography*. He was pleased with her piece after she had made a few of the changes he suggested. 'I think you have done Mrs B very well . . . Substantially, in spite of my criticisms, I really think it very well done indeed.'[126] She had written it under the strain of intense, recurring headaches compounded by financial anxiety. And then, in April, she fell victim to a series of attacks of sciatica.

The pain was intense and Anny had to abandon her work. Morphine proved the only relief from her agonies. She inhabited a nightmare world, governed by pain and peopled by the spectre of the Banker's Book and the ghost of General Gordon who seemed to take possession of her leg at night.[127] A nurse was brought in. Richmond devotedly sat up with her, brought her cups of tea, and comforted her in the middle of the night. When the pain lessened, he played patience by her bedside. But by the time she had begun to recover, her hair had turned white, and she was never again entirely free from pain for very long.

Julia and Leslie now suggested the Ritchies should take 11 Hyde Park Gate South, half of which was owned by Anny. That would immediately halve the rent. Anny was touched by the Stephens' concern and their offer, but neither she nor Richmond jumped at it. Their dithering was cut mercifully short by Pinkie and Mrs Ritchie, who persuaded them to move into Southmead, the large house at Wimbledon which Mrs Ritchie had made the family home. It was a generous offer, and Anny and

Minny with Laura in her arms.

Minny, Laura and Troy.

Laura with a doll.

Julia Jackson, April 1867,
by Julia Margaret Cameron.

Laura as a girl.

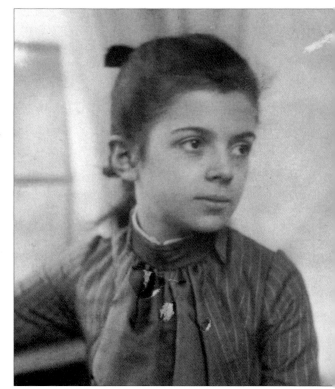

Anny reading.

Eleanor Tennyson.

Lionel Tennyson.

A cartoon version of
Frank Warre Cornish.

Anny at Aix-les-Bains.

Richmond in 1877.

Anny with irises.

Eleanor as a widow.

Richmond in the India Office.

Anny reading in her chair.

Richmond agreed at once. Richmond let Rosary Gardens for £200 a year to Mrs Kepple. But the move to Southmead meant that the intimacy of their independent married life was over. This was the beginning of yet another pattern in their marriage.

At this time, Richmond was aware of Lionel Tennyson's troubles, which coincided with his own. By now, Lionel was determined to leave the India Office, which he hated, at the first opportunity. But some other appointment must be found.

Years before, the Marquess of Dufferin and Ava had asked Tennyson to write some verses to be illuminated in Helen's Tower, a charming gazebo he had built in memory of his mother at Clandeboy, his estate in the north of Ireland. Now, Lord Dufferin had been appointed Viceroy for India. Never considering, or not caring, that it might be out of step with accepted protocol, Lionel's mother, Emily Tennyson, wrote to Lord Dufferin, and asked him whether he couldn't find some appointment for Lionel in his retinue.[128] Lord Dufferin couldn't, but in May 1885, he suggested that if Lionel could get leave from the India Office, he recommended a tour of India. It wasn't a job, a position, or an appointment. Lionel didn't mind: it would get him out of the office, out of England and, he hoped, out of a dreadful hole.

Like Richmond, Lionel had got himself into a financial mess, and now his marriage was endangered. Since the birth of their third son, Michael, a sickly child, he and Eleanor had drifted apart. Eleanor was a born flirt, and Lionel had recently been very much taken up by the young Margot Tennant. 'The difficulty of married life,' he wrote in his diary, 'at least to sensitive people, is to soften down their angles which cause constant irritation and destroy the health and peace of love. It is not so much that married people get tired of each other, but often they become uneasy in each other's presence.'[129] It was arranged that Lionel should have five months' leave from the India Office, and that he and Eleanor would leave their three small boys in Scotland with Eleanor's aunt, Lady Frances Baillie. When they set sail late that blustering October, they left the unresolved tangle of their troubles behind them, never dreaming of what lay ahead.

22

Southmead was a substantial house with various outbuildings and a large garden in the new, gentrified suburb of Wimbledon, next to the Common. Mrs Ritchie, who spent most of her time in her blue bow-windowed parlour upstairs, was genuinely pleased for Richmond to bring his family to live with her and her unmarried daughter Pinkie. Even so, she might have been forgiven for having second thoughts when Anny arrived prone with another attack of sciatica, and both the children suffering from measles.[130] But she remained undaunted, and gave them all a very heartfelt welcome.

Anny and Richmond were given spacious rooms on the ground floor for their daily use, and upstairs, Richmond had a dressing-room and a study leading out of Anny's bedroom so that he could work on the papers he brought back from the office and still be near her. The children had a nursery and a large yellow schoolroom where they played, kept a jackdaw in a wicker cage, and received very inadequate lessons from their governess.[131]

For Anny, the move was a great relief. She was released from the charade of responsibility for household duties and it was not in her nature to resent not being the mistress of her house. Except for the happy interlude at Young Street, she had always shared her homes, first with Minny and then with Leslie, ever since her father's death. She could see that for the children Southmead was paradise. They grew to love their grandmother and their Aunt Pinkie, and other relations who swarmed about the place. When he had time, Richmond took them for long walks across the Common, and they came flying back, rosy and well, bursting to tell Anny their adventures. The change was harder on Richmond, as he took much longer getting to and from work, catching a late train home when he was dog-tired.

Richmond was a much more typical product of the age he lived in than Anny, and it was a blow to his *amour propre* to forgo being paterfamilias in his own home. He appeared impassive, but he was deeply worried about Anny. At times it seemed as though a proper marriage had eluded him. The strain he felt under was occasionally intense, and the pretence of ordinary happiness he felt compelled to demonstrate exhausted him. He could not bear to wound Anny. He knew that she could never have been nursed so satisfactorily as at Southmead. And things could have been much worse. Under Mrs Ritchie's aegis, Southmead had a strong family atmosphere, ordered yet lively. Richmond and Anny knew they were lucky that they and the children could be absorbed into it. Richmond played golf, came home to read poetry aloud to her, settled into his role in the structure of things.

The hardest thing for Anny was not being able to take a more active part. She was often forced to keep to her bed and was plagued by general ill-health. But she had always been very fond of Pinkie, and now developed a very close intimacy with her mother-in-law, Mrs Ritchie. 'The whole house was pervaded with an atmosphere of dignified comfort. Cosy armchairs covered in flowing shiny chintz, big coal fires. A grand piano where Pinkie played sonatas.'[132] Reading aloud to Mrs Ritchie, listening to Pinkie playing the piano, watching the children tearing around the garden, Anny grew to love the place and, in the intervals between pain, became an influential member of the clan. '. . . There were so many people at Southmead, so many interests, Willy's children, our children, Cornishes & Freshfields all coming & going, all our friends & the Ritchies' friends & servants & retainers . . . & it all made such a crowd, friendly, harmonious, but incoherent & not very easy to describe.'[133]

While she was still in her sickroom, late that first spring at Southmead, she learnt that Lionel Tennyson was dangerously ill in India. He died on board ship, and was buried at sea before reaching Aden. The blow hit Anny very hard. She had known and loved Lionel since he was a child, and equated his sudden smile and infectious high spirits with the idyll that had been Freshwater. At first, they only knew the bare facts. The news trickled in very slowly. He had caught the fever. The doctors bungled things. He had pneumonia. Eleanor had moved him to Calcutta from Barrackpore. They stayed at Government House. The Dufferins were dismayed. Lord Dufferin had warned them of the dangers of malaria and made them promise to take quinine every day. He wrote distractedly to Lionel's parents. The doctors operated on Lionel's liver. His only chance was to leave the torpid heat of India, and hope that the sea-change would effect a miracle.[134] Margie Ritchie went to see them off at Calcutta, but she could not tear herself away, and travelled on with them until the ship docked at Ceylon.[135]

And then the rumours began to fly. They reached Anny and Richmond, who were trying to comfort each other for the loss of their friend. Eleanor had danced on deck all night, and flirted with the gentlemen on board while Lionel lay dying and Margie sat with him, trying to nurse him back to life.[136] After Margie left the ship and it steamed on to the Red Sea, Lionel was brought on deck from the stupefying heat of the cabin and died while singing hymns. He died beneath the merciless sun, and was committed to the deep the same night under 'a great silver, solemn moon'.[137] The rumours were malicious, but Richmond and Anny knew enough about the Tennysons' marriage to have some idea how they came about. Anny had loved Lionel, and she was fond of Eleanor and mourned for her. As for thinking of his parents' grief, it was more than she could contemplate without shuddering, although Emily, she knew, would find comfort from her faith. 'Such sorrows are beyond words. There are no words for such a loss.'[138] Later, Tennyson did mourn his son in verse:

> And now the Was, the Might-have-been,
> And those lone rites I have not seen
> And one drear sound I have not heard,
>
> Are dreams that scarce will let me be,
> Not there to bid my boy farewell,
> When That within the coffin fell,
> Fell — and flash'd into the Red Sea,

Beneath a hard Arabian moon
And alien stars. To question why
The sons before the fathers die,
Not mine! and I may meet him soon.

All that summer, and for most of the autumn, Anny was ill and in considerable pain. Richmond took her down to Ramsgate to take a cure, and they both held high hopes of it. '. . . There is no knowing what revivals may not be in store,' she wrote to Pinkie optimistically.[139] The change was not as dramatic as she had hoped, but for the first time in months she was able to walk without cringing in every bone. '. . . Richmond walked from Deal to Dover yesterday by the cliffs, and I (no less enterprising) walked down to the port and back, to see him off without an ache. This is the first time I have walked without any pain at all, and how I did enjoy it. The wind blew, six vulgar delightful steamers started off on their different ways, the sun, the shrimpers, the conjurors, the revivalist all came out on the sands.'[140]

Like a young girl, she delighted in the regained use of her legs, 'the most perfect invention there ever was for getting about'. Blanche went down to join her at Ramsgate. She, too, was in need of a cure. She had just given birth to her eighth child, Cecilia, and was beginning to suffer from what turned out to be a long and severe nervous breakdown. Although very fond of each other, Blanche and Anny had always had their little contentions, vying in their different ways for very much the same things, and could only overcome their difficulties by acknowledging them and laughing at them. They spent hours on the sands, sitting in deck chairs and writing long letters. They would become utterly engrossed in their writing, looking up to be half irritated, half amused by the other's presence. Blanche was in a pitiful state, her beauty crumpled, her face grown sallow and, rather to her surprise, Anny found that caring for her did her a power of good. When Blanche grew distracted and failed to order a cab, Anny delightedly hailed one for her, '*forgetting* my own handicap as I hurried along'.[141]

Her next decision was to go to France. It had been a long time since Anny had been abroad by herself, and it was in a spirit of trepidation mingled with adventure that she decided to take the waters at Aix-les-Bains. Her long illness had deprived her of all that old confidence she felt when she travelled independently during Minny's marriage to Leslie; her own marriage had fostered a feeling of dependency on Richmond. She would miss him. She would miss the children. But she was loath to lose the benefits to her health she had begun to feel at Ramsgate. Before she left, she conferred a million charges on Richmond. He was to look after everything: keep her informed about the children; about Mrs Ritchie's health; forward her letters; write to her constantly; look after himself. The most pressing charge she laid on him, however, was to look after Eleanor. She bitterly regretted she couldn't do so herself. She foresaw a multitude of difficulties awaiting the young widow to do with probate, with lawyers, with moving house, and all kinds of nuisances which Richmond would be the ideal person to disentangle. Richmond promised. Anny left for Aix-les-Bains with a lighter heart.

Situated on the shores of the Lac du Bourget, high up in the Savoie, and famous for its medicinal sulphurous springs, Aix-les-Bains looked more like a fashionable resort than a health spa. It was only on closer inspection that one noticed that many of the well-dressed visitors were disabled, that they walked stiffly, leaning on canes, or were driven in invalid carriages along the shores of the lake. There were enclaves of Germans and Russians

and English, and they tended, in the fashion of foreigners abroad, to keep their small worlds apart. There were grand hotels, and cafés under the trees crowded with ladies in bustles sitting at little tables and sipping the famous water.[142] It was a microcosm of society, and its habitués seemed as concerned with the details of its hierarchy and etiquette as they were with the benefits of the sulphur. Anny had a good many friends in the English contingency. The actress Fanny Kemble was staying in a beautiful apartment at one of the more select hotels, and presided over her salon hung with blue silk curtains. Mrs Cameron's sister Virginia, the Countess of Somers, was there. Queen Victoria's daughter, Princess Louise, together with a good many ladies-in-waiting, occupied the first floor of the same hotel where Anny stayed. 'I see great bouquets like teetotums all down the passage, which, I suppose, are tributes to H.R.H.'[143]

For her part, Anny was thankful she had stopped at Paris to get her new gowns made up. She enjoyed the petty absurdities within the community as much as anything, and could not help being reminded how her father had been amused by the intrigues at the Court of Weimar during his long stay there after leaving Cambridge. The atmosphere and charm of the place did as much to restore her as did the waters, which tasted very nastily of rotten eggs. She went to the baths every day. After the treatment, she explained in a letter to her mother, 'You are wrapped up in a blanket & carried right off by two porters who bring you up to your very bedroom.'[144] After a prescribed rest, she would join the other ladies sipping the beastly water at their favourite café, and glory in her surroundings. 'The Lake is so heaven blue and the sky so lake clear, and the vines seem to dance in rings with garlands of green and gold, and the little town glitters all day long in the sunshine.'[145]

She could not help being flattered when Princess Louise picked her out as a companion and took her on afternoon drives in her carriage. Anny found the Princess rather quaint and very charming. On one of their outings, they drove along a dusty road, with a lady-in-waiting on the back seat, until they reached a little farmhouse where they all got out. The Princess told Anny that nobody knew who she was, but she often went to see the old woman who lived there. They went into a low-ceilinged kitchen, where the table was partly laid for supper and an old woman was stirring potato soup over the fire. 'I'll stir the potatoes,' said the Princess. 'You can go about your business.' 'Then I'll finish laying the supper,' said the little old woman. After a while, the Princess began to play with the kitten. Through the window, they could see the carts coming back from the fields. The twilight began to fall and there was a sound of distant thunder. The old woman lit the lamp and her son came in, hungry after his work in the fields. The lady-in-waiting alerted the Princess to the storm, and they got up to go. It was a scene so much like a fictitious episode that Anny might have written herself, she could hardly believe it to be true. 'I thought to myself this is a fairy tale, a real cottage, and a real Princess stirring potatoes, and *me* looking on.'[146]

In asking Richmond to help Eleanor, Anny had been remarkably short-sighted. Eleanor had always held immense appeal for Richmond. Very attractive, young, sexy, and just then extraordinarily vulnerable, she represented the epitome of everything that Anny was not and which Richmond had been denied by his marriage. If Eleanor was devastated by Lionel's death, Richmond himself was at a singularly low ebb, with his defences down. He could not admit it to Anny, and hardly dared to admit it to himself, but his marriage had not turned out as he had hoped – although what he had hoped remained too vague and idealistic a concept even for

him to put into words. But if he was not disillusioned by Anny's continued ill-health and the consequent swiftness of her aging, the upheaval of
their living arrangements and the disorder of their finances, he was still
sensible of being drained by exhaustion. Far from being immune to
Eleanor, he became addicted to her charms. That she was his best friend's
widow only enhanced her in Richmond's eyes. He spent increasingly long
hours with her. Often, he spent the night in town, his letters to Anny
becoming more frequently 'dated by his midnight office lamp'.[147] A situation evolved which he could no longer ignore: he and Eleanor had fallen
in love. For Richmond, this was disastrous.

Richmond was too conscientious to cast off Anny for Eleanor. He
knew that he still loved Anny, that his feelings for her were genuine and
that, whatever happened, he would remain inextricably bound to her for
the rest of his life. But his love for her had altered and he had long
outgrown the starry-eyed emotions he had felt as a schoolboy. It went
against the very fibre of his soul as a gentleman to deceive Anny. He was
bound to tell her.

She seemed to take the news very calmly. Richmond was never quite
sure how much Anny already knew, how much she had guessed, and Anny
never told anyone. Much later, she destroyed any mention of the matter
in her private papers and almost everything she had overlooked, her daughter burned.[148] There remains only one small scrap which had enclosed
another letter, an explanation from Eleanor written long after the event,
and subsequently destroyed. Even so, people knew. They talked. Things
leaked out. It was in the nature of that small society of overlapping circles.
The affair was not forgotten in a hurry.

Even if she had suspected what was going on, Anny's apparent imper-
turbability was deceptive. She was shattered by Richmond's declaration.
All at once it seemed as though the basis of her existence had been axed
into splinters. She acted instinctively and decisively. She played upon
Richmond's sense of honour. She told him he must make up his mind.
She could wait. She sent him down to Brighton to reach a decision.

He knew then that it was hopeless. He had no choice at all. If he went
off with Eleanor, the scandal would be shocking and society unforgiving.
It would be an outrage for Thackeray's daughter to be abandoned for the
Poet Laureate's daughter-in-law. He and Eleanor would be banished to
some obscure foreign town to eke out a dingy and possibly embittered
existence. He would have to leave his children, as well as the establishment which had become the pivot of his life, the India Office, and everything which it stood for. He knew that if he had only cared lightly for

Eleanor, as many men in his walk of life cared for their mistresses, that might have proved, however awkward, an acceptable solution. But his feelings ran deeper and Eleanor reciprocated them. Their desire to build a new life together was very strong. Brooding over the matter at Brighton, Richmond capitulated as gracefully as he knew how. Two days after he had confronted Anny with the facts, he sent her a postcard, addressing her as 'Dearest Wife . . .'[149] He was only thirty-two.

Their marriage survived. Anny knew that her ill-health had played a part in the affair and she didn't hold it against Richmond. 'My health was so broken all this time that I was not able to keep up any regular ways – perhaps if I had been well I might have failed equally.'[150] But they never regained that easy footing which, if they had not taken exactly for granted, they had presumed on. Anny was always conscious how much she was indebted to Mrs Ritchie's tact and kindness. Curiously, it was largely because they were living at Southmead in less intensely intimate conditions, that they were able to build up their trust more easily than if they had been alone. Far from exiling Eleanor from their circle, it was important for all of them that friendship with her should be maintained and seen to be beyond reproach. The Tennyson children continued to play with the young Ritchies, and when Eleanor eventually remarried, her husband, Augustine Birrell, the writer and politician and a man of immense charm, became a good friend of both Richmond and Anny.[151]

Although the Ritchies and Birrells succeeded in patching things up so that no visible frayed edges were discernible, Richmond continued to have affairs with other women. Anny knew about them. She could scarcely help it, since nearly all his lovers belonged to their social circle. None threatened her marriage as Eleanor had, for the simple reason that Richmond was not in love with them. But Anny could not help finding it embarrassing when she and Richmond and one of his most enduring mistresses, Mrs Murray-Smith, were constantly guests at the same dinner parties, meeting in the drawing-rooms and at the tea-tables of the many friends they held in common. Anny was no prude, but she would have preferred it if Richmond could have found consolation in other quarters. However, she also knew him well enough to see that he would never find satisfaction unless it were provided by a woman from his own milieu. She accepted the situation with uncommon grace and understanding. Richmond was not ungrateful. Many years afterwards, probably in the late 1890s, he wrote this letter:

Pinkie has been talking to me about Eleanor, who has been pouring out to her. I wrote her a line myself when she left S in which I said she knew my life had not been spoilt, thanks to you, & that when I saw her with her children, I could not but hope that the difficulties of her life had been lightened . . . I know now by experience that nothing I can do is of any avail, which is the pity of it. And I will be all right in a day or two. Only if you don't mind I shan't come till Monday, when I shall have had two days to myself.

Don't you be frightened but write to me about yourself & the children. Next week I shall rise up & wash my face & eat like King David. There is no book like the Bible. But no man can deliver his brother or make agreement for him: for it cost more to redeem their souls, so he must leave that alone for ever. If I hadn't had you for an anchor, God knows what would have become of me.[152]

It was well over a year since Leslie had drawn Anny's attention to Laura's increasingly worrying condition. Anny's own ill-health and the trouble with Eleanor had obscured her horizons. In July 1885, Leslie was sufficiently anxious about Laura to call in the specialist, Langdon Down, and ask his opinion.[153] It was a gloomy one and Leslie didn't like it. He had to brace himself to accept the dismal future prophesied for his daughter.

Laura was now nearly sixteen. She was able to read passages from books like *Robinson Crusoe*, but it was difficult to know quite what she made of them. Her behaviour had grown so unpredictable as to be alarming. She veered between extremes of apathy and violence without any apparent cause. It seemed unlikely that she could remain at home. The three Duckworth children were now adolescent and the four young children by Julia and Leslie's marriage were growing rapidly. Julia did her best by Laura, but she did not love her. She had never relinquished the demands made on her by her own immediate family and innumerable friends and relations. George Duckworth, though still a schoolboy, took Leslie to task for having burdened his mother with looking after Laura. George thought it was too much for her. Leslie agreed, but he couldn't believe that Laura should be sent to an asylum, or 'that it would be good for her to be with idiots'.[154] He refused to give up hope easily. 'All I can say is that I shall not give up making her do what she can do because she *may* advance & equally because as soon as she is left to herself she falls back & becomes more apathetic & babyish.' By November 1886

Laura was sent for several months a year to be looked after by a Miss Searle in the country.

Leslie loved Laura, but he didn't know how to show it. Since Minny's death, Laura had known no unconditional love except for Anny's, and since Anny had moved to Southmead, they saw each other less often. Yet Laura was not altogether incapable. When she was being looked after by Miss Searle, she was put on a train to St Ives in Cornwall, where Leslie and Julia were expecting her. It was a long and complicated journey and when Leslie met the train at the junction, he discovered her luggage but couldn't see Laura, who was carried on by mistake to Penzance. She had to spend the night there, asked the porter what to do, and the station-master sent her to a temperance inn.[155] She showed remarkable presence of mind. At one time, years later, when Anny went to see Julia and Leslie at Hyde Park Gate South, Laura was there. When she saw Anny she rushed into her arms and remained in her embrace. She knew that Anny loved her, and was the only person who ever showed her any physical affection.

When Laura was finally committed to Earlswood Asylum at Redhill in Surrey under the care of Langdon Down, Anny went to see her quite often and occasionally had her to stay at Wimbledon. She was very good to Laura, but often found her visits to the asylum very distressing. Laura's fate was the tragedy of Leslie's life. 'Poor child – everything about her is inexpressibly sad to me.'[156] Her life was a long drawn-out disappointment, unremarked, and for many years ignored.*

With regard to her own family, Anny had no aptitude for teaching. Ill-health was sufficient reason to dismiss the inadequate governess and send the children to a day school close by, the South London College at Putney.

---

* Laura lived in a mental hospital at York for many years. She died at The Priory, a mental institution near Roehampton on 9 February 1945. Her inheritance – over £7,000 – was divided between her surviving half-brother and sister, Adrian Stephen and Vanessa Bell, neither of whom had seen her for many years. Anny had continued to have Laura to stay occasionally, and after her death, Laura used to go and stay with Hester. Belinda Norman-Butler, Anny's granddaughter, can remember Laura quite clearly. 'She was perfectly all right, really. Of course, she had some companion to look after her. She was craggy-looking, with the Stephen nose, like Leslie's. She was tall and thin and dressed in black lace. She was utterly sweet to us. She was *nice* to us. When we broke something once, I remember she helped us to pick up the pieces of some china we had smashed. She laughed and was kind, and didn't scold us.'

Hester was a clever child, quick to learn. Billy was a happy-go-lucky boy with a sunny nature, but he hadn't inherited Richmond's brilliance and they worried that he wouldn't do well at Eton, unable to live up to his father's reputation. Anny's friend, Lady Strachey, recommended Sedburgh in the West Riding of Yorkshire. It was a good choice. Later, he went to Trinity, Cambridge, more as part of the expected course for a young English gentleman, than from any academic leanings.

Always in quest for a cure for her arthritis, Anny was frequently away at Aix-les-Bains, Vichy, Malvern and Bath. She was a great believer in the benefits of ozone and sea air, which she always found did her good. The school holidays became occasions when they could all be together as a family, and Richmond could usually get away from the India Office to be with them. In the late summer of 1887, for example, they went to Aldeburgh on the Suffolk coast. They took a house right on the sea. The waves came practically up to the door at high tide, and the children were in seventh heaven, collecting starfish and crabs, and bathing. Anny, however, always connected things to old associations: she couldn't help thinking of Dickens and seeing even this holiday through his descriptions of them. 'A Pickwick Inn and Bar, a dark stable yard and Sam Weller with a lantern, and home by the sea walk, with the sailors talking together in the blackness, and then a little home interior, a lamp, the children peacefully playing at cards, and Estelle stitching – finally my room, my lamp, the fire lighting up the little square den and the sea washing and washing.'[157]

One of her father's closest friends, the poet Edward FitzGerald, had died eight years before, and now Dr Aldis Wright, a bumbling old Trinity Fellow, had started to edit FitzGerald's letters. Aldis Wright, who was known as 'Always Right', was not a particularly imaginative man, but since Anny had known FitzGerald very well, he naturally approached her and she agreed to help him. While she was at Aldeburgh, she met FitzGerald's niece, Annie Kerrich, a delightful old lady called Miss Lynn who had played with FitzGerald on the beach as a child, and Mr Basham the fish-monger. As part of the treatment for her arthritis, Anny had entirely given up eating red meat, and lived on chicken and quantities of fish. Mr Basham not only sold some of the best and freshest fish she had ever eaten, but had known FitzGerald very well. 'He is a handsome, charming, gentle-man by birth, he keeps himself by his fish-shop and Mr FitzGerald gave him his boat. We take little walks together and he carries his shrimps and talks quite enchantingly.'

From Aldeburgh, Anny took the children to Yarmouth, where they stood on the sands and watched the herring boats come in. Richmond had had to return to London and the India Office. One night, when a terrific storm blew up and the waves banged on the shore, Anny read *David Copperfield* aloud to the children: they listened spellbound as the wind and rain crashed about the house. The seaside had effected its cure, temporarily at least. 'I came a wreck and am going back with a new jib-boom, new sails and a new rudder.'

When Aldis Wright's collection of unpublished work by FitzGerald came out there was a furore. Aldis Wright had stupidly included a letter by FitzGerald in which he declared, 'Mrs Browning's death is rather a relief to me, I must say no more Aurora Leighs, thank God!' Browning was still alive, and he was understandably furious, wretched and indignant. He dashed off a poem seething with rage and published it in *The Athenaeum*:

To Edward FitzGerald

I chanced upon a new book yesterday:
I opened it and where my finger lay
'Twixt page and uncut page, these words I read
– Some six or seven at most – and learned thereby
That young FitzGerald, whom by ear and eye
She never knew, thanked God my wife was dead.
Ay, dead! and were yourself alive, good Fitz,
How to return your thanks would task my wits:
Kicking you seems the common lot of curs –
While more appropriate meeting lends you grace:
Surely to spit these glorifies your face –
Spitting from lips once sanctified by hers.

The London literary scene being what it was, most of Browning's surviving friends had also been friends of FitzGerald. It was all very unpleasant and embarrassing. Being a mere mortal, even if her sympathy was 'little short of the angels', Anny got caught up in it, trying to smooth things out. Emily Tennyson, who had been very fond of FitzGerald, sympathised: 'I wish Aldis Wright had not only omitted those words, but I wish that he had told people that FitzGerald lived for a time in a house in his Father's park on five shillings a week that he might give the rest of what he had to the poor. A man so kind never would have written those words had he thought they would be made public, or misunderstood by him to whom they were addressed.' The matter blew over. However outrageous Browning found FitzGerald's words, they had never been meant to be read by him, and the world would surely be a poorer place if people could not write freely to one another without fear of a breach of confidence.

An added worry was Aunt Jane: Anny's compassion for her aunt was mingled with despair. None of her efforts to help her succeeded. Now she learned that Aunt Jane was ill at Clifton. She travelled down by train, and arrived to find the old lady very bewildered, hardly knowing who she was. Anny stayed at a hotel and arranged for a professional nurse to stay with her aunt. Next, it was decided to admit Aunt Jane to a Home. Anny took her there and, after a dismal parting, went back to her hotel, sad and worn out. Almost immediately one of the staff from the Home arrived to tell her Aunt Jane had run away. Presently, she was discovered with a friend who had taken her in. More distressed and anxious about Aunt Jane than she cared to admit, Anny telegraphed Richmond who came at once. Suddenly, everything seemed much better. They decided that Aunt Jane would probably be happier with her friend, who was willing to look after her, than in the Home.

Then Mrs Ritchie fell ill. By the autumn of 1888 it was noticeable to all of them that she had grown very weak. On 1 November, Anny went out driving in her victoria to have lunch with a friend, and when she came home the maid said Mrs Ritchie had been taken very ill and had been asking for her. The doctor came. A nurse was called in. The family began to assemble. The next night, Anny found it difficult to sleep and went at six in the morning to Mrs Ritchie's room, where the nurse said that she had had a very bad night. But she looked very calm, and when Anny asked her if her presence troubled her, she said she liked Anny being there and 'a great light like a wing came into the eastern sky & she lay looking at it'.[158] Anny gave her a little brandy and water and then went back to her own room. Later, she was woken by Richmond standing by her bedside. He lay down half fainting on Anny's bed. Afterwards, Gussie told Anny that Richmond had remained in the room while his mother had been laid into her coffin.

His mother's death came as a severe blow to Richmond. 'In his deep heart he is so tender & so afraid of showing it or shamming that it makes him seem stern & cold when he is not one bit.'[159] His hard work at the India Office, his anxiety about Anny's health, the difficulties in their marriage, culminating in grief for his mother which he found impossible to express, proved too much for him. Richmond broke down and he was forced to take notice of his doctor and stay away from the India Office for most of that winter. He was not a difficult or demanding individual. He merely withdrew. But the retreat into his shell did not make life easy for Anny, and if it had not been for the trust they still held, despite all the strain that had been put upon it, the situation might have been beyond them both. They found that the recipe was to be extraordinarily kind to each other: it was a strategy that worked and one which came naturally to them both.

They delighted in reading aloud to each other in French as well as English, frequently pausing to look up a footnote or verify a fact. They spent hours discussing the merits of their favourite music and often played to each other on the piano, calling Pinkie in to confirm her version of someone else's rendering of a time-honoured classic, or a lesser known jingle. Very slowly, Richmond began to recover his lost ground as he and

Anny deliberated which books to order from Mudie's, how best to entertain their guests and simultaneously beat the Banker's Book. At the same
time, they surprised each other by their shared contentment at their altered,
but regained feeling of togetherness. In so doing, Anny realised that the
key to Richmond's character lay not so much in his early brilliance as in
his steadfast patience and attention to detail.

The sameness of Richmond's daily routine and the demands made of
him by the India Office, together with his social and domestic obliga-
tions were beginning to take their toll. He found conformity convenient.
The solidity of his life was reflected in his surroundings: in mahogany
sideboards, leather trunks, plush cushions, and a set of the Classics bound
in yellow calf with endpapers of Florentine marbling. If Anny was a late
developer, Richmond had been precocious. Now he was growing stout
and middle-aged, even though he was only thirty-four. If his doctor
ordered him to play golf, his tailor was obliged to insert gussets. He was
beginning, very gradually, to resemble a well-oiled porpoise. Innumerable
dinners, whether eaten at the club, at home, or in company at other
people's tables had expanded his girth, for the dinners were invariably
lengthy and composed of quantities of courses. Turtle soup might be
followed by turbot, roast leg of mutton and floury potatoes, braces of
pheasant accompanied by bread sauce seasoned with nutmeg and cloves,
and then steamed puddings, Nesselrode puddings and Cabinet puddings,
and the finest of English cheeses. And, of course, there were balloons of
brandy and the best Havanas whose smoke wreathed around his after
dinner statements. 'If I have succeeded at my work, it is because I have
stuck to it,' he said. And then he might join the ladies in the drawing-
room, or revert to the contents of the red boxes he invariably brought
home, whatever the hour, from the India Office. The fate of the sub-
continent of India was contained in those red boxes, and Richmond would
peruse the matter late into the night.

23

Anny never attempted to write another novel after *Mrs Dymond* in 1885.
It was a good note to end on. Many of her readers thought it her finest
work. Quite why she stopped writing fiction is a puzzle which Anny
herself didn't bother to pursue. Perhaps maternity fulfilled her old need
to invent imaginary worlds. Perhaps she simply didn't want to. It may

have had something to do with Richmond's affair with Eleanor, or it might have had something to do with all these reasons. Anny never disguised the fact that she was deeply superstitious, and there are elements in the plot of *Mrs Dymond* which she might have seen later to be uncomfortably close to reality. She had conceived the idea of her novel before her marriage and it took a long time to germinate. It is concerned not only with her heroine Susannah's yearning for her mother and her own salvation from 'mental suicide', which she finds against the violent background of Paris during the Commune of 1870 – a scene which Anny was exceptionally well qualified to describe – but with the relationship between Michael and Mary Marney. Like Anny, Mary is a considerably older wife married to a handsome, if feckless, man, attracted to younger women. 'People's lives as they really are and people's lives (for all their experience of the past) as they imagine them to be, are very different. And yet reality has often a great deal more spirit and inventions in it than the most romantic daydreams – it is less gracious, less *poseur* than one's imagination, but at the same time it is a great deal more amusing and original.'[160]

Anny may not have been aware of it, but she could not have written more succinctly about herself if she had tried. She had a genius for living and her life was far more interesting than anything she ever wrote. Her talent for writing fiction was genuine, but she never mastered the discipline of her craft. Her frequent flashes of perception are original and illuminating, but despite their considerable charm, each one of her novels is flawed and suffers from a lack of structure. Her plots waver and her tendency to indulge in lengthy passages of flowery description, together with her frequent use of the present tense seriously impair her novels. And yet Virginia Woolf, writing of Anny's virtues as a novelist, exclaimed: 'How is it possible . . . that a writer capable of such wit, such fantasy, marked by such a distinct and delightful personality, is not at least as famous as Mrs Gaskell, or as popular as Anthony Trollope? How has she escaped notice all these years? By what incredible oversight have we allowed passages which can only be matched in the classics of English fiction to be so hidden beneath the modern flood that the sight of them surprises like the flash of a jewel in a dust heap?'[161]

Virginia had known Anny all her life and, like her siblings, the children of Leslie and Julia Stephen, she always called her 'Aunt Anny' – although, in fact, Anny was only truly aunt to poor Laura. Anny's influence on Virginia was considerable, but although it was not in Virginia's nature to be guilty of nepotism, her assessment of Anny as a novelist is overrated.

She did concede that none of Anny's novels was a masterpiece, but she went too far when she claimed that they 'offer us a world unlike any other when we are setting out upon one of our voyages of the imagination. We doubt whether since the death of George Eliot in 1880 the same can be said of the work of any other Englishwoman'.[162] It is a pity that Virginia made such an extravagant statement, and it is unfair and absurd to put Anny in the same league as George Eliot or Elizabeth Gaskell. For while none of Anny's novels is comparable to *Middlemarch*, *Cousin Phyllis* or *Wives and Daughters*, such books of hers as *The Story of Elizabeth*, *The Village on the Cliff* and *Old Kensington* can still be read with pleasure and offer a highly idiosyncratic view of a now vanished world.

Anny stopped writing fiction, but she never stopped writing. She couldn't. She was a natural and compulsive writer and continued to write until the end of her life. Her last book, a collection of biographical essays called *From Friend to Friend*, was published posthumously in 1919. Earlier, she had shown herself to be mistress of a fine, if miniaturist art, which she made all her own. She had already published, in 1883, her essay on Tennyson and her contribution to *The Dictionary of National Biography*, her article on Elizabeth Barrett Browning. She followed these up with memoirs of Ruskin, Browning, Millais and Adelaide Sartoris amongst others. She was in the privileged position of having known her subjects intimately. 'My father lived in good company, so that even as children we were not always conscious of our privileges. Things certainly strike children oddly, partially and for unexpected reasons. They are so busy in early life with all that is going on on every side, that one person or another person, the visitor in the drawing-room, the tortoiseshell cat on the garden wall, the cook's little boy who has come to partake of cold pudding, all seem very nearly important one as the other. Perhaps I should not have been so much impressed by my first conscious sight of a poet, if I had then realised all the notabilities who came to our house from time to time.'[163] As a direct result of her first-hand knowledge of her subjects, her tone is intensely personal and often reveals as much about her own perception and state of mind as it does about the person she is describing.

Chapters from Some Memoirs, published in 1894, an episodic collection of autobiographical essays describing events and people of distinction she had known during her childhood, is one of her most interesting developments. She writes, as she so often did, from a double standpoint. The child she was is recalled by the woman she had become. These memoirs are extraordinarily vivid, for Anny possessed all her life a remarkable ability to recall. She never dismisses the folly of her own childish self but, viewing the child over her adult shoulder, she shows a fond forbearance. 'There is often a great deal more of the past in the future than there was in the past itself at the time. We go back to meet our old selves, more tolerant, forgiving our mistakes, understanding it all better, appreciating its simple joys and realities.'[164] Her portrait of the actress Fanny Kemble, in particular, is not merely memorable, but is a typical example of Anny's propensity to go through the looking-glass beyond the past she starts to describe into the past her subject now recalls. She describes Fanny Kemble making *As You Like It* come miraculously alive in her own drawing-room, and then goes on without a break to Mrs Kemble's own recollection of listening to her own aunt, the actress Sarah Siddons, recreating the witches' scene in *Macbeth*. 'The sense of storm and mystery and power was all around, Mrs Kemble said. One can imagine the scene, the dark-eyed maiden sitting at the feet of the great actress and receiving initiation from her failing hands.'[165]

Anny wrote more personally still. Much earlier, in that dreary winter after her father's death when she and Minny had been moving between Putney and Freshwater before they bought the house at Onslow Gardens, Anny had, purely for her own reasons, written a private and largely auto-biographical memoir. She wrote it from 1864-1866, and called it her ClaspBook. It was a large, leather-bound volume which had a brass clasp so that she could lock it. It is a tribute of love to her father, whom she recalls in a series of vignettes, brushing his hair, gesturing with his hands, and laughing at her and Minny as he poured the tea. It is also an intensely private journal where she agonises retrospectively about her past behav-iour and might-have-beens if only her father was still alive. It is a curious document, remembering her father and the life she and Minny led with him, interspersed with her own doubts, her grief, her guilt and her need to be loved. Its singularity lies in the tone she chose to adopt. Anny was twenty-six and already a published author, but she writes in the voice of a lonely child. And yet, whilst plaintive, it lacks self-pity. It conjures the image of a dutiful child taking infinite pains over the tiny, exacting demar-cations on a sampler picturing the past, to be worked in the neatest, microscopic stitches.

After Minny's death and shortly after her marriage to Richmond, when she was already expecting the birth of Hester, Anny wrote a second version of the ClaspBook early in 1878. It is dedicated to Laura. It was a common practice to dedicate a memoir to a member of the next generation. Anny may have intended Laura to read it one day, even though the child was already showing disturbing symptoms of mental deficiency. But at the time of writing this version of her memoir, Anny had no more idea than

Leslie how severe Laura's condition would prove to be. Whilst it covers the same ground as the original, it is the work of a more objective and more mature writer. If it lacks some of the spontaneity of the earlier version, it is more of a piece, and ends with a striking recollection of Minny – here called Mommee, as Laura's mother – as a child. 'I was 9 & Mommee was 6 when we came to live in Young Street with our Papa. It was winter-time & a nice fire was burning in the drawing-room & all the old *Punch* books were out upon the table & some day you must come over the old house & see the room Mommee lived in. I think she liked the garden best of all. She used to dance about on the little green lawn & her long thick curls used to shine so, that I used to look out of the window at them; sometimes she would turn round & round as quick as she could go & then her hair would seem like a burning bush.'[166]

Her finest achievement in the field of biographical recollection is indisputably the *Notes and Introductions* she wrote for the republication of Thackeray's works in the *Biographical Edition*, published in thirteen volumes between 1898-99. Although Thackeray had died intestate, he had made it perfectly clear to Anny that he did not want any biography of him to be written. 'Papa said when I drop there is to be no life of me, *mind* this & consider it as my last testament & desire.' As half in love with the memory of her father as she had been with him when he was alive, Anny felt bound to respect this. Like many writers, she was fed and nurtured by the past. She kept it alive in her essays, vignettes and memoirs. In 1894, when she accepted Reginald Smith's offer to write the biographical prefaces to the new edition of her father's work, she saw a way round the embargo which did not offend her sense of filial fidelity, while supplying the public with a much wanted portrait. These evocative, 'magnanimous and gentle' pen portraits won great praise and proved immensely popular.[167] Swinburne, whom she still saw occasionally, strolling over Wimbledon Common and staring at ponds, wrote in *The Quarterly Review* of her *Introductions*, 'To the exquisite genius, the tender devotion, the faultless taste and unfailing tact of his daughter, we owe the most perfect memorial raised to the fame and to the character of any great writer on record by any editor or commentator or writer of prefaces and preludes to his work.'[168] Anny took great care not only with her introductions, but also with the presentation of the volumes themselves. 'One thing I do think we might with advantage borrow from the various Melville Editions – printing the yellow facsimiles to each novel in turn. It gives a certain character to the books to appear with their old dress & habit.'[169] It was a felicitous thought and the result was a success.

Virginia Woolf thought so too. She may have exaggerated Anny's qualities as a novelist, but she was not wide off the mark when, in her obituary of Anny for *The Times Literary Supplement*, 6 March 1919, she wrote:
'She will be the unacknowledged source of much that remains in men's
minds about the Victorian age. She will be the transparent medium through
which we behold the dead. We shall see them lit up by her tender and
radiant glow. Above all and for ever she will be the companion and inter-
preter of her father whose spirit she had made to walk among us not
only because she wrote of him but because, even more wonderfully, lived
in him. It would have pleased her well to claim no separate lot for herself,
but to be merged in the greater light of his memory. Praise of her own
work would have pleased her, to realise with what a benediction many
are today turning to the thought of her, thanking her not only for her
work, but thanking her more profoundly for the bountiful and magnanimous nature in which all tender and enchanting things seemed to grow
– a garden, one might call it, where the air blew sweetly and freely and
the bird of the soul raised an unpremeditated song of thanksgiving for
the life that it had found so good.'[170]

As she made clear, Virginia appreciated Anny's loveable, if occasionally
bewildering character – qualities which are reflected in Anny's writing.
While Virginia paid tribute to the woman she had both admired and
ridiculed since childhood, she adopted a vein of hyperbole as if the unre-
strained enthusiasm of Anny's own writing was contagious. 'To embrace
oddities and produce a charming, laughing harmony from incongruities
was her genius in life and letters . . . She was a mistress of phrases which
exalt and define and set people in the midst of a comedy . . . And the
music to which she dances, frail and fantastic, but true and distinct, will
sound on outside our formidable residences when all the brass bands of
literature have (let us hope) blared themselves to perdition.'[171]

In her novel *Night and Day*, which Virginia submitted to her publisher
and half-brother Gerald Duckworth in April 1919, shortly after Anny's
death, Virginia based the character of Mrs Hilbery on Anny and the likeness is remarkable. Virginia knew it. 'My only triumph in *Night and Day*
is that the Ritchies are furious with me for Mrs Hilbery,' she wrote to
her sister, the painter, Vanessa Bell.[172] In the novel, Mrs Hilbery is the
mother of the heroine Katherine and, very much as Anny would have,
she brings her daughter and Ralph together, convinced of the power of
romantic love. 'Ideas came to her chiefly when she was in motion. She
liked to perambulate the room with a duster in her hand, with which she
stopped to polish the backs of already lustrous books, musing and romanc-

ing as she did so. Suddenly the right phrase or the penetrating point of view would suggest itself and she would drop her duster and write ecstatically for a few breathless moments; and then the mood would pass away, and the duster would be sought for and the old books polished again. These spells of inspiration never burnt steadily, but flicker over the gigantic mass of the subject as capriciously as a will-o'-the-wisp, lighting now on this point now on that . . . And yet they were so brilliant, these paragraphs, so nobly phrased, so lightning-like in their illumination, that the dead seemed to crowd the very room.'[173]

Although Anny's health had failed, she still did not feel her age. Her enthusiasms and observations were those of a much younger woman, keenly involved with the absurdities of the minutiae of life. 'I wonder if anyone has turned up for you in your great solitude,' she wrote to Margie, who was temporarily all alone in her great palace on the Ganges. 'I do hope so – anyhow things turn up, *oneself* turns up, and one has no idea of the unexpected corners one has, until one's been alone a little.'[174] She went on seeking relief at the health resorts so favoured by her doctors, and enjoyed the quaint picturesque foreign towns and the society she met there.

One visit was made to Scotland on the invitation of Lady Colevile, a sister of Lady Strachey and a charming and exceptionally musical woman. Childless, she became the patron of many painters whose work she admired and who were known personally to her and to Anny. Lady Colevile invited Anny and her family to Rothiemurchus, the home of her mother Lady Grant, hoping that the clear air at Rothiemurchus, near Aviemore in the Highlands, would help to cure Anny's continuous headaches. Anny was enchanted by the place '& its clan of Grants & unmarried daughters', by the deer forest, the running streams and the purple heather.[175] There was a great house party and Anny, despite her sciatica, spent an entire day with Hester practising hornpipes and Scottish reels. The Grants gave a great Highland ball, with guests coming far and wide from across the moors to attend. Anny loved it and astonished everyone by her ability to foot it with the best of them, even though she had to stay in bed with sciatica for three days afterwards. But the wild beauty of her surroundings helped to make the pain bearable, and it had been so much fun she felt it was worth it.

Since Mrs Gaskell's death in 1865, Anny had remained on close terms with her daughters, Meta and Julia. She delighted in a visit to them at Manchester in May 1891:

'O what kind ladies!

O what a delicious dinner!

O what a nice room!

O how extraordinarily rejuvenated and cheered I feel!'[176]

Meta was waiting in a brougham at the station, and they drove back to find lunch ready, with pheasant jelly, Apollinaris water and champagne. Anny enjoyed being spoiled by the Gaskell sisters, who took her sight-seeing and to the Town Hall to see the paintings by Ford Madox Brown. They thought nothing too good for her, and arranged a luncheon party in her honour. The guests included Mr Wilkinson, a self-made philan-thropist, and the anarchist, Prince Kropotkin.* The Gaskell girls had briefly told Anny about their guests. She found herself being taken into lunch-eon by an unassuming little man, and proceeded to make herself as agree-able as she could.

'I. What a striking city this is!

He. Indeed.

I. What a magnificent Town Hall!

He. Really, I have never been there.

I. (nervously) How proud you must be of the great work and achieve-ments of Manchester.

He. I take no interest in them.

I. Not in that lovely new church I saw yesterday with Miss Gaskell?

He. I am an Atheist!

I. (still more nervous) And do you care for the great canal?

He. Not at all, I am an Anarchist!

I. Good gracious, would you destroy everything?

He. Yes, I am a Nihilist!'

Luckily, the real philanthropist, Mr Wilkinson, had overheard the conver-sation and burst out laughing at the quandary Anny had got herself into. She ended by liking Prince Kropotkin very much, and he gave her a description of anarchy 'that was more like Heaven upon earth than anything else, with laws of order, peace and beauty enforced by a vast army of Christian-hearted atheists'.[177]

Concerned as she was with her own health, it came as a shock in 1889 when Richmond, who had been suffering from attacks of vertigo, was

* Prince Pyotr Alexeivich Kropotkin (1842-1921). Revolutionary, geographer and zoologist, he had recently settled in England after having been imprisoned for five years in France for anarchism. He stayed in England until the revolution of 1917, when he returned to Russia. His idea of anarchy was a gentle one based on mutual trust in a peaceful society. Anny's description of Kropotkin's ideal is a very accurate one.

diagnosed with Menière's disease. The symptoms were unpleasant and bewildering and he heard imaginary sounds like oceans roaring in his ears. He was ordered away from work until he recovered, and Julia lent them the Stephen holiday house at St Ives in Cornwall. Anny had taken Richmond's good health for granted far more than she realised. Now she never felt safe, became prey to anxiety and grew as nervous as a weathercock in an east wind.

Richmond bore it patiently, but the noises in his ears interfered with his listening to music, which was one of his chief pleasures. When he returned to the India Office, nothing could persuade him to lighten his duties there. Anny continued to be anxious, although she was reassured by Pinkie and Gussie, who constantly visited and who had a heartening effect on Richmond.

★

Who says, 'Youth's a stuff will not endure?' It lasts as long as we do,
and is older than age. For those moments of eager life, of seeing and
being, come back to us, and we babble of green fields and live among
them to the very end.

ANNE THACKERAY RITCHIE TO HESTER RITCHIE.

Anny had always been linked to the past through her attachment to
her father, but her affection for her mother was no less enduring. For
fifty-three years now, Isabella had been keeping a tenuous hold on life,
leading a sheltered existence in professional care. Anny had continued to
see her and care for her needs and had written to her regularly. Her letters
to Isabella were tender and solicitous, although a note of wistfulness occasionally crept in. One of Anny's greatest sources of happiness was that as
her mother grew older, she became calmer, and her old attacks of mental
anguish and frenzy seemed to fade away. She now occasionally came to
stay with Anny at Wimbledon for short periods, and if these visits were
rays of light in the obscurity of Isabella's life, they gave Anny a pleasure
she had never dared hope for. To see Isabella sitting outside in a wicker
chair in the garden, chattering away to Billy and Hester, fulfilled Anny's
very strong desire for continuity. She was moved to see how much Isabella
was at ease in the children's company, able to enter into their small follies
and grand schemes. When she stayed with the Thompsons at Leigh-on-
Sea on the Essex coast, Isabella composed letters to Anny which Mrs
Thompson wrote out for her in her neat, old-fashioned, sloping hand.
'So Billy has attained his 9th year . . . and is learning the carpenter's art.
It must be very interesting. I recollect having 2 country hats made for
me out of wood shavings . . . We have been employed making all sorts
of shirts and chemises, and planting our usual potatoes and a good many
sticks for future fruits. And now the evening shades prevent me so with
love & kisses I must conclude ever your affect Mammy I. G. Thackeray.'[178]
And then, on 10 January 1894, Anny received a telegram from the
Thompsons saying that Isabella had fallen ill and asking Anny to come at
once. She left by the early train and reached Leigh at two o'clock. It was
damp and freezing cold, and Anny was chilled to the marrow. She found
Isabella unconscious, but still breathing. She sat beside her, holding Isabella's
small hand within her own, and it seemed to her then that their clasp of
hands, her larger one enfolding her mother's tiny, delicate one, epitomised
the history of their relationship. Julia Stephen, with her uncanny way of
being present at other people's deathbeds, appeared and sat with Anny,
lending silent support. After she left, Anny remained alone with Isabella

270

for the long vigil of watching her through the night. She saw the dawn come in. Mrs Thompson brought her some tea and the doctor came. Suddenly, Isabella's face changed. It seemed to Anny as if the room was full of light, and that Isabella looked like a young girl. She gave three long breaths and then she died. She looked beautiful and serene. The Thompsons, the doctor and Anny all stood round her bed. Anny made the arrangements for her mother's funeral and then she came away.

Isabella had been Anny's last link with her immediate family and the past. She took the train back to town. It was the loneliest journey she ever made in her life. Richmond met her at the station, and she stopped on the way home to order black to be made up into mourning. As they passed the newspaper-seller at Earl's Court, she looked up and saw splashed on the hoardings, DEATH OF MRS THACKERAY.[179] For the rest of the world, it was a surprise to learn that Mrs Thackeray had still been alive. For Anny, it was a critical break with the past.

★

> Grey goose and Gander,
> Waft thy wings together
> And carry the King's good daughter
> Down the One-Strand river.
>
> ANON.

Even though her hair had turned white when she was ill, it was only after Isabella's death that Anny began to feel her age. Old age suited her. She enjoyed the homage of youth and grew very gracefully into a grand old lady, radiating sympathy and kindness. Anny had never been a beauty as a girl, but there was something very splendid about her in her last years and her charm, which had always been very evident, became more endearing than ever. As the years passed, her friends and family died, leaving Anny a survivor on the rock of a vanishing age.

The last time Anny saw Julia, she watched her walk away from the corner of the street. Julia walked with her back very straight and turned to give Anny one last bright, kind look. 'She was walking away for ever.'[180] Anny and Richmond had been going to dine at Hyde Park Gate, but Stella wrote to say her mother was ill with rheumatism, and on 5 May 1895, Anny received a telegram saying that Julia was dead.

The Stephen household was plunged in gloom. Anny proved herself a loyal friend to Leslie. She went to see him very often, tried to cheer him, even a little. When he was ill and wretched, she did rouse him from his misery by going straight to his bedside, saying brightly, 'Well Leslie – Damn – Damn – DAMN!' which succeeded in making him laugh instead of groan. No one else would have dared.[181]

In 1898, Billy went up to Trinity, Cambridge, and Richmond received the Companion of the Order of the Bath. Anny chose not to attend when he received the insignia, which was pinned to his lapel by the Duke of Connaught. Nine years later, in 1907, he was knighted in recognition for his unstinting services at the India Office. Richmond was closely involved in negotiations with Tibet after Sir Francis Younghusband's armed mission to Lhasa in 1903–4, as well as with the Anglo-Russian Convention which, with the British Entente with France, enabled Britain to face the German danger of 1914. But Richmond did not live to see the consequences. He died in 1912 from pneumonia, complicated by overwork and Menière's disease. He was fifty-eight. His career had been distinguished even though he never reached the brilliant heights of glory his friends had predicted.

Anny had never envisaged surviving Richmond, but her natural moral courage stood her in good stead. During the First World War, the house in Cheslea where she was living was bombed, but she remained undaunted.

With her old friend Katie Collins, now Perugini, she ran a bookstall selling rare editions and valuable manuscripts donated to help the war effort. Billy became the apple of her eye, and she became a doting grandmother to his children. For the rest of Anny's life, Hester was her willing slave, and after her death Hester devoted herself to her mother's memory – not, as Anny had done, in a spirit of illumination but, sadly, to eclipse her own personality. To the rest of the family, Anny became known, and is still referred to, as Aunt Anny.

Despite the tragedies which beset her throughout her life, Anny had a rare and felicitous quality which enabled her to overcome her sorrows; she never grew bitter, and kept her sympathetic good humour to the end of her days. She was sitting out in the garden one afternoon with Pinkie, who asked her if she had really loved Richmond. 'Not enough to say no,' was her answer.[182]

She died quite suddenly, in Hester's arms, at The Porch at Freshwater, to which she had retired in 1916, on 26 February 1919. She was eighty-two. For her funeral, Hallam Tennyson lent the embroidered pall that had covered his father's coffin. After a service at St Agnes Church at Freshwater, the cortège left in the moonlight by the night boat to ferry Anny for the last time from the island. She was buried beside Richmond at Hampstead. Later, a commemoration stone was erected on the Isle of Wight at St Agnes Church. Its inscription reads:

> Her writing reveals the inheritance of Genius,
> Her life the inspiration of loving kindness.

Notes on Anny's Journals
and Photograph Album

In order to simplify things I have kept to the custom first established by Anny's daughter Hester, of referring to Anny's journals as such – as did Anny's first biographer, Winifred Gérin, in her book, *Anne Thackeray Ritchie*, 1981. But the term is misleading, for they are not really journals at all in the sense that Virginia Woolf's diaries or Katherine Mansfield's journals are. When I first saw them I was bewildered. I had been to visit Anny's granddaughter, Belinda Norman-Butler. She gave me lunch in her elegant house in a quiet backwater of Kensington and we spoke about Anny at length. Afterwards, she led me to a polished tallboy and showed me the drawers where she kept Anny's journals. Most generously, she also pointed to Thackeray's desk (with a brass plate bearing his name attached to it) and indicated that I could use it to work on. I was eager to start.

The journals before me consisted of about a dozen little books hard bound and covered in Florentine marbled paper. The entries were written in black ink, in a flowing, cursive script, often difficult to decipher, which I recognised immediately and which made my heart sink. It was definitely Anny's writing, but Anny's writing in old age which was not at all the same as when she was a young woman. Clearly, she had copied these entries from an earlier source. After some perusal, it became evident that she had copied out entries from her pocket-books – the kind of small engagement books where one might write down an appointment with the dentist or a dinner date – and then add to the note if one felt the inclination. According to Hester, Anny had copied these out in 1895, when she was working on her biographical introductions to her father's work. She added to the original, using phrases she had written earlier in the reminiscences of other people that she had published. Occasionally, she stuck in a few lines she had cut out from a letter. She did not stick them in with glue but with the white, perforated paper saved from a sheet of postage stamps – her equivalent of our Sellotape. The result was a mishmash of the past recalled at different times and from different points of view. The original pocket-books had either been destroyed by Anny or by Hester after Anny's death.

After my initial disappointment, I realised that the small bound books lying on the desk were evidence of how Anny felt about her past and how she incorporated it into her present. It was not so much that she tinkered about with the past for posterity, but that she never let go of her memories and her view of the past inevitably changed with time. She did not reinvent her life, but presented it differently on different occasions, rather as a shirt first seen on a man's back is recognised later as a piece in a patchwork quilt.

On one of my subsequent visits, Belinda handed me a sheaf of paper on which Hester had typed out excerpts from Anny's journals which she used later in her *Letters of Anne Thackeray Ritchie*, 1924. The kaleidoscope twisted once more. Hester's editing completely distorted Anny's rewritten journals. She took phrases and sometimes complete sentences, but altered the punctuation and style, thus changing the meaning of her mother's recollections. Hester did this for posterity and her corruption of Anny's writing was an error of judgement which did Anny a grave disservice. It was not remedied until 1994, just after I had started my research on this book, when the late Lilian Shankman's *Anne Thackeray Ritchie's Journals and Letters*, edited by Abigail Burnham Bloom and John Maynard was published. It is a masterly piece of scholarship and an invaluable reference book for anyone interested in Anny and her circle. But what Shankman calls Anny's journals are not these little notebooks, but the two memoirs she wrote in 1864-5 and 1878 which Anny herself referred to as The ClaspBooks (and I have followed her in this). Shankman never got to see the journals in Belinda Norman-Butler's tallboy.

What might have intrigued Shankman, and certainly did Abigail Burnham Bloom, when I met her in New York a few years later, was the condition of Anny's photograph album, which I first saw just after Belinda had made a gift of it to Eton College Library together with the Ritchie letters. I looked at these with Michael Meredith, the Librarian, and Linda Fowler. What fascinated all three of us was the photograph album, with its embossed cover and leaves of thick black pasteboard, typical of a Victorian family collection. The photos had been glued in such a slapdash way that the excess of cow-gum was visible on the page. Here were all the great and famous by whom Anny had been surrounded for most of her days – Carlyle, Tennyson, Joachim and Browning – but some of the likenesses had been hacked out with savage little cuts probably made with a pair of sewing scissors, the kind with handles shaped to resemble a stork. Sometimes the cut went right through the page, so that great holes appeared on the face of the surviving image on the reverse. There was no clue as to who had been removed, or why. In one instance, the removal had been clumsily pasted over with a cutting from *The London Illustrated News*. We could only conjecture that the photograph had been considered too compromising or that it had been mounted and framed separately. There was something desperate and sad about the album and we all thought it was Hester who had disfigured it. Sadly, it seemed that Hester felt no compunction in changing images of the past, whether in the journals or the album, whereas Anny herself had always remained faithful to the first impression, and never failed to illuminate her readers with her changing perceptions of former times.

The THACKERAY & RITCHIE *Families*

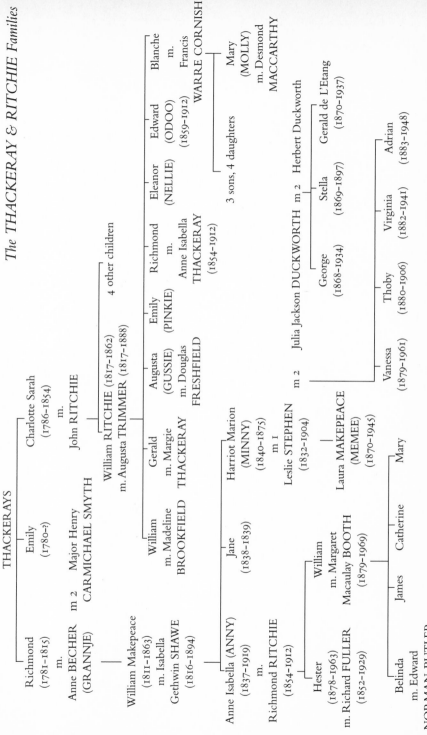

THACKERAYS

Richmond (1781–1815)
m.
Anne BECHER (GRANNIE)

Emily (1780–?)
m 2 Major Henry CARMICHAEL SMYTH

Charlotte Sarah (1786–1854)
m.
John RITCHIE

William Makepeace (1811–1863)
m. Isabella Gethwin SHAWE (1816–1894)

William RITCHIE (1817–1862)
m. Augusta TRIMMER (1817–1888)

4 other children

William m. Madeline BROOKFIELD

Gerald m. Margie THACKERAY

Augusta (GUSSIE) m. Douglas FRESHFIELD

Emily (PINKIE)

Richmond m. Anne Isabella THACKERAY (1854–1912)

Eleanor (NELLIE)

Edward (ODOO) (1859–1912)
WARRE CORNISH

Blanche m. Francis

Mary (MOLLY) m. Desmond MACCARTHY

3 sons, 4 daughters

Anne Isabella (ANNY) (1837–1919)
m.
Richmond RITCHIE (1854–1912)

Jane (1838–1839)

Harriot Marion (MINNY) (1840–1875)
m 1
Leslie STEPHEN (1832–1904)
m 2
Laura MAKEPEACE (MEMEE) (1870–1945)

Julia Jackson DUCKWORTH m 2 Herbert Duckworth

Gerald de L'Etang (1870–1937)

George (1868–1934)

Stella (1869–1897)

Vanessa (1879–1961)

Thoby (1880–1906)

Virginia (1882–1941)

Adrian (1883–1948)

Hester (1878–1963)
m. Richard FULLER (1852–1929)

William m. Margaret Macaulay BOOTH (1879–1969)

Belinda m. Edward NORMAN-BUTLER

James

Catherine

Mary

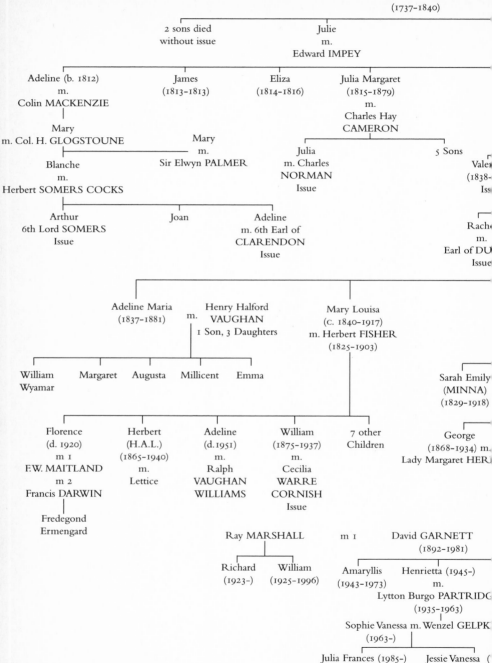

Ambrose Pierre
Antoine
CHEVALIER de L'ETANG
(1737-1840)

2 sons died
without issue

Julie
m.
Edward IMPEY

Adeline (b. 1812)
m.
Colin MACKENZIE

James
(1813-1813)

Eliza
(1814-1816)

Julia Margaret
(1815-1879)
m.
Charles Hay
CAMERON

Mary
m. Col. H. GLOGSTOUNE

Mary
m.
Sir Elwyn PALMER

Julia
m. Charles
NORMAN
Issue

5 Sons

Vale
(1838-
Iss

Blanche
m.
Herbert SOMERS COCKS

Arthur
6th Lord SOMERS
Issue

Joan

Adeline
m. 6th Earl of
CLARENDON
Issue

Rach
m.
Earl of DU
Issue

Adeline Maria
(1837-1881)

m.

Henry Halford
VAUGHAN
1 Son, 3 Daughters

Mary Louisa
(c. 1840-1917)
m. Herbert FISHER
(1825-1903)

William
Wyamar

Margaret

Augusta

Millicent

Emma

Sarah Emily
(MINNA)
(1829-1918)

Florence
(d. 1920)
m 1
F.W. MAITLAND
m 2
Francis DARWIN

Herbert
(H.A.L.)
(1865-1940)
m.
Lettice

Adeline
(d.1951)
m.
Ralph
VAUGHAN
WILLIAMS

William
(1875-1937)
m.
Cecilia
WARRE
CORNISH
Issue

7 other
Children

George
(1868-1934) m.
Lady Margaret HER

Fredegond
Ermengard

Ray MARSHALL

m 1

David GARNETT
(1892-1981)

Richard
(1923-)

William
(1925-1996)

Amaryllis
(1943-1973)

Henrietta (1945-)
m.
Lytton Burgo PARTRIDG
(1935-1963)

Sophie Vanessa m. Wenzel GELPK
(1963-)

Julia Frances (1985-)

Jessie Vanessa (

se Blin de GRINCOURT
eat-great grandaughter of
Marie Monica)
(1767–1866)

Adeline
m.
ames PATTLE

Virginie
m.
Samuel BEADLE

Sarah
(1816–1887)
m.
hoby PRINSEP

Maria
(1818–1892)
m.
John JACKSON MD
(1804–1887)

Louisa Colebrook
(1812–1873)
m. Henry Vincent
BAYLEY
(1816–1873)

Sophia
(1819–1911)
m. John DALRYMPLE
7th Bt
(1824–1888)
Issue

lice
Charles
RNEY

2 other sons

Maria m. Charles
MACNAMARA

7 Children

Virginia
(1827–1910)
m.
Charles SOMERS COCKS
3rd Earl Somers

Laura
m.
Sir Thomas
TROUBRIDGE
Issue

Isabel
(1851–1921)
m.
Lord Henry SOMERSET
1 Son

Adeline
(d. 1920)
m.
George RUSSELL
10th Duke of BEDFORD

William MAKEPEACE THACKERAY
(1811–1863)
m.
Isabella SHAWE

Herbert
UCKWORTH
(1833–1870)

m 1

Julia
(1846–1895)

m 2

Leslie
STEPHEN
(1832–1904)

m 1

Harriet Marian
(MINNY)
(1840–1875)

Anne Isabella
(ANNY)
(1837–1919)
m.
Richmond RITCHIE
(1854–1912)

Stella
(1869–1897)
Jack HILLS

Gerald
(1870–1937)
m. Cecil SCOTT CHAD

Laura
MAKEPEACE
(MEMEE)
(1870–1945)

Hester   William
(BILLY)

an Grant
5–1978)

gelica
18–)

Vanessa
(1879–1961)
m.
Clive BELL
(1881–1964)

Thoby
(1880–1906)

Virginia
(1882–1941)

Adrian
(1883–1948)
m. Karin

es   Nerissa
-)   (1946–)

Julian
(1908–1937)

Quentin m. Anne Oliver POPHAM
(1910–1999)

Julian
m.
Jenny
Scott
3 Children

Virginia
m.
William
NICHOLSON
3 Children

Cressida

The STEPHEN Family

James STEPHEN (c. 1733–1779) m. Sibella MILNER

Sarah CLARKE, née WILBERFORCE (d. 1816) 2 m James (1758–1832) m 1 Anna (Nancy) STENT

James (1789–1859)
m. Jane VENN (MILADY)
(1791–1875)

6 other children

Herbert Venn
(1822–1846)

Francis Wilberforce
(1824–1825)

James Fitzjames (FITZY)
(1829–1894)
m. Mary CUNNINGHAM

Caroline Emilia (MILLY)
(1834–1909)

Katherine
(1856–1924)

Herbert
(1857–1932)

James Kenneth
(JEM)
(1859–1892)

Harry
(1860–1945)

Helen
(1862–1908)

Rosamund
(1868–1951)

Dorothy
(1871–1965)

William Makepeace THACKERAY
(1811–1863)
m.
Isabella SHAWE

LESLIE
(1832–1904)

m 1

Julia JACKSON
(1846–1895)

m 2

Herbert DUCKWORTH
(1833–1870)

Harriet (MINNY)
(1839–1875)

Laura (MEMEE)
(1870–1945)

Anne Isabella (ANNY)
(1837–1919)
m.
Richmond
RITCHIE

George
(1868–1934)

Stella
(1869–1897)

Gerald
(1870–1937)

Vanessa
(1879–1961)

Thoby
(1880–1906)

Virginia
(1882–1941)

Adrian
(1883–1948)

William
(BILLY)

Hester

Acknowledgements

I owe a particular debt of gratitude to the following: Belinda Norman-Butler for her generosity, patience and hospitality; Linda Fowler (to whom this book is dedicated) and Michael Meredith of Eton College Library for their remarkable generosity, help, support and hospitality; the late Quentin Bell whose discussions with me about the people in this book were great fun and very instructive, and Olivier Bell for her support and generosity in sharing her unrivalled knowledge of aspects of the subject; Jane Martineau and Willy Mosteyn-Owen for their great kindness, help and hospitality; Richard and Jane Garnett for their consistent practical help and moral support; Linda Garnett for her criticisms and laughter; Fanny Garnett for her timely rescue and critical benevolence; Nel Garnett for her spirited advice; Angelica Garnett for her encouragement; Mark Divall for his immense help and patience; Frances Partridge for her imaginative support and critical benevolence; Dr Brian Hinton for his consistent support, critical benevolence and hospitality and for sharing his profound knowledge of Dimbola and the Isle of Wight with me; Sue Fox for her perception and generosity; Garth Carter for his encouragement, help and imaginative criticism; Professor John W. Bicknell for sharing his immense knowledge about Leslie Stephen with me over the years, allowing me to use his meticulous research, and for his hospitality when I stayed with him for an unforgettable few days on Little Deer Isle, Maine; Phyllis Hatfield for her constant support, advice and generosity; Jenny Uglow for her patience and the way in which she made the editing of this book an enjoyable and illuminating education, as well as everybody at Chatto & Windus, particularly Alison Samuel, Poppy Hampson, Ruth Warburton, and to Gertrud Watson for her typing and to Vicki Robinson for the index.

I am indebted to the following individuals for help, advice, inspiration and encouragement of many kinds: the late Noël Annan; Rebecca Aaronson; Liz Anderson; Alan Bell; Julian and Jenny Bell; Sarah Browns Berger; Abigail Burnham Bloom; John Beaumont; Nicola Beauman; Tony Bream; Tony and Frances Bradshaw; Tim Card; L'Abbé Hector Carissimo; Annie Castle; Nicole Cauet; Jeremy Crowe; Adrian and Dora Firth;

Katharine Fedden; Vivienne Dazin; Drs. Sue and Jeremy Dawson; the Divall family; Professeur and Mme François Gallix; Oliver Garnett; Diana Gunn; Joanna Goldsworthy; Anthony J. Hall; Rosalie Harrison; the late Professor Kaspar Locher and Caroline Locher; Willie Landles; Ulla Larson-Steel; Julian Lethbridge; Annie Hole; Magooshe Fielding; Paul and Terry Harter; Robert Kee; Alice Mauron; Patrick McCaughey; Hugh Millais; the Revd. St John H. Mullett; Suzanne Nield; Sophie Partridge; Dr Donald Rau; Lucy and Andrew Rawlinson; John and Agnès Ritchie; France Richaud; Robert Skidelsky; John and Caroline Sullivan; Frances Spalding; Georgia Tennant; the late John Willitt and Anne Willitt; the late John Wynne; John Wyse-Jackson; the Villardo family.

Among the many archivists, librarians and curators who have contributed to this book, I owe first and foremost an immense debt of gratitude to Michael Meredith, Librarian of Eton College Libarary, and the staff: Linda Fowler, Nick Baker, Philippa Grimstone, and Penny Hatfield, who all went out of their way to help me far beyond the call of duty and made my research at Eton a highly pleasurable experience; to the Provost and Fellows of Eton College for permission to use illustrative material from their archives and Chris J. Parker for photographing it; Dr Brian Hinton and Ron Smith and the staff of the Julia Margaret Cameron Trust for their support and generosity; Judy Coates and the staff of the Victoria and Albert Museum; Stephen Crook of the Berg Collection, New York Public Library; Russell Roberts of the National Museum of Photography, Bradford; Rebecca Aaronson and the staff of the Society for the Preservation of New England Antiquities, Boston; Angela Child of the Tennyson Research Centre; Helen Young of University College, London; Inez Lynn, Librarian, and the staff of the London Library; John Wyse-Jackson and the staff of John Sandoe (Books) Ltd; Deborah Protheroe at Oxford University Press; Bertrand Horrocks and the staff of the National Portrait Gallery; Susie Kocher at the Science and Society Picture Library, the Science Museum, London; Sarah Woolf and the staff of the American International University in London; Jeremy Crowe of the Society of Authors.

I am also grateful to the following: Olivier Bell for the use of a document by Minny Thackeray Stephen relating to Laura Stephen's progress; Olivier Bell and Angelica Garnett (Virginia Woolf); Alan Bell for permission to quote from his edited *Sir Leslie Stephen's Mausoleum Book*; Professor John W. Bicknell for allowing me to quote from his research dossier and permission to quote from his 2 vols of *Selected Letters of Leslie Stephen*; the British Library (Leslie Stephen and Julia Duckworth); the Literary Executors of Molly MacCarthy (Molly MacCarthy); Richard Garnett for permission to quote from the unpublished diaries of MAM Marshall; Belinda Norman-Butler for permission to quote from and making available to me journals, memoranda and notebooks by Anne Thackeray Ritchie.

Abbreviations and
Short Bibliography

Abbreviations

AIT Anne Isabella Thackeray
JD Julia Duckworth
LS Leslie Stephen
MS Minny Thackeray Stephen
RR Richmond Ritchie
Fuller Hester Fuller, *Letters of Anne Thackeray Ritchie*, edited by Hester Fuller, John Murray, 1924
Bicknell *Selected Letters of Leslie Stephen*, edited by John W. Bicknell, Macmillan 1996
Eton Ritchie Papers at Eton College Library.
MB *Sir Leslie Stephen's Mausoleum Book*, with an introduction by Alan Bell, Clarendon Press, Oxford, 1977

Unpublished works, and manuscript sources

Journal of Anne Thackeray, courtesy Belinda Norman Butler.
Letters between Anne Thackeray, Minny Stephen, Leslie Stephen, Richmond Ritchie, and various members of the Ritchie family at Eton College Library, courtesy Eton College.
The 'Calendar Correspondence', letters between Leslie Stephen and Julia Duckworth, courtesy the British Library.

Works by Anne Thackeray Ritchie

The Story of Elizabeth, London: Smith, Elder & Co., 1863. (Novel) Published also in Leipzig by Bernhard Tauchnitz; republished with *Old Kensington,* Thoemmes Press, 1995.

The Village on the Cliff, London: Smith, Elder & Co., 1867. (Novel) Published also in Leipzig by Bernhard Tauchnitz.

Five Old Friends and a Young Prince, London: Smith, Elder & Co., 1868. (Short stories) Published also in Leipzig by Bernhard Tauchnitz.[*Published as Fairy Tales for Grown Folks.* Boston: Loring, n.d.]

To Esther and other Sketches, London: Smith, Elder & Co., 1869. (Short stories)

Old Kensington, London: Smith, Elder & Co., 1873. (Novel) Published also in Leipzig by Bernhard Tauchnitz. Republished with *The Story of Elizabeth*, Thoemmes Press, 1995.

Toilers and Spinsters and other Essays, London: Smith, Elder & Co., 1874. (Essays)

Bluebeard's Keys and Other Stories, London: Smith, Elder & Co., 1874. (Short stories) Published also in Leipzig by Bernhard Tauchnitz.

Miss Angel, London: Smith, Elder & Co., 1875. (Novel) Published also in Leipzig by Bernhard Tauchnitz.

From an Island and Some Essays, Leipzig: Bernhard Tauchnitz, 1877. (A story and essays) (Boston: Loring, n.d.) [The story appeared previously in *Story of Elizabeth* and eleven of the twelve essays in *Toilers aand Spinsters.*]

Da Capo and Other Tales, Leipzig: Bernhard Tauchnitz, 1880. (Short stories)

Madame de Sévigné, London: Blackwood & Sons, 1881. (Biography)

Miss Williamson's Divagations, London: Smith, Elder & Co., 1881. (Six short stories, four published in *Da Capo and Other Tales.*)

A Book of Sibyls, London: Blackwood & Sons, 1883. (Essays)

Miss Angel and Fulham Lawn, London: Smith, Elder & Co., 1884. (Rpt. of *Miss Angel*, with addition of *Fulham Lawn.*)

Mrs Dymond, London: Smith, Elder & Co., 1885. (Novel)

Records of Tennyson, Ruskin, and Browning, London: Macmillan & Co., 1892. (Reminiscences) Published also in New York by Harper and Brothers.

Lord Amhurst and the British Advance Eastwards to Burma, Oxford: Clarendon Press, 1894. (Biography written with Richardson Evans.)

Chapters from Some Memoirs, London: Macmillan & Co. 1894. (Memoirs, title changed to *Chapters from Some Unwritten Memoirs* in Harper edition.) Published also in New York by Harper and Brothers, and in Leipzig by Bernhard Tauchnitz.

Blackstick Papers, London: Smith, Elder & Co.; New York: G. P. Putnam's
  Sons, 1908. (Essays)
From the Porch, London: Smith, Elder & Co., 1913. (Essays)
From Friend to Friend, London: Smith, Elder & Co., 1919; New York: E. P.
  Dutton, 1920. (Essays, published posthumously)

Major introductions, prefaces, reminiscences, biographical essays, attached to works by other authors

Introduction to *The Orphan of Pimlico* by W.M.Thackeray. London: Smith,
  Elder & Co., 1876.
Memorial preface to *Poems & Music* by Anne Evans. London: Kegan Paul
  & Co., 1880.
'Elizabeth Barrett Browning'. *Dictionary of National Biography*, 1886.
Preface to *Cranford* by Elizabeth Gaskell. London: Macmillan & Co., 1891.
Introduction to *The Fairy Tales of Madame d'Aulnoy*. London: Lawrence &
  Bullen, 1892.
"Reminiscences". Lord Tennyson and His Friends: A Collection of Photographs
  by Julia Margaret Cameron and H.H. Cameron, London:
  T. Fisher Unwin, 1893; New York: Macmillan & Co., 1893.
Introduction to *Our Village* by Mary R. Mitford. London: Macmillan &
  Co., 1893.
Introductions to the following works by Maria Edgeworth. London:
  Macmillan & Co.:
  Castle Rackrent and the Absentee, 1895.
  Ormond, 1895.
  Popular Tales, 1895.
  Helen, 1896.
  Belinda, 1896.
  The Parents' Assistant, 1897.
'Reminiscence', *Life and Letters of Frederick Walker*, edited by John G. Marks.
  London: Smith, Elder & Co., 1896.
Biographical introductions to *The Works of William Makepeace Thackeray*,
  Biographical Edition, 13 vols. London: Smith, Elder & Co., 1898-99.
'Some Recollections of Millais', *Life and Letters of Sir John Millais*, edited
  by John Guille Millais. Vol. II. London: Smith, Elder & Co., 1899.
Preface to *A Week in a French Country House*, by Adelaide Sartoris. London:
  Smith, Elder & Co., 1902.
'Recollections of G.J. Cayley', *The Bridle Roads of Spain*, by G.J. Cayley,
  London: T. Fisher Unwin, 1908.

Biographical introductions to *The Works of William Makepeace Thackeray*, Centenary Edition, 26 vols. London: Smith, Elder & Co., 1910-11.

Introduction to *W.M.Thackeray and Edward Fitzgerald: A Literary Friendship. Unpublished Letters and Verses* by W.M.Thackeray, London: privately printed by Clement Shorter, 1916.

Secondary sources

Alison Adburgham, *Shops and Shopping 1800-1914*, George Allen & Unwin Ltd, 1964; Barrie & Jenkins Ltd, 1984.

Noel Annan, *Leslie Stephen, The Godless Victorian*, London: Weidenfeld and Nicolson; New York: Random House, 1984.

Rachel Barnes, *The Pre-Raphaelites and Their World*, Tate Gallery Publishing, 1998.

John Beaumont, ed., *The Chevalier de l'Etang (1757-1840) and his descendants the Pattles* by Sir Hugh Orange, The Julia Margaret Cameron Research Group.

Alan Bell, ed., *Sir Leslie Stephen's Mausoleum Book* with an Introduction by Alan Bell, Oxford: Clarendon Press, 1977.

Quentin Bell, *Virginia Woolf: A Biography*, 2 vols., Hogarth Press, 1972.
On Human Finery, Revised edition, Hogarth Press, 1976.
Ruskin, Hogarth Press, 1978.

Vanessa Bell, *Sketches in Pen and Ink by Vanessa Bell*, edited by Lia Giachero, Hogarth Press, 1997.

John W. Bicknell, ed., *Selected Letters of Leslie Stephen*, vols. I and II, Macmillan, 1996.
'*Mr. Ramsay was Young Once*', essay.

Charles and Frances Brookfield, *Mrs Brookfield and her Circle*, 2 vols., Sir Issac Pitman & Sons Ltd, 1905.

William E. Buckler, *The Victorian Imagination, Essays in Aesthetic Exploration*, The Gotham Library, New York University Press, 1980.

Julia Margaret Cameron, *Victorian Photographs of Famous Men and Fair Women* by Julia Margaret Cameron, with introductions by Virginia Woolf and Roger Fry; preface and notes by Tristram Powell, Hogarth Press, 1973.
The Herschel Album, An Album of Portraits by Julia Margaret Cameron presented to Sir John Herschel, with prefaces by John Hayes and Colin Ford, National Portrait Gallery, London, 1975.
A Victorian Album. Julia Margaret Cameron and her Circle, edited by Graham Ovenden with an introduction by Lord David Cecil, Secker and Warburg, 1975.

Anny

For Beloved Sister Mia, An Album of Photographs by Julia Margaret Cameron fom the Hochberg-Mattis Collection; University of New Mexico Art Museum, 1994.

Annals of my Glass House. Photographs by Julia Margaret Cameron, text by Violet Hamilton. Ruth Chandler Williamson Gallery, Scripps College, with University of Washington Press, 1997.

Julia Margaret Cameron, The Complete Photographs by Julian Cox and Colin Ford, Thames and Hudson, 2003.

John Carey, *Thackeray: Prodigal Genius*, Faber and Faber 1977.

'How They Destroyed Thackeray', *Sunday Times*, 10 April 1983, reprinted in *Original Copy*.

Hugh and Mirabel Cecil, *Clever Hearts: Desmond and Molly MacCarthy*, Gollancz, 1990.

Ronald Chapman, *The Laurel and the Thorn, A Study of G.F.Watts*, Faber and Faber, 1945.

Rupert Christiansen, *Tales of the New Babylon, Paris 1869/1875*, Sinclair Stevenson, 1994.

Clarence Cook, *The House Beautiful*, Charles Scribner's Sons, New York, 1881, reprinted by Dover Publications, 1995.

Cornishiana, published privately, 1935; republished as part of *Bensoniana and Cornishiana*, Settrington Stonthrough Books, 1999.

Anthony Curtis, *Before Bloomsbury*, The 1890's Society, London.

Caroline Dakers, *The Holland Park Circle, Artists and Victorian Society*, Yale University Press, Newhaven, 1999.

George du Maurier, *Trilby*, Osgood, McIlvaine & Co., 1895.

Margaret Forster, *William Makepeace Thackeray – Memoirs of a Victorian Gentleman*, Quartet Books, 1980.

Charles Elmé Francatelli, *The Modern Cook, A Practical Guide to the Culinary Art in all its Branches*, Richard Bentley and Son, 1896 (29th edition).

Elizabeth French Boyd, *Bloomsbury Heritage: Their Mothers and Their Aunts*, Hamish Hamilton, 1976.

Hammersley & Hester Thackeray Fuller, *Thackeray's Daughter*, with an Introduction by Desmond MacCarthy, Euphorion Books Dublin, 1951.

Hester Fuller, ed., *Letters of Anne Thackeray Ritchie*, John Murray, 1924.

Three Freshwater Friends, Tennyson, Watts & Mrs. Cameron, with foreword by Belinda Noman Butler, ed. Elizabeth Hutchings; Hunnyhill Publications, 1994.

Derek Hudson Gambit, *Munby: Man of Two Worlds. The Life and Diaries of Authur J. Munby (1828-1920)*, USA, 1972.

Winifred Gérin, *Anne Thackeray Ritchie*, Oxford University Press, 1981.

288

Barbara Hardy, *Tellers and Listeners, The Narrative Imagination,* The Athlone Press, London University, 1975.

Augustus J. C. Hare, *The Story of my Life,* George Allen, 1900.

F.W.J. Hemmings, *Culture and Society in France 1848–1898,* B.T. Batsford, 1971.

Brian Hinton, *Immortal Faces: Julia Margaret Cameron on the Isle of Wight,* Isle of Wight County Press and County Council, 1992.

Amanda Hopkinson, *Julia Margaret Cameron,* Virago, 1986.

Molly Hughes, *A Victorian Family 1870-1900,* Sidgwick & Jackson, 1990.

Elizabeth Hutchings, *Discovering the Sculptures of George Frederick Watts, O.M., R.A.,* Hunnyhill Publications, 1994.

Pat Jalland, *Death in the Victorian Family,* Oxford University Press, 1996.

Henry James, *Letters of Henry James,* ed. Leon Edel, Vol 11, 1978.
William Wetmore Story and his Friends, 1903.

Mary Kennedy, *The Paris Commune,* William Collins & Co. Ltd, 1979.

Hermione Lee, *Virginia Woolf,* Chatto and Windus, 1996.

P[hilip] L[eigh]-S[mith], *Record of an Ascent, A Memoir of Sir Richmond Thackeray Ritchie,* Dillon's University Bookshop Ltd, 1961.

Jean O. Love, *Virginia Woolf, Sources of Madness and Art,* University of California Press, 1977.

Jeremy Maas, Paula White Trimpe, Charlotte Grere et al., *Victorian Fairy Painting,* ed. Jane Martineau, Royal Academy of Arts, 1997.

Mary MacCarthy, *A Nineteenth Century Childhood,* William Heinemann Ltd, 1924.

Jane Marcus, ed., *Virginia Woolf and Bloomsbury: A Centenary Celebration,* London: Macmillan; Bloomington: Indiana University Press, 1987.

Joy Melville, *Julia Margaret Cameron, Pioneer Photographer,* Sutton Publishing, 2003.

Victoria Olsen, *From Life: Julia Margaret Cameron & Victorian Photography,* Aurum Press, 2003.

Thomas Love Peacock, *The Novels of Thomas Love Peacock,* ed. David Garnett, Rupert Hart-Davis, 1948.

Gwen Raverat, *Period Piece: A Cambridge Childhood,* reprinted by Faber and Faber, 1960.

Gordon N. Ray, *The Letters and Private Papers of William Makepeace Thackeray,* 4 vols., Oxford University Press, 1946.
Thackeray: The Uses of Adversity (1811-1846), Oxford University Press, 1955.
Thackeray: The Age of Wisdom (1847-1863), Oxford University Press, 1958.

S.P. Rosenbaum, *Victorian Bloomsbury. The Early Literary History of the Bloomsbury Group,* Vol. 1, Macmillan, 1987.

Adelaide Sartoris, *A Week in a French Country House*, preface by Lady Ritchie, Smith, Elder & Co, 4th impression, 1909.

Arthur Severn, *Professor Arthur Severn's Memoir of John Ruskin*, edited by Mames S. Dearde, George Allen & Unwin, 1967.

Lillian F. Shankman, *Anne Thackeray Ritchie Journals and Letters*, edited by Abigail Burnham Bloom and John Maynard, Ohio State University Press, 1994.

Clare Sheppard, *Lobster at Littlehampton, an Edwardian Childhood*, Tabb House, 1995.

M.C.M. Simpson, *Many Memories of Many People*, Edward Arnold, 1898.

Leslie Stephen, *Hours in a Library*, republished in 3 vols., with an introduction by Jonathan Steinberg, Folio Society, 1991.

Howard O. Sturgis, *Belchamber*, with an Introduction by Alan H. Harris, Gerald Duckworth & Co. Ltd, 1904.

Virginia Surtees, *Jane Welsh Carlyle*, Michael Russell, 1986.

D.J. Taylor, *Thackeray*, Chatto and Windus, 1999.

Emily Tennyson, *The Farringford Journal of Emily Tennyson 1853-1864*, edited by Richard J. Hutchings and Brian Hinton, Isle of Wight County Press, 1986.

Ann Thwaite, *Edmund Gosse, A Literary Landscape*, Oxford University Press, 1984.

Emily Tennyson; The Poet's Wife, Faber and Faber, 1996

Laura Troubridge, *Memories and Reflections*, William Heinemann Ltd, 1925.

Jenny Uglow, *Elizabeth Gaskell, A Habit of Stories*, Faber & Faber, 1993.

Helen Valentine, ed., *Art in The Age of Queen Victoria*, Treasures from the Royal Academy of Arts Permanent Collection, Royal Academy of Arts with Yale University Press, 1999.

Stephen Winsten, *Salt and his Circle*, with a preface by Bernard Shaw, Hutchinson & Co., 1951.

Sylvia Wolf, *Julia Margaret Cameron's Women*, The Art Institute of Chicago and Yale University Press, 1998.

Virginia Woolf, *Night and Day*, Gerald Duckworth & Co., 1919.

The Letters of Virginia Woolf, edited by Nigel Nicolson and Joanne Trautmann, 6 vols., Hogarth Press, 1977-84.

The Diary of Virginia Woolf, edited by Anne Olivier Bell and Andrew McNeillie, 5 vols., Hogarth Press, 1977-84.

Freshwater, a Comedy, edited by Lucio P. Ruotolo, Hogarth Press, 1976.

Moments of Being, Unpublished Autobiographical Writings, edited by Jeanne Schulkind, Harcourt Brace, 1978.

Other sources

The Life and Times of Queen Victoria, vol 2. Cassell & Co Ltd (n.d.).
The Young Englishwoman Magazine. Various vols., nineteenth-century.
The English Illustrated Magazine, Macmillans, 1887.
Fashion Design, A Pepin Press Design Book, 1997.
Paths of Glory: or a Select Alphabetical and Biographical List. Illustrated with Line Drawings of their Monuments, of Persons of Note Commemorated at the Cemetery of All Souls at Kensal Green, The Friends of Kensal Green Cemetery, 1997.

Notes

Part I - The Desolate Sisters

1. WMT to Mrs Baxter, Ray, vol. IV, p. 236.
2. AIT to Mr and Mrs Synge, LF, p. 146 (letter 46 Fales).
3. AIT, ClaspBook, LFS, p.126.
4. Charles Collins Ray, vol. IV, p. 296.
5. Mrs Simpson, *Many Memories of Many People*, 1898, pp.109-10.
6. Ibid.
7. WMT, quoted as saying this to Mrs Kemble by Rhoda Broughton, Fuller, p.119.
8. AIT, *Chapters from Some Memoirs*, p. 79.
9. AIT, ClaspBook, LFS, p. 125.
10. Ibid.
11. Ibid.
12. Information from the V & A and see Pat Jalland, *Death in the Victorian Family*, p.194.
13. AIT Journal.
14. Ibid.
15. No clearer example of the attitude then prevalent is expressed than in Elizabeth Gaskell's novel, *North & South*, when Margaret Hale proposes to accompany her father to her mother's funeral. Mr Hale replies, 'You! My dear, women do not generally go.'
    'No: because they can't control themselves. Women of our class don't go, because they have no power over their emotions, and yet

are ashamed of showing them. Poor women go, and don't care if they are seen overwhelmed with grief. But I promise you, Papa, that if you let me go, I shall be no trouble. Don't have a stranger, and leave me out. Dear Papa! If Mr Bell cannot come, I shall go. I won't urge my wish against your will, if he does.'
'Mr Bell could not come. He had the gout.'

16. WG, p. 141.

17. John Carey, 'How They Destroyed Thackeray', *Original Copy*, p. 125.

18. *The Express Newspaper*, WG, p. 141.

19. The Wilberforces: William Wilberforce (1759-1833) British politician, evangelist and philanthropist, he was responsible for the abolition of the slave trade in the West Indies in 1807 and died one month before the Slavery Abolition Act was passed. His evangelical belief led him to persuade the English upper classes to practise 'Real Christianity' and set an example to the poor.

    The Venns: John Venn (1759-1813), Anglican clergyman, became a prominent member of the wealthy group of families with ardent religious and social views who were known as the Clapham Sect.

20. AIT, ClaspBook, LFS, p. 124.

21. Letter from Isabella to Mrs Carmichael-Smyth, Ray, Vol. I, p. 462. 'I tried to persuade him not to go, but it seems as if I was always to damp him.'

22. AIT, ClaspBook, LFS, p. 132.

23. WMT to Mrs Carmichael-Smyth, Ray, Vol. IV, p. 271.

24. AIT, *Chapters from Some Memoirs*, p. 20.

25. Isabella was diagnosed as suffering from schizophrenia and post-puerperal depression. See Stanley Dobbs, MD in his Appendix to Ray's monumental work on Thackeray, quoting E.A. Strecler and F.G. Ebaugh, 'Psychoses Occurring during Puerperium', *Archives of Neurology and Psychiatry*, Ray, Vol. IV, p. 238.

26. AIT, Journal.

27. Emily Tennyson, *Journal*, edited Richard J. Hutchings and Brian Hinton, p. 13.

28. AIT, *From Friend to Friend*, p. 5.

29. *The Chévalier de l'Étang (1757-1840) and his descendants, the Pattles*, by Sir Hugh Orange, revised, edited and recast by John Beaumont (Julia Margaret Cameron Research Group, Research Document 2000). Thérèse's maternal great-great-grandmother was a Bengali lady called Marie-Monica.

30. Family legend as told to the author by Vanessa Bell who was the

granddaughter of Maria Jackson, née Pattle and great-niece of Mrs Cameron. See also the revised version of *The Chévalier de l'Étang.*

31. AIT, *Alfred, Lord Tennyson and his Friends*, p. 13.
32. R. Chapman, *The Laurel and the Thorn*, 1945, p. 50.
33. Julia Norman, letter to Julia Margaret Cameron, *Annals of My Glass House*, p. 11
34. AIT, Journal.
35. A.C. Hare, *The Story of my Life* (1896-1900), Vol. II, p. 224.
36. Emily Tennyson, *Journal*, quoted in Anne Thwaite, *Emily Tennyson: The Poet's Wife*, p. 347.
37. Ann Thwaite, *Emily Tennyson: The Poet's Wife*, Letter from Charles Dodgson (Lewis Carroll) to Graham Daykyn, tutor to both the Tennyson boys.
38. AIT, Journal.
39. Ibid.
40. Ibid.
41. Ibid.
42. WMT to AIT, Ray, Vol. III, p. 141.
43. AIT, Journal. Amy Crowe had been companion to the sisters before she married their cousin, Captain Edward Thackeray, with whom she went to live in India. She was the daughter of Thackeray's friend, the painter, Eyre Crowe.
44. AIT, ClaspBook, LFS, p. 208. M. Monod was a distinguished French Calvinist preacher to whom Mrs Carmichael-Smyth sent both her granddaughters for spiritual guidance whilst they stayed with her in Paris.
45. AIT, Journal.
46. Ibid.
47. Ibid.
48. AIT, ClaspBook, LFS, p. 126. Mr Longman was Thomas Longman (1804-79), London publisher and partner in the firm established by his father.
49. Ibid., p. 131.
50. AIT, Journal.
51. Foreword by Belinda Norman-Butler to AIT, *From an Island*, p. 1.
52. AIT, Preface to Adelaide Sartoris, *A Week in a French Country House*, p. xvii.
53. Ibid., p. xi.
54. Letter from Sir Henry Taylor to his father, quoted in Amanda

Hopkinson, *Julia Margaret Cameron*. Sir Henry Taylor (1800-1886), colleague of Sir James Stephen at the Colonial Office, close friend of Mrs Cameron and Tennyson, author of *Philip Van Artevelde*, married Theodosia Spring-Rice, poet daughter of Lord Monteagle, and aunt of Victor Marshall.

55. AIT, Preface to *A Week in a French Country House*, p. xix.
56. AIT, Journal, version collated by her daughter, Hester Fuller.
57. AIT, Journal.
58. AIT, *Tennyson, Ruskin and Browning*, p. 53.
59. AIT, Journal.
60. Ibid.
61. AIT to Mrs Cole, Letter 44 Ray/Morgan, LFS, p. 143. The 'horrid thing' was the final settling of Thackeray's estate. Sir J.W. Lubbock of Lubbock and Company, 11 Mansion House Street, was Thackeray's banker.
62. Obituary of Mr Prescott, *The Times*, Wednesday, 3 May 1865.
63. WMT to Mrs Frederick Elliott, Ray, Vol. IV.
64. AIT, Journal.
65. Ibid.
66. Ibid.
67. AIT, *Chapters From Some Memoirs*, p.133.
68. AIT to Jane Shawe, Letter 45 Ray/Morgan, LFS, p. 144.
69. AIT to Mrs Baxter, Ray, Vol. IV, p. 298.
70. AIT, Journal, and a reading of Vizetelly, *Glances Back Through Seventy Years*, Ray, Vol. IV, p. 302.
71. AIT, Journal: the source for all quotations for this trip unless otherwise specified.
72. AIT to Mrs Fanshawe, Fuller, p. 124.
73. AIT, Journal.
74. AIT, Letter to Reginald Smith, Fuller, p. 260.
75. AIT, Journal.
76. WMT, Letter to Mrs Carmichael-Smyth, quoted by John Carey, *Original Copy*, 'How They Destroyed Thackeray', p. 125.
77. AIT, Letter to Mrs Baxter, Ray, Vol IV, p. 304. The three people were Anny, Minny and their grandmother.
78. AIT, Journal.
79. Family legend as told to the author variously by Belinda Norman-Butler, Jane Martineau, Duncan Grant and others. WMT's half-sister later became Mrs James Blenchynden.
80. AIT, ClaspBook, LFS, p. 139.

81. Ibid. *The Christian Year* by John Keble (1792-1866).
82. AIT, Journal.
83. AIT to Mrs Synge, Letter 48 Fales, LFS, p.149.
84. Unidentified. Possibly 'The End of a Long Day's Work', published in *The Cornhill*, August 1864, which Anny may have written at Clarence House on a visit to the Prescotts. Anny refers to the letter from George Eliot in her journal, but the letter has not survived.
85. *The Cornhill*, May 1860.
86. Rhoda Broughton, Fuller, p. 118.
87. All quotations from *The Story of Elizabeth*, 1863 edition.
88. *The Athenaeum*, 41, 25 April 1863, anonymous review.
89. All quotations from *The Village on the Cliff*, 1867 edition.
90. Anthony Trollope, *Autobiography*.
91. AIT, Journal.
92. AIT to George Smith, Fuller, p. 127, and AIT, Journal. Benjamin Jowett (1817-1892), Master of Balliol College, Oxford, and Regius Professor of Greek and translator of Greek.
93. AIT to Walter Senior, Fuller, p. 125.
94. Ibid.
95. Ibid.
96. DNB, article by Julia Stephen.
97. AIT to Walter Senior, Fuller, p. 127. The cousin is unidentified, possibly one of the Irvines.
98. AIT, *Records of Tennyson, Ruskin and Browning*, p. 54.
99. AIT to George Smith, Fuller, p. 128.
100. Obituary of the late Mr Prescott, *The Times*, Thursday, 4 May 1865; article in *The Times*, 'The Suicide of Mr Prescott', Wednesday, 3 May 1865.
101. AIT, Journal
102. AIT to J.E. Millais, Fuller, p. 128.
103. Quentin Bell, *Virginia Woolf*, Vol. I, p. 6.
104. LS, *MB*, p. 9.
105. Charles Kingsley (1819-75). Better known as the author of *The Water-Babies,* his blank verse drama *The Saint's Tragedy* deals with the clash between humanity and asceticism. It is a brilliant piece of Anti-Tractarian writing, heavily influenced by Carlyle and also, oddly enough, by Maurice, both of whom were well acquainted with Leslie.
106. Noel Annan, *Leslie Stephen, The Godless Victorian*.
107. Caroline Emilia Stephen to F.W. Maitland, in F.W. Maitland, *Life of*

Sir Leslie Stephen and Noel Annan, *Leslie Stephen, The Godless Victorian*, p. 44.

108. Oliver Wendell Holmes, Jr (1841-1935), lawyer, judge and legal scholar, he was later appointed to the Supreme Court of the United States where he was renowned for his original opinions and the convincing powers of his argument. James Russell Lowell (1819-91), poet, critic, scholar, editor, politician and statesman. In 1880 he became United State Minister to Britain where he served with distinction and enjoyed Leslie's continued friendship. It was during his term of office in London that he became unofficial godfather to Leslie's youngest daughter, Virginia. Charles Eliot Norton (1827-1908) was an influential art critic and writer, much travelled in Europe. All three of these men were close friends and were greatly esteemed by the intellectual Boston society of the period.

109. LS to James Russell Lowell, 13 January 1865, Bicknell, Vol. I, pp. 27-8.

110. Russell Gurney (1804-78), Recorder of the City of London from 1856-1878, he married Leslie's cousin, Emilia Venn and became a member of the close Stephen family circle.

111. Shelley, 'Prometheus Unbound', quoted in LS's *The Playground of Europe*.

112. Elizabeth Gaskell (1810-1865), writer and author of *Wives & Daughters, Mary Barton, North and South, Cousin Phyllis, Cranford*, etc. She had known Thackeray but their friendship was an uneasy one, although she was very fond of both Anny and Minny.

113. AIT, Journal.

114. Edward FitzGerald (1809-83) poet and translator and close friend of WMT.

115. AIT, ClaspBook, LFS, p. 139.

116. Sir John Everett Millais (1829-96), Pre-Raphaelite painter who studied at the Royal Academy from the age of eleven. He became enormously popular. His marriage to Ruskin's wife, Effie Grey, caused a tremendous controversy.

117. LS, MB, p. 9.

118. The Married Women's Property Act was passed in 1870 when it gave women greater rights, but not amended until 1882 when it gave married women the right to own their own property and assets.

119. Vanessa Bell, *Memoir Relating to Mrs Jackson, Sketches in Pen and Ink*, ed. by Lia Giachero, Hogarth Press, p. 50.

120. AIT, Journal. Francis Warre-Cornish (1839-1916) author, Vice-Provost and Librarian at Eton College.

121. AIT to MS, 1869, Eton. I am indebted to Michael Meredith, Librarian at Eton College Library, for drawing my attention to this.

122. AIT, Journal.

123. *The Life and Letters of Sir John Everett Millais*, by John Guille Millais, Vol I, p. 276.

124. AIT, Journal.

125. Ibid.

126. AIT, Letter to George Smith, Murray Archives, WG, p.157.

127. AIT, Journal.

128. AIT, quoted in *Thackeray's Daughters*, Hammersley and Fuller, p106.

129. Ibid., p. 107.

130. Derek Hudson, *Munby, Man of Two Worlds: The Life and Diaries of Arthur J. Munby*, 1828-1920, p. 233. Walter Pollock was the son of the distinguished jurist and legal writer, Sir Frederick Pollock.

131. AIT, Journal.

132. Jeanie Senior, née Hughes, was the sister of Tom Hughes, author of *Tom Brown's Schooldays* and of Harry Hughes, a student of Leslie's at Cambridge who died tragically young. She married Nassau John Senior (1822-91), son of the economist Nassau William Senior (1790-1864) and childhood friend of Leslie's.

133. Quentin Bell in conversation with the author.

134. LS, *MB*, p. 10.

135. AIT, Journal.

136. LS, *MB*, p. 10.

137. Details and quotations for this trip are all taken from AIT Journal, unless otherwise noted.

138. AIT, Journal and LS, *MB*, p.10.

139. LS, *MB*, p. 11.

140. Gwen Raverat, *Period Piece*, p. 260.

141. LS, *MB*, p. 11.

142. Ibid.

143. Ibid.

144. AIT, Journal.

145. LS, *MB*, p. 11.

146. AIT, Journal.

147. Lady Stephen's Journal; quoted in Bicknell.

148. LS to Oliver Wendell Holmes, Jr, Bicknell, Vol. I, p. 32.

149. LS to MS, Eton and Noel Annan, *Leslie Stephen, The Godless Victorian*, p. 63.

150. LS to Oliver Wendell Holmes, Jr, Bicknell, Vol. I, p. 37.

151. AIT, Journal.
152. AIT/Tennyson, *The Village on the Cliff*, p. 318.
153. MS to Mrs Fanshawe, LFS, p. 156, and Ray, *Thackeray and his Daughter*, p. 143.
154. AIT, Journal.
155. LS to MS, Bicknell, Vol. I, p. 38.
156. Ibid.
157. AIT, Journal.
158. AIT, Journal, and *Life of Frederick Walker*.
159. LS to Oliver Wendell Holmes, Bicknell, Vol. I, p. 47.
160. Ibid.
161. AIT, Journal.
162. AIT to MS, Eton.
163. AIT, Journal.
164. Herman Merivale, Murray Archives, quoted in WG, p. 159.
165. AIT to MS, Eton.
166. AIT to MS, Eton.

Part II - A Nest of Gentlefolk

1. AIT, Journal.
2. AIT to MS, Eton.
3. Jane Martineau in conversation with the author.
4. LS to JD.
5. Virginia Woolf, Obituary of Lady Ritchie, *Times Literary Supplement*, Thursday, 6 March 1919, quoted in WG, p. 279.
6. George Eliot, Letter to a friend, LFS, p. 69.
7. AIT to MS, Eton.
8. Ibid.
9. Madeleine Wyndham, society hostess – there is a splendid portrait of her by G.F. Watts in a dress patterned with sunflowers. Lady Pollock was the wife of Sir Frederick Pollock, editor of the Law Reports, later Corpus Professor of Jurisprudence at Oxford. The Pollocks were great friends of the Stephen family, and were well known to the Thackeray sisters.
10. AIT to MS, Eton.
11. MS to AIT, Eton. All quotations on this trip are from Minny to Anny (Eton, undated) unless otherwise noted.
12. LS to Oliver Wendell Holmes Jr. 'We went to Switzerland & revisited my dear old mountains & to you – being out of the possi-

bility of preaching – I may whisper that I felt certain pangs at staying at the bottom, instead of bounding from peak to peak over the fathomless abysses of the glaciers. However, I had, as you will believe, a glorious time, notwithstanding.' Bicknell, p.52.

13. LS to AIT, Eton.
14. Fournel, quoted by Rupert Christiansen, *Tales of the New Babylon, Paris 1869–1875.*
15. AIT to MS, Eton.
16. Belinda Norman-Butler in conversation with the author.
17. AIT to MS, Eton.
18. MS to AIT, Eton.
19. LS to AIT, Eton.
20. MS to AIT, Eton.
21. LS, *MB*, p. 16.
22. MS to AIT, Eton.
23. LS to AIT, Eton.
24. MS to AIT, Eton.
25. MS and LS (joint letter) to AIT, Eton.
26. LS to Oliver Wendell Holmes, Jr, Bicknell, Vol. I, p.53.
27. Ibid., p. 56.
28. Later General Sir Edward Bruce Hamley, intimate friend of the Rothschilds, Prescotts, Proctors and WMT. A Southern sympathiser during the American Civil War.
29. AIT, Journal.
30. Benedetto Marcello (1686-1739). Composer born in Venice. Best known for his *Estro poetico armonico*, 8-vol. collection of the Psalms of David, and his prolific keyboard and instrumental sonatas. It was probably a keyboard sonata that Mrs Prescott was playing.
31. MS quoted by LS, *MB*, p. 15.
32. LS to Julia Duckworth, Bicknell, Vol. I, p. 215.
33. LS to Oliver Wendell Holmes, Jr, Bicknell, Vol. I, pp. 60-1.
34. Noel Annan, *Leslie Stephen, The Godless Victorian*, p. 180.
35. AIT to Lucy Baxter, Letter 54, Columbia, LFS, p. 175.
36. Virginia Woolf, *Collected Essays*, Vol. IV, p. 77: 'Leslie Stephen'.
37. LS, *MB*, p. 23.
38. A.C. Benson, *Memories and Friends.*
39. Miss Mitford, quoted in Henry James, *William Wetmore Story and his Friends.*
40. See Nathan Appleton, *Memoir of the Hon. Abbott Lawrence*, Massachusetts Historical Society (Boston, 1856), pp. 4-5.

41. Unidentified, but very likely descended from the donors who set up the Dexter Lectureship at Harvard in the early nineteenth century. I am grateful to Professor John W. Bicknell for this speculation.
42. MS to AIT, Eton. All quotations on their American stay are taken from this source unless otherwise noted.
43. Noel Annan, *Leslie Stephen, The Godless Victorian*, p. 56.
44. LS to AIT, Eton.
45. Ibid.
46. LS to AIT, Eton.
47. MS to AIT, Eton.
48. Leon Edel quoting Henry James.
49. 'All the same, I like to remember, for it gives humanity to his austere figure, that he was so struck, so normally and masculinely affected by Mrs Langtry's beauty, that he actually went to the play to see her. Otherwise, he never went to the play.' Virginia Woolf about her father, Leslie Stephen, quoted by Noel Annan in *Leslie Stephen, The Godless Victorian*, p. 100.
50. MS to AIT, Eton.
51. LS to AIT, Eton.
52. MS to AIT, Eton.
53. LS to AIT, Eton.
54. Ibid.
55. Ibid.
56. MS to AIT, Eton.
57. MS to AIT, Eton. Minny was not to see that the bustle would create its own impediments. 'Whereas in the 1860s a lady's skirts were too wide for her to pass up a narrow stairway, in the 1880s they were so tight that she might not mount a steep flight of stairs.' Quentin Bell, *On Human Finery*, p. 110.
58. LS to AIT, Eton.
59. Ibid.
60. Ralph Waldo Emerson (1830–82). Poet, essayist and transcendentalist in philosophy whilst a rationalist in religion and advocate of spiritual individualism. He was living at Concord, Cambridge, when the Stephens were in Boston: a meeting between him and the Stephens was arranged, but cancelled because Emerson's brother was dying. Margaret Sarah Fuller (1810–50) writer, feminist and revolutionary who was one of the circle of transcendentalists who gathered around Emerson. Her *Woman in the Nineteenth Century* is a pioneering work of American feminist writing. She died in a ship-

wreck after having taken part in the abortive Italian Revolution of 1848. Her dates make it clear that Mrs Baxter was regaling Minny with an old piece of gossip.

61. LS to AIT, Eton.
62. MS to AIT, Eton.
63. Martin Duberman, *James Russell Lowell*, p. 463, quoted in Bicknell, Vol. I, p. 69.
64. MS to AIT, Eton.
65. LS to AIT, Eton.
66. AIT, Journal.
67. AIT to George Smith, Fuller, p. 133.
68. Emily Tennyson's Journal quoted in Thwaite, *Emily Tennyson, The Poet's Wife*, p. 456.
69. AIT Preface to Adelaide Sartoris, *A Week in a French Country House*, p. xlii.
70. AIT to George Smith, Fuller, p. 133.
71. AIT, Journal.
72. LS to AIT, Eton, undated fragment from 16 Onslow Gardens, convincingly dated winter 1869 in Bicknell, Vol. I, p. 64.
73. George Smith, quoted WG, p. 257.
74. LS, AIT, Journal, and Noel Annan, *Leslie Stephen, The Godless Victorian*, p. 65.
75. AIT to MS, Eton.
76. Ibid.
77. Ibid.
78. AIT, *Tennyson, Ruskin and Browning*, p. 76.
79. *Unknown to History* is the title of one of many of Charlotte M. Yonge's historical romances.
80. AIT to MS, Eton, and quoted in Fuller, p. 138.
81. 'Rome in the Holy Week', *Pall Mall Gazette*; Letter I, 6 April 69, Letter II, 7 April 1869: 'Sola', *Cornhill*; 'Moretti's Campanula', *Cornhill*, Part I 20 (July 1869); Part II 20 (August 1869).
82. AIT to MS, Eton.
83. Ibid.
84. Ibid.
85. Ibid.
86. Leigh Hunt (1784-1859). Poet and essayist, he edited the Liberal magazine *The Examiner* which Byron, Keats and Shelley all contributed to. A friend of WMT's, Anny had met him in her child-hood. Thomas Huxley (1825-95), biologist and foremost expounder

of Darwinism to which he added an anthropological perspective in *Man's Place in Nature*. He coined the term 'agnostic'.

87. William Spottiswoode (1825–93). Mathematician, physicist and publisher, he succeeded his father as head of the publishing firm Eyre & Spottiswoode. He did original work in polarisation of light and electrical discharge of gases and wrote a mathematical treatise on determinants (*Cambridge Biographical Encyclopaedia*).
88. Henry James, *William Wetmore Story & his Friends*, p. 255.
89. AIT to MS, Eton.
90. The author is indebted to Michael Meredith for this information.
91. AIT, Journal.
92. AIT to MS, Eton.
93. LS to AIT, Eton.
94. MS to AIT, Eton.
95. *Record of an Ascent*, a memoir of Sir Richmond Ritchie by P. L-S. p. 7.
96. AIT, Journal.
97. Noel Annan, *Leslie Stephen, The Godless Victorian*, p. 72.
98. Family saying attributed to LS and quoted by him in *MB* and various papers.
99. AIT, Journal.
100. 'Little Paupers', *Cornhill*, September 1870.
101. LS, *MB*.
102. In her Journal, AIT makes it clear that she was at tea with the Merivales at Guildford and that Mr Merivale read the news from *The Times*. In a letter to Fitzy, she says that she was with Lady Stephen at Guildford.
103. AIT, Journal.
104. Unidentified. Presumably one of the many young Marshall cousins living nearby.
105. AIT, Journal.
106. I am indebted to Susan Campbell for this information.
107. AIT Journal, and Fuller, p. 141.
108. AIT, Journal.
109. Ibid.
110. JS quoted by LS, *MB*, p. 42.
111. Ibid.
112. Ibid.
113. Ibid.
114. AIT to James FitzStephen, Fuller, p. 142. Achille Bazaine (1811–88), Marshal of France, trapped by the Prussians at Metz, and surrendered

after a siege of 54 days, for which he was later court-martialled and imprisoned in 1873. He escaped a year later and fled to Spain.

115. LS to Oliver Wendell Holmes, Jr., Bicknell, Vol I, p. 101..
116. Ibid.
117. AIT to J.F. Stephen, Fuller, p.145..
118. Ibid.
119. LS to MS, Bicknell, Vol. I, p.82, and Eton.
120. MS to JS Stephen, quoted Bicknell, Vol. I, p.18
121. AIT to J.F. Stephen, Fuller, p.145.
122. AIT, Journal.
123. Ibid.
124. Ibid.
125. Rupert Christiansen, *Tales of the New Babylon: Paris 1869-1875*, p.240. For a fascinating and detailed account of Paris under siege and the Commune, see Christiansen and also Mary Kennedy, *The Paris Commune*.
126. AIT, Journal.
127. Ibid.
128. Mrs Dilke, wife of the statesman Charles Dilke. Much later, Anny noted in her Journal that she had been subpoenaed to appear as a witness in the Dilke trial and that Richmond got her out of it. I have been unable to elucidate this, or to find out why she should have been implicated in it. She knew the Dilkes and various other people involved in the case, but why she should have been involved remains a mystery. In 1876 when Anny and Leslie moved to Hyde Park Gate South, they became neighbours of the Dilkes, but this is not an adequate explanation.
129. AIT, *Mrs Dymond*, 1885.
130. Told to the author by Vanessa Bell, Julia Margaret Cameron's great-niece.
131. RR to AIT, Eton.
132. AIT, Journal.
133. For an invaluable record of *Victorian Fairy Painting*, see the catalogue (editor Jane Martineau) for the exhibition of that name, shown at Burlington House, 13 November 1997-8 February 1998.
134. AIT, Journal. Anny is misquoting Jane Austen, who wrote in a letter to her sister, Cassandra, 'By the by, as I must leave off being young, I find many Douceurs in being a sort of Chaperone for I am put on the Sofa near the Fire & can drink as much wine as I like.'
135. LS to Oliver Wendell Holmes, Bicknell, Vol. I, p. 109.

136. AIT, Journal.
137. AIT to RTR, Eton.
138. LS to Oliver Wendell Holmes, Jr, Bicknell, Vol. I, p. 111.
139. AIT to RTR, Eton.
140. AIT, Journal.
141. AIT, *Old Kensington*, p. 14: all quotations from 1873 edition.
142. Ann Thwaite, *Emily Tennyson: The Poet's Wife*, p. 487.
143. RTR to J.E. Nixon, Eton. Nixon was an old Etonian, who, though he never taught at Eton, was variously a Classical lecturer at King's College, London 1871-4, Fellow of King's College, London 1878 and Gresham Professor of Rhetoric at London University, 1881-1914. Nixon lived mainly at Windsor and, highly musical and gifted with a rare talent to impart knowledge (the Classics), was an important early influence on Richmond. See *Alumini Cambridgiensii*, ed. J.A. Venn, Part II, 1752 to 1900, Vol. IV (Cambridge, 1951).
144. Ann Thwaite *Emily Tennyson: The Poet's Wife*, p. 488.
145. AIT to RTR, Eton.
146. AIT, Journal.
147. MS to AIT, Eton.
148. Ibid.
149. AIT, *Tennyson, Ruskin and Browning*, p. 282.
150. MS to AIT, Eton. Nobody did fish in the Cam in those days, since the drains at Cambridge left the river notoriously polluted.
151. MS to AIT, Eton.
152. AIT, *Tennyson, Ruskin and Browning*, p. 286.
153. Ibid.
154. AIT, Journal.
155. AIT to RTR, Fuller, p. 151, and Eton.
156. AIT, Journal.
157. AIT to Hallam Tennyson, Fuller, p. 150, and Eton.
158. AIT, Journal.
159. Ibid.
160. AIT to Emily Ritchie, Eton.
161. AIT, Journal.
162. Ibid.
163. Ibid.
164. MS to AIT, Eton.
165. Ibid.
166. LS to Charles Eliot Norton, Bicknell, Vol. I, p. 128.
167. MS to AIT, Eton.

168. AIT, Journal.
169. AIT, *Miss Angel*, p. 170.
170. AIT, Journal.
171. Henry James, writing in the *New York Tribune*, quoted by Rupert Christiansen in *Tales of the New Babylon, Paris 1869-1875*, p. 395.
172. AIT, Journal.
173. AIT to RTR, Eton and Fuller, p.154.
174. MS to AIT, Eton. It was quite a socially accepted practice for people to drop in unexpectedly, even at dinner time. It was not at all odd of Julia, nor was the fact that she did not eat with them.
175. MS to AIT, Eton.
176. John Morely (Viscount Morely of Blackburn , 1838-1923). Philosopher, journalist and friend of Leslie. A fellow-agnostic.
177. MS to AIT, Eton.
178. Ibid.
179. Ibid.
180. AIT to MS, Eton.
181. AIT, *Miss Angel*, p. 46.
182. AIT, Journal. *Accapare*: to take over or corner the market (*Collins Concise Italian Dictionary*).
183. AIT to MS, Eton.
184. AIT, Journal.
185. Ibid.
186. Ibid.
187. AIT to RTR, Eton.
188. RTR to AIT, Eton.
189. MS to AIT, Eton.
190. AIT, Journal.
191. AIT to RTR, Fuller, p. 167, and Eton.
192. Ibid.
193. AIT, Journal.
194. Ibid.
195. AIT to Augusta Freshfield, Fuller, p. 165 and Eton.
196. AIT to LS, Fuller, p. 164, and Eton.
197. AIT to Augusta Freshfield, Fuller, p. 165, and Eton.
198. AIT, Journal.
199. LS, *MB*, p. 22, ' I was sitting at home with her in perfect happiness and security'.
200. AIT, Journal.
201. Ibid.

Part III - Intimate Relations

1. *MB*, p. 24.
2. AIT, Journal.
3. AIT to Mrs Baxter, LFS, Letter 62, Columbia, p. 183.
4. LS to Charles Eliot Norton, Bicknell, Vol. I, p. 70.
5. Ibid.
6. Ibid.
7. AIT to RTR, Eton.
8. AIT, Journal.
9. P. L–S, *Record of an Ascent: Memoir of Sir Richmond Thackeray Ritchie*, p.8.
10. AIT to RTR, Eton.
11. Ibid.
12. Mary MacCarthy, *A Nineteenth-Century Childhood*, p. 22.
13. LS, *MB*, p. 43.
14. Apart from Minny's money, he acquired the valuable manuscript of *Vanity Fair*, the illustrated manuscript of *Lord Bateman*, and a dowry for Laura which later reverted to his family. Noel Annan, *Leslie Stephen, The Godless Victorian*, p. 72.
15. RTR to AIT, Eton.
16. LS, *MB*, p. 22.
17. AIT, Journal.
18. AIT to RTR, Eton.
19. LS, *Wordworth's Ethics, Hours in a Library*, Vol. II, p. 279.
20. Diary of MAM Marshall, unpublished memoir.
21. Victoria Alberta Alexandrina Gordon. Her father was the second son of the 4th Earl of Aberdeen.
22. AIT, Journal.
23. AIT to RTR, Eton.
24. LS to Charles Eliot Norton, Bicknell, Vol. I, p. 177 and LS to JD.
25. AIT, Journal.
26. AIT, *Tennyson, Ruskin and Browning*, p. 83.
27. Ibid, p. 87.
28. Ibid.
29. Isabelle Maison was the niece of Mr Dommez, the business partner of Ruskin's father. In his youth, Ruskin had been deeply enamoured of Isabelle. See *Thackeray's Daughter*, Hester Fuller and Violet Hammersly for correspondence between Anny and Ruskin about Isabelle Maison.
30. AIT to RTR, Eton.

31. AIT to George Smith, Fuller, p.174, and Eton.
32. Ibid.
33. LS, *MB*, p. 42.
34. AIT, Journal.
35. James Bryce, Viscount, historian and fellow alpinist of Leslie's.
36. AIT, Journal.
37. Ibid.
38. Ibid.
39. Ibid.
40. Ibid.
41. Ibid.
42. LS, *MB*, p. 45.
43. Ibid, p. 43.
44. Ibid, p. 44.
45. Ibid, p. 43.
46. MS to AIT, Eton.
47. LS, *MB*, p. 45.
48. Howard Sturgis, *Cornhill*, November 1919, quoted WG.
49. LS to AIT, Eton.
50. From *In the Valley of Cauteretz* (1861 and published in *Enoch Arden*, 1864). Leslie did not remember it accurately. The entire poem reads:

> All along the valley, stream that flashest white,
> Deepening thy voice with the deepening of the night,
> All along the valley, where thy waters flow,
> I walk'd with one I loved two and thirty years ago.
> All along the valley, while I walk'd today,
> The two and thirty years were a mist that rolls away;
> For all along the valley, down the rocky bed,
> Thy living voice to me was as the voice of the dead,
> And all along the valley, by rock and cave and tree,
> The voice of the dead was a living voice to me.

51. AIT, Journal.
52. Ibid.
53. LS, *MB*, p. 47.
54. AIT to RR, Eton.
55. AIT, Journal.
56. The Biographical Introduction to *The Novels of Peacock*, ed. David Garnett.

57. AIT to RR, Eton.
58. LS to AIT, Eton, and Bicknell, Vol. I, p. 204.
59. Ibid, p. 206.
60. Much later, whilst writing *The Mausoleum Book*, Leslie inaccurately attributes this row to have been between Fitzy and Frank.
61. LS to AIT, Eton.
62. AIT, Journal.
63. Ibid.
64. Remark made years later by Thoby Prinsep's great-nephew, Thoby Stephen.
65. AIT, Journal.
66. Ibid.
67. AIT, *From an Island*, p. 299.
68. AIT, Journal.
69. LS to JD.
70. LS, *MB*, p. 55.
71. Ibid.
72. MS to AIT, Eton.
73. LS, *MB*, p. 71, and Jean O. Love, *Virginia Woolf Sources of Madness and Art*, p. 162.
74. LS to JD.
75. Ibid.
76. Ibid.
77. JD to LS.
78. I am indebted to Professor John Bicknell for pointing out that Fräulein Klappert was recommended by Mary Stephen and not, as has been previously stated, by the Huxleys.
79. LS to JD.
80. AIT, Journal.
81. LS to JD.
82. AIT, Journal.
83. (Pinkie) Emily Ritchie to Emily Tennyson, Fuller and Hammersly, *Thackeray's Daughter*, p. 154.
84. Ibid.
85. LS to JD.
86. AIT to RTR, Eton.
87. AIT, Journal.
88. P. L–S, *Record of an Ascent, A Memoir of Sir Richmond Thackeray Ritchie*, quoting Edward Lyttleton, p. 13.
89. AIT, Journal.

90. AIT to Mrs Ritchie, Eton.
91. AIT, Journal.
92. Isabella Thackeray to AIT (written down supposedly to her dictation by Mrs Thompson), Eton.
93. Virginia Woolf, *Moments of Being, A Sketch of the Past,* p. 81.
94. Number 27 Young Street has been demolished. Number 13, where Anny and Minny went to live with Thackeray after being brought up by their grandmother in Paris, is still standing. The interior has been very little changed since Thackeray's day, although the garden is now part of the depot for Barker's Department Store. I am indebted to Sarah Woolf and the staff of the American International University in London, who allowed me to go over the house at my leisure.
95. AIT, Journal.
96. Ibid.
97. Ibid.
98. Henry James, *Letters*, ed. by Leon Edel, Vol. 2, p. 209.
99. Ibid, p. 211.
100. Ann Thwaite, *Emily Tennyson, The Poet's Wife*, p. 490.
101. AIT, Journal.
102. Lionel Tennyson to Mary Gladstone, quoted in Ann Thwaite, *Emily Tennyson, The Poet's Wife*, p. 552.
103. Ann Thwaite, *Emily Tennyson, The Poet's Wife*, p. 537.
104. AIT, Journal.
105. Ibid.
106. Ibid.
107. Ibid.
108. RTR to AIT, Eton.
109. AIT, Journal.
110. LS to AIT, dated 16 January 1878, Bicknell, Vol. I, p. 229, and Eton.
111. Ibid.
112. LS to JD.
113. JD to LS.
114. AIT, Journal.
115. Ibid.
116. Anna Laetitia Barbauld (1743-1824) was the author of several works for children and a supporter of radical causes – *Epistle to Wilberforce*. Her poem 'Eighteen Hundred and Eleven' prophesies the decline of British supremacy and the rise of American prosperity. Amelia Opie (1769-1853), friend of Mme de Stael, Sheridan and Sidney Smith, was a prolific novelist and poet, and author of such popular

verse as 'The Orphan Boy', and 'The Felon's Address to his Child'.
Maria Edgeworth (1768-1849), Irish novelist and woman of letters,
author of *Castle Rackrent, Ormond*, etc., and of many improving moral
tales for children, including *Rosamund and the Purple Jar*, and the
popular anthology, *The Parent's Assistant*.

117. AIT, Journal.

118. Richard Doyle (1824-1883) also illustrated Leigh Hunt's *Pot of Honey*,
Ruskin's *King of the Golden River*, William Allingham's *In Fairyland*.
He had great success with his highly original fairy pictures. Some
of them were vast and portrayed hundreds of fairies in minute detail.
He died suddenly of an apoplexy at the Athenaeum Club.

119. AIT, Journal.

120. AIT to George Smith, Fuller, p. 188, and Eton.

121. AIT to Emily Ritchie, Eton.

122. AIT, Journal.

123. Ibid. In her Journal, Anny says it was the National Gallery, but she
may have got it wrong. It would make more sense if she had taken
it to Sir Henry Cole to get it mended at the Victoria & Albert
Museum. Anny was not always reliable.

124. Ibid., and Mary MacCarthy, *A Nineteenth Century Childhood*, p. 7.

125. AIT, Journal.

126. LS to AIT, Bicknell, Vol. II, p. 332, and Eton.

127. AIT, Journal.

128. See Ann Thwaite, *Emily Tennyson, The Poet's Wife*, p. 556.

129. Lionel Tennyson, Diary, quoted in Ann Thwaite, *Emily Tennyson, The
Poet's Wife*, p. 560.

130. AIT, Journal.

131. Ibid.

132. Ibid.

133. Ibid.

134. Ibid. Other biographers of Anny Thackeray (Fuller, Gérin, and
Shankman) have suggested that Anny learned the news of Lionel's
death while taking the waters at Malvern or at Aix-les-Bains. In her
Journal, Anny indicates that it was at Southmead and, given the
dates, I am inclined to take her word for it. Just because one biographer is repeated by another, doesn't make a statement more true.

135. I am indebted to Ann Thwaite, see *Emily Tennyson, The Poet's Wife*,
for most of my information concerning Lionel's death.

136. Information from conversation with Belinda Norman-Butler.

137. Eleanor Tennyson, as reported by Mary Gladstone to Hallam

Tennyson, quoted in Ann Thwaite, *Emily Tennyson, The Poet's Wife*, p. 564.

138. Emily Tennyson to Edmund Lushington, quoted by Ann Thwaite in *Emily Tennyson, The Poet's Wife*, p. 563.
139. AIT to Pinkie, Emily Ritchie, Fuller, p.193, and Eton.
140. Ibid.
141. AIT, Journal.
142. AIT to RTR, Eton.
143. Ibid.
144. AIT to Isabella Thackeray, LFS, p. 235.
145. AIT, Journal, and AIT to RTR, Fuller, p.194, and Eton.
146. RTR to AIT, Fuller, p. 196, and Eton.
147. Phrase used by Belinda Norman-Butler in conversation with the author, also used by WG, who equally had the benefit of conversations with Belinda Norman-Butler. Jane Martineau has used this phrase as well, in conversation with the author.
148. According to Belinda Norman-Butler, and apparent to the author.
149. Told to the author by Belinda Norman-Butler. Also quoted by WG, p. 215, and LFS, p. 216.
150. AIT, Journal.
151. Augustine Birrell (1850-1933) statesman and writer. He was Liberal MP for West Fife (1889-1900) and Bristol North (1906-18), President of the Board of Education (1905-7) and Chief Secretary for Ireland (1907-16), resigning after the Easter Rising of 1916. Author of *Obiter Dicta*, volumes of gently biting essays, etc.
152. RTR to AIT, Eton.
153. J.L.H. Langdon Down (1828-96), Medical Superintendent of Earlswood Asylum for the Imbecile and Weak-minded. Down's syndrome is named after him.
154. LS to AIT, Bicknell, Vol. II, p. 333, and Eton.
155. Ibid., p. 363.
156. Ibid.
157. AIT to Pinkie, Emily Ritchie, Eton.
158. AIT, Journal.
159. Ibid.
160. AIT, *Mrs Dymond*, 1885, p. 95.
161. Virginia Woolf. A. Lady Ritchie (Obituary), *Times Literary Supplement*, Thursday, 6 March 1919.
162. Ibid.
163. AIT, *Chapters From Some Memoirs*, p. 1.

164. Ibid.
165. Ibid, p. 207.
166. AIT, ClaspBook, LFS, p. 212. The ClaspBook has been published and edited with an introduction by Lilian F. Shankman in *Anne Thackeray Ritchie, Journals and Letters*, ed. by Abigail Burnham Bloom and John Maynard, Ohio State University Press, 1994.
167. WMT on Anny's character, Ray, Vol. II, p. 789.
168. Swinburne, *The Quarterly Review*, July, 1902.
169. AIT to W. J. Williams at Smith & Elder, 18 September 1910, LFS.
170. Virginia Woolf, *TLS*, 6 March 1919.
171. Virginia Woolf, 'The Enchanted Organ', *The Nation & the Athenaeum*, 15 March 1925 (Review of Hester Fuller's *Letters of Anne Thackeray Ritchie*, 1924).
172. Virginia Woolf to Vanessa Bell, *The Letters of Virginia Woolf*, ed. Nigel Nicolson and Joanne Troutmann, Vol. II.
173. Virginia Woolf, *Night and Day*, 1919, p. 36.
174. AIT to Margaret Ritchie, 1889, Fuller, p. 208.
175. AIT, Journal.
176. AIT to RR, Eton, Fuller, p. 215, and AIT, Journal.
177. Ibid.
178. Isabella Thackeray to AIT, Eton.
179. AIT, Journal.
180. Ibid.
181. See Alan Bell, Introduction, LS, *MB*, p. xxv.
182. Conversation with Belinda Norman-Butler.

Index

Minny's letter, as a girl in 1855, to Gussie and Blanche Ritchie

'. . . I must write & tell you that I am very glad to think how happy you will be soon when one day you hear a carriage stop at the door & and you run out to meet all the ladies & gentlemen who are coming up the stairs . . .

1 Félicie, 2 Annette, 3 Mrs Trimmer, 4 Jane,
5 Charlotte, 6 Blanche, 7 Gussie